Entrepreneurship Development and Business Communication

Entrepreneurship Development and Business Communication

VASANT DESAI
Director,
Visvesvaraya Institute of
Socio-Economic Research (VISER),
Mumbai.

Dr. URMILA RAI
Ex-Principal,
Narsee Monjee College of
Commerce and Economics,
Vile Parle, Mumbai.

Himalaya Publishing House
ISO 9001:2008 CERTIFIED

First Edition : 2004
Reprint : 2010
Reprint : 2013
Reprint : 2017

Published by : Mrs. Meena Pandey for **Himalaya Publishing House Pvt. Ltd.,**
"Ramdoot", Dr. Bhalerao Marg, Girgaon, Mumbai - 400 004.
Phone: 022-23860170, 23863863; **Fax:** 022-23877178
E-mail: himpub@vsnl.com; **Website:** www.himpub.com

Branch Offices :

New Delhi : "Pooja Apartments", 4-B, Murari Lal Street, Ansari Road, Darya Ganj, New Delhi - 110 002.
Phone: 011-23270392, 23278631; Fax: 011-23256286

Nagpur : Kundanlal Chandak Industrial Estate, Ghat Road, Nagpur - 440 018.
Phone: 0712-2738731, 3296733; Telefax: 0712-2721216

Bengaluru : Plot No. 91-33, 2nd Main Road Seshadripuram, Behind Nataraja Theatre, Bengaluru - 560 020.
Phone: 08041138821; Mobile: 09379847017, 09379847005

Hyderabad : No. 3-4-184, Lingampally, Besides Raghavendra Swamy Matham, Kachiguda, Hyderabad - 500 027.
Phone: 040-27560041, 27550139

Chennai : New No. 48/2, Old No. 28/2, Ground Floor, Sarangapani Street, T. Nagar, Chennai - 600 012. Mobile: 09380460419

Pune : First Floor, "Laksha" Apartment, No. 527, Mehunpura, Shaniwar Peth (Near Prabhat Theatre), Pune - 411 030.
Phone: 020-24496323, 24496333; Mobile: 09370579333

Lucknow : House No. 731, Shekhupura Colony, Near B.D. Convent School, Aliganj, Lucknow - 226 022.
Phone: 0522-4012353; Mobile: 09307501549

Ahmedabad : 114, "SHAIL", 1st Floor, Opp. Madhu Sudan House, C.G. Road, Navrang Pura, Ahmedabad - 380 009.
Phone: 079-26560126; Mobile: 09377088847

Ernakulam : 39/176 (New No. 60/251), 1st Floor, Karikkamuri Road, Ernakulam, Kochi - 682011.
Phone: 0484-2378012, 2378016; Mobile: 09387122121

Bhubaneswar : 5 Station Square, Bhubaneswar - 751 001 (Odisha).
Phone: 0674-2532129; Mobile: 09338746007

Kolkata : 108/4, Beliaghata Main Road, Near ID Hospital, Opp. SBI Bank, Kolkata - 700 010. Phone: 033-32449649; Mobile:07439040301

Printed at : Shri Krishna Offset Press Delhi.

PREFACE

Entrepreneurship is an important aspect of the business and industrial growth of a modern nation. The spirit of entrepreneurship is marked by enthusiasm, persistence and ability to seek opportunities. It is at the core of all commercial and industrial activity.

One need not have a business and financial background in order to be a successful entrepreneur. But an entrepreneur must have the ability to assume risk and take opportunities for profit and advantage. The best way to minimize the risk is to prepare oneself for the road that lies ahead.

Although everyone may not be an entrepreneur at heart, it is possible to acquire most of the skills and abilities which are necessary for success in business. The business climate of our country is fast improving and many individuals and families are venturing into enterprises, small and big. Knowledge and understanding of entrepreneurship are a necessary part of today's business education.

Business Communication is today an integral part of business and management education. Success in business and industry depends largely on a person's ability to build and sustain relationships with different sections of society, customers, suppliers, employees and people at large in and outside the market. Communication skill is all the more important for service industries whose success depends not only on the quality but also on the manner and the style in which the service is rendered; the human relationship is as important as the quality.

This book covers the syllabus for the paper in Entrepreneurship and Business Communication for the B.Com degree course of Kolkata University. It would also be useful to entrepreneurs who are about to start business and to those who are already in business.

The authors welcome feedback and suggestions from teachers, students and other users of this book.

— **AUTHORS**

CONTENTS

WHAT'S SIZE – IT ENTREPRENEURS

The new breed of IT entrepreneurs does not want to follow the venerated footsteps of Infosys, TCS, Wipro, Satyam. Instead, they are creating a new business model that takes them straight to the top of the value chain. The new companies have two things in common—a narrowly defined niche and a skew towards products. They are confident, ambitious creative, innovative and raring to go.

We present FOUR varied examples from the new breed of entrepreneurs on the horizon.

HEALTH IS WEALTH

AMRIT S. CHOPRA

MEDICOM SOLUTIONS
Founder: Amrit S. Chopra
Niche: Healthcare Informatics
Revenues: Rs. 3000 lakh
No. of employees: 250

He is the only entrepreneur in this series who has grey hair. While we're in no way trying to underline the age of Amrit S. Chopra, the idea is to drive home the point that, unlike the others, Chopra turned entrepreneur late in his career. He was with IBM till 1977, and also worked with Tata Burroughs for a while.

While in Oman, working for a firm called Oman Computing Services, he was asked by the Ministry of Health to advise on IT solutions for a hospital there. Not being satisfied with the given solution, he went to the concerned minister who told him to find a better solution. He found the answer in a Dutch firm, specialising in health-care. Purely by chance, that firm at the time was moving out of this area and so in 1992 along with OCS he founded Medicom.

The area has well-entrenched billion-dollar companies, so Medicom evolved a strategy that saw them working in the Middle East, South Asia and South Africa. Today the firm has already completed 140 implementations in 14 countries. Explains Ashwini Kumar, EVP Medicom: "We knew that the US was not our initial market, since India and Indians were not known for work at the high end. We therefore went to markets where there was more of a level playing field."

The Indian background came in handy in these regions. For example, in South Africa they were looking for a technology that could not only be scaled up but could also be scaled down. The bigger companies from the developed world assume a certain level of IT, and Medicom's versatility enabled it to bag the contract.

FITTING THE BILL

INFOZECH

ANKUR LAL

Founder: Ankur Lal
Niche: CRM, billing and settlement solutions for packet based converged networks
Revenues: Rs. 500 lakh
No. of employees: 50

Ankur Lal has never been one to let an opportunity go a-begging. The luckiest break he got was while studying electrical engineering at IIT Delhi. He managed an internship with a relatively unknown start-up in the US. He impressed them so much that the company gave him a project to take back to India. No wonder, when he finally graduated, a regular job was not what he wanted. And so in 1991 Infozech was born.

Lal still remembers the early days when he would pay money to make sure his firm appeared high on Google searches for offshore telecom software development. There was a time when 50 per cent of the firm's business was coming through the net. But with the dotcom bust, the profits made in 10 years of operations evaporated in eight months.

The big opportunity came while working on a telecom billing and customer care project. His firm decided to buy back from the client what they had developed and convert it into a product. With a little help from CDC, UK—$ 1 million to be exact—the product development work was taken forward.

Doesn't it worry him at all that his firm is in a sector that was hit the most in the IT downturn? Lal is quick to point out that the telecom domain is also the one that is rebounding the fastest. Today his firm has alliances with Microsoft and Cisco, and these firms in turn refer Infozech to the system integrators that they work with.

OUT OF THE BOX

NET4NUTS

Founders: Chirag Patel and Neerav Parekh
Niche: Wireless Middleware Solutions
Revenue: Rs. 50 lakh
No. of employees: 27

After studying and working in the US - like most scions of Indian business families—Chirag Patel returned to India to work in the family's edible oil business in Ahmedabad. However, he soon realised that his heart lay in technology. And so, along with an old classmate Neerav Parekh, a computer science graduate from Stanford, he formed NET4NUTS in 2000.

Their idea was simple — increasing dependence on the internet meant a lot of chaos in terms of managing various resources. Getting a Yahoo address book, Hotmail account and mobile to work in sync was quite impossible. It was (as Patel puts it) driving everyone 'nuts.' It was a problem they felt would only get worse, so they formed NET4NUTS with the idea of making these services complement each other.

By the end of 2001, with the $1 million funding they got from the World Bank — promoted GVFL, their product 'AVTAAR' was ready for launch. The timing could not have been worse — 9/11 happened ten days before the scheduled launch. The ensuing tech downturn meant there were no takers for their technology, which was seen as a next-generation product with long-term benefits, and not really a need of the times.

Patel says: "People had stopped investing in technology; no one had a cheque book ready." So they resorted to free trials but even that didn't prompt companies to invest. Finally, they came up with an ASP model where they implemented and ran the product for the client and got paid according to the end use.

TAKING A CALL

SUBEX SYSTEMS

SUBHASH MENON

Founders: Subhash Menon and Alex PJ
Niche: Telecom software solutions
Revenues: Rs. 7000 lakh
No. of employees: 250

In 1992, Subhash Menon, along with classmate Alex PJ set up Subex with Rs. 20,000 loaned by an ex-employer. The two started by selling imported infrastructure products to cellular operators in India. That gave them a foretaste of what it means to compete against MNCs like Agilent (then part of HP). They graduated to software services and today develop their own products. Recalls Menon: "At that time it was difficult to get a Rs. 1 lakh loan from a bank. It was an uphill task with customers too, as we had no experience."

Once the company entered the product space, each customer was used as a stepping-stone. Menon explains: "Indian companies are not known for products in the advanced space. Also, telecom companies are conservative in choosing who they work with as they can't afford downtime." Even in India they initially did not get a warm response, especially since big players like HP, Ericsson and Alcatel were well-entrenched.

It was the consistent focus on implementation that got them a foothold in the market. the first major breakthrough was with Hutch in Mumbai. Since then, there's been a build-up of credibility. From handling 70-80 mn transactions a day, their product today handles networks with 300 mn transactions a day.

Having gained experience in India, Subex has quickly expanded overseas. Today, only 10 per cent of revenues come from India. Their first product specialised in fraud management. Where once the two main products of the company were me-toos, today Subex is working on a new-to-the world product.

Chapter - 1

THE CONCEPT OF ENTREPRENEURSHIP

Introduction

A decade is not even a punctuation mark in human history, much less in an ancient country like India. Yet the 1990s were a defining decade for the Indian economy and in particular for corporate India. Though its spirit plagues us even today, the licence raj was officially dismantled and the lives of many changed dramatically.

The journey of India Inc. is, above all, the journey of its men and women—those who lead the charge into the new era of competition and globalisation. We have accordingly divided these entrepreneurs into four sections: The Recreators, Pathbreakers, The Pioneers, and the The Gamblers.

The first is a generation of entrepreneurs who had the foresight to adapt their old family run business to the modern era. The next group laid the foundation for new business opportunities during the final years of the command economy and saw the fruition of their unrelenting efforts during the 1990s. They were followed by another generation of nimble entrepreneurs who quickly used the social and economic changes of the 1990s to make their fortunes. The final category consists of a brash, new breed of entrepreneurs who see opportunities in new lifestyles and global marketplaces. They might make it big—or they might burn.

The Concept

The concept of entrepreneurship is a complex phenomenon. Broadly, it relates to the entrepreneur, his vision and its implementation. The key player is the entrepreneur. Entrepreneurship refers to a process of action an entrepreneur (person) undertakes to establish his/her enterprise. It is a creative and innovative response to the environment.

Entrepreneurship is, thus, a cycle of actions to further the interests of the entrepreneur. In this chapter, the concept of entrepreneurship and the related issues are analysed, and discussed.

One of the qualities of entrepreneurship is the ability to discover an investment opportunity and to organise an enterprise, thereby contributing to real economic growth. It involves taking risks and making the necessary investments under conditions of uncertainty and innovating, planning and taking decisions so as to increase production in agriculture, business, industry, etc.

Entrepreneurship is a composite skill, the result of a mix of many qualities and traits. These include imagination, the readiness to take risks, ability to bring together and put to use the other factors of production, capital, labour, land, as also intangible factors such as the ability to mobilise scientific and technological advances.

A hard practical approach is necessary to be able to implement and manage a project by securing the required licences, approvals and finance from governmental and financial agencies. The personal incentive is to make profits from the successful management of the project. A sense of cost consciousness is essential for the long-term success of the enterprise. However, both are different sides of the same coin. Entrepreneurship lies more perhaps in the ability to minimise the use of resources and to put them to maximum advantages. Without an awareness of quality and desire for excellence, consumer acceptance cannot be achieved and sustained. Above all enterpreneurship today is the product of teamwork and the ability to create, build and work as a team. The entrepreneur is the maestro of the business orchestra, wielding his baton to which the band is played.

What is Enterpreneurship?

Entrepreneurship is the propensity of mind to take calculated risks with confidence to achieve a pre-determined business or industrial objective. In substance, it is the risk-taking ability of the individual, coupled with correct decision-making. When one witnesses a relatively large number of individuals in generation after generation of a particular community, who engage themselves in the industrial or commercial pursuits and appear to take risks and show enterprise, it is acknowledged to be a commercial class. The 'commercial class' is a myth just like that of the so-called 'martial race.' There are neither for all-time, martial races nor commercial classes. Communities, which once appeared to be martial in spirit have, in later periods, emerged as mercantile societies. Those who were once more concerned with and relished trade, are seen later in history to have taken to the profession of the sword. Today, it is quite evident to anyone that national communities which have developed world-wide industrial and consequently commercial interests are militarily powerful; nay, great industrial powers have today become super-military powers as well. Enterprise is manifested in different ways the capacity to take risks independently and individually, with a view to making profits and seizing an opportunity to earn more in the market-oriented economy, is the dominant characteristic of modern entrepreneurship. Enterprise, ready for the pursuit of business and responsive to profit by way of producing and/or marketing goods and commodities, to meet the expanding and diversifying actual and potential needs and demands of the customers, is what constitutes the *entrepreneurial essence*. But this kind of sensitivity of enterprising citizen throws up a species of entrepreneurs, that is mostly mercantile in outlook and performance. In underdeveloped countries like India, a new species of entrepreneurs is desirable, because here economic progress has to be brought about along with social justice. Entrepreneurship in India, has therefore, to serve the national objective. There is an apparent conflict between social objectives and economic imperatives. This conflict has to be resolved first by the individual entrepreneur in his own mind before achieving economic growth. This includes industrial development, as one of the instruments of attaining the social objectives. A high sense of responsibility is thus an essential attribute of emergent entrepreneurship in India.

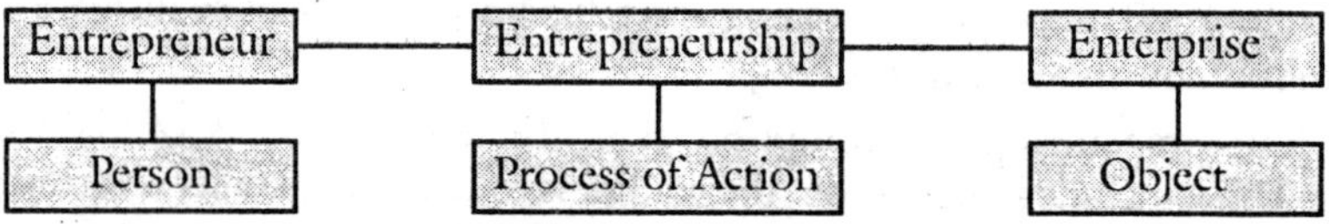

Fig. 1.1 : Concept of Entrepreneurship

Stimulation of Entrepreneurship

Entrepreneurship development is probably one of the most elusive, complicated and perplexing issues in the promotion and growth of small enterprises. Recently, a number of development agencies have been involved, in the process. However, in spite of all these efforts, there have been only a few partially successful programmes and many colossal failures in the field.

The stimulation of entrepreneurship is a function of both internal and external variables. The presence of certain personal qualities in an individual is a requisite. Some of the findings about entrepreneurs in Nepal are as follows:

(a) Mainly there are two types of entrepreneurs: the Government and private individuals.

(b) In a family-run business the entrepreneur is owner as well as manager. Entrepreneurs are frequently found to have parents who were engaged in business-related occupations. Membership in certain communities (Mewass, Marwadies, Gurung etc.,) is highly correlated with entrepreneurship.

(c) Many people who migrated from the hills to the southern part of the country (Terai) and returned have become entrepreneurs and

(d) In the family business, a change is taking place. Now educated young members are becoming entrepreneurs rather than heads of the family who are generally old.

Definition

Entrepreneurship is a multi-dimensional function defined differently by different authorities. Centillion was the first to use the term 'entrepreneur.' He portrayed an entrepreneur as one discharging the function of direction and speculation. J.B. Say, moving along in the French (Centillion) tradition, was the first to assign the entrepreneur a position in the economic process. According to him, an entrepreneur's function is to combine the factors of production into producing an organism. But to Adam Smith, the father of political economy, the entrepreneur was a proprietary capitalist, a supplier of capital and at the same time, a manager, intervening between labour and the consumer. Adam Smith also treated him as employer, master, merchant and undertaker, but explicitly identified him with the capitalist. Schumpeter was decidedly the first economic thinker to have assigned the entrepreneur a key role in the process of economic development. In Schumpeter's system, entrepreneurship is essentially a creative activity. The entrepreneur is the innovator who introduces something new into the economy. The innovation may be a method of production, not yet tested by experience in the concerned branch of manufacture, or a product with which consumers are not yet familiar, or a new source of raw material or a market hitherto unexploited or other innovations in the strict sense of the term.

According to him, entrepreneurs are business leaders and not simple owners of capital. They are men of vision, drive and talent, who spot opportunities and promptly seize them for exploitation. It will not be out of place to mention here that the innovators concept of entrepreneurship cannot exclusively be depended upon in underdeveloped countries. In these countries business leaders who promote many large and small enterprises and adapt western techniques of production and distribution to the prevailing conditions in their own industries are entrepreneurs of no mean significance. They may not be innovators in the true sense of the term but they are men of great vision and effective industrial leaders who transform the economic landscape of their countries. People like

Jamsetji Nusserwanji Tata, M. Visvesvarayya, G.D. Birla, Jamnalal Bajaj, Laxmanrao Kirloskar and other visionaries, builders and thinkers laid the foundation for a modern industrialised India. Professor Bert F. Hoselitz calls them *imitative entrepreneurs*, and regards their existence as quite purposeful in a mixed economy. "Coupled with all historical experiences of Western Europe, it appears to be safe to assume", he writes, that "small and medium-scale entrepreneurs are likely to play an important role in developing countries for several decades, provided these developing nations permit a private sector of enterprise in the industrial, commercial and financial field at all."

Besides, in South-East Asian countries, at the pre-take-off stage, the need is for more promoters, risk-takers and business organisers than for innovators. In the emerging economies, employment creation is a far more immediate goal for entrepreneurs than technological innovation. As Professor Jan Tinbergen points out: "The best entrepreneur to any developing country is not necessarily the man who use much capital, but rather the man who knows how to organise the employment and training of his employees. Whoever concentrates on this is rendering a much more important service to his country than the man who uses huge capital."

Box 1.1

My Best Lesson In Leadership

What's the secret to building a great organisation? How do you sustain consistent growth, profits, and service in an industry that can, literally, change overnight ? And how do you build a culture of commitment and performance? I can answer all that in two words: be Yourself.

That's both a simple and a profoundly difficult goal. It means spending less time building an organisation in which personality counts as much as quality and reliability. Southwest Airlines has the reputation being the wild-and-crazy guy of commercial aviation. Yet, in many ways, we are the most conservative company in our industry. We have always paid as much attention to out financial fitness in good times as in bad. But you can't lead by just the numbers.

At far too many companies, when you come into the office, you put on a mask. You look different, talk different, and act different, which is why most business encounters are bland and impersonal. But we try not to hire people who are humourless, self-centred, or complacent. So, when they come to work, we want them—not their corporate clones. They are what makes us different from other airlines and, in most enterprises, different is better.

Culture defines personality. If you create an environment where people truly participate, you don't need control. They know what needs to be done, and they do it. We're not looking for blind obedience. We're looking for people who, on their own initiative, want to be doing what they're doing because they consider it to be a worthy objective. They know that our company's success rests with them—not with me.

Personality is strategy. Over the years, we've developed not only a different strategy, but also a different strategic planning-process. Basically, we just don't do it. In an industry where a two-week plan is likely to become obsolete, to spend days debating whether we're to serve Trenton, New Jersey, in 2005 is a meaningless exercise. So, rather than trying to predict what we'll do, we try to define who we are, and what we want in terms of market niche, operational strategy, and financial health. Obviously, you manage a $25-billion company differently than you do a $ 25 million company. But you change practices—not principles. You remember that systems are not masters. And that nothing comes ahead of your people.

Working for a worthy cause. Because our low-fare strategy is central to who we are, our employees are enormously cost conscious. But you need to spend more time on the intangibles than on the tangibles to create that kind of buy-in. We're not afraid to talk to our people with emotion. One of or managers once said: "The important thing is to take a brick-layer and make him understand that he's building a home." So, we constantly hold up examples of customer-experiences and employee-efforts to make a difference.

Building employee-partnerships. Our most important tools for building employee-partnerships are job-security and a stimulating work-environment. And, as it turns out, providing job-security imposes additional discipline because, if your goal is to avoid lay-offs, you hire sparingly. But it's not enough to try to assure people a job; equally important is allowing them to feel liberated when they come to work. To foster problem-solving and co-operation, for example, we have the Walk-A-Mile programme, in which any employee can do another's job for a day.

Training is another way you forge partnerships. Our most important training is in how to lead. My best lesson in leadership came during my early days as a trial lawyer. Wanting to learn from the best, I went to see 2 of the most renowned litigators in San Antonio try cases. One sat there, never objected to anything, was very gentle with witnesses, and established a rapport with the jury. The other was an aggressive, thundering help-raiser. And both seemed to win every case. That's when I realised that there are many different paths—not one right path. That's true of leadership as well.

People with different personalities, different approaches, and different values succeed not because one set of values or practices is superior, but because their value and practices are genuine. And when you and your organisation are true to yourselves—when you deliver both results and a singular experience–customers can spot it from 30,000 feet.

Herb Kelleher

Importance of Entrepreneurship

From classical economics to the post-keynesian analysts, the role of the entrepreneur has been surveyed and observations, theories and pronouncements advanced. Not only were pure economists involved in this endeavour, but also prominent social theorists such as Marx, Weber, Sombard and Veblen.

In general, contemporary economists agree that the entrepreneur is a business leader and that his role in fostering economic growth and development is a pivotal one. At present, however, there is no consensus at to what constitutes the essential activity which makes the entrepreneur a crucial figure, while some economists have identified the basic entrepreneurial requirements of production resources, the provision of capital or the introduction of innovations. Professor, James R. Omps of the International Institute of Entreprenology, Honolulu, Hawaii, in his paper entitled "*Entreprenology, the Critical Factor in Nation Development*", has this to say:

"In all crisis situations, there is one critical factor. There is one factor in each situation that can be cited as being the straw that broke the camel's back! In listing some of today's possible critical factors, such familiar words and phrases as limited natural resources... food... energy all would emerge. A question may be phrased thus:

"What is the critical factor?"

Over-population?

Food shortages?

Energy shortages?

Lack of technology? or

All of the above?

"Many factors have been proposed ... and yet is it possible that the most critical factor has not been recognised? What is this factor that has either been stifled or totally ignored? It is a relatively untapped source... that of qualified individuals with peculiarly unique aptitudes for innovation ... for change, aptitudes, in other words, for using present day technology in ways yet unheard of or perhaps even unthought of. The critical factor is a dire shortage of the appropriate economic innovator and implementor... the Entreprenologists."

In the words of A.H. Cole, entrepreneurship is the purposeful activity of an individual or a group of associated individuals, undertaken to initiate, maintain or organise a profit-oriented business unit for the production or distribution of economic goods and services.

McClelland describes the innovative characteristics of the entrepreneurial role. The entrepreneurial role, by definition, involves doing things in a new and better way. A businessman who simply behaves in a traditional way is not an entrepreneur. Moreover, an entrepreneurial role calls for decision-making under uncertainty. If there is no significant uncertainty and the action involves applying known and predictable results, then entrepreneurship is not at all involved.

McClelland, like others, identified two characteristics of entrepreneurship. First, doing things in a 'new and better way.' This is synonymous with the innovative characteristics mentioned by Schumpeter and secondly, decision-making under uncertainty, i.e., risk as identified by Cantillon. McClelland more explicitly emphasised the need for achievement or achievement-orientation as the most directly relevant factor for explaining economic behaviour. This motive is defined as a tendency to strive for success in situations involved and of one's performance in relation to the same standard of excellence.

In other words, entrepreneurship means the function of creating something new, organising and coordinating and undertaking risk and handling economic uncertainty. Higgins defines the term thus, "Entrepreneurship is the function of seeing investment and production opportunity, organising an enterprise to undertake a new production process, raising capital, hiring labour, arranging for the supply of raw materials and selecting top managers for the day-to-day operation of the enterprise."

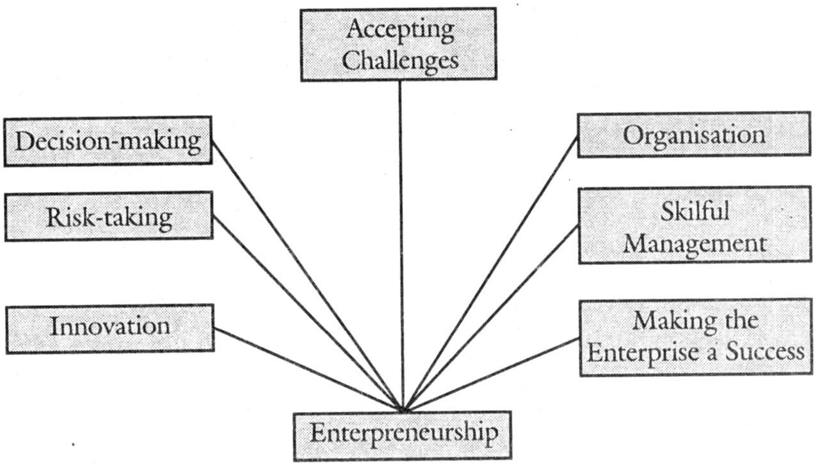

Fig 1.2 : Characteristics of Entrepreneurship

According to Peter Drucker, "Entrepreneurship is neither a science nor an art. It is a practice. It has a knowledge base. Knowledge in entrepreneurship is a means to an end. Indeed what constitutes knowledge in practice is largely defined by the ends, that is, by the practice." Entrepreneurship is considerably less risky, if the entrepreneur is methodical and does not violate elementary and well-known rules.

Innovation and entrepreneurship are thus needed in society as much as in the economy, in public-service institutes as much as in business. It is precisely because innovation and entrepreneurship are not 'root and branch' but 'one step at a time', a product here, a policy there, a public service yonder; because they are not planned but focussed on this opportunity and that need; because they are tentative and will disappear if they do not produce the expected and needed results; because, in other words, they are pragmatic rather than dogmatic and modest rather than grandiose—that they promise to keep any society, economy, industry, public service or business flexible and self-renewing.

Thus, entrepreneurship is a complex phenomenon. "Some think of entrepreneurs primarily as innovators, some chiefly as managers of enterprises, some as bearers of risks and others place a major emphasis on their function as mobilisers and alloacators of capital." In the Indian context, however, an entrepreneur may at best be defined as a person (or a group of persons) responsible for existence of new business enterprises.

Features of Entrepreneurship

The main features of entrepreneurship are as follows:

1. ***Economic :*** It involves the creation and operation of an enterprise.
2. ***Creative :*** It involves innovative process. A catalytic agent.
3. ***Purposeful :*** It is a goal-oriented activity seeking to earn profits.
4. ***Risk bearing :*** Risk is an inherent and inseparable element of entrepreneurship.
5. ***Organisation :*** It involves organisation building capabilities.
6. ***Human Relations :*** Ability to work with other people and signing responsibility is a key to success.
7. ***Flexibility :*** Flexibility is the hallmark of a successful entrepreneur.

8. *Innovation :* Entrepreneurship is an innovative function.
9. *Skills :* It calls for special skills to handle the situation as it unfolds.
10. *Values :* It is an attempt to create value recognition of business opportunities to bring a project to fruition.

Thus, entrepreneurship is a multi-dimensional concept. It is an art as well as a science.

Phases of Entrepreneurship Development

Broadly, entrepreneurship development consists of the three following phases:

(a) *Initial Phase :* Creation of awareness of entrepreneurial opportunities based on survey.

(b) *Development Phase :* Implementation of training programmes to develop motivation and management skills.

(c) *Support Phase :* Infrastructural support of counselling and assistance to establish a new enterprise and to develop existing units.

Box 1.2

CEO Survival Kit

Digital devices rule Chugh's life. Not surprising. His company helps machines talk to one another.

Cellphone: Nokia 6210. It is my constant companion, as my wife says. I largely use it for phone calls—and SMS, especially during long, laborious meetings.

Laptop: Toshiba Tecra 8100 — It is the key to my survival. I use it in the office, in flight, any time I am away from home, at least three to four hours a day. I have dispensed with the desk-top PC. (After all) our business runs off the net.

PDA: I rely on my good old Palm IIIxE. I store schedules when I travel, and some spreadsheets. A true friend away from home.

Telephone: Cisco 7960 IP phone. Just one integrated infrastructure. No complex manuals, just simple English.

Manoj Chugh, CEO, Cisco India

Causes of Slow Growth

Entrepreneurship growth is slow in India and that of women's entreprenership is still slower and negligible due to discouraging social factors such as unfavourable family background, lack of education, dual role of women, lack of aptitudes and training, absence of individualistic spirit, lack of freedom to choose a job according to ability, influence of sex, caste, kinship, custom and family burden etc. All these retarding causes are due to the unfavourable socio-economic conditions and tradition-bound society.

The *economic factors* retarding entrepreneurship growth are inadequate infrastructural facilities, shortage of capital and technical know-how, inadequate transport and communication facilities, absence of cheap and regular supply of power and raw materials. These constraints exist more in rural areas. The *environmental factors* discouraging entrepreneurship are unstable state governments, lack of security, absence of ideal market conditions and business and corruption in administration.

Stimulants to Entrepreneurship

A variety of social, economic, political and cultural factors are stimulating entrepreneurial activity and thus generating more robust economic development. These stimulants are as follows:

1. An increasing focus on capital formation. Availability of capital is a stimulant to an entrepreneur to start a new firm and/or give birth to a new idea.
2. The ability to transform scientific and technical developments through new institutional development is a second factor.
3. A third stimulant is supportive government programmes.
4. Availability of required training and input is ranked fourth.
5. A collaborative relationship between business and research and their direct attempts to transfer technology to the market place may provide stimulus to a number of entrepreneurs who seek the opportunity to commercialise their ideas and
6. Finally, an endeavour to create an environment conducive to innovation will provide a much-needed stimulant to entrepreneurial activities.

The innovation centre provides technological evaluation, entrepreneurial assessment and other related levels of assistance to entrepreneurs.

Entrepreneurship and Economic Growth

Economic development of any region is an outcome of purposeful human activity. A man assumes various roles in the development process, namely, as organiser of human capital, natural material resources, worker and consumer. He stands at the center of the whole process of economic development. According to Schumpeter, economic development consists of "employing resources in a different way", in making a new combination of the means of production. The entrepreneur locates ideas and puts them into effect in the process of economic development.

According to Baumol, an entrepreneur is a Shumpeterian innovator and something more than a leader. The entrepreneur, according to him, occupies a crucial place in the process of economic development.

Schumpeter further says that economic growth depends on the rate of applied technical progress (i.e., innovation) and rate of technical process in the economic field which in turn depends on the supply of entrepreneurs in society. Thus the entrepreneur becomes the agent of change in society.

In the Schumpeterian model, entrepreneur is an innovator and the supply of 'innovative entrepreneurs' depends on the necessary social and economic overheads. These economic and social overheads are very poor in backward regions which causes a shortage in supply of entrepreneurs. In this connection, we can refer to David McClelland who explained the development of entrepreneurship in terms of human motivation to achieve or need for achievement. McClelland's hypothesis is that a society with a generally high level of achievement will produce more energetic entrepreneurs, who, in turn, accelerate the process of economic development.

In the Indian context, entrepreneurship has yet another dimension. An entrepreneur may not necessarily be an 'innovator' but an 'imitator' who would copy the organisation, technology, or products of innovators from other developed regions. His role as imitator

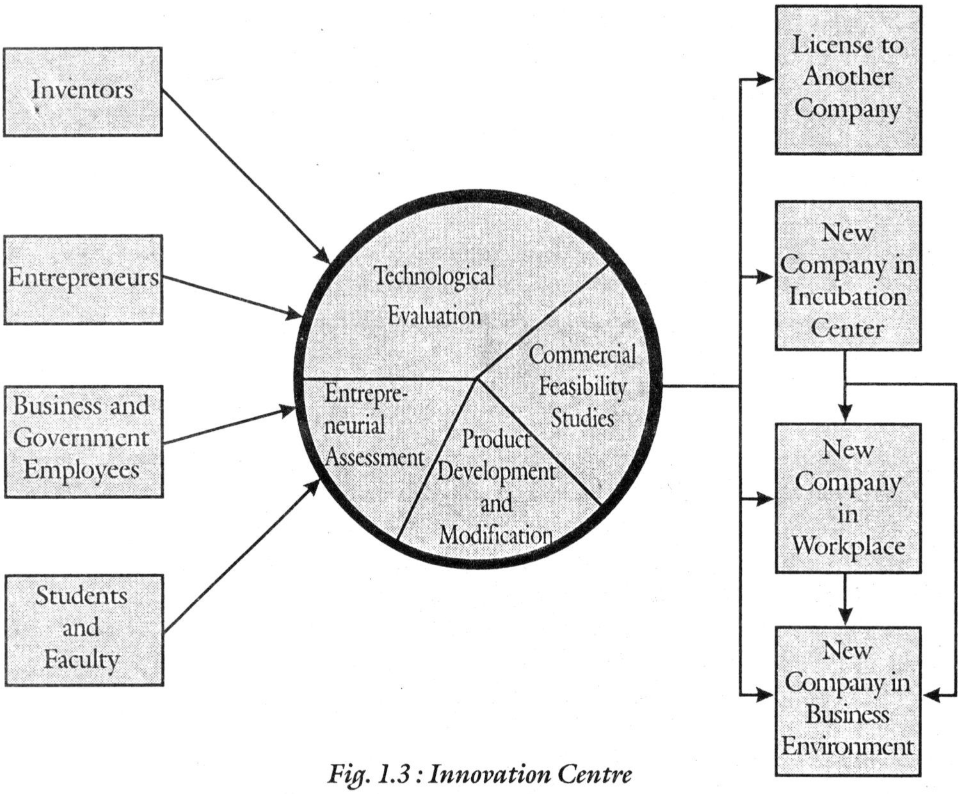

Fig. 1.3 : Innovation Centre

is likely to be guided and controlled by the various constraints and conditions peculiar tothis area of operation and the factors under which he conducts his minimal modest industrial activity.

Other social scientists, notably Max Weber, have talked of the importance of entrepreneurship and expressed the view that creative and entrepreneurial energies are generated by the adoption of exogenously supplied beliefs which in turn produce intense efforts in occupational pursuits and accumulation of productive assets leading to the manufacture of goods and services. According to him, entrepreneurs are a product of the particular social conditions in which they live and it is the society which shapes the personality of individual entrepreneurs.

John Kunkel believes that the behavioural pattern of individuals is important for development and such a pattern can be influenced by external stimuli so as to alter it in the manner we want it. In other words, if we want more people in society to behave as entrepreneurs, we can bring about such behaviour on their part by appropriate alterations in the social environment so as to influence them to take to entrepreneurial pursuits. Like Weber, Cochran and Young underscore the importance of society in shaping the entrepreneurial personality and consider that ingredients in the emergence of entrepreneurs are cultural values, role expectations, social tensions and inter-group relations in society.

Entrepreneurs are an important source of economic development. It is, therefore, suggested that there must be a motivational training programme to develop entrepreneurs and measures must to be taken to modify the environment to stimulate entrepreneurial behaviour among individuals. There are thinkers who believe that "Schumpeterian entrepreneurs are needed in underdeveloped countries for rapid economic development."

Entrepreneurs are to be innovators who must change the production function and bring about rapid development. It is only through entrepreneurs that substantial development can be brought about.

In a mixed economy, the government tries to remove the evil of monopoly capitalism by placing some restrictions. It may curb the growth of monopolies and introduce workable competition which is essential for the optimum use of the available resources. The mixed economy tries to solve the problem of distribution of goods and services in a better way than the capitalist economy. The government tries to level up the incomes of the poor people and level down those of the rich. This is done by fiscal measures, fixation of minimum wages and salaries and improvements in the environment of the people.

The role played by an entrepreneur is significantly important in a mixed economy as it permits the growth of both the public and the private sectors. In the private sector, the profit motive acts as an incentive to the entrepreneur and market mechanism plays its own role and this establishes the role of the entrepreneur in the mixed economy.

Entrepreneurship has great importance in various economic systems. It is all the more important under capitalism and mixed economy where not only are the responsibilities of the entrepreneur in production and distribution are recognized but the objectives of the growth of business and profit maximisation is also attained. Therefore, the importance of entrepreneurship stands beyond challenge in every economic system, except under socialism where it appears in a different form. Yet, entrepreneurship prevails in all economic systems in one form or the other.

Small-scale Industries as Seed-beds of Entrepreneurship

Small-scale industries contribute significantly to the strengthening of the industrial structure, many articles can be produced economically on a small-scale, with some even more economically than on a larger scale. Efficient small-scale industries can be linked with large enterprises in complementary relationship, e.g., ub-contracting. One of the most obvious benefits of such relationship is that it expands the industrial bases by efficiently utilizing resources, scarce or otherwise.

Also, small-scale industries may serve as seed-beds of entrepreneurship. They serve a newly industrialising country not only by their output of goods but also by functioning as a nursery of entrepreneurial and managerial talent. The almost infinite diversity of products and services that may be developed and produced by the small-scale industry sector also demands a commensurate development of skills—a desirable basis for long-term development of a diversified industrial structure in the region. Already skilled technicians, foremen and workers are induced, motivated and are often able to set up their own small-scale industrial enterprises. Generally, they offer the most promising means of promoting entrepreneurship among the people from different walks of life, especially those with limited financial resources and scant technical and managerial experience, thus establishing a wide base for rapid industrialisation. This role of small-scale industries is of decisive importance in any economy, where the industrial structure consists of a few large-scale and medium-sized industries (many of which are foreign-owned) on the one hand, and of large number of traditional industries such as artisans, handcrafts and cottage industries on the other.

The lack of a middle group of modern small-scale industries is a factor of an imbalance in the industrial structure. Such a lack also contributes to the stagnation of the economy as a whole. As a general rule, neither the government nor foreign investors are interested in owning and operating small-scale establishments. Therefore, to promote small-scale industries is to promote rural industrial private enterprise, specifically to create a new class of indigenous industrialists throughout the countryside.

Small-scale industries play a useful role in regional development and industrial dispersal. Indeed, one of the pivotal problem confronting many countries in the world today in the task of social modernisation is how to disperse sources of economic activities so that development should become general, rather than concentrated in larger cities and capital. In a country that sanctions free enterprise, the movement of economic activities cannot easily be directed as the government would want it to be. Instead, we witness the tendency of capital to centralise itself in already developed areas.

Factors Influencing Entrepreneurship

Peter Heydeman, Science Counsellor in the U.S. Embassy here, is very much impressed with the role small business play in the process of innovation in the U.S. economy. He explained how 'incubators' are used successfully in the United States to encourage small entrepreneurs.

The problem is how best to help small entrepreneurs translate the results of laboratory research into marketable product, to transform a new scientific concept into a commercial product. Simply put, 'incubators' are very basic facilities offering shared secretarial services, space for conducting a retail or manufacturing business, and a few simple machine tools. But, and this is very important, incubators offer advice and consultation on subjects with which most budding entrepreneurs are unfamiliar: business and finance planning, market development, government regulation. Incubators have indeed greatly helped small manufacturers to develop new products. Recent studies show that such enterprises are the main source of innovation in U.S. industry.

The idea of incubators of technology is relatively new, "five or six years old", says Heydemann. This is because until recently it was felt that U.S. industry would forever remain in the forefront, without any competition. But things changed rapidly. So, realising that "the 6000 plus national laboratories could not possibly service all the one-and-a-half million or so small entrepreneurs," individual American states took it upon themselves to help local industry through their technological support and development organisations.

Incubators are very often attached to state university systems as universities have much of the technical and non-technical information that needs to be fed to entrepreneurs. Moreover, state universities have increasingly come to believe that apart from their traditional role, they must also promote industrial activity in their areas of operation.

State authorities in turn help by enabling businessmen to cut through red tape, provide low-interest loans to develop prototypes, undertake market research and generally assist in brining a new product to the consumer. "Some notion of the magnitude of this support can be had from the fact that last year alone, the federal and state governments together spent more than $ 2,000 million in encouraging small business." Many private sector companies also provide incubator facilities, though at a comparatively higher cost.

Another important aspect of incubators is that experts do not make any business decisions for their clients. They only provide guidelines and advice on product development, engineering, pilot production and in identifying markets.

Among the businesses in which incubators are making a significant contribution, says Heydemann, "are light manufacturing in matter technologies, retail and wholesale trade and, finally research and development in emerging technologies."

The success rate or incubators has been salutary in the number of new jobs created, the enlarged tax base for state revenues and in the export of manufactures. In short, incubators are bringing new vigour and vitality to America's industrial renaissance and are once more giving the country a competitive edge.

Problems

The task before the national leadership today is to industrialise a predominantly agricultural society, where capital is scarce and labour is plentiful. Again, modern industry implies a style and a method of work which are quite at variance with the traditional culture and modes of social behaviour in the underdeveloped countries. So, the hole structure of society has to undergo a considerable structural and institutional change commensurate with the needs of the situation.

The Gap between the indigenous arts and even the improved crafts, on the one hand, and imported and also indigenous technology, on the other, is wide enough and is further widening day after day with the explosion of innovative research. Furthermore, the economy has been historically and unavoidably polarized between a few mighty industrial centres and the far-flung rural areas. With all the progress during the two decades and a half, the national economy is beset with all kinds of shortages and scarcities of inputs, most vital to new entrepreneurs, when they launch their small or tiny units. Besides, they have, at times, to contend and compete with well established small, medium or large industrial units in the same lines of production. Newly emerging industries, particularly those of the first-generation entrepreneurs, even in the underdeveloped economies, are slowly but certainly tending to become high investment industries and the entrepreneurs have to battle against the formidable force of hostile elements, such as (i) erratic shortages of raw materials, (ii) flourishing black market, (iii) prices rigged up by monopolists, (iv) administrative maldisribution, (v) gaps between official promise and performance, (vi) inefficiency of industrial management,(vii) irresponsible attitude to work, (viii) rising cost of capital and credit, (ix) deficient and arrogant institutional banking, (x) inadequacy of common service, (xi) primitive wholesale and retail trade outlets and others. New entrepreneurship in India has to be cherished in this environment.

Box 1.3

Now Consider This

When defining a new role for education, executives should ask themselves the following questions:

What Should be on our Learning Agenda?

- Key concepts that underpin our values and beliefs
- Key capabilities to be developed in live initiatives
- Key conditions that must be in place for performance

Which initiatives have the potential for big impact ?

- Initiatives that are high value-at-stake
- Initiatives that are high on our corporate agenda
- Initiatives in which it is important to reinforce high standards

Which experiences offer opportunities for simulation and learning ?

- Issues that span multiple business units
- Business cases that highlight difficult trade-offs
- Potential scenario that are likely to be encountered

What do we need to get started ?

- A clear learning agenda
- Alignment around business and educational priorities
- The right experience to execute

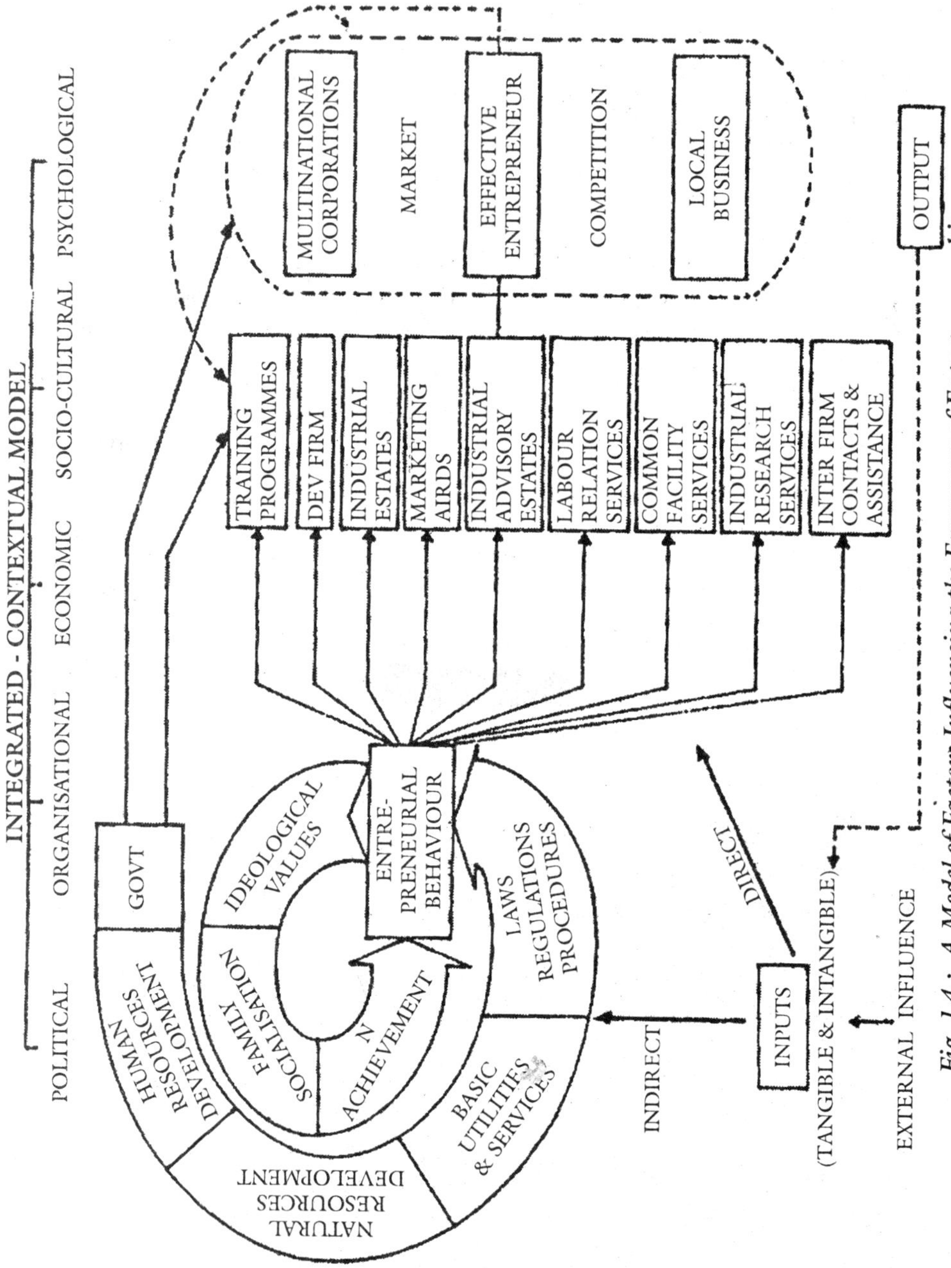

Fig. 1.4 : A Model of Factors Influencing the Emergence of Entrepreneurship

Box 1.4

Entrepreneurship Beyond Borders

The ability to spot opportunities and do business beyond borders is increasingly becoming the defining trend that will separate the entrepreneur from the rest. Government de-regulation is opening national borders for commerce. Trading and investing beyond national borders is now common and is either the salvation or the death knell of the Indian economy. We have an enviable domestic market and that in itself is a threat unless domestic enterprises shake themselves out of their comfort zones and gear up to face the pressures of competition from across the border, now made easier, thanks to the World Trade Organisation (WTO).

India and other developing countries will continue to oppose and seek amendments to the WTO proposals that prohibit developing countries from following the same policies that developed countries pursued to make their domestic enterprises internationally competitive. But the WTO threats are real. The trick, if one is to survive and prosper, will be to identify emerging threats before they become real and then prepare for them. It will be equally important to learn to spot opportunities before they arise, and take advantage of them. Success comes to those who are able to take advantage of opportunity. Alexander Graham bell said: "When one door closes, another door opens; but we often look so long and so regretfully upon the closed door that we do not see the ones that open for us." In business, opportunity knocks once; it usually does not lean on the doorbell.

Competition from across the border will affect high-cost producers, and perhaps even decimate entire industries, especially in the small-scale sector. India already finds itself in a situation of jobless growth. Where will new jobs be generated?

However, the alternative for job-seekers is to create their own jobs. Entrepreneurship in India (outside of family-controlled businesses) is largely necessity-based, not opportunity-driven. Entrepreneurs in this country have traditionally not been looked up to as role models. It is still widely believed that you cannot become a successful entrepreneur in this country without bending the rules. But this view is slowly changing, thanks to the success of Indian entrepreneurs in the infotech industry. They have fired the imagination of a whole new generation, and entrepreneurship is now a desired career option. Industries where entrepreneurship has flourished are IT, drugs, and pharmaceuticals.

The comparable advantage of developing countries will expand beyond low labour costs. This trend is a clear warning to those who are basking in the comfort of apparent demand for their products and services. If the industry is so complacent, then where is the opportunity for innovation?

The present stage of entrepreneurship development programmes as a factor contributing to the industrialisation of backward and other areas needs a proper direction and organisation for making it more effective and purposeful. The contribution of entrepreneurship development programmes is very uneven among different region and definite programmes need to be chalked out to bring about some degree of uniformity and upgradation. Before these problems are tackled, some important issues need immediate attention, for example: (i) structure and composition of entrepreneurship development programmes; (ii) areas of operation; (iii) fixing of priorities; (iv) follow-up; (v) spatial dispersal of the entrepreneurship development programmes; (vi) training and (vii) financing pattern.

Apart from these, some of the operational problems experienced in the course of implementing the entrepreneurship development programmes are listed below:

(1) Past experience has shown that the supporting agencies/organisation either tend to be slipshod in the first phase or are less interested in the third phase which means that the programme fails to tap the entrepreneurial potential of the area or the trained entrepreneurs do not receive the support and counselling which they need most.

(2) Most of the existing support organisations meant for maintenance operations are not for innovative functions. There is also an element of cynicism. A reorientation in the attitude of supporting organisations is called for.

(3) Poor investment on the part of institutions as also trainees and wrong selection of target groups contributed largely to the failure of the number of entrepreneurship development programmes.

(4) Experience reveals that entrepreneurial failures are mostly due to incompetence and poor management.

(5) It is also said that there is an inability to identify the needs of institutions and differences of opinion prevailed amongst the practitioners and also amongst trainees.

(6) It is also stated that there is a low institutional commitment for local support to the entrepreneurs. There is also a very low level of involvement in the marketing of the products of units.

(7) Non-availability of various input, i.e., raw materials, power etc., and infrastructure support, combined with poor follow-up by the primary monetary institutions resulted in the failure of entrepreneurship development programmes.

(8) It is also states that there is ill-planned training methodology, inconsistency in the programme design, its content, sequence and theme and that the focus of the programme is not clear.

(9) Training institutions do not have much concern for the objective of identification and selection of entrepreneurs and the follow-up after training.

(10) Some institutions are still debating whether to have a proper identification and selection of entrepreneurs for preparing successful entrepreneurs.

(11) Those involved in and concerned with selection and follow-up activities have either limited manpower support or a narrow linkage with other support agencies.

(12) It is also said that there are no standard curricula even in terms of broad modules being adopted by interventions.

(13) A majority of institutions engaged in the entrepreneurship development programmes are themselves not convinced of what they are doing as the task is delegated by the government. As a result, the social objective aimed at is not achieved.

(14) Perpetual ambiguity in the objectives of entrepreneurship development programmes seems to have percolated to the grassroots level with significant deterioration in terms of content and interest.

(15) In has also been realised that absence of an appropriate industrial and commercial climate coupled with lack of information and access to relevant technology as acted as a great handicap and

(16) Mechanical implementation of entrepreneurship development pregrammes, as is happening in many cases, will not solve the problem. The mechanical approach may help them (entrepreneurs) to initiate the entrepreneurial development activity but they may not be able to manage and expand it successfully.

Obstacles

There are a variety of obstacles which inhibit entrepreneurship : an unwillingness to devote organisational abilities to business purposes, restrictive effects of customer and tradition, lack of reaspone to monetary incentives, low status of businessmen, high risk involved in new enterprises, absence of vertical mobility in the social structure, market imperfections which deny potential entrepreneurs the resources they need for organising new production units, and arbitrary changes in the administration of laws by the government; all of which make the environment too uncertain for entrepreneurs. N.H. Leff has put it as follows: "Absence of entrepreneurship (in LDCs) is generally attributed to alleged socio-cultural rigidities."

Robert L. Garner has observed that "development is a state of mind. People have to develop themselves before they can change their physical environment and this is a slow process ... it involves change in relations between classes and races. It requires improvement of governmental organisations and operations; the extension of social institutions, schools, courts and health services. Habits of thoughts and conduct are the most stubborn obstacles to development."

Motivation, abilities and a congenial environment, which promote entrepreneurship, are lacking in India. If the motives and abilities are weak, then it becomes all the more essential to have a more congenial environment. But in India the right environment is also lacking. The stimulation of entrepreneurial abilities is a complicated long-term sociological problem. The social organisations represented by such major institutions as caste, joint family, rural village, and school are more favourable for the development of entrepreneurship. In India all these are not conducive to the development of entrepreneurship.

In underdeveloped countries, the functions of a person in entrepreneurial capacity include innovation, promotion, capital provision and risk-bearing, management, assembling materials and labour.

He lacks the help of markets for components, materials, labour, capital markets which have already standardised products and trained workers. He also lacks the communication network, specialised industrial newspapers and magazines. Sociologists and anthropologists distinguish many types of family in terms of who lays down the law and where the newly married couples live. The vertical family under which young adults continue to live with one set of parents after marriage and contribute earnings to a common pool, has a distinctly inhibiting effect on many of the factors affecting economic development such as mobility, saving, risk-taking, even willingness to work more for higher rewards.

Labour supply curves may bend backwards with respect to wage increases because of limits on economic aspirations, or because the personal incentive is dulled by the necessity to contribute all the work while sharing its fruits. The incentive to take risks in entrepreneurship is blunted in the same way. The institutional framework of a community determines the scope of an individual's efforts. If the institutions are favourable, willingness to make efforts is encouraged and grows; and if this willingness is strong, institution will be remodeled to accommodate these changes.

If religious attitudes and institution encourage discipline, hard work, efficiency, honesty and thrift among its followers, the social climate will impel people to apply their minds to increasing productivity to acquire wealth and to improve their social prestige and power. Most religions, as prevailing in India, consider the existing order of the universe as sacred and try to make people believe that. Ethical beliefs discourage the spirit of enquiry, experimental and scientific outlook among members of the society. A religion which permits and encourages rationality and a scientific attitude is conducive to technological improvements and dynamism in social relations and social attitudes. A desire to discover the causes of things is the most effective motivating force behind inventions, discoveries and innovations in physical, as well as in social spheres.

Box 1.5

The Winners

When disaster struck Manohar Krishna, it struck hard. He lost his job, his wife had just given up her job to look after their newborn, and the couple was suddenly asked to vacate their flat. It would've been easy to get frustrated but the Krishnas were made of sterner stuff. Leaving their child in Krishna's brother's care in Mumbai, the couple moved in with friends as they tried to make sense of their lives.

With an enthusiastic accomplice in former colleague Pankaj Malhotra, Krishna decided to set up shop on his own. "We saw our job loss as an opportunity to try out our own ideas", recalls the 38-year-old. With about Rs. 2 lakh pulled in primarily from provident fund savings, the two set up Kam Marketing, to sell a plethora of products, including lawn mowers, shoeshine machines and mail-openers.

The search for the perfect product finally ended at Chennai's TTG Industries: the 'Retriever', a manual drain cleaner. Krishna took up the Pune agency: "I knew that towns everywhere had innumerable choked drains. That meant an opportunity."

In March 1991, they got their first break. The Air Force station in Pune had been struggling with a blocked pipeline for over a month. Krishna took the Retriever over for a demo, and was rewarded with a Rs. 12,000 purchase order. In three months, Kam had sold 10 drain cleaners and bagged the agencies for Mumbai and Gujarat. That first full year, Kam's revenues were an impressive Rs. 12 lakh. By year three, they had logged Rs. 1 crore, with a client list that included hotel chains, large corporates and municipal corporations.

At this point, Krishna realised that if TTG withdrew the product, they would be struck again. That's when they

A Pipedream Come True

People find their destinies in the most unusual places. This man found his in a clogged drainpipe.

— **Naren Karunakaran** (15 Jul 1998)

business : *drain cleaning systems*

company : *Kam Avida*

launched : *1991*

starting capital : *Rs. 2 lakh*

turnover in 1998 : *Rs. 4 crore*

roped in Porusasp Dadchanji, a former Merchant Navy engineer, and reinvented themselves as Kam Avida Enviro Engineers Pvt Ltd. The company began to manufacture a range of drain cleaning systems, from manual units to massive truck-mounted units that cost Rs. 4-20 lakh. In fiscal 1998, revenues touched Rs. 4 crore and markets expanded to Europe. Kam had arrived.

Intoxicating as growth is, Krishna's biggest reward is still the heartfelt thank you that comes when the drain finally clears up with a satisfying gurgle.

The View From Up There

Adventure-tour operator Rani Puri, the only woman in adventure tourism, has made it to the top in more ways than one. An avid trekker from childhood, she worked at Sita Travels and Cox & King's for seven years before getting frustrated with a schedule that meant she could not trek anymore. She decided to quit and get out on her own.

Puri launched Rucksack Tours in 1986, and for several months, did nothing but dash off letters to all former clients and hope for a response. Then, Puri took her most resolute plunge into business by investing every last paisa in a small office. The 200 sq. ft. office cost Rs. 1.8 lakh. At this point, Puri was fighting several battles—doubts in her ability to succeed, her family's fears and the gender bias prevalent in the market.

The first booking came in 1987, and earned her Rs. 2 lakh. Within a year of launch, turnover had touched Rs. 4 lakh. Former colleague Shashank Gupta, later her husband, joined her now and they set about growing the business. By 1994, turnover had touched Rs. 70 lakh. And Puri feels great about being the woman on top.

For some people, scaling mountains is just business as usual. Meet this passionate adventure enthusiast.

— **Chumki Bharadwaj** (12 Jul 2000)

business : *adventure tourism*
company : *Rucksack Tours*
launched : *1986*
starting capital : *Rs. 1.8 lakh*
turnover in 2000 : *Rs. 50 lakh*

Entrepreneurial Management

Entrepreneurship is not 'natural', it is not 'creative.' It is work. Entrepreneurship and innovation can be achieved in any business. But they must be striven for. They can be learnt, but they require effort.

Specifically, entrepreneurial management in an existing business requires policies and practices in four major areas:

1. The organisation must be made receptive to innovation and willing to perceive change as an opportunity rather than as a threat. It must be organised to do the hard work of the entrepreneur. Policies and practices are needed to create an entrepreneurial climate.

2. Systematic measurement or, at least, appraisal of a company's performance as entrepreneur and innovator is mandatory, as well as built in learning to improve performance.
3. Entrepreneurial management requires specific practices pertaining to organisational structure, to staffing and managing, and to compensation, incentives, and rewards.
4. There are some 'don'ts', things not to be done in entrepreneurial management:
   (a) not to mix managerial units and entrepreneurial ones and
   (b) innovative efforts that take the existing business out of its own field are rarely successful. Innovation should not be 'diversification'.

A business that wants to be able to innovate, wants to have a chance to succeed and prosper in a time of rapid change, has to build entrepreneurial management into its own system. It has to adopt policies that create, throughout the entire organisation, the desire to introduce the habits of entrepreneurship and innovation.

The Next Big Leap

By the first phase of liberalization, modern management practices began to establish themselves in some family-run firm. As society and the economy changed, it was no longer enough to keep old firms going: it was obvious they needed to be recreated to fit the new moulds.

The biggest warning to the business family was served by the rise of the Indian middle class. With new money and new desires borne on satellite television, new markets were created by a rising tide of entrepreneurs. Many were people who came from communities not previously known for entrepreneurship. They were sons of austere middle-class clerks, bankers, professionals and farmers.

The first wave of entrepreneurship spread to small towns where business folk churning out things like bicycle parts and gaskets began to reach out to the world beyond. They created some of the markets we take for granted today: from housing finance to cheap television sets to private airlines. They were pathbreakers.

But the flaws of liberalisation also meant that to be really successful, the new breed of entrepreneur need to know how to work the system. The result is that many of the people who came out of nowhere since the late 1980s excel at schmoozing their way to the top.

It is time for all of India's entrepreneurs, new and old, to shrug off the chains — perceived or otherwise. While there are a lot of infrastructural problems that must be solved, there is no denying the fact that we need to do much more ourselves. Thinking global is not just about setting up operations in other countries or acquiring companies. It is about having the passion, the zeal, the confidence to beat anybody and everybody, whether at home or in the new markets beyond our shores.

Every point of growth that we witness today is qualitatively better than all the growth we witnessed in the era since Independence. That's because everything the Indian entrepreneur achieves today is in the face of increasing competition.

Vision for Future

The entrepreneurship that contributes in a modest way to critical economic and social needs of the country and always strive to attain global leadership in all of its major initiative. This is the vision for future.

Pursuing this vision, over the next few years, entrepreneurs will pursue a strategy of :

- Reinforcing competitive advantage of existing business through new capacities and synergistic acquisitions.
- Scaling sizeable opportunities in the core sectors.
- Forward integrating into retailing transportation fuels and creating new customer experiences.
- Addressing the significant information and communications market opportunity in India and in the world.
- Leveraging its strong balance sheet, cash flows and managerial capacity to create value by adding new capacities, acquisitions and turnaround of under performing assets.
- Developing strategic alliances in technology and product-market domains with global majors.
- Fostering new higher education institutions for knowledge creation and sharing.
- Leveraging its formidable strengths beyond Indian borders.
- Reorienting the best practices to enhance productivity and quality (Q).
- In addition to manufacturing products venture into developing manufacturing systems.
- From having a manufacturing orientation to providing technical solutions.
- From being an intermediate goods producer to being a final goods and services provider.
- From licensing technology to developing technology.
- From being an intellectual property user to an intellectual property creator.
- In addition to operating in India to being a global company.
- From building financial equity to fostering social equity.

This change will entail creating new organisational competencies such as:

- Creating a customer-centric organisation.
- Developing new products and technologies.
- Exploring and producing new products to meet the new generation's expectations.
- Fostering and sustaining globally oriented management talent.
- Training the human resources to harness the opportunities.
- Encouraging intrapreneurship.
- Focusing on Research and Development for sustainable development.
- Imbibing new technology to enhance the value of the product.
- Focusing on business ethics in managing the enterprises.
- Managing customer-oriented supply chains.
- Developing and protecting intellectual capital.
- Managing strategic technology and product-market relationships.

Managing diversity in businesses, technologies, export markets and people is the primary challenge for Reliance, as it marches ahead in realising its vision.

Conclusion

Entrepreneurship is an attitude of mind which can take risks but calculated ones; a true entrepreneur is one who can see possibilities in a given situation where others see none and has the patience to work out the idea into a scheme to which financial support can be provided. It is one of the catalytic activities fostering initiative, promoting and maintaining economic activities for the production and distribution of wealth. The stimulation of entrepreneurship is a function of both internal and external variables. In developing countries, there is no dearth of ideas, but there is a real scarcity of men with the right blend of vision and practical sense to become successful entrepreneurs. The objective of the programme is to identify such people and to provide them with the support needed to make them a success. They then become 'demonstration models' to the community; and once the right climate is generated, entrepreneurship becomes a way of life.

Industrial growth in a country is achieved through a 'mix' of large and small industry; the entrepreneurship for the former comes through the large companies often in collaboration with the multinationals. Simultaneously, economic growth also depends upon the level of development and use of information systems in the country.

In fact, the small-scale industry sector is considered as an ideal nursery for the rapid growth and development of entrepreneurship. But, alas, there are only a handful of entrepreneurs in the true sense of the term in this sector. The men who will set up small industry units have to come from within the country and the community; they are 'local' in the true sense and their success, therefore, has a much greater impact on generating the right climate for successful entrepreneurship.

Programmes for developing entrepreneurship must recognise that, ultimately, the change they seek to induce is attitudinal; it is more than just providing information, land or money. It is to provide new goals so that a motivated young person is no longer content to take up a secure job which will assure him a modest income, but seeks bigger challenges in setting up and running his own business. The risks are greater but so are the rewards, both in a monetary sense and psychologically, in the feeling of confidence and pride it generates in the person. It is through the effort of such persons that a small industry can become a dynamic sector of the economy and hence, the effort made to develop such persons is well worth the money and labour. The need of the hour is the growth of entrepreneurship in the country to accelerate the process of economic growth. According to Peter Drucker, the entrepreneurial strategy is as important as purposeful innovation and entrepreneurial management. In a way society needs entreprenurship on a normal, steady and an ongoing basis. Just as management has become the specific organ of all contemporary institutions, and the integrating organ of our society and of organisations, so innovation and entrepreneurship have to become an integral life-sustaining activity in our organisations, our economy and our society.

This requires of executives in all institutions to make innovation and entrepreneurship a normal, ongoing, *everyday activity, a perceptive in their own work and in that of their orgnisation. Entrepreneurship is the cornerstone of the emerging economic scene in the world.*

CASE STUDIES

Sarda Plywood

'To be the best rather the biggest.'

Sarda Plywood was incorporated by a young, innovative entrepreneur Shri P. D. Chitlangia way back in 1964. He was a great visionary and envisioned that wood would be a scarce raw material in future. Therefore, he started the production of plywood and block boards. He set up the first factory of the Group at Jeypore (Assam), in the timber rich havens of the Northeast.

Durobord was the flagship brand of the company. Buoyed by the huge commercial success of this brand, the company grew from strength to strength, and slowly but surely captured the plywood market in India, with strongholds in northern and western India.

In the late 1980s the mantle of responsibility shifted from Shri P. D. Chitlangia to his two sons Jaydeep Chitlangia and Sudeep Chitlangia. Both of them were hands-on practitioners and well versed with the market dynamics, and the demands of the consumer. It was under their expertise that the company started manufacturing brand, which encompassed wide areas of application. Whatever the product or service the emphasis was always on quality.

Through the years, Sarda has instituted their very own demanding performance standards, realising that quality is solely defined from the customer's perspective. This single focus commitment of providing the consumer with the finest quality plywood at a reasonable price has held the company in good stead over the years. All products are manufactured using state of the art technology, are ISI certified, and made to go through stringent quality control tests. Every stage of the manufacturing process is painstakingly supervised and rigid quality control tests are applied, to ensure excellence in the final product.

In 1996, the Supreme Court ruling dealt a severe blow to the company. At that point of time the company was the single largest veneer factory in the country, and the sudden closure of the factory was a huge setback for its proprietors. During the next few years, the company regrouped and opened a state of the art factory at Rajkot and an ancillary unit at Nagpur.

Today the Sarda Group has spead its roots far and wide in the country. From its humble beginnings in the Northeast, the Group has blossomed into a diversified business group, encompassing several manufacturing activities. It has a plethora to brands under its umbrella, which have over the years created a niche for themselves in their respective segments. Durobord, Pumaply, Duroply, Natures' Signature to name just a few. Moreover, all these products are made from 100 per cent imported raw materials.

As the new millennium unfolds, Sarda Plywood looks forward with confidence, and the past merely hints at the accomplishments they are confident of seeing in future.

Vista Flooring

Vista Levoler is a leading interior fashion products manufacturer, which offers a great variety of creative opportunities. It believes in meeting the high and ever changing demand of its customers, innovation and introduction of new products and concepts. One can choose from a wide range of stylish floorings from Vista Floor Fashions which is a trusted household name in the creation of innumerable outstanding products available in a variety in natural wood designs, which are easy to install and maintain. A commitment towards providing complete solution in the field of interior factions, it has introduced Vista laminated wooden flooring.

Vista laminate wooden flouring gives a warm, natural, classy, and a distinctive look to interiors. It is made of high density fiber board, with high performance melamine laminate, and high abrasive silica for wear resistance on the top and melamine polymer film to back it. Vista is the lone laminate flooring that comes with unique underlay material" **Hush Factor"**, a special engineered material that reduces the noise level by absorbing sound, in interiors. Thermal resistance helps to keep interiors cool in summer and warm in winters. The flooring is available in two ranges: the Classic collection comes with 12 decors at a cost of Rs. 140 per sq ft (for heavy residential and moderate commercial applications) and the Royal collection with six decors at a cost of Rs. 160 per sq ft (for heavy residential and general commercial applications).

Vista recently launched Vista Valls laminate wooden ceiling and wall paneling with Vista Exotic, the economy range of laminate wooden flooring. The products cost around Rs. 111 per sq ft.

These latest products are meant for new constructions and renovations of both residential as well as commercial use. In the commercial sector, the products meant for clubs, hotels, restaurants, auditoriums, small offices, conference halls, gymnasium and aerobic centers. Happy shopping!

Artisans at work on the snazzy outfits SEWA are becoming famous worldwide

A ONE-WOMAN REVOLUTION, SEWA

Businesswoman of the Year 2003

Ela Bhatt

When a group of women workers from the informal sector in Ahmedabad dared to form a union in the early 1970s, little did they know that they were penning history. Even as cynics scoffed, these women went ahead to set up the Self Employed Women's Association (Sewa). They were led singularly by the courage and conviction of Ela Bhatt, the founder general secretary of the association. What began then as a trade union in small numbers is today the country's largest primary union with over seven lakh members. It is revered as one of the exemplary economic revolutions of the world and Elaben had since build over 18 innovative market institutions for the women of India.

These institutions have been instrumental in providing market access to thousands of small and medium businesswomen in India. They epitomise a Utopian blend of grandness of scale coupled with social values and viable financial principles.

One may call Sewa a trade union for record's sake. But more than that, it is a movement which imbibes the essence of the labour movement, the women's movement and the co-operative movement. As is rightly said, 'It is difficult to imagine a solution to a problem which people think does not exist.' However, Elaben defined the quandaries of vendors, hawkers, junk-smiths, garment makers *et al.* and charted the path for their deliverance. In her own words, "Capital formation at the grassroots is a must for women to gain equal access and stake in national wealth building. These institutions save, pool, transfer and generate wealth for and with women."

To know the institutions better, Elaben has built a business development federation of 86 women's service co-operatives with an annual turnover of Rs. 18 crore. She has built six district producers' federations of 1,200 self-help groups covering three lakh rural women workers and a co-operative saving bank of two lakh women entrepreneurs, with a turnover of Rs. 400 crore. There is also a maternal and health insurance programme covering one lakh home-based producers and other women; a national trade facilitation centre for 40,000 agriculture and non-farm rural women; a direct market outlet for 35,000 women artisans, with a turnover of Rs. 60 crore; and women's banking services in 18 states reaching 80,000 women with a Rs. 30-crore credit each year through 150 NGOs. There is a quality improvement network of 17 key micro-credit providers in India, a women's business development service and so on. Not surprisingly Ms Bhatt was conferred the Millennium Lifetime Achievement Award by Ficci, a representative body of trade and industry, in '00.

Trained in English literature and law Ms Bhatt taught at SNDT University before moving on to head the women's wing of the Textile Labour Association (TLA) during the 1960s. TLA's original purpose was to assist women belonging to households of mill workers and was focused largely on training and welfare activities. On an appeal from women workers, it was decided to set up a trade union for self-employed women and Sewa was born in December 1971. Sewa later moved out of the aegis of TLA and is today perhaps a larger entity than its parent.

Awards like the Roman Magsaysay Award for 'Community Leadership' in 1977; the Susan B. Anthony Award for National Integration in 1982; the Right Livelihood Award for Changing the Human Environment in 1984; and the Women in Creation Award from Alliance de Femme of Paris in 1990 have all celebrated the vision of Ms Bhatt. She was awarded the Padmashree in 1985 and Padmabhushan in 1986.

ENTREPRENEUR OF THE YEAR, 2003

V. G. Siddhartha

You could just call him 'Mr Indian Coffee.' Better known for setting up the country's first fine coffee-cafe chain under the Cafe Coffee Day banner, he is today present in every phase of Indian coffee — from cultivation to consumption. The cuppa you drink at Cafe Coffee Day could be from berries that grow on the 5,000 acres his family owns in the coffee growing heartland of Karnataka. And they may have been processed in the family's own curing works.

He set up India's first fine coffee cafe on Bangalore's Brigade Road in 1996. Today, there are 125. In 1995, he started retailing coffee through 30 outlets where beans were roasted and ground before the consumer. Today, there are 350. He is one of India's leading coffee exporters, shipping out around 20,000 tonnes a year under the holding company Amalgamated Bean Coffee Trading (ABCL). His latest foray is into the packet filter-coffee market.

Even for such a stimulating beverage, that's a lot of coffee. His family has been growing coffee for 120 years, but it's 42-year-old V. G. Siddhartha who has gone places with the berry. His philosophy: value-add at every stage.

The liberalisation of coffee-marketing India, which began in 1992, gave Siddhartha an opportunity he was hungry for. For 50 years from 1942, coffee growers had to pool their beans with the Coffee Board, a system which mitigated against quality upgradation. In 1992, growers were permitted to sell up to 20% of their produce under an internal sales-quota. That process gained momentum and by 1996, pooling with the Coffee Board was phased out.

Siddhartha was quick off the mark. In 1993, he set up ABCL. Within a few years, ABCL had become one of the country's leading coffee exporters, helped by the boom in global prices following the mid-1994 frost in Brazil, the world's leading coffee producer. India's coffee-export business took off, through a bulk of shipments was in a bean and green form. Coffee is, however, one of the most price-volatile commodities globally. To insulate against this, Siddhartha realised he had to brand coffee. In 1995, ABCL launched what were then known as Coffee Points where the customer in Bangalore and Chennai could buy freshly ground and roasted coffee. In 1996, he launched the first fine coffee cafe on Bangalore's Brigade Road combining coffee drinking with surfing the net.

Today, the business model is no longer just an internet-and-coffee-based one. Everything if focused on the youth market in an attempt to live up to Cafe Coffee Day's promise that 'A lot can happen over a cup of coffee!'.

Through its four divisions — exports, vending machines, retail points, and cafes — ABCL has helped pioneer India's coffee revolution. The 10-year-old ABCL, which ended its first year of operations with a turnover of Rs. 10 crore, crossed the Rs. 200-crore mark for, 02-03 and expects to touch Rs. 250 crore for the current fiscal. If net profits have not risen in tandem (Rs. 1 crore for the first year of operations to Rs. 3 crore for this fiscal), it could be due to the frenetic pace of expansion over the past 30 months. However, Siddhartha feels numbers alone cannot convey the excitement of these years.

Chapter - 2

CHARACTERISTICS OF ENTREPRENEURS

Introduction

An entrepreneur who has a high level of administrative capability, flair for decision-making, is skilled at computation, delegation and organisation, good at communication and has a sound technical knowledge stands a much better chance of success than his counterpart who possesses none or a low level of these basic qualities. It is the possession of these scarce qualities which confers an advantage on an entrepreneur. Besides these qualities, however, the entrepreneur also needs either to be himself a generalist so that he can discharge his function with out delegation, or to possess delegation and organisational skills.

The entrepreneurial qualities are to some extent innate. But not all of them are entirely so. Some can be enhanced by training, or simply by experience. For example, analytical ability and computational skill can be enhanced by education at school and university, while practical knowledge and foresight can be enhanced by the general experience of everyday life. Entrepreneurial careers will be strongly influenced by the desire to enhance qualities which are scarce, yet difficult to obtain through delegation, because of the problems involved in screening for them. Of the two indispensable qualities of the entrepreneur, imagination is almost entirely innate, while foresight, though to some extent innate can be enhanced by varied experience. Imagination and foresight are the scarce qualities which are difficult to analyse and quantify. The skills of delegation and organisation, though to some extent innate, can be enhanced by varied experience. Imagination and foresight are the scarece qualities which are difficult to analyse and quantify. Delegation skill and organisation skill, though no essential are highly desirable whenever large-scale decision-making is contemplated. These too are qualities which can be enhanced through experience.

The characteristics of an entrepreneur that contribute to success are the results of his achievement motivation. The characteristics of achievement motivated persons as identified by McClelland have been discussed in the chapter on 'Future of Entrepreneurship in India.' A successful entrepreneur must be a person with technical competence, initiative, good judgement, intelligence, leadership qualities, self-confidence, energy attitude, creativity, fairness, honesty, factualness and emotional stability.

1. *Mental ability:* Mental ability consists of intelligence and creative thinking. An entrepreneur must be reasonably intelligent, and should have creative thinking and must be able to engage in the analysis of various problems and situations in order to deal with them. The entrepreneur should anticipate changes and must be able to study the various situations under which decisions have to be made.

New Generation of Indian Entrepreneurs

2. *Clear objectives:* An entrepreneur should have a clear objective as to the exact nature of the business, the nature of the goods to be produced and subsidiary activities to be undertaken. A successful entrepreneur may have the objective to establish the product, to make profit or to render social service.
3. *Business secrecy:* An entrepreneur must be able to guard business secrets. Leakage of business secrets to competitors is a serious matter which should be carefully guarded against by an entrepreneur. An entrepreneur should be able to make a proper selection of his assistants.
4. *Human relations ability:* The most important personality factors contributing to the success of an entrepreneur are emotional stability, personal relations, consideration and tactfulness. An entrepreneur must maintain good relation with his customers if he is to establish relations that will encourage them to continue to patronise his business. He must also maintain good relations with his employees if he is to motivate them to perform their jobs at a high level of efficiency. An entrepreneur who maintains good human relations with customers, employees, suppliers, creditors and the community is much more likely to succeed in his business than the individual who does not practice good human relations.
5. *Communication ability:* Communication ability is the ability to communicate effectively. Good communication also means that both the sender and the receiver understand each other and are being understood. An entrepreneur who can effectively communicate with customers, employees, suppliers and creditors will be more likely to succeed than the entrepreneur who does not.

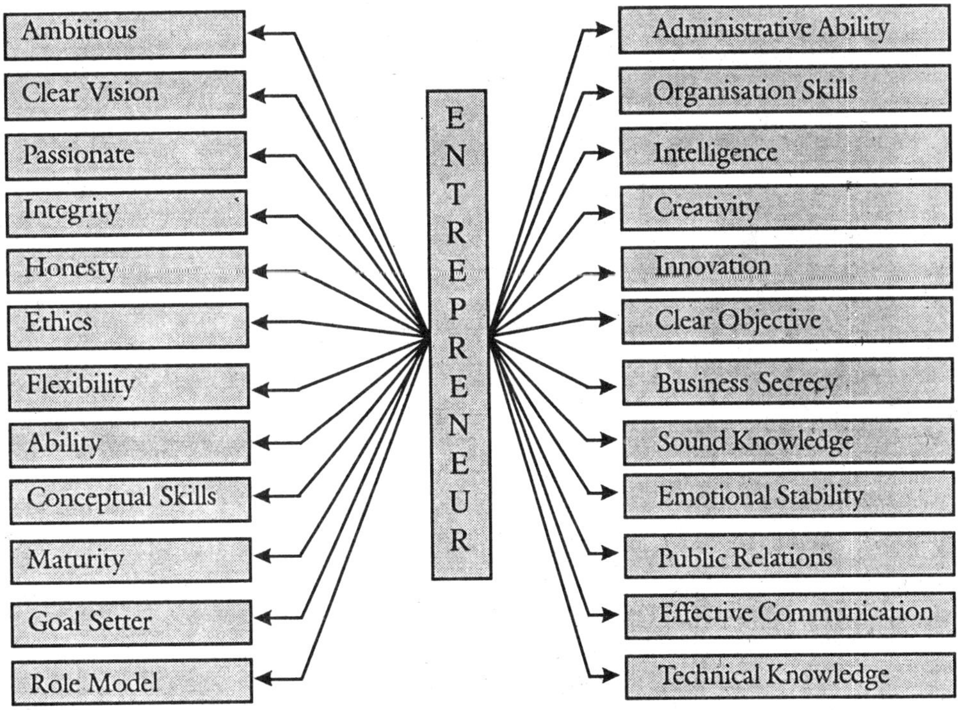

Fig. 2.1 : Characteristics of an Entrepreneur

6. *Technical knowledge:* An entrepreneur must have a reasonable level of technical knowledge. Technical knowledge is the one ability that most people are able to acquire if they try hard enough.

The Mark of A Leader

What separates wining organisations from the also-rans? Winning organisations share certain financial attributes. Companies consistently ranked in the top quartile of the S & P 500 maintain annual revenues-growth of 12 per cent and 16 per cent operating returns on assets. Gains achieved by simply slashing payroll and expenses are seldom sustained in the long run. Likewise, erstwhile winners who fail to keep pace with change, and thereby destroy billions of dollars in shareholder value, are severely punished.

Companies such as General Electric, Allied Signal, PepsiCo, Intel, and others are led by people who personally and methodically nurture the development of other leaders at all levels of the oganisation. Even if you, as a leader, are smart enough to anticipate and prepare for massive economic and social shifts, you cannot response to the ground-level demands of the moment without the energy, commitment, and ability of people throughout the organisation. Effective leaders recognise that the ultimate test of leadership is sustained success, which demands the constant cultivation of future leaders.

Three Keys for Leading. The ability to develop the leadership of others needs 3 things: a teachable point of view, a story for your organisation, and a well defined teaching methodology.

To succeed as a leader, you must be able to talk clearly and convincingly about who you are, why you exist, and how you operate. This means you need to have ideas on products, services, distribution-channels, customers and growth. But you also need something I call e^3: emotional energy and edge. Winning leaders seem naturally to generate positive emotional energy in others. They also have the edge to face reality, and take tough decisions. All 3 components of leadership — good ideas, appropriate values, and positive energy and edge — are part of the package you resent to those you hope to develop. How you apply these essential elements of leadership has changed in important ways in recent years.

The basic cognitive form in which people organise their thinking is the narrative story. There are 3 kind of stories that leaders can tell. There's the "who I am" story, in which leaders describe themselves. There's the "who we are" story, in which you articulate for your constituents what their identity is. But the most important leadership tale is the "where we are going" story. To be a great teacher, you have to be a great learner. Most effective teachers and leaders will tell you that they grow as much as those they teach and lead. The process of teaching can be quite simple; it starts with having a conscious system for interacting with people.

Learning to Teach. The current conventional wisdom in leadership–development programmes is to develop a set of competencies for what a good leader is, and then, to figure out a way to develop people around those competencies. At the end of the day, the competencies develpoed in these programmes look similar : integrity, trust, knowing how to overcome resistance. What's missing is the leaders themselves teaching their colleagues — not leaving the teaching to others, or talking about somebody else's values.

Practice What You Teach. The military has understood this for years. You need someone who has hands-on expertise, credibility, and a teachable point of view about how to develop others' capabilities. To compete in the 21st Century, leaders need to build not just a learning organisation, but a teaching organisation — one with the capacity to build leaders.

Making Training Pay. Most leadership-training springs from the question, Are leaders born or made? and is designed to prove that the latter is correct. It's an age-old, pointless debate. The answer is, obviously, both. Any organisation that takes the time to get more leadership out of people is going to be ahead of its competitors. Are all managers candidates for the top job? Of course not. But can they be a lot better than they are now? Absolutely.

Leaders who invest personally in the process of developing future leaders are also building the most precious of organisational assets. The long-tern success of leaders cannot be measured by whether they win today or tomorrow. The measure will be whether or not their company is still winning 15 years from now, when a new generation of leaders has taken over.

Noel Tichy

An entrepreneur who has a high level of administrative ability, mental ability, human relation ability, communication ability, and technical knowledge stands a much better chance of success than his counterpart who possesses low levels of these basic qualities. Brilliant men with first class degrees from universities shy away from becoming entrepreneurs because the one thing they cannot be taught is coping with human emotions.

Robert D. Hisrich has identified a few more capabilities or personal characteristics that an entrepreneur should possess. According to him, the entrepreneur must have an adequate commitment, motivation, and skills to start and build a business. The entrepreneur must determine if the management team has the necessary complementary skill to succeed. Some key characteristics of a successful entrepreneur are:

Motivator : An entrepreneur must build a team, keep it motivated, and provide an environment for individual growth and career development.

Self-confidence: Entrepreneurs must believe in themselves and the ability to achieve their goals.

Long-term involvement: An entrepreneur must be committed to the project with a time horizon of five to seven years. No ninety-day wonders are allowed.

High energy level: Success of an entrepreneur demands the ability to work long hours for sustained periods of time.

Persistent problem-solver: An entrepreneur must have an intense desire to complete a task or solve a problem. Creativity is an essential ingredient.

Initiative: An entrepreneur must have initiative, accepting personal responsibility for actions, and above all make good use of resources.

Goal setter: An entrepreneur must be able to set challenging but realistic goals.

Moderate risk-taker: An entrepreneur must be a moderate risk-taker and learn from failures.

These personal traits go a long way towards making an entrepreneur a successful man/woman. However, no entrepreneur possesses total strengths. In such cases, he acquires and/ or associates and thus strengthens his enterprise.

Success Depends on...

Building value propositions for customer groups
Dealing with competitors as business partners
Tracking and analysing customer database for trends
Setting up strong front-end solutions units

Potential Pitfalls are...

The absence of product specific sales teams
Managing culturally diverse alliance partners
Focusing on volumes rather than profits
Keeping up the pace of new product launches

Entrepreneurial Initiative

Recent data on entrepreneurial initiative and self-employment reveal a few problems. To overcome these problems it is essential to develop entrepreneurial skills for which the entrepreneur has to initiate the process of development. This is a challenging task. This unprecedented, perpetual change with unlimited barriers makes entrepreneurial initiative in the future more significant and more dynamic.

This means that entrepreneurial initiative is a strategic process which embodies calculated strategic choices. There are strategies open to the entrepreneur himself in terms of industry choice and individual and resource-task fit, and there are strategies open to the regulators and support agencies in terms of industrial policy tools, incentive and explicit stimulation of industrial sector or branches. A conceptual framework that contains both dimensions will provide a convenient base for analysis and possible policy action.

Encouraging entrepreneurial initiative is an issue applicable to both developed and developing countries and the search for effective means is proceeding in earnest. The analysis has dealt with a way of viewing the constraints embodied in the process of creating a new business or manufacturing operation.

The slow pace of the propensity to enterprise is mainly due to the existence of a tangible set of barriers prohibiting the process of entry into, continuity in, and an eventual exit from a business venture of a would-be entrepreneur if it is a function of forces that one may view as barriers limiting full-fledged business performance. There many be *entry barriers, survival barriers and exit barriers.*

Entry barriers are those forces limiting access to identified business opportunities and capitalisation on these opportunities. Survival barriers are constraints on the conditions essential for the small business entity. Exit barriers are constraints limiting the termination of small industrial ventures that have outlived their business viability or the growth of such ventures to a different size category.

The existing entry barriers are:

1. A cultural bias in identifying and managing the entrepreneurial development process.
2. Limited industry-specific data and insufficient market information.
3. Limited effectiveness of the infrastructural base.
4. Existence of visible and invisible obstacles to entry of a specific societal group (e.g., women) into business.
5. Unorganised capital market and traditional feasibility assessment processes.
6. Unsympathetic and cumbersome government attitude.
7. Hostile environment.
8. Limited access to technology.

Observed survival barriers include the following:

1. A behavioural pattern that could impair basic managerial practices.
2. Constraining practices within the capital market. The threatening shadow of changing technology.
3. The threatening shadow of changing technology.
4. Limited learning.
5. The cultural management of resources.
6. Failure of guidance agencies to guide.
7. Scarce information and limited dissemination of that information.

Identified exit barriers include:

1. The emotional commitment of the entrepreneur to his venture.
2. Specialised assets, sunk funds.
3. The increasing demand for managerial skills.
4. Fear of failure.

Barriers, single or combined are said to have an impact on to strategic and long-term planning perspective of the small entrepreneur and could, equally, have an impact on the government's promotional policies within the sector. Low entry and low survival industries (or industrial branches) could provide policymakers with an area for quick and intensive intervention. At the other extreme, industries with high entry barriers and high survival barriers, can probably be regarded as low priority areas that deserve a different kind of attention, i.e., barrier adjustment instead of enterprise development. The relationship between entry and exit barriers could lead to a similar set of conclusions. One of those conclusions is the advisability of the management of enterprise flow and the early identification of the potential for switching (a form of exit), or planned divestment. Again this can prove valuable for government policies for small industry promotion at the national and regional levels.

Progress in economic development and technological diversification does not happen accidentally or haphazardly. In a hyper competitive environment, the economic renaissance of an area depends on a city's or region's ability to address critical needs. To sustain the momentum of positive economic growth, communities must establish programmes for investment in a viable public private infrastructure. This includes not only meeting the other essential infrastructure needs such as roads, water, and services but also providing for educational needs and diversified cultural amenities.

A vibrant financial environment is essential for continued economic development. This includes sophisticated banking community that understands the unique problems and needs of emerging companies, especially technologically based companies, and an expanding venture capital industry that can address the requirements of high-risk ventures. Only in this way can an area ensure diversified opportunities for entrepreneurs.

A pool of capable people hold the responsibility for economic development. A community, therefore, has to find ways to ensure a locally-trained workforce with a minimum reliance on imported services. As needs are supplied locally there are more opportunities for entrepreneurs. By responding to a rapidly changing environment, it engenders a dynamic entrepreneurial spirit.

Motivation

Motivation is an indispensable function of management. When man is at work, he cannot be forced to work like a machine. He is a human being who has his dignity, self-respect, values, sentiments and aspirations apart from the economic status. Under such circumstances the efficiency of the enterprise is related not merely to the efficiency of sophisticated machines installed but more importantly upon the satisfaction and the spontaneous desire of man to put his mind and heart into the work. This spontaneous urge to involve in work is not merely relate to monetary awards or assignment of position or the direction to perform the duty or even the fear of punishment but to the mechanics and system of motivation.

Motivation encompasses complex aspects of human behaviour to which contribution has been made by sociologists, social anthropologists, psychologists and business executives. This concept has its roots in motives within a person which induce him to behave in a particular manner. Generally speaking, the concept of motivation is by an large psychological which "relates to those forces operating within the individual employee or subordinate which impel him to act or not to act in certain ways" —

" *Motivation refers to the way in which urges, drives, desires, aspirations, strivings or needs direct, control or explain the behaviour of human beings.*"

This is a deep-seated definition of Motivation. It includes three things:

(i) The urges, drives, desires, aspirations, strivings or needs of human beings influence human behaviour.

(ii) The factors which influence human behaviour — psychological, sociological, economic or managerial.

(iii) The efficiency of such behavour — this may be tested by the resultant action. Whether this behaviour has directed, controlled or implemented the desired action.

If the entrepreneur feels motivated his behaviour will bring about the desired action.

Here, one reaches the most crucial point in the Regional or District Development Strategy of the under developed regions. The development agency with all the institutions concerned, will have to formulate a motivation programme and by continuous and ingenious methods, involve people in the process of development so that they acquire new attitudes and confidence to enter into new activities and to show the propensity of enterprise. Appropriate values will have to be inculcated and risking capacity be cultivated. Unless this aspect is given its due weightage in the Development Plan, in spite of all the incentives, most of the projects will hardly make much progress. Development is the consequence of motivated people.

Motivational factors constitute the inner urge present in an individual which continuously demands from him to do something new and unique as also to perform better than others. The motivational factors again are compressed of three basic elements– entrepreneurial motivation, personal efficiency and coping capability. The achievement motivation is also termed *efficiency motivation*. McClelland and Winter have made considerable studies and concluded that what motivates a person to do something new or something to seek better is the inner urge which directs him towards such ends. This urge also force a person to use the resources efficiently than to be negligent of it. Also important is the power of motivation which is really the urge to have control over others and to direct their course of activities towards the end which one seeks to attain. These motivational factors induce the person to undertake entrepreneurial activities which relate to creating a new business where there was none. This also means to excel the performance in carrying out any acivity by striving through persistent efforts unlike others who do not have sufficient capacity for hard work.

What Makes Entrepreneurs?

Access to capital, positive attitude, and favourable regulations, says an Accenture survey.

THIS SHOULD COME AS NO SURPRISE: The US is perceived as the most enterprising country. And neither should this: India is seen as the most enterprise-unfriendly nation. So what accounts for this huge disparity in entrepreneurial success? According to a survey done by Accenture on entrepreneurship, no matter where in the world a company is located or does business, certain basic aspects must be in place for an entrepreneurial climate to evolve, these include: access to capital, the right regulatory and tax environment, and positive social and cultural attitudes towards entrepreneurship.

The survey — which spanned 18 months and 22 countries, including India — reveals that the US is overwhelmingly seen as the most entrepreneurial country, with Japan coming a clear, albeit distant, second. Interestingly, while executives in the US chose their country as the most entrepreneurial nation, very few Japanese executives thought likewise of their country, and virtually no other executives of other countries chose their own country.

Countries that stand out as having positive social attitudes to entrpreneurship include the US, Canada, Singapore, Taiwan and Netherlands. Art of the social acceptability of entrepreneurs is tied up with cultural attitudes to wealth and success. For instance, in India, when talking about entrepreneus and their will to succeed, the chairman of Triveni Engineering, Dhruv Sawhney, says : "As a society we tend to suspect motives rather than encourage them."

According to the survey, most executives in Indian do not perceive their country to be highly entrepreneurial. Only 5 per cent mentioned India as the most entrepreneurial country, with half citing the US, while over four-fifths thought that India was far behind the country they regarded as the most entrepreneurial.

Bureaucratic problems are seen by three-quarters of Indian executives as one of the impediments to progress, with 78 per cent citing a lack of incentives against a global average of 63 per cent. Also, in India, entrepreneurship seems to be associated above all with leadership. Top executives see entrepreneurial organisations as those driven by strong leaders with propensity for risk taking. The survey doesn't say this, but give India another decade for entreprenuship to take risk.

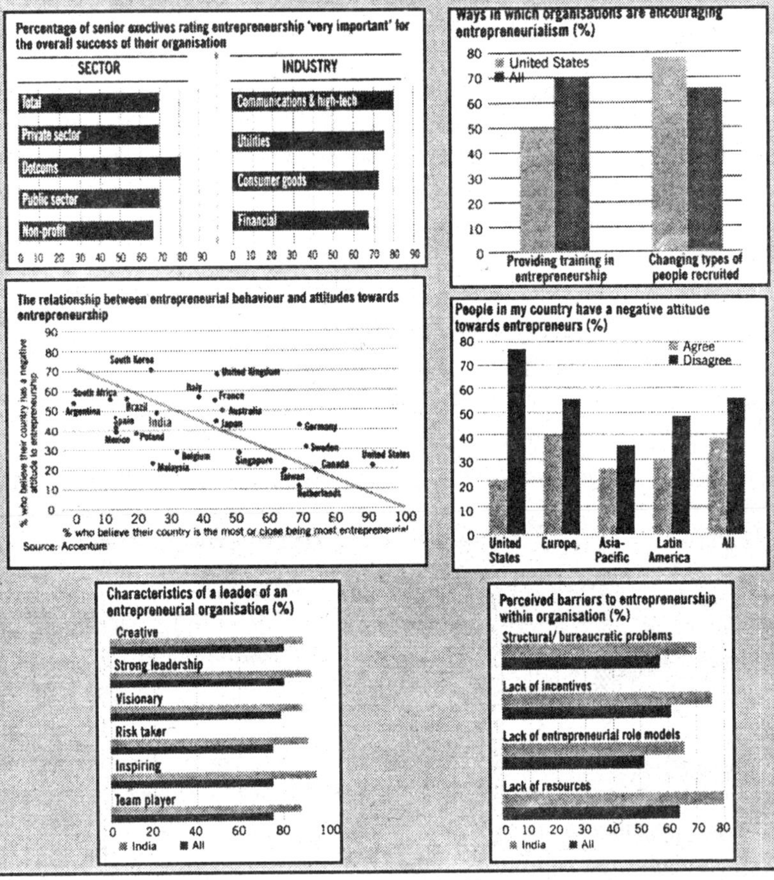

What Makes an Entrepreneur?

What makes an entrepreneur is the combination of various factors that have enabled the personality formation right from the childhood as also the psychological urge that exists intensively in the person. These psychological processes which lead men to set up on their own a successful business enterprise beginning the very early life and have cumulative effect. The influence of early childhood and other social roles are determinate factors for the formation of that personality which motivates an individual towards becoming an independent businessman or entrepreneur.

In the case of persons who take up jobs, it has always been found that they have secured success in the established organisations. These people do not have a rejection towards the established institutions and neither do they attempt to rebel against the traditional path to success. On the other hand, an entrepreneur fails to achieve educational success through the established organisations and this is because of the general rejection of the established organisations at all levels. People who tend to like security and not uncertainty gets more satisfied by taking up jobs which are less risk-oriented and hence are not motivated towards building up their own industrial enterprise.

Men who establish new business are men who have right from the childhood faced a different set of environment in their family, school and other social situations. Research studies have indicated that successful entrepreneurs identify acrisis before they venture into new entrepreneurial activities. Even in their childhood most of them had threatening non-supportive and disgusting adult figures who had much say in their social and economic life. Most of these have a childhood of impoverishment and stress. Economic deprivation also works as a motivational factor towards creating something on their own and free oneself from the clutches of oppressing forces which attempt to kill their spirit of individualism. Thus it has been found that creating a successful new business is not due to an isolated incidence in the life of an individual but it has been as a result of learned response to their total social, emotional and economic environment.

The family background plays an important role in building up personality necessary for turning into an entrepreneur later in life. In family situations where security and non-risk bearing activities are encouraged right from childhood, the individual likes to be more security-oriented rather than attempt on his own in areas where adventures and uncertainty conditions prevail. Also in families where deep attachments and emotional relationships are encouraged, it has been found that the child growing under such situations tends to take up activities which are more security-oriented than risk-oriented. Since in most of the middle-class families, attachment and security-oriented activities are encouraged despite seeking academic excellence, it itself does not help the person to develop a deep urge to be independent and create a framework required for enjoying autonomy.

As a result of this attitude building, many bright graduates shy away from placing themselves in open positions but instead choose to stay in the established organisations because they have developed a favourable attitude towards the establishment. On the other hand, the entrepreneurial personality would rather face the impersonal forces of the economy than cope with inter-personal relations of the established organisations. Due to this characteristic of an entrepreneur, they tend to shift from job to job till they have finally found a field of activity in which they will ultimately have a say and also enjoy the happenings of events by their sheer will, determination and efforts.

While people who take up jobs prefer to see success in the traditional and highly structured roles in the established undertakings, entrepreneurs, on the other hand, prefer to have a different approach toward success and be unique in their own way. They find more satisfaction in their creative faculties getting an opportunity to express themselves fully rather than submitting themselves to forces which are already structured and rigid. The bright graduates may very often lack creativity and are not in a position to break through the undifferentiated mask of circumstances and make something of their own.

The entrepreneurs, on the other hand, find such situations extraordinarily challenging and attempt with determination and persistence to come out of this web of oppressing factors, which tend to keep him in the rigid framework. Thus we find entrepreneurial characteristics are formed through a combination of various social, economic and psychological factors to which the person becomes subjected right from childhood. These factors reinforce in him the urge to excel others and seek satisfaction in creating on his own a new enterprise instead of seeking a security-oriented job. in the absence of these reinforcing elements which go into the formation of the entrepreneurial personality, however bright a person may be in the academic life, it is not a guarantee that he would also become a successful entrepreneur. Something more than mere academic excellence is a pre-requisite for becoming an entrepreneur of success and repute. These requisites are embodied in the various qualities that the entrepreneur must have basically within himself in order to establish himself as a successful entrepreneur. But many graduates do lack in these qualities.

Conclusion

A number of entrepreneurial managers have attempted to identify the true nature of the entrepreneur and entrepeneurship in the post industrial revolution era. The definition has, therefore, undergone changes with changes in the socio-economic environment and will continue to *undergo changes* with the changing times. However, some basic essentials of innovation, risk-taking, vision and oganising skill continue to be the four pillars on which the edifice of the entrepreneurial concept has to rest.

An ideal entrepreneur is one who combines values in the market economy; that profit do not somehow preclude ethical behaviour; that growth is possible even if political patronage is not used to bend rules and cut corners, and quite simply that pursuit of wealth can be a principle and mannerly one. He takes with him the interest of his people, his country, his natural resources, the ecology and sees that his enterprise becomes a catalytic agent of development. There is, thus, a need for true entrepreneurs, who do not work for incentives, infrastructure, government support; but build their enterprises, harness the sources and develop. They adopt a responsible value driven corporate philosophy for their enterprises and /or business activities. As such, there is no dispute among economists and social thinkers about the urgent need for the emergence of the entrepreneurial society as a forerunner of accelerated development of the economy in an integrated manner.

CASE STUDY

Designed to Succeed

At 25, with a promising career ahead of her on the creative teams of advertising majors such as Contact and Mudra, Sonia Manchanda chose to walk away to set up Esign, a design hotshop. Ask her why and she replies : "No guts, no glory." When she started off her design consultancy business in 1997, she made this her leitmotif.

Why did she choose to break away ? "In a large agency, I had no control over my design output. I'd ask if we could print on paper napkins, and the production manager would just turn around and say no." Freshers on the creative team, she says, were expected to write copy, sketch visuals and go home. There was little involvement with the total design process. Which was not what this NID graduate was looking for.

Take Off. So, Manchanda did the next best thing. And that was to set up shop on her own. It wasn't easy. Newly wed, she and husband Girish Raj had just moved to Bangalore. The young couple had no savings that could be used to start a business. Investing Rs. 20,000/- on peripherals and with an old 386 computer, Manchanda started work from one room in her new home.

Says Manchanda : "For a woman in the world of start-up business, insecurity is a very real fear." She couldn't refuse to take on even the most unsavoury clients. Bereft of the support structure that a corporate office provides, Manchanda found herself adrift. And, for the first few months, she found herself running from pillar to post, getting printouts from a neighbouring computer centre, meeting clients, and at the same time creating top notch design work.

Manchanda's creative work coupled with astute money management and some luck, saw Esign post a healthy turnover of Rs. 35 lakh in just three years, with profits after tax of Rs. 8.7 lakh. The company had by now signed up retained contracts with four major clients, and Manchanda began to hire more talent to take her creative team to eight members.

Most people would have rested on their oars now and let the business drift along. Being on a retainer meant companies would pay up every month but would only throw Esign occasional scraps of work that often had little to do with design. Manchanda was making money, but her business was going nowhere. "We were being underutilised, and one day I decided I'd had enough and just stopped sending in the retainer bills," she says. With contracts on hand worth between Rs. 50,000 and Rs. 2 lakh a month, it was not an easy decision to take.

Designed To Succeed

A young designer decides that she can be more creative running her own business.

— Sonia Manchanda

business : *design consultancy*

company : *Esign*

launched : *1997*

starting capital : *Rs. 20,000 + 1 computer*

current turnover : *Rs. 6 crore*

secret of success : *'no guts, no glory'*

Bold break. Instead of being on a retainership, Manchanda wanted clients to hire Esign as design consultants and pay per project. For many clients, this went against the grain, and they severed business ties with Esign. Naturally, this left the company with acute cash flow problems. Luckily for Manchanda, husband Raj was by then heading advertising agency McCann Erikson in Bangalore, and was earning enough to be able to support Esign. For six months, the couple pumped in over Rs. 2.5 lakh of their personal funds to keep the company going, while Manchanda aggressively scouted around for new assignments.

Says Raj, who was by then the primary sounding board for the start-up: "The insecurity led to the making of a totally new work culture." Pantaloon, the retail major and now one of Esign's largest clients, asked for a visual merchandise design for one of its stores — an order worth around Rs. 70,000. But Manchanda scented opportunity and went far beyond her brief to design a communication package for the entire chain using both visual and print media.

Intrigued, Pantaloon asked her to design the 'look' for a proposed hypermarket, the now-ubiquitous Big Bazaar. As they had no Indian examples to draw from, the couple invested in a trip to Singapore to study the malls there. Says Raj: "It paid off. Revenues from that client alone are now worth Rs.50 lakh."

There has been no looking back ever since. With capitalised billings of Rs. 5 crore. It was time for Esign to acquire a business chief. Says Raj: "Once Esign could afford me, I quit my job to oversee business and finance, so that Sonia and her team could focus on what they do best, top-notch design."

Manchand's go-for-broke approach to business is, however, not reflected in finance management at Esign, which is run on the lines of a thrifty household. The only outstanding debt exposure after seven years was Rs. 1 lakh from an old computer loan.

Now, with business booming, Esign is raising debt finance of Rs. 45 lakh for a new design studio to house the 15 member team and to Esign mascot Zena, a blue-black Great Dane. By betting everything to realise a deep-rooted conviction, Manchanda transformed a tiny SoHo into a business with potential.

ANNEXURE 1

BUSINESS SKILLS INVENTORY

The following inventory will help you to assess your strengths and weaknesses as a future small business owner. In this exercise, you need to identify how much knowledge and /or experience you have in relation to each of the skills listed in the inventory. These are the most important skills that you will need to start and run you further contracting business. They have been grouped under various management functions representing the key roles that you will have to play as a business owner.

It is important that you realistically examine your background knowledge and your experience in these key roles. The success of your business depends on how well you are prepared to assume these roles.

Rate yourself on a four-point scale and circle the figure that you feel most accurately represents your explanation of each category:

1. No knowledge, no experience
2. Some knowledge, but no experience
3. Some experience
4. Much experience

Question: How much knowledge or experience do you have in relation to each skill listed in the investory?

I. Marketing the Construction Firm	***Your Ratting***			
• Identify Construction firm.				
• Determine the territory within which you will operate.	1	2	3	4
• Determine the types of customers you will serve	1	2	3	4

• Use Statistics of India as information to assess the size of the target market.	1	2	3	4
• Design a questionnaire to identify potential customers and their needs.	1	2	3	4
• Choose a location for the business.	1	2	3	4
Give yourself an overall rating reflecting your level of Competency in identifying your target market.	1	2	3	4
II. Competing with Others				
• Find out how well your competitors are doing	1	2	3	4
• Analyse how the competitors obtain their contracts	1	2	3	4
• Determine how your firm will be different from the competitors.	1	2	3	4
Give yourself an overall rating reflecting your level of competency in competing with others.	1	2	3	4
Pricing Your Services				
• Set a competitive hourly labour rate.	1	2	3	4
• Prepare an estimate of the costs for providing your services.	1	2	3	4
• Submit bids with/without cost-escalating clauses.	1	2	3	4
• Negotiate contracts with other parties.	1	2	3	4
Give yourself an overall rating reflecting your level of competency in properly pricing your services.	1	2	3	4
Promoting Your Business				
• Develop promotional strategy	1	2	3	4
• Design Promotional materials	1	2	3	4
• Prepare a budget for advertising	1	2	3	4
• Use quality of workmanship and customer service as a promotional tool.	1	2	3	4
Give yourself an overall rating reflecting your level of competency in promoting your future construction firm.	1	2	3	4
III. Managing Finances				
1. Borrowing Money				
• Determine how much many is needed to start and run your business.	1	2	3	4
• Forecast the need for additional capital or cash.	1	2	3	4
• Identify appropriate sources for shot-term/ long-term financing.	1	2	3	4
• Negotiate loans.	1	2	3	4
Give yourself an overall rating reflecting your level of competency in borrowing money.	1	2	3	4

2. Managing Money

• Do book-keeping.	1	2	3	4
• Establish and use financial controls.	1	2	3	4
• Set up a cost control system for separate jobs or contracts.	1	2	3	4
• Analyse overhead costs.	1	2	3	4
• Prepare profit and loss statements and balance sheets.	1	2	3	4
• Prepare budgets.	1	2	3	4
Give yourself an overall rating reflecting your level of competency in managing money.	1	2	3	4

3. Analysing Financial Statements

• Prepare a cash flow analysis.	1	2	3	4
• Prepare a break-even analysis.	1	2	3	4
• Understand profit and loss statements and balance sheets.	1	2	3	4
Give yourself an overall rating reflecting your level of competency in analysing financial statements.	1	2	3	4

4. Handling Credit and Collection

• Understand current credit policies in the construction industry set by sub-contractors, general contractors and developers.	1	2	3	4
• Design accounts payable and receivable aging systems.	1	2	3	4
• Use various collection techniques.	1	2	3	4
• Know how and when to commence legal action, file a lien, go to small Claim Court.	1	2	3	4
Give yourself an overall rating reflecting your level of competency in handing credit and collection.	1	2	3	4

IV. Organising the Business

1. Handling Legal Issues

• Choose the appropriate: proprietorship, partnership, incorporation.	1	2	3	4
• Write a partnership agreement.	1	2	3	4
• Write a valid contract with general contractors, Sub-contractors and/ or clients.	1	2	3	4
• Determine appropriate terms for a leasing agreement.	1	2	3	4
• Use the litigation process or other alternatives to resolve construction disputes.	1	2	3	4
• Choose a lawyer who can understand your legal problems.	1	2	3	4
Give yourself an overall rating reflecting your level of Competency in handling legal issues.	1	2	3	4

2. Complying with Government Regulations

- Obtain appropriate business licences and permits. 1 2 3 4
- Comply with federal, provincial and municipal tax laws. 1 2 3 4
- Comply with the Labour Code: minimum wage, payment of wages, holidays, hours of work, Human Rights code, Worker's Compensations Board. 1 2 3 4

Give yourself an overall rating reflecting your level of competency in complying with government regulations. 1 2 3 4

3. Insuring Your Business

- Purchase proper insurance coverage for important business risks. 1 2 3 4
- Select an insurance broker or company. 1 2 3 4
- Obtain performance bonds. 1 2 3 4

Give yourself an overall rating reflecting your level of competency in insuring your business. 1 2 3 4

V. Managing Business Operations

- Buy supplies from the best sources at the best price possible (including discount). 1 2 3 4
- Buy reliable equipment with adequate warranties. 1 2 3 4
- Negotiate contracts with suppliers. 1 2 3 4
- Use techniques for controlling materials inventories. 1 2 3 4
- Set up quality control procedures to ensure quality of workmanship. 1 2 3 4
- Coordinate own work schedule with the schedule of other trades people on the same project. 1 2 3 4
- Set up a system for recording work orders. 1 2 3 4

Give yourself an overall rating reflecting your level of competency in managing your business operations. 1 2 3 4

VI. Managing People

- Develop a job description. 1 2 3 4
- Interview applicants for jobs available. 1 2 3 4
- Provide employees with feedback on their performance. 1 2 3 4
- Supervise and motivate employees. 1 2 3 4
- Train employees. 1 2 3 4
- Schedule workers on a daily or weekly basis. 1 2 3 4
- Work effectively with other trades on a construction job. 1 2 3 4

Give yourself an overall rating reflecting your level of competency in managing people. 1 2 3 4

The skills for which you have rated yourself as 1 or 2 represent your weakness. Before you start your business, you should plan on acquiring these skills or find a partner who has such expertise. You must also plan to improve those skills which are rated 3.

In any case, attempting to develop or improve your skills as you run your business may be very costly and lead to bankruptcy. There will be numerous tasks to accomplish and they will put high pressure on your ability to make your business profitable. If you are not sufficiently prepared and organised to have them done, you will soon fall behind and the problems will rapidly pile up with no relief in sight.

The skills which you rated as 4 represent the strengths that will contribute to the success of your future contracting business.

You should not expect to be equally strong in all the functions necessary for operating a business. However, knowing your weaknesses will allow you to see assistance for solving problems requiring those skills.

Consult the overall rates you have assigned to the main functions listed in the inventory (there are 13 overall rates). List your four strongest management functions and your four weakest management functions.

Strongest management functions:

....

....

Weakest management functions:

....

....

ANNEXURE 2

RANKING ENTREPRENEURIAL TRAITS CENTRE

No single entrepreneur possesses all the traits or characteristics described earlier nor are all those characteristics needed to be successful. But which of the traits and characteristics are most commonly shared and most important for success?

In order to assess what you believe to be important entrepreneurial abilities, complete the following quiz. Rate the characteristics on a scale of 1 to 5. A rating of 1 indicates little importance, and a rating of 5 indicates great importance.

Characteristics

	Little importance 1	2	3	Great importance 4	5
1. A strong need to achieve					
2. A visionary					
3. A need to associate closely with others					

4. Ability to focus on people and process
5. Ability to get along with employees
6. Ability to motivate and build relationships
7. A willingness to tolerate uncertainty
8. Good physical health
9. A high level of energy
10. Singleness of purpose
11. A willingness to take risks
12. Drive to be ahead of others
13. Ambition
14. Self-confidence
15. Innovation
16. Ability to chart a course of direction
17. Ability to lead effectively
18. Patience
19. Ability to strive
20. A strong desire for money
21. Being well-organised
22. Thirst for knowledge and adequate reading habit
23. A desire to create
24. A desire to adopt active attitudes towards goals
25. A need for power
26. Perseverance
27. Commitment and hard work
28. Self-reliance
29. Abundant common sense
30. Desire and willingness to take the initiative
31. Competitiveness
32. Versatility
33. Desire to share knowledge/experience
34. Quality consciousness
35. Desire to add value
36. Honesty
37. Progressive approach
38. Flexibility
39. Ability to change
40. Uniqueness.

Now that you have rated the various entrepreneurial characteristics, rank the characteristics in order of importance in you opinion under one of the following three categories:

(a) Most important for success (include those characteristics that you numbered 4 and 5)

(b) Important for success (include those characteristics that you gave a rating of 3)

(c) Least important for success (include those characteristics that you rated as 1 and 2)

Most Important	Important	Least Important
....	....	....
....	....	....
....	....	....
....	....	....
....	....	....
....	....	....

The idea is not just to work to finish a task but rather to work well and to savour each step you take up to the mountain you've chosen. Then, when you reach the top, you won't feel spent from all the effort. In fact, you won't even feel you've arrived. Instead, you'll feel refreshed and invigorated by what you've accomplished, and you'll find yourself looking for the next peak to conquer.

Taken together, mission, vision and a set of unique traits form the bedrock of entrepreneurship. They allow them to help shape their future. Mastering the discipline of innovation will require organisations to learn from one another.

Ranking entrepreneurial traits will definitely guide the entrepreneurs, particularly first generation entrepreneurs to recognize their deficiencies and move ahead with speed in this competitive environment.

Chapter - 3

DIFFERENT FORMS OF ENTREPRENEURSHIP

Introduction

In the previous chapter, we have analysed the concept of entrepreneurship and its significance over the centuries, particularly in the post industrial revolution period. In modern times stress has been laid on the entrepreneur. Entrepreneurial development is the thrust area of development planners, economic thinkers and policy makers. What is more, the entrepreneurs has emerged as a *kingpin* of development.

"An entrepreneur is a person who discovers new ideas and business opportunities, brings together funds to establish a business, organises and manages its operations in order to provide economic goods and services for the public. Entrepreneurs have strong convictions, self motivation, the will to grow and prosper tremendously and also the courage to go bankrupt if they fail in their venture. But in the majority of cases, they start with nothing but entrepreneurial ability and end with positive results."

By and large, entrepreneurs are found in every economic system and in every form of economic activity as well as in other social and cultural activities. They are found amongst artisans, labourers, artists, importers, exporters, engineers, supervisors, bankers, industry, professionals etc. They are also found among farmers, fishermen, forest workers, tribals and so on. Some writers have also identified entrepreneurs among politicians, theologists, philosophers and bureaucrats.

Box 3.1

A Fair Path to Success

Sunita Ramnathkar, a chemistry graduate and housewife, set up a factory in Andheri, a distant suburb of Mumbai with a net capital of Rs. one lakh in 1982. Over a span of 12 years, the company, Fem Care Pharma Pvt. Ltd., has come a long way and has crossed Rs. 3.5 crore turnover mark with its key products. Its first product was 'Fem Instobleach.' Today the company has broadened its product base. Fem has succeeded in carving a niche for itself in all its product lines. While the distribution of the other products in the Fem range are handled by 450 stockists, sales and marketing for the Pharma range is via medical representatives and is restricted to Karnataka, Maharashtra and Madhya Pradesh. And Fem has been developing its expertise in niche marketing developing into a fine art.

After all, whatever the generic name of the product, the success of a brand depends on how the consumer values it.

Broadly, entrepreneurs are classified into those from a business community and others. This chapter attempts to analyse different types of entrepreneurs in business as well as in different faculties of understanding. On the basis of his study of American agriculture, Clarence Danhof classified entrepreneurs into four categories, namely, Innovative Entrepreneur etc. The other classification is based on technology, economic activity and market economy.

Economists' View

In economic analysis, entrepreneurial functions are supposed to be directed towards the materialistic objective of maximisation, though its foundations may be of a high order such as spiritual, patriotic, social, psychological or ethnic. Entrepreneurial activity is a form-giving activity—giving form to the wishes of the society, to ideas, to the efforts of factors and to the raw material to be processed.

J.B. Say states that to rationally combine the forces of production into a new producing organisation is the function of the entrepreneur. J.S.Mill lists superintendence, control and direction as entrepreneurial functions.

Superintendence

To assemble the means, turn out maximum at minimum cost and to supervise the work.

Control

The flow of goods, use of finance, utilisation of machinery and the activities of subordinates.

Direction

An entrepreneur is a goal-oriented person; he has to keep the organisation constantly on the path to his objective. His is an activity of producing in the present what the future will demand. Mill also emphasised managerial and administrative functions of an entrepreneur according to Marshall. Organisation-building capacity is the most critical skill expected of an entrepreneur according to Marshall. Mill assigns to the entrepreneur the functions of risk-bearing, innovation and management. To Cantillion, an entrepreneur is an uncertainty-bearer buying at a fixed price and selling at an uncertain one.

Kirzener viewed the entrepreneur as a dilsequilibrating force. It is the alertness to unnoticed opportunities which creates a tendency of the ever-circular flow of equilibrium. Harvey Leibenstein states, "Entrepreneur is an individual or group of individuals with four major characteristics. He connects different markets; he is capable of making up market deficiencies (gap-filling); he is input complete and he creates or expands time-binding, input-transforming entities (firms)."

To Schumpeter, innovation is the sole function of an entrepreneur. It cover the introduction of new goods, a new method of production, a new market, a new source of supply of raw materials or half-manufactured goods and a new organisation of any industry for the creation of monopoly position or breaking it. The function of the entrepreneur is to reform or revise the pattern of production. So, Schumpeter has given a social context to the activity, a psychological objective to be attained and a functionality spearheading development of the community. Lazarfeld as also Meier and Baldwin concur with Schumpeter.

B.F. Hoselitz reports, "The primary function of entrepreneurship is the investment of time, capital and energy in economically significant pursuits; the emphasis is on decision-making in its various aspects."

Harbinson enumerates four functions : The undertaking or managing of risks and handling of economic uncertainty; planning and innovation; coordination, administration and control and routine supervision. Ability to build an organisation is, perhaps, Harbinson adds, the most precious of all entrepreneurial skills. Redlich's threefold division of function is: (i) capitalist—employing the factors and buying raw material, setting up the organisation; (ii) managerial—innovation, supervision, and coordination of productive activities and (iii) entrepreneurial—decision-making. Benjamin Higgins lists seeing opportunities for introduction of new techniques or new products and exploitation of new resources and organising factors of production into an enterprises to take advantage of these opportunities as essential for economic development.

B.C. Tandon discusses the function of an entrepreneur in a developing economy in the context of economic, legal, political and cultural environment. Accordingly, the entrepreneur must possess (a) capacity to assume risk and self-confidence; (b) technological knowledge, alertness to recognize opportunities, willingness to accept change and ability to initiate; (c) ability to Marshall resources and (d) talent for organisation and administration. He has to have tact, patience, sagacity, power of observation and ability of discrimination. He should have the capacity to pick and choose associates and subordinates and wisely delegate authority to inspire loyalty. He must be able to multiply 'himself' effectively. Tandon describes an entrepreneur as an 'ideal-type' rather than as a 'social-type.' Knight identifies entrepreneurship with control and responsibility.

The economic functions described above isolate the entrepreneur from the economic environs, social milieu and political ethos in which he functions. Maximization is taken as the pole star in his voyage. It seems to be conveniently assumed that he is abundantly provided with all the resources and the market readily absorbs what he puts into it. Reality is, however, full of bottlenecks and hurdles which are ignored in the above-mentioned works. Small industry is a natural habitat of the entrepreneur where his role is like that of a stoker who keeps the fire burning. Economic functioning takes no notice of this.

Sociologists' View

Sociologists consider the entrepreneur as a role player corresponding to the role expected by society. Wishes of the society are exhibited through customs and taboos, rewards and restraints, ethnic values and child-rearing practices, nationalistic attitudes and patriotic inculcations and protestant ethics. He is conditioned by the social milieu to which he belongs. According to Peter Marries, to assemble or reassemble from what is available, a very concrete kind of imagination, to see what others have missed, sensitivity to business and social environment, zest for industrial development and entrepreneurial courage are the factors that make an entrepreneur. According to Flavia Derossi, coordination at every stage — inception, maintenance and expansion — is the function of an entrepreneur. She feels an entrepreneur needs two qualities : (i) An optimistic belief that there is a possibility of change, the environment can be mastered and he himself can introduce the required change. He finds difficulties challenging and stimulating; he thrives on them. And (ii) As a participant the dynamic area of industry, he seizes upon new problems as opportunities for testing one's own capabilities.

Psychologists' View

Among psychologists, Frank Young describes an entrepreneur as a change-agent. K.L.Sharma maintains that entrepreneurs are men who exhibit qualities of leadership in solving persistent professional problems; but those persons likewise demonstrate eagerness to seize unusual opportunities. They have a business gambler's itch. T. V. Rao and Udai Pareek describe entreprenership as a creative and innovative response to the environment. The entrepreneur is goal-oriented rather than means-oriented. He must not only have a high capacity for risk-taking but must also have a high capacity for risk-sustaining which is a function of a high degree of self-confidence.

In sum, the foregoing description of the functions of an entrepreneur presents the profile of a functionary. Economists present him as a perceiver of otherwise unnoticed opportunity, an organisation builder, adapter of new profitable activity and beneficiary thereof. Sociologists present him as a personality moulded by various practices of social enforcement and values imbibed in him. Psychologically, entrepreneurship is a vigorous application of the person's energies towards long-cherished goals.

Large firms, both large industrial undertakings and multinational units — are now such a dominant form of business enterprise in most countries that we are sometimes likely to forget that this is a comparatively recent development. The Industrial Revolution was accomplished largely through small-scale industries — entities with modest capital, a few score workers at most, owned and managed by a single individual or family. In fact, industrialisation made its warily beginning in the small sector. Really large-scale organisations emerged slowly, and their explosive growth did not take place until the firstly half of the present century. In spite of rapid growth of large enterprises and multinationals and the scale of economics, in recent years, however, there has been renewed interest in and appreciation of the value of small and medium enterprises, and efforts have been made to encourage them and create a better climate for their successful operations in the hope that they would reduce the nation's dependence on imports and promote greater decentralization of economic activity in the country. At the same time, it may be possible for individual entrepreneurs to achieve a greater sense of identity with local community. This apart, the small-scale sector has been given due importance in the developing countries on account of their employment potential.

The Importance of Small Industry

Small industries are as essential link in the chain of the Indian economy. They serve the consumer and meet the needs of other businesses, large, medium and small (tiny). While they may not be able to match the product variety and production volume of large firms, they can compete with them in regard to price and service and in specialised segments of particular markets, and increase the range of available alternatives. The cottage industries excel in artistic production, which is intrinsic of Indian culture and civilization.

Large-Scale Vs. Small-Scale

If large-scale industries are capital-intensive with a comparative long gestation period, small-scale industries are employment-intensive. Cottage, village or other traditional industries help to preserve a productive system which is the product of historical evolution and, at the same time, embody certain cultural and aesthetic values. The evolution of an integrated pattern of all sizes of industrial units is as much due to certain compulsions of the economic situation—under-employment in rural areas and unemployment in urban areas—as to the democratic political system.

Distinction between Industry (Large & Medium) and Small-Scale Industries

Medium and Large Industries	*Small-Scale Industries*
Under Industries Development and Regulation Act (IDRA) 1951, all the industrial undertaking (large and medium) included in Schedule I of the Act are subject to licensing and registration with Government within a prescribed time limit.	Industrial undertakings covered by the small-scale sector required to be registered as SSI units with Directors of Industries or State and Union Territories for purpose of allocation of scarce raw materials, power supply, taxation as also for statistical purposes.
No new industrial unit could be established or substantial expansion to and diversification to produce new items by existing units can be effected without a licence.	SSI undertakings are, however, outside the purview of IDRA, being in the centralised sector. For their expansion, and diversification, they are governed by the rules and regulations enacted by the State Governments and directives issued by the Director of Industries.
Government could order an investigation in respect of any scheduled industry or undertaking if, in its opinion, there had been an unjustifiable fall in the volume of production in the industry or undertaking or marked deterioration in quality or increase in price without any justification or cause serious injury or damage to consumers.	Government intervention is somewhat less pronounced as compared with units under IDRA. However, the Small Industries Development Organisation (SIDO) which has been entrusted with the main task of development of small-scale industry in India. SIDO acts as a policy formulating, co-ordinating and monitoring agency for development of small-scale industries.

Medium and Large Industries	*Small-Scale Industries*
In the event of an industry no carrying out the directions, the Government could take over its management.	SSI units are not generally governed by the Government directives such as take-over by the Government, in the event of deterioration of output, quality, etc.
Though the Industries Development & Regulation Act (IDRA) does not distinguish large and medium units, normally an undertaking whose investment is more than Rs. 25 lakhs and less than Rs. 1 crore is considered a Medium Industrial Undertaking and those with investment of Rs. 1 crore and above are reckoned as large industrial undertaking.	An undertaking with fixed investment in plant and machinery not exceeding Rs. 100 lakhs is a small-scale unit. The investment limit is Rs. 1100 lakhs for ancillary industries. Those units with investment less than Rs. 10 lakhs in plant and machinery are classified as tiny sector within the overall framework of small-scale industries.
Organisationally, by and large, medium-scale units are closely held and private limited, whereas large units are normally public limited. Public ownership has given added status to large industrial undertakings.	Ownership of small-scale industries, by and large, is proprietary or partnership. The ownership and control in small-scale industry vest in the hands of a few proprietors who have a major stake in the undertaking promoted or purchased by them.
Engaged in manufacturing and processing activities on a large-scale (mass production). Large/medium units generally have a higher input of technology and capital. Relatively they are more capital-intensive.	Generally, SSI units are in less capital-intensive/intermediate technology areas, which are labour-intensive. The number of reserved items stood at 832 as at the end of January 1982. While by the very definition, SSI units cannot be capital-intensive, they have of late, entered into technologically sophisticated lines like electronics.
Large units converge more around metropolitan and urban areas, where all the basic infrastructural facilities are available. (They are, by and large, infrastructure oriented).	SSI units are more amenable to dispersal and decentralised growth. As such, they are located in cities as well as in rural and semi-urban centres with the minimum availability of infrastructural facilities.
Large and medium industries by and arge, require proportionately larger areas for their location, wherever they may be established.	In contrast, many an SSI units function in vertical industrial estates in cities and horizontal industrial estates in other areas. Thus, they economise the use of land which is quite scarce and limited.
The very large industries generally belong to MRTP Groups or foreign companies. Medium industries, by and large, are the growth of SSI units.	Generally, there are no links with foreign companies and do not belong to MRTP companies.

Medium and Large Industries	*Small-Scale Industries*
Large and medium industrial undertakings have a greater exposure to professional management.	In a large number of cases, traditional or intermediate technology is employed. While professionals have entered into SSI sector, in a majority of cases the organisational management continues to be traditional and professionalism has yet to be inducted in full measure.
Large and medium industries are basically market oriented. They produce goods for the mass.	SSI basically caters to the need of the people and /or large industries in their areas of operation. 33884 items have been reserved for exclusive purchase from SSI units.
These industries are prone to modern technology aimed at increased productivity and attractive wages.	SSI sector offers resistance to change that surfaces on occasion and stands and leads to unemployment and halts progress all round.
Different jobs are handled by a chain of specialised and /or professional skilled people.	All management functions at all levels—executive, administrative, productive, supervisory, clerical and even skilled and common labours—are carried out by the entrepreneurs.
Training is imparted in specialised institutions and modern modes of management are implemented to derive varied benefits.	Training is generally imparted in the industry. One has to learn by trial and error methods.
Village industries have to absorb the shocks of the market consumer preference and other internal and external resources. There are only two options left: (1)wind up the shops or (2) changeover to other occupation. For example, a rural artist, if not successful, becomes an agricultural labour. Alternatively rural industrial family may migrate to cities in search of new avenues.	In the event of an industry in the organised sector not carrying out the directions, the Government could take over its management.
Rural industries in the decentralised sector are a not capital intensive. It is, by the large, a household enterprise, wherein the whole family toils for subsistence. With the extension of rural electrification, a large number of tiny sector industries with investment less than Rs. 2 lakhs in plant and machinery have been established.	Though the Industries development and Regulation Act (IDRA) does not distinguish large and medium units, normally an undertaking whose investment is more than Rs. 25 lakhs and less than Rs. 1 crore is considered a Medium Industrial undertaking, and those with investment of Rs. 1 crore and above are reckoned as large industrial undertakings.

Medium and Large Industries	*Small-Scale Industries*
The question of organisation and ownership does not much matter. Rural industries are household industries and invariably proprietary concerns. The entire family has a stake in the undertaking promoted by them.	Organisationally, by and large, medium-scale units are closely held and private limited, whereas large units are normally public limited. Public ovenrship has given added status to large industrial undertakings.
Some of the rural industries are as old as human civilisation. Modern technology has not made much impact because of the adherence of its artisans to the age-old techniques and tools. Unlike reservation of industries for small-scale industries sector, rural industries are not restricted by any number. Village industries are many and varied.	Engaged in manufacturing and processing activities on a large-scale (mass production). Large/medium units generally have a higher input of technology and capital. Relatively they are more capital intensive.
Rural industries sprawl over the rural areas. They depend mainly on the availability of raw material locally or are service industries, depending upon the skill and artistic talents handed over from one generation to another. Of late, some of the rural industries are mechanised and have improved their productivity. For example, Indian handicrafts are famous throughout the world because of their exclusive look, beauty and capability to attract and appeal to human mind	Large units cover more around metropolitan and urban areas, where all the basic infrastructural facilities are available. (They are, by and large, infrastructure oriented).
Rural industries are invariably household industries. The courtyard or a portion of the house/ hut forms the area of operation. Thus they economise the use of land. Location of rural industries does not pose any problem.	Large and medium industries , by and large, require proportionately larger areas for their location, wherever they may be established.
Large and medium industrial undertakings are capital intensive, per employee investment being over Rs. 25,000—varying between Rs. 25,000 and Rs. 5 lakhs.	Per employee investment is around Rs. 6,000. SSI are basically employment intensive.
Comparatively long gestation period.	Short gestation period.

Rural Industries Vs. Organised Industries

Yet another relevant classification is of rural industries vs. organised industries. Aprat from location, rural industries are quite different from the industries in the organised sector. They use simple tools, skilled and unskilled labour, simple methods of management and do not maintain any accounts. By and large, rural industries are vocation rather than units run for profit. Rural industries also differ from the modern concept of small-scale industries wherein the ceiling on capital investment in plant and machinery is fixed at Rs. 20 lakhs. In contrast, modern technology, machines and modern concept of management have not touched rural industries. Of the total 736,943 small units financed by the commercial banks, 437,718 were rural industries—321,771 were artisans, village and cottage industries and 115,947 tiny sector units. The average amount outstanding for each village industries stood at Rs. 1,597 as compared to Rs. 14,231 for tiny sector and Rs. 84,230 for other SSI units.

Distinction between Decentralised (Rural) and Centralised Industries

Decentalised Industries	*Centralised Industries*
Decentralised rural industries sector is required to be sponsored by the Khadi and Village Industries Commission. However, a large number of industries are not registered and not governed by any rules and regulations, units engaged in the production of choir goods are required to be registered with the Coir Boards according to the Coir Industry (Registration and Licensing) Rules, 1958.	Under Industries Development and Regulation Act (IDRA) 1951, all the industrial undertakings (large and medium) included in Schedule I of the Act are subject to licensing and registration with the Government within a prescribed time limit.
Rural Industries are outside the purview of Industrial Development and Regulation Act. Expansion/diversification is, by and large, determined by the local as well as nearby urban market.	No new industrial unit could be established or substantial expansion and diversification to produce new items by existing units can be effected without a licence.
There is no Government intervention. KVIC is one of the institutions, which has been entrusted with the main task of development and promotion of 24 types of village industries, provides direction and coordinates the activities, under an Act of Parliament.	Government could order an investigation intersect of any scheduled industry or undertaking if, in its opinion, there had been an unjustifiable fall in the volume of production in the industry or undertaking or marked deterioration in quality or increase in price without any justification or cause serious injury or damage to consumers.

Different Segments of SSI have been defined as under:

Small Scale Industrial Undertakings: As per Government of India Notification No. 857(E), dated 10 December, 1997, an industrial undertaking in which the investment in plant and machinery, whether held on ownership terms or on lease/hire-purchase basis does not exceed Rs. 30 million is graded as small-scale industrial undertaking.

Ancillary Industrial Undertaking: An industrial undertaking which is engaged or is proposed to be engaged in the manufacture or production of parts, components, sub-assemblies, tolling or intermediates, or the rendering of services is termed as ancillary undertaking. The ancillary undertaking has to supply or render or propose to supply or render not less than 50 per cent of its production or service, as the case may be, to one or more other industrial undertakings. The investment in plant and machinery, whether held on ownership terms or on lease or on hire purchase, should not exceed Rs. 30 million.

Tiny Enterprises: A Unit is treated as tiny enterprise where investment in plant and machinery does not exceed Rs. 2.5 million, irrespective of the location of the unit.

Women Entrepreneurs' Enterprises: An SSI unit/industry related service or business enterprise, managed by one or more women entrepreneurs in Proprietary concerns , or in which she/ they individually or jointly have a share capital of not less than 51 per cent as Partners/Share Holders/Directors of Private Ltd. Company/Members of Co-operative Society is treated as Women Entrepreneurs' enterprise.

Small-Scale (Industry related) Service and Business Enterprises (SSSBEs): Enterprises rendering industry-related service/ business with investment up to Rs. 0.5 million in fixed assets, excluding land and building, are called SSSBEs.

Export oriented units (EOU): A unit with an obligation to export at least 30 per cent of its annual production by the end of third year of commencement of production and having investment ceiling in fixed assets—plant and machinery—up to Rs. 30 million is regarded as an EOU.

The definition of SSI is linked to the question of ownership. SSI units cannot be controlled or owned or be a subsidiary of any other industrial undertaking. This implies that in Proprietary/Partnership firms, the combined investment of all the units set up by the same proprietor/partners should not exceed the total investment limit fixed for an SSI. As regards the formation of an SSI as a limited company, the equity investment by other companies in SSIs should not exceed 24 per cent.

The objectives of such classificatory changes are aimed at:

- Facilitating and boosting the growth of SSI in the private sector.
- Promoting SSIs within the framework of the social and economic policy of the country.
- Encouraging technology modernization among existing units.
- Aiding technically qualified entrepreneurs to set up new units with advance technology.
- Improving product standards.
- Creating opportunities for in-house R&D.
- Providing greater thrust to export.

Small industry has been subjected to various controls and regulations in terms of the IDR Act, 1951 and other relevant statutes. The restriction on ownership is unique in the Indian context and has been introduced primarily to prevent large companies from obtaining fiscal and other concessions by setting up of SSI units as "Fronts." This also discourages the misuse of incentives by establishing more than one SSI unit, in the same line of production, by the same set of entrepreneurs.

An attempt has been made to analyse the quantitative increase in investment ceiling in plant and machinery from the year 1966 to 1997 by segregating the inflation component from the increase in current prices so as to calculate the effective enhancement in real terms. The upper investment ceilings in plant and machinery both for the SSI and ancillary units, at different points of time are presented in Table 3.1.

Table 3.1

Investment Ceilings in Plant and Machinery

(Rs. million)

Year	*SSI*		*Ancillary*	
	Nominal	*Real**	*Nominal*	*Real**
1966	0.75	0.95	1.00	1.26
1975	1.00	0.58	1.50	0.87
1980	2.00	0.85	2.50	1.05
1985	3.50	1.06	4.50	1.34
1991	6.00	1.18	7.50	1.48
1997	30.0	3.17	30.00	3.17
2000	10.00	1.02	10.00	1.02

*The nominal asset values have been deflated by the wholesale price index (WPI) for machinery and transport equipment at 1970-71 prices.

Source: Ministry of Industry, GOI

With the help of deflation of nominal asset values at 1970-71 prices, it is observed that:

1. The ceiling of investment in plant and machinery for SSI in real terms, has remained relatively unchanged from 1966 to 1991. For subsequent years from 1991 to 1996, it would further come down in real terms before increase in the ceiling in 1997.
2. For the greater part of the seventies and early eighties the upper threshold of investment in plant and machinery for both SSI and ancillary units was below the 1970-71 level, in real terms.
3. The revision of the ceiling in 1991 did not make much of a difference in real terms.
4. It was only the last revision in the investment criterion of 1997 that had provided opportunities for small units to undertake higher investment for technology upgradation, product standardisation, R&D facilities and building competitiveness.

The Government of India has since decided to lower the investment ceiling from Rs. 30 million to Rs. 10 million.

SMEs in other Countries

In India, there exists no definition of medium enterprises and as such, there is no specific definition for small and medium enterprises (SMEs). What prevails here, is only the concept of small-scale, ancillary and tiny industry which are related to the historical value of the investment in plant and machinery.

In other countries, SMEs are defined on the basis of both quantitative and qualitative elements, such as, the number of workers employed and /or annual turnover or the level of fixed investment. However, employment is an omnipresent criterion for determining the size of the unit in these countries. The prevailing definitions in some countries are listed in Table 3.2.

Table 3.2

Definition of SMEs in Asia and other Countries

Country	*Category of Industry*	*Criteria/ Country's Official Definition*	*Measure*
North America			
USA	Very Small Enterprise	<20 employees	Employment
	Small Enterprise	20-99 employees	
	Medium Enterprise	100-499 employees	
Canada		Independent firms having < 200 employees	Employment
Latin America	Manufacturing		
Mexico	Micro	< 15 employees and gross income / sales < US $ 175,000	Employment and gross income/sales
	Small	15-99 employees and gross income/sales < US $ 175,000	
	Medium	100-249 employees and gross income /sales < US $ 3,500,000	
Europe			
Belgium	SME	Annual staff average of 50 employees, annual turnover (VAT excluded) ECU-4.2 million, balance sheet total of ECU 2.1 million	Employment and annual turnover
Denmark	Manufacturing	<500 employees. Production units with more that 5 employees	Employment
France	SME	10-499 employees	Employment
Germany	SME	< 500 employees	Employment
Greece	Small Enterprises	<50 employees	Employment
	Medium Enterprises	50-500 employees	
Ireland	SME	<500 employees	Employment
Italy	Small Enterprises	<200 employees	Employment
Netherlands	Small Enterprises	<10 employees	Employment
	Medium Enterprises	10-100 employees	

Table 3.2 (Contd.)

Portugal	SME	<500 employees <Esc 2400 million in sales (value for 1993) is not controlled more than 50 percent of any company (nor does it hold more than 50 percent of any other company).	Employment and sales value
Spain	Small Enterprises Medium Enterprises	<200 employees <500 employees	Employment Employment
Sweden	SME	Autonomous firms with < 200 employees	Employment
Switzerland	SME	No fixed definition	
United kingdom	SME	No fixed definition	
Asia China	SME	Depends on product group usually <100 employees: investment ceiling 30 million Yuan (US$ 8 million)	Employment & investment
Indonesia	SME	<100 employees	Employment
Japan	Manufacturing Wholesale Trade Retail Trade and Services	< 300 employees or asset capitalisation < 100 million yen <50 employees or asset capitalisation <30 million yen < 50 employees or asset capitalisation < 10 million yen	Employment and assets
Korea	Manufacturing Services	<300 employees < 20 employees	Employment
Malaysia	SMIs Sis Mis	<75 full time workers or with a shareholder fund of <RM 2.5 million (US$1 million) Manufacturing establishments employing between 5 and 500 employees or with a shareholder fund upto RM 500,000. Manufacturing establishments employing between 50 and 75 full time employees or with shareholders' fund between RM 500,00 to RM 2.5 million.	Employment and shareholder fund
Singapore	Manufacturing Services	<S$ 12 million fixed assets <100 employees	Fixed assets Employment

Table 3.2 (Contd.)

Taiwan	SMEs	In manufacturing, mining and construction—invested capital is <NT$ 40 million or regular employees to be <200	Employment or invested capital
	SSEs	In manufacturing and construction sales turnover <NT$120 million or regular 20	Employment or sales turnover
Thailand	Labour intensive sectors Capital intensive sectors	<200 employees <100 employees	Employment
Vietnam	SME	No fixed definition generally < 200 employees	Employment
Brunei	SME	0-100 employees	Employment
Hong Kong	SME	Manufacturing enterprises with fewer than 100 employees and non-manufacturing enterprises with fewer than 50 employees.	Employment
Australia	Manufacturing Services	Small enterprises < 100 employees Medium enterprises < 20 employees	Employment Employment

Sources:

1. Handbook on Foreign Direct Investment by Small and Medium sized enterprises Lessons from Asia, UNCTAD, Geneva, 1998.
2. Globalization and Small and Medium Enterprises (SMEs)–Vol. I Synthesis Report OECD.
3. Industry Division, Government of Hong Kong Special Administrative Region.
4. Small and Medium Business Administration, Government of Korea.

Powerlooms

The unorganised powerloom sector largely meets the clothing needs of the country's population. This sector contributes approximately 54 per cent to the total cloth production (excluding the cloth produced by non-SSI, weaving and hosiery/knitting units). According to the 1997-98 Annual Report of the Ministry of Textiles, as on December 31, 1997, there were 15,23,336 powerless units in the country. The powerless sector in India manufacture 10 billion square metres of cloth in 1996-97 and employed 7.08 million persons. In view of the rising export share of this sector, the Government has, in 1997, increased the export quota of fabrics and readymade garments for powerloom units [exporting to quota countries covered by the Multi-Fibre Agreement (MFA)].

There are 13 Powerloom Service centres under the Textile Commissioner and 32 Power loom Service Centres under the Textile Research Associations/ State Government Agencies. These Centres train workers, develop new designs and test samples, the sub-sector is assisted and governed by the Textile Commissioner in the Ministry of Textiles. Powerlooms are required to get the approval of the capacity of their units before installing machinery for weaving textile cloth. Under the Textile (Development and Regulation) Order, 1993, every person installing powerlooms in the SSI sector is required to file an information memorandum with the authorised officer. Currently, the powerloom census data is being compiled by NCAER.

Traditional Industries

Handicrafts

Handicrafts embody the traditional skills of artisans who use a variety of materials — wood, metal, clay, ivory, cloth, etc., to produce consumer articles as well as decorative or artistic products. Today, only artistic and decorative articles are classified as handicrafts. The all India Handicrafts Board is responsible for the development of this industry, while the Handlooms and Handicrafts Export Promotion Corporation promotes exports from this sub-sector. This industry alone employs 7.6 million persons according to Annual Report of Handicraft Board, and is of special significance in the country's economy as regards foreign exchange earnings.

The promotion of handicrafts industries rests with State Governments but various schemes at the Central level are directed by the Development Commissioner (Handicrafts). The important products from this sector are hand knotted carpets, printed textiles, art metalwares, cane and bamboo crafts, woodwares, etc. Exports of handicrafts including hand knotted carpets were of the order of Rs. 56,290 million during 1996-97 and Rs. 64,580 million during 1997-98. The main items, exports of which increased during 1997-98 were *zari* and *zari* goods, art metalwares, woodwares, hand printed textiles, scarves and hand embroidered/ crocheted goods.

Handlooms

Handloom form a part of India's heritage and exemplify the richness and artistry of the weavers. The 1997-98 Annual Report of the Ministry of Textiles states that the handloom industry is the largest direct and indirect employer (more than 3.0 million weavers and 12.4 million other persons) among the traditional industries. The production of handloom fabrics was 7,862 million square metres in 1997-98 and contributes to nearly 23 per cent of total cloth produced in the country. The hand weaving of cloth from yarn (produced by the mills) forms an important segment of rural industry with respect to geographical spread, employment and exports. The Development Commissioner (Handlooms) in the Ministry of Textiles at the centre and separate Directorates in most of the States are responsible for development of handloom sector. These offices implement numerous schemes for the promotion of the handloom industry. Currently, the data for Handloom sub-sector are compiled by NCAER.

The Handloom (Reservation of Articles for Production) Act, 1985 aims at protecting the interests of weavers. Under this Act, 11 textile articles are presently reserved for exclusive production by handloom units (as per the Government notification dated July 26, 1996).

Sericulture

India is the second largest producer of silk in the world. There are four main varieties of silk produced in the country, viz., mulberry(91.7 per cent), *eri* (6.1 per cent) *tasar* (1.6 per cent) and *muga* (0.6 per cent). Sericulture is an agro-industrial activity based on mulberry and non-mulberry silk production and provides gainful occupation to about 6 million persons in the rural and urban areas. There is substantial involvement of women workers in this industry. The production of raw silk in 1996-97 was 14,126 tonnes (estimated to have increased to 15,061 tonnes in 1997-98). The certified exports of silk items during the year 1996-97 was Rs.8,804.4 million (likely to have increased to Rs. 9,262.9 million during 1997-98). This activity is concentrated in the states of Karnataka, Andhra Pradesh, Tamil Nadu, West Bengal, Madhya Pradesh, Tamil Nadu, West Bengal, Madhya Pradesh, Jammu and Kashmir, Uttar Pradesh, Assam and Orissa.

The Central Silk Board (Ministry of Textiles) was constituted in 1949 to oversee the development of this sector. The Board provides basic training, extension and seed support to the units and also certifies the quality of silk goods for export.

Coir

Coir, obtained from coconut husk, involves operations like netting, spinning and weaving and is a traditional cottage industry located in conconut producing states. It forms an important cottage industry in the coastal districts of Karala, Tamil Nadu, Karnataka, Andhra Pradesh, West Bengal, Orissa, Maharashtra, Assam, Goa, etc. The Coir Board, under the Department of Small Scale Industries and Agro and Rural Industries (SSI and A&RI) Government of India, assists the industry in increasing exports and in improving the quality of coir products.

The coir industry in India consists of two distinct segments, viz., white and brown fibre. This sector employs a total of 0.5 million persons, of which 0.36 million are in the State of Kerala itself. The production of coir fibre was 263,300 metric tonnes (MT) in 1995-96 and 276,000 MT in 1996-97. The other coir products, such as, coir yarn, rope, curled and rubberised coir registered a production of 138,600 MT in 1995-96 and 147,300 MT during 1996-97. Out of a total of 6,531 coir units registered with the Coir Board as on March 31, 1997, the State of Kerala alone accounted for 5124 registered coir units. Exports of coir and coir products from India during 1995-96 and 1996-97 were valued at Rs. 2,070 million and Rs. 2,130 million, respectively.

Khadi and Village Industries

Hand woven cloth from hand spun yarn is known as Khadi. Along with certain specific village industries such as food processing, forest based raw materials and other miscellaneous manufacturing activities, Khadi comes within the purview of the statutory body known as the Khadi and Village Industries Commission (KVIC). This agency operates under the Department of SSI A&RI in the Ministry of Industry. The Khadi and Village Industries (KVI) sector has much scope for utilising local skills and resources by providing employment to rural artisans and women workers in the rural and semi-urban areas.

The KVI Sector employed a total of 6 million persons in 1996-97. The production of Khadi cloth in 1996-97 was 125 million square metres (msqm). The production originating from village industries was valued at Rs. 421,200 million for the same period.

Table 3.3

Performance of Village and Small Industries Sector

	Production (Rs. Crore)		*Employment (Lakh nos.) as at end-March*		*Exports (Rs. crore)*	
	Actuals 2000-01	*Anticipated 2001-02*	*Actuals 2001*	*Anticipated 2002*	*Actials 2000-01*	*Anticipated 2001-02*
Modern SSIs						
SSIs	645,496	697,522	186	192	59,978	62,377
Powerlooms	26,157	28,250	42	43	5,853	6,146
Sub-Total	671,653	725,772	228	235	665,831	68,523
Traditional Industries						
Khadi	562	580	14	15	Neg.	Neg.
Village Industries	6,273	6,775	53	56	33	35
Handlooms	15,197	15,500	124	125	1,761	1,796
Sericulture	1,728	1,901	54	56	2,122	2,228
Handicrafts	55,804	61,384	99	104	9,271	10,610
Coir	1,250	1,350	5	5	314	320
Sub-Total	80,814	87,490	349	361	13,501	14,989
Total	**752,467**	**813,262**	**577**	**596**	**79,332**	**83,512**

Neg. : Negligible

Note : Figures for 2001-02 are provisional and are based on estimates made by respective departments and SIDBI.

Source : Office of the DC (SSI), Commissioner Textiles, KVIC, DC-Handlooms, Central Silk Board, Handicrafts and Coir Board.

Classification of Entrepreneurs

Entrepreneurs in business are broadly classified according to the types of business, use of professional skill, motivation, growth and stages of development. The various types of entrepreneurs are classified in Fig. 3.1.

According to the types of business

1. Business entrepreneur
2. Trading entrepreneur
3. Industrial entrepreneur
   - (i) Large
   - (ii) Medium
   - (iii) Small and
   - (iv) Tiny
4. Corporate entrepreneur
5. Agricultural entrepreneur
   - (i) Plantation
   - (ii) Horticulture
   - (iii) Dairy
   - (iv) Forestry
6. Retail entrepreneur
7. Service entrepreneur

According to the use of technology

1. Technical entrepreneur
2. Non-technical entrepreneur
3. Professional entrepreneur
4. High-tech entrepreneur
5. Low-tech entrepreneur

According to the motivation

1. Pure entrepreneur
2. Induced entrepreneur
3. Motivated entrepreneur
4. Spontaneous entrepreneur

According to the growth

1. Growth entrepreneur
2. Super-growth entrepreneur

According to the stages of development

1. First generation entrepreneur
2. Modern entrepreneur
3. Classical entrepreneur

According to area

1. Urban entrepreneur
2. Rural entrepreneur

According to gender and age

1. Men entrepreneurs
2. Women entrepreneurs
   (i) Young entrepreneurs
   (ii) Old entrepreneurs
   (iii) Middle-aged entrepreneurs

Others or unclassified

1. Professional entrepreneurs
2. Non-professional entrepreneurs
3. Modern entrepreneurs
4. Traditional entrepreneurs
5. Skilled entrepreneurs
6. Non-skilled entrepreneurs
7. Imitating entrepreneurs
8. Inherited entrepreneurs
9. Forced entrepreneurs
10. National entrepreneurs
11. International entrepreneurs
12. Bureaucratic entrepreneurs
13. Entrepreneur entrepreneurs
14. Immigrant entrepreneurs

Fig. 3.1:Classification of Entrepreneurs

The above classification of entrepreneurs is not exhaustive, for it aims at highlighting the broad range of entrepreneurs found in various businesses and professions. We shall now discuss in brief, each type of entrepreneur.

Based on the Type of Business

Entrepreneurs are found in various types of business occupation of varying sizes. We may broadly classify them as follows:

Business Entrepreneurs: Business entrepreneurs are individuals who conceive an idea for a new product or service and then create a business to translate their idea into reality. They tap both production and marketing resources in their search to develop a new business opportunity. *They may set up a big establishment* or a small business unit. They are called *small business entrepreneurs* when found in small business units such as a printing press, textile processing house, advertising agency, readymade garment unit or confectionery. In a majority of cases, entrepreneurs are found in small trading and manufacturing business and entrepreneurship flourishes when the size of the business is small.

Trading entrepreneur: He undertakes trading activities and is not concerned with the manufacturing work. He identifies potential markets, stimulates demand for his product line and creates a desire and interest among buyers to go in for his product. He is engaged in both domestic and overseas trade. Britain, due to geographical limitations, has developed trade through trading entrepreneurs. These entrepreneurs demonstrated their ability in pushing many ideas ahead which promoted their business.

Industrial Entrepreneur: Essentially a manufacturer, he identifies the potential needs of customers and tailors product or service to meet marketing needs. He is a product-oriented man who starts in an industrial unit because of the possibility of making some new product. The entrepreneur has the ability to convert economic resources and technology into a considerably profitable venture. He is found in any industrial unit such as the electronics industry, textile unit, machine tools or video cassette making unit and the like.

Corporate Entrepreneur: He is a person who demonstrates his innovative skill in organising and managing a corporate undertaking. A corporate undertaking is a form of business organisation which is registered under some statute or Act which gives it a separate legal entity. A trust registered under the Trusts Act, or a company registered under the Companies Act are examples of corporate undertakings. He is thus an individual who plans, develops and manages a corporate body.

Agricultural Entrepreneur: Agricultural entrepreneurs undertake such agricultural activities as raising and marketing of crops, fertilisers and other input of agriculture. They are motivated to raise the productivity of agriculture through mechanisation, irrigation and application of technologies for dry land agriculture. They cover a broad spectrum of the agricultural sector and include agriculture and allied occupations.

Based on the Use of Technology

The application of new technology in various sectors of the national economy is essential for the future growth of business. We may broadly classify these entrepreneurs on the basis of the use of technology as follows:

Technical Entrepreneur: A technical entrepreneur is essentially an entrepreneur of the 'craftsman type.' He develops goods of new and improved quality because of his craftsmanship. He concentrates more on production than marketing. He does not care much to generate sales by applying various sales promotional techniques. He demonstrates his innovative capabilities in matters of production of goods and rendering services. The greatest strength which the technical entrepreneur has is his skill in production techniques.

Non-technical Entrepreneur: Non-technical entrepreneurs are those who are not concerned with the technical aspects of the product in which they deal. They are concerned only with developing alternative marketing and distribution strategies to promote their business.

Professional Entrepreneur: A professional entrepreneur is a person who is interested in establishing a business but does no have interest in managing or operating it once it is established. A professional entrepreneur sells the running business and starts another venture with the sales proceeds. Such an entrepreneur is dynamic and he conceives new ideas to develop alternative projects.

Based on Motivation

Motivation is the force that influences the efforts of the entrepreneur to achieve his objective. An entrepreneur is motivated to achieve or prove his excellence in job performance. He is also motivated to influence others by demonstrating his power thus satisfying his ego.

Pure Entrepreneur: A pure entrepreneur is an individual who is motivated by psychological and economical rewards. He undertakes an entrepreneurial activity for his personal satisfaction in work, ego or status.

Induced Entrepreneur : Induced entrepreneur is one who is induced to take up an entrepreneurial task due to the policy measures of the government that provides assistance, incentives, concessions and necessary overhead facilities to start a venture. Most entrepreneurs are induced entrepreneurs who enter business due to financial, technical and other facilities provided to them by state agencies to promote entrepreneurship. A person with a sound project is provided packaged assistance to his project. Today, import restrictions, and allocation of production quotas to small units have induced many people to start a small-scale industry.

Motivated Entrepreneur: New entrepreneurs are motivated by the desire for self-fulfillment. They come into being because of the possibility of making and marketing some new products for the use of consumers. If the product is developed to a saleable stage, the entrepreneur is further motivated by reward in terms of profit.

Spontaneous Entrepreneur: These entrepreneurs start their business out of their natural talents. They are persons with initiative, boldness and confidence in their ability which motivate them to undertake entrepreneurial activity. Such entrepreneurs have a strong conviction and confidence in their ability.

Based on Growth

The development of a new venture has a greater chance of success. The entrepreneur enters a new and open field of business. The customers' approval to the new product gives him psychological satisfaction and enormous profit. The industrial units are identified as high growth, medium growth and low growth industries and as such we have 'Growth Entrepreneurs' and 'Super Growth Entrepreneurs.'

Growth Entrepreneurs: They necessarily take up a high growth industry. These entrepreneurs choose an industry which has sustained growth prospects.

Super-Growth Entrepreneurs: Super-growth entrepreneurs are those who have shown enormous growth of performance in their venture. The growth performance is identified by the liquidity of funds, profitability and gearing.

Based on Stages of Development

Entrepreneurs may also be classified in relation to the stage of development.

First-Generation Entrepreneur: A first-generation entrepreneur is one who starts an industrial unit by means of an innovative skill. He is essentially an innovator, combining different technologies to produce a marketable product or service.

Modern Entrepreneur: A modern entrepreneur is one who undertakes those ventures which go along with the changing demand in the market. They undertake those ventures which suit the current marketing needs.

Classical Entrepreneur: A classical entrepreneur is one who is concerned with the customers and marketing needs through the development of self-supporting ventures. He is a stereotype entrepreneur whose aim is to maximise his economic returns at a level consistent with the survival of the firm, with or without an element of growth.

Women Entrepreneurs

In 1988, for the first time, the definition of 'women entrepreneurs' enterprise' was evolved that applied to an SSI unit/industry-related service or business enterprise, managed by one or more women entrepreneurs in proprietary concerns, or in which she/they individually or jointly had a share capital of not less than 51 per cent as partners/ share holders/ directors of a private limited company/members of a cooperative society, as a Women Enterprise.

Women entrepreneurs have been on the Indian business scene for quite some time now and have achieved remarkable success. However, their number in relation to the overall number of small scale enterprises is still very small. One of the reasons for this is the initial hesitation and inhibition, both familial and social, due to the traditional perception of the women's role. Moreover, like any other entrepreneur, any first generation woman entrepreneur has to compete in the business against those already well established.

Women entrepreneurs, as a group, came into prominence in the late 1970s. The information contained in the Second All Indian SSI Census 1987-88 shows that about 7.7 per cent of small enterprises were owned by women. Industry group-wise the most popular activity for women entrepreneurs was food processing followed by garment making. Realising their great untapped potential, the Government has been making concerted efforts to channelise the skills and talent of women towards economic and business generating activities.

Women Entrepreneurs

The incredible element in **Jashwantiben Popat's** work is that at a time when women entrepreneurs were unheard of in India, she, along with a group of women, came up with a simple idea for a simple product, and used it not just as a successful business model, but as an instrument of social transformation as well.

Sulajja Firodia Motwani

Lila Poonawalla

Kiran Mazumdar Shaw

In spite of the many setbacks, here's a woman who has succeeded in a man's sphere. That too, in a field like biotechnology, which is geared towards global benefit.

The work that **Ela Bhatt** has done to spawn women entrepreneurs unleash their creativity and fire power, is indeed worthy of emulation.

Sunanda Singhania

New Age Women

In barely one generation, our culture has experienced two momentous changes in tandem. Rigid work-structures that provided relative stability and prosperity for 150 years have given way to a more fluid post-industrial economy. Women are, for the first time, assuming positions of influence in business and public life, the confluence of these transformations has enormous indications for the future. The study of women's lives assesses the impact that the social and economic revolutions are having in at least 3 realms of public life: career development and training, commercial and social entrepreneurship, and the new physical, social, and spiritual communities that are reshaping cultures.

The new meaning of careers. Most women today are, have been, or will be part of the paid workforce. They may take 2, or 5, or even 10 years away from their jobs to raise children, to work art-time, or to volunteer for community organisations, but most eventually return to full-time work. In a rigid industrial system, where one gets an education, works for 35 years, and then retires, taking several years off is destructive to one's work-life. But, women's traditional pattern of taking time away from work give them an edge in adapting to the difficult, but increasingly common career-transitions. Women who have chosen to make a career change after taking a few years off often re-examine the nature of their work in the light of more mature personal and professional goals. When they return to the workplace, they have a better sense of who they are, and what they want to do.

The new market for training. The demand for continuing education programmes among well-educated adults is growing. Although men receive most of the dollars spent on corporate training, according to the US Department of Labour, women are the largest consumers of outside training, whether public seminars, college courses, or personal development programmes,. Women more actively seek out such training opportunities. They are more willing to spend their own money and, thus, take responsibility for their own training.

Cities on the edge. The profound changes in how we live and work are closely tied to where we live and work. Today, the massive commercial, office, and residential developments in outlying areas — dubbed edge cities by writer Joel Garreau—dominate the landscape. These communities are much more complex and self-contained than the suburbs of the 1950s, and provide a new stage for the twin revolution of gender participation, and technological and economic transformation.

The new forms of affiliation. Many people are approaching their current jobs as an opportunity to lay the foundation for a second or third career. People who rely for their sense of pride, enjoyment, and personal mastery on their work are not going to want to bow out at 70. One outlet for displaced employees — and women, in particular — is entrepreneurship. More than one-third of all small business are now owned by women. They are a manifestation of what Charles Handy calls the work portfolio, encompassing the many jobs we will hold in our lives as well as the family and educational commitments we will pursue. Often, these social and commercial ventures are done part-time at home as people cobble together diverse casserole careers that suit their own needs and interests. Again, women are leading this social shift.

Community and non-profit. Volunteer work is beginning to assume a more professionalism character. This is evident among women who manage the health problems of a child or family-member. The result is an unparalleled growth in the influence and sophistication of volunteer enterprises. The challenge for organisations is to engage the hearts and minds of their people at this level to draw the same kind of commitment and energy that people devote to their voluntary activities.

The intentional community. The dual revolutions in social and economic behaviour are having a clear impact on individuals and organisations. As never before, people are defining their own vocations — sometimes, 2 or 3 at a time — as well as their organisational affiliations. The most accomplished people see themselves as part of a self-selected network; yet, as also being larger than that network. For organisations, such once-peripheral issues such as flextime, childcare family leave, employee-training and development, community-service, and work-redesign are emerging as important competitive tools. That these were largely dismissed as women's issues just a few years ago is indicative of the extent to which women are leading today's workplace revolution.

In the end, women's greatest contribution to our changing world may be their insistence on breaking the mould rather than just fitting in. This has forced them to devise new strategies and improvisations that are collectively reshaping our world.

Women Owned Proprietory Enterprises

Industry Group	*Rural*	*Urban*	*Total*	%
Food Products	161.72	40.88	202.60	9.49
Beverages, Tobacco & Tobacco Products	396.61	131.41	528.02	24.72
Cotton Textiles	202.24	44.29	246.53	11.54
Wool, Silk & Synthetic Fibre	33.40	10.13	43.53	2.04
Jute, Hemp, and Meats Textile	33.36	7.84	41.20	1.93
Hosiery and Garments	324.28	44.50	368.78	17.27
Wood Products	292.47	58.29	350.76	16.42
Paper Products and Printing	10.81	17.87	28.68	1.34
Leather Products	0.83	5.31	6.14	0.29
Rubber & Plastic Products	47.85	49.40	96.85	4.54
Chemical & Chemical Products	5.53	7.05	12.58	0.59
Non Metallic Mineral Products	11.77	4.98	16.75	0.78
Basic Medical Industries	0.07	0.44	0.51	0.02
Metal Products	1.03	5.16	6.19	0.29
Machinery Parts Except Electrical	0.04	1.10	1.14	0.05
Electrical Machinery & Parts	0.37	0.87	1.24	0.06
Transport Equipment & Parts	0.03	0.66	0.69	0.03
Miscellaneous Mfg.Industries	127.91	46.96	174.87	8.19
Service Not Elsewhere Classified	0.42	2.62	3.04	0.14
Repair Services	1.87	3.59	5.46	0.226
Other Repair services	0.07	0.09	0.16	0.01
Total	1652.28	483.44	2135.72	100.00

Source: Survey of Manufacturing Enterprises, 1994-95.

Other Types

Innovating Entrepreneurs: Innovating entrepreneurship is characterised by aggressive assemblage of information and analysis of results, deriving from a novel combination of factors. Men/women in this group are generally aggressive in experimentation and exhibit cleverness in putting attractive possibilities into practice. One need not invent but can convert even old established products or services, by changing their utility, their value, their economic characteristics, into something new, attractive and utilitarian. Therein lies the key to their phenomenal success. Such an entrepreneur is one who sees the opportunity for introducing a new technique or production process, a new commodity, a new market, a new service or even reorganisation of an existing enterprise.

Imitative Entrepreneurs: Imitative entrepreneurship is characterised by readiness to adopt successful innovations by innovating entrepreneurs. They first imitate techniques and technology innovated by others.

A New Class

In step with India's liberalisation process, entreprenurship has received a boost. In the last two decades, even the composition of the entrepreneurial class has seen a sea change as an increasing number of a whole new class of entrepreneurs has been born. The new entrepreneur is educated, sometimes qualified abroad, is keyed into the frontiers of technology, aware of the latest in the production techniques, generally conscious of current management systems and is relatively well versed in marketing and quality control. He is thus, in full command of himself.

More importantly, this class of entrepreneurs is active all over the country and harvesting the fruits of a liberalised economy.

1998 New breed of first-gen entrepreneurs born; IT professionals quit jobs to explore Net-based business opportunities. Venture capital firms pitch in. **1999** The spread of the Internet helps professionals set up SOHOs. Principal beneficiaries: journalists, web designers, programmers, ad and PR people, copywriters, fund managers, research analysts. **2000** Dotcom bust wipes out many webpreneurs. Chastened, they return to the corporate world; VC activity slows down. **2001** Action in biotech and bioinformatics; select VCs focus on these new areas; there's less hype now. **2002** Outsourcing spawns new business-ops and start-ups in IT-enabled services. Also in the limelight: HR services like training and retirement benefits management. **2003** India ranks second among 37 countries in the annual Global Entrepreneurship Monitor index for entrepreneurial activity, but government policy, infrastructure, finance remain big hurdles.

Information : Strategic Catalyst of Entrepreneurial Transformation

With all the recent attention paid to information as a strategic entrepreneurial resource, it is possible to overlook that which is simple and obvious: that information is a commodity that enterprises are run by people. Businesses do no make decisions, people do. The right information coming at the right time and place in an appropriate context leads to an informed decision, and an informed decision is always better than a blind one.

This is not in itself a new phenomenon. What is new is the requirement that entrepreneurs in every enterprise, entrepreneurs in every major corporation, government body or large institution responsibly navigate their organisations through a more rapidly changing and complex environment, with more uncertainty, more viability, a greater number of stakeholders and wider range or choices than has ever been the case before.

This kind of environment demands a leadership that can anticipate the future impact of relevant trends, current decisions and evolving possibilities. It requires that both leaders and followers be prepared to redirect and mobilise an organisation in quick responses to the opportunities presented by shifting markets, diversifying needs, evolving technology and changing social norms.

In the past, we tended to think of human resources as only arms and legs. More recently and more importantly, we have begun to realise the tremendous potential represented by minds and their capacity to grow, adapt, learn and innovate. If we are to capitalise on the full capacity of people to think and create, then we must begin to view information, communication and the technology on which they are based as another critical human resource.

Another emerging aspect of the potential of human resources is the recognition that our employees are not the only human resources available to us. Instead, we should be viewing an expanded set of stakeholders and their human potential as well. It is a simple and obvious fact that our shareholders, customers, suppliers and the communities in which we operate are made up of people too. We tend to overlook the obvious potential role information can play in the development of mutually beneficial relationships, with each of these stakeholder groups. All we have said about the value and potential of information and communications as human resource can be applied as well to our relationships with other organisations, the public and the market place.

In the past few years, we have all seen numerous articles focussing on the concept of competitive advantage, but only a few have envisioned the power of using information as a competitive weapon. There seem to be two overriding strategies: one is to bundle information or technology into the company's products, electronically connecting with suppliers or with customers to place orders, invoice, pay bills and the like. This is the area where a number of well-known successes have been documented. A second was to achieve a competitive advantage through information is by delivering information capacity that allows the business to lead, manage and utilies its resource in a manner superior to others in the industry.

Distinctiveness in the future will come from leveraging and creatively bringing to bear value-adding forms of information, communication and technology to achieve excellence in:

- Strategic market intelligence, by combining factual, data-based trends with human judgment and learning;
- Personal excellence as a result of leveraging the uniquely human qualities of judgements, experience, insight and creativity to our internal and external relationships;
- Product and service excellence, by adding information components to the product or service bundles we offer in the market place;

- Functioning excellence, by creating fluid networks unbounded by the constraints of time, technology, structure or geography and
- Stakeholder excellence, due to the extension of organisational boundaries to connect with external stakeholders in new ways, so as to add mutual value and influence.

The power of information to make an impact upon people on an individual and collective basis is real. It is the challenge we face apply to new thinking to the extended uses of information as a catalyst for excellence. After all, it is thinking that drives behaviour, and behaviour in turn drives results; and it is information that moulds thinking toward new, higher results. We are all convinced that this in an integrated and escalating process that gains substance through time and that our task as leaders is to make this gain a reality.

Entrepreneurship and Intrapreneurship

Intraprenership or intrapreneuring or corporate entrepreneurship is the process by which other new ventures are born within the confines of an existing corporation. It involves expansion by exploring new opportunities through new combination of existing resources. The concept of intrapreneurhsip requires that top executives inside the company should be encouraged to be entrepreneurs within the enterprise rather than go outside.

Entrepreneurship can be differentiated from intrapreneurship in the following ways:

1. An entrepreneur is an independent businessman whereas an intrapreneur is semi-dependent on the promoters/owners of the corporation.
2. An entrepreneur himself raises the necessary capital from various sources and guarantees the return to investors/creditors. On the other hand an intrapreneur neither raises the capital nor guarantees any returns to the suppliers of capital.
3. An entrepreneur bears full risks of his business whereas an intrapreneur does not fully bear the risk of the business he develops and operates.
4. An entrepreneur operates from outside whereas an intrapreneur is an organisation man operating from with in the organisation.

Phaneesh Murthy

Vivek Paul

M.S. Banga

Sunil Alagh

INTRAPRENEURS

Conclusion

It should be noted that private entreprenurship has to harmonise economic opportunities with social and moral responsibility. As wise people have said, unless the pursuit of wealth is integrated with the pursuit of *Dharma*, there could be no lasting prosperity and peace, whether within a country or among nations. The highly developed countries have realised that aggressive entrepreneurship without an ethical base can produce more harm than good, more misery than happiness and more destruction than creation. *Harmonised planning of economic and moral values is a long-drawn-out process, but the goal has to be kept in mind constantly*. One should remain optimistic that entrepreneurship in India will develop on these lines, to promote India's economic development on a sound basis, as an integral part of the world economy. The burst of creativity and innovation in emerging technological industries holds tremendous promise for economic development and technological business growth. When talent is linked with technology, people recognise and then push viable ideas and the entrepreneurial process is under way.

Liberalisation and the new economic policy have thrown open the doors for every entrepreneur to seek his own fortunes and thus contribute his mite to the growth of the economy. In a way, the new economic policy has been fostering the spirit of entreprenurship. Human capital and infrastructure provide the two major assets in a global economy. The states are striving to provide a framework that will improve investment, infrastructure, agriculture and industry. They have endeavoured to dovetail industrial growth with creation of employment and balanced development. The country has a vast pool of skilled manpower and there is no dearth of entrepreneurs.

In this time of rapid economic development and technological change, entrepreneurial spirit can be a unique and important advantage, but only if we learn to use it. The entrepreneurs are the agents of change and our hope for the future. In fact, the entrepreneur always searches for change, responds to it and exploits it as an opportunity.

Chapter - 4

THE ROLE OF ENTREPRENEURS

Introduction

The world is rapidly changing, and unless we are also to change our attitudes and approaches, there is a real danger that a country of India's size and potential will become peripheral in the context of the world's economy. The process of development includes creation of infrastructure and setting up and management of public utilities. Non-conventional energy sources have to be developed on a commercial scale. Similarly, application of modern scientific techniques in agriculture and horticulture is essential for providing a sound base for a more rapid growth of employment and income generation. There is also a need for rapid industrial growth which is well distributed and multi-directional. Apart from land, labour and capital, there is greater need for entrepreneurs to strive for growth on an ongoing basis. In this context, an attempt has been made in this chapter to analyse the nature and importance of entrepreneurs.

Entrepreneurial Functions

A successful entrepreneur recognises the commercial potential of a product or service, designs operating policies in marketing, production, product development and the organisational structure. He carries out the whole set of activities of the business. He has a high capacity for taking calculated risks and has faith in his own capabilities.

According to some writers, the functions of an entrepreneur are co-ordination of business management of an enterprise, risk-taking, controlling the enterprise, innovation for change, motivation and other related activities. In reality, an entrepreneur has to carry out a combination of these in keeping with time and the environment. Truly, the entrepreneur has to react to new ideas, demands and exploit the opportunities, and thereby contribute to technical progress. He is thus a nucleus of high growth of the enterprise.

Box 4.1

The Trusted Leader

Enterprises cannot hope to build long-term success unless they cannot build trust with their clients and customers, and they cannot build trust with clients and customers unless they have leaders who can help trust permeate through all levels of the organisation. Thus, trust must become a discipline that is managed along with strategy and operations. Unfortunately, most advice on the subject treats trust as a character/personality trait, synonymous with trustworthiness, which keeps it in the realm of the abstract and does not offer much in the way of concrete points of action.

The Trusted Leader fills that gap by presenting trust as the outcome of very tangible processes and tools that upper management can use to make trust an explicit component of their leadership behaviour. Based on their extensive, highly specific research and experience with a wide range of organisations, Galford and Drapeau present a comprehensive, practical guide for senior leaders that identifies the critical types of trust they need to master, offers a practical formula for building organisational confidence, analyses the obstacles to trust, and demonstrates how crises, restructuring and mergers can be transformed into trust-building experiences.

The benefit of moving leaders beyond the subjectivity of being trustworthy to the concrete procedures for actively creating and maintaining a culture of trust. Seen from this perspective, trusted leadership requires "developed talent and considerable skill," and this work provides a model relevant to that task.

As the basis for this model, Galford and Drapeau identify strategic, organisational, and personal as the three types of trust found inside the organisation. Strategic trust is the faith people have in their organisation's ability to do things right, in terms of its goals and strategies. Organisational trust is their conviction in the company's processes and decision making. And, personal trust is the employees' confidence in the leader as an individual. Although personal trust can exist without organisational trust, there needs to be a modicum of personal trust in order to have organisational trust. And, though confidence in goals and strategies can exist without there being any confidence in goals and strategies can exist without there being any confidence in the leader or in processes and decisions, strategic trust without the other two means trouble for the future.

Building personal trust involves moving through several stages, beginning with the establishment of a connection with someone and ending with a commitment to act in concert with that person to achieve a goal. Organisational trust is a composite that derives from an amalgam of lots of personal trust that develops in wide range of individuals. And, it is the processes and traditions to which these individuals adhere. Accordingly, organisational trust equals aspirations, plus abilities and actions, multiplied by alignment and articulation, divided by resistance. For organisational trust to exist, all five variables must not only be present, they must play off each other. The five variables must be united, as a whole, against resistance.

SEEKER, captures the essence of personal and organisational trust. Leaders must: **S**how they understand the needs of the person or group; **E**stablish the guiding principles of how they will operate; **E**xplain the resources they will use in this endeavour; **K**eep the principles they have articulated; **E**ngage in constant, honest, two-way communication; and **R**einforce their words through consistent behaviours.

It's model that effectively and consciously frames leadership practices so that they proactively free people to do their work, fuel passion, provide focus, foster innovation, and improve productivity. In this way, trust and trusted leadership become the drivers of the organisaation's long-term success and profitability.

An entrepreneur is expected to perform the following functions:

1. Assumption of Risk: the entrepreneur assumes all possible risks of business. A business risk also involves the risk due to the possibility of changes in the tastes of consumers, techniques of production and new inventions. Such risks are not insurable. If they materialise, the entrepreneur has to bear the loss himself. Thus, risk-bearing or uncertainty still remains the most important function of an entrepreneur. An entrepreneur tries to reduce the uncertainties by his initiative, skill and good judgement.

2. Business Decisions: The entrepreneur has to decide the nature and type of goods to be produced. He enters the particular industry which offers him the best prospects and products and produces whatever commodities he thinks will pay him the most, employing those methods of production which he considers most profitable. He effects suitable changes in the size of the business, its location, and techniques of production and does everything that is needed for the development of his business.

3. Managerial Functions: The entrepreneur performs the managerial functions which are different from entrepreneurial functions. He formulates production plans, arranges finance, purchases raw materials, provides production facilities, organises sales and assumes the task of personal management. In a large establishment, these functions are delegated to the paid managerial personnel.

4. Function of Innovation: An important function of an entrepreneur is 'innovation.' He conceives ideas for improvement in the quality of a production line. He considers economic viability and technological feasibility in bringing about improved quality. The introduction of different kinds of electronic gadgets is an example of such an innovation of new products. Innovation is an ongoing or intermittent activity not a one-time policy.

Box 4.2

The Power of Innovation

National Pride Symbolises the convergence of the aspirations of our people with the political vision of the country. Over the last decade, there has been a great shift in national pride—for the better. In the 1990s, national pride emphasised our past achievements. Today, it's about our confidence in the future. In the past, we basked in the glory of our forefathers, but today we perceive ourselves as creators of new history, directing our own destinies. The "Made in India" label is no longer something that we need to defend. Rather, it is something that we can project with a sense of national pride. Information technology has provided India with a powerful branding platform, which has raised national pride to an all-time high. We've gone from being a non-brand to being a known-brand.

In the coming decades, Brand India will only get more powerful. As information, innovation, and imagination will be the prime drivers of the new knowledge economy. And India—as a rich reservoir of these attributes—is ideally placed to emerge as its new leader.

Research and development (R & D) is the soul of this emerging domain and India exhibits global advantage through its large reservoir of scientific talent, engineering prowess in process development and manufacturing, and rapidly developing clinical research capabilities.

The entrepreneurial function can be performed by different kinds of people under different economic systems. In principle, the entrepreneur could be a planner in a socialist economy, or even a priest or king in a traditional society. In practice, entrepreneurship is closely identified with private enterprise in a market economy.

An entrepreneur performs many useful functions. He undertakes venture, assumes risk and earns profit. He is the man strongly motivated to achieve success. He is self-confident in his entrepreneurial abilities and exploits opportunities wherever and whenever they arise.

The entrepreneur can identify opportunities to start a business either as a manufacturer or as a distributor, for entrepreneurship exists in every field of economic endeavour. Manufacturing activities require a relatively high capital investment and a greater degree of entrepreneurial abilities than distribution activities. Entrepreneurship has also been developed in the trading sector. Britain, for example, has developed trading entrepreneurship while Germany and Japan have developed industrial entrepreneurship. A manufacturing entrepreneur demonstrates his entrepreneurial talents by bringing out new products while a trading entrepreneur performs his entrepreneurial functions in creating demand for the business in which he deals.

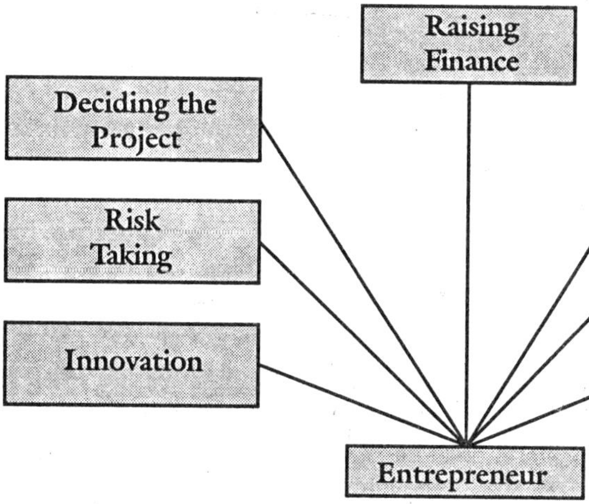

Fig. 4.1 Entrepreneurial Functions

Decision-making

Arther H. Cole described an entrepreneur as a decision-maker and attributed the following function to him:

- The determination of those objectives of the enterprise and the change of those objectives as conditions required or made advantageous;
- The development of an organisation, including efficient relations with subordinates and all employees;
- Securing adequate financial resources and maintaining good relation with existing and potential investors;
- The requisition of efficient technological equipment and the revision of it as new machinery appeared;
- The development of a market for the products and the devising of new products to meet or anticipate consumers' demand and
- The maintenance of good relations with public authorities and with society at large.

Modern writer on this subject have outlined the following three broad functions of an entrepreneur:

- Innovation

- Risk-taking and
- Organisation and management of business so as to maintain leadership and control over it.

Innovation means "doing new things or the doing of things that are already being done in a new way." It includes new processes of production, introduction of new products, creation of new markets, discovery of a new and better form of industrial organisation. Risk-bearing means making provisions for capital in order to enable the entrepreneur to establish and run the enterprise. An important function of an entrepreneur is to reduce uncertainty in his plan of investment and expansion of the enterprise. Thus innovation may occur in the following forms:

- Introduction of a new good, that is, one which consumers are not yet familiar with, or of a new quality of good.
- Introduction of a new method of production, that is one not yet tested by experience in the branch of manufacture concerned, which need by no means be founded upon a discovery scientifically new and can also exist in a new way of handling a commodity commercially.
- Opening of a new market, that is, a market into which the particular branch of manufacture of the country in question has not previously entered, whether or not his market has existed before.
- Conquest of a new source of supply of raw materials or half-manufactured goods, irrespective of whether this source already exists or whether it has first to be created.
- Carrying out of the new organisation of any industry, like the creation of a monopoly position (for example, through trustification) or the breaking of a monopoly position.

Before coming to other functions, it is necessary to clarify how innovation differs from the two other notions with which it is sometimes confused: *research and invention.*

The aim of research is to produce knowledge, that of innovation to produce objects which work and can be sold. Since it is inspired by different objectives, innovation can be completely independent of research. It is not based on the same skills. Even the relevant information required on markets, on patents and on management has little to do with research. Innovation may be based on the application of knowledge produced by research but it may also be purely empirical: indeed practice often precedes theory and innovation may open the way to research as (the stem engine did for thermodynamics, or the computer for programming). Moreover, many innovations are not based on research but on ingenious combinations of existing materials and components.

Invention too is different from innovation. An invention becomes an innovation only when it is embodied in a product which can be successfully marketed. History abounds in examples of bankrupt inventors whose brainchild took hold years later. The innovator, on the other hand, is the person who come on the scene at the right moment to find the missing element in an invention which will make it eminently marketable. Thus it is always difficult to identify the true innovator. Several individuals or organisations may simultaneously claim the authorship of ideas or inventions which have given rise to innovation.

Innovation cannot be confined to a simplistic scheme. Facts show that small and medium firm, at least in some countries, can make a very significant contribution to technical prosperity. For instance, it is estimated that firms of less than 1000 workers and individual inventors were responsible for more than 40 per cent of the major innovations appearing in the United States in the early 1970s. This innovation potential can be explained by the advantages enjoyed by small firms over large ones.

Steps to Improved Innovation

Innovation means different things to different people. For some, it means new product ideas or new manufacturing processes that lower delivered costs. The manager may define it broadly as a strategic and profitable management of change. Still others think in terms of developmental stages: idea, implementation and diffusion throughout the market lace. Many entrepreneurs appreciate the need for innovative thinking and implementation in every area, from human resources management to transportation. All these require special planning, implementation, and control. More importantly, the entrepreneurs today recognize that careful management of innovation can go a long way towards assuring real growth, competitiveness and profitability.

Arthur Young and the Institute for Innovation have created a group of powerful analytical tools that assist entrepreneurs to innovate and change.

Role of Entrepreneurs

Entrepreneurs, on the other hand, as Schumpeter and many others have pointed out, are distinct from business owners and managers. They are essentially strategic innovators, seeking profitability with growth. Promoting entrepreneurship, in that sense, is intrinsically different from promoting small-scale industry.

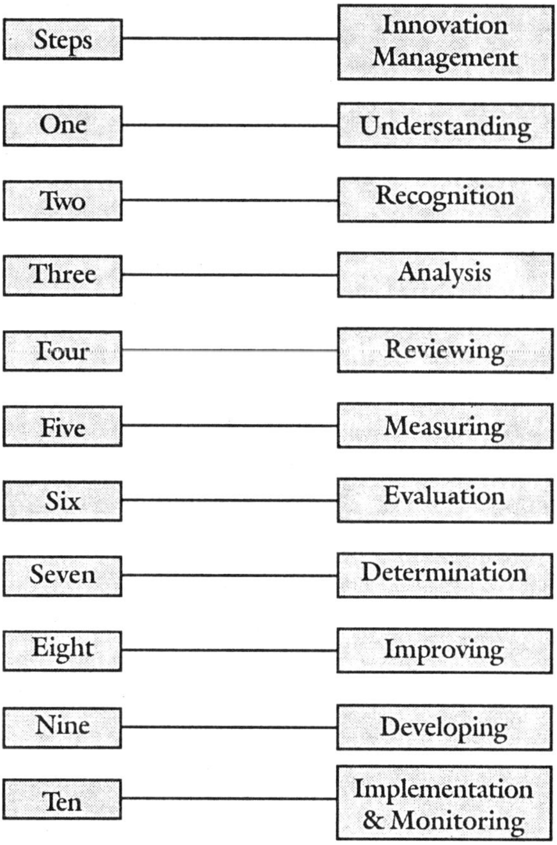

Fig. 4.2 : Ten Commandments of Improved Innovation Management

If any small business in the developed countries has received special attention, it is because it has been the fountainhead of innovation and creativity. Studies have brought out that a large number of innovations have come from small, rather than large business. As these innovative firm entered the market, they made profits and created jobs. In the U.S. Presidents Jimmy Carter and Gerald Ford emphasised that small business created 60 per cent of the new jobs in the United States. And this employment generation was due to its better financial performance. Similarly, the Bolton Committee, 1971, and the Wilson Committee, 1979, also concluded that the small business in the U.K. had higher profitability than any large business.

The studies on entrepreneurship also point out that, "most of the risk in entrepreneurial management lies not in misperception of opportunity, but in trying to pursue opportunity, without adequate resources. One of the fundamental errors of large corporations, on the other hand, is over commitment of resources."

MANAGERS AND ENTREPRENEURS

Both managers and entrepreneurs are answerable for producing results. The results are, of course, different. In their respective result areas, the buck stops with them. While they can delegate, they are finally accountable.

Both have to produce results through people working with them though they deal with different sets of people. They are not effective in the long run, if they are loners.

Both are decision-makers but the decisions are different as their tasks vary.

Both have to operate under constraints which are also understandably different.

To be effective in their respective roles, both have to follow sound principles of management like planning, staffing, delegation and control. The focus of these management tools may vary depending upon the ultimate purpose.

The table summarises the similarities, focussing on the different perspectives within each similarity.

A successful organisation needs both enterprise and management. The entrepreneurial role may be played by the Chief Executive and his team of top-level executives, the managerial role by the middle-level and joint-level executives.

Box 4.3

Keshav (L) & Vikram Anand

Parijat Agrochemicals

In 1990 the brothers Anand were small-time traders in pesticides. Today, their company Parijat, operates in 50 countries and boasts a turnover of Rs. 75 crore.

Table 4.1

Similarities between Managers and Entrepreneurs

Area of Similarity	*Differing Focus*	
	Manager	*Entrepreneurs*
To produce results	Results of today, this month, this year. Short-term and medium-term.	Result of tomorrow, next year and coming five years. long-term and very long-term.
To produce results through people	Have usually to handle people oriented to day-to-day management of nitty-gritty and nuts and bolts type—men of details.	Have to deal with people who can conceptualize with aggregate perspectives—strategists.
To take decisions	Operational and administrative decisions, which have a bearing on short-term and medium-term results.	Mostly strategic decisions, involving growth through expansion, diversification, takeovers and mergers.
To co-operate under constraints	The constraints are usually organisational, i.e., those within an organisation like machine capacity, labour productivity, routing and scheduling, information availability, financial limitations etc.	The constraints are usually environmental which lie outside an organisation like the policy of financial institutions, import policy, licencing policy, infrastructure constraints etc.
To follow sound principles of management	The principles are more oriented towards internal administration and control like delegation, accountability, responsibility, planning, budgeting, reporting and information system.	The principles are with reference to macro-social aspects like social responsibility, equal opportunity, employment, ethical advertisement practices, adherence to government policies etc.

Box 4.4

PROFESSIONAL MANAGERS

Programmed Promotion

S. Balaji, is the 34-year-old vice-president of Polaris Software Labs who spearheads its strategic business units in the insurance sector.

Balaji was born in Dindigual near Madurai. A graduate from BITS, Pilani, he joined Nucleus Software in 1990 and was based in Bombay. "Then Citi India was our only client and since it was based in Bombay, Nucleus also provided most of its services from here," he says. "This is where I started as a programmer analyst." In 1993, Nucleus Software was renamed Polaris Software Labs. As time went by business grew, and Balaji was sent to Chennai. He was subsequently promoted to assistant vice-president. But Balaji is more nostalgic about the opportunity that followed, that of setting up for Polaris a base in Australia. "Setting up a new business in a new country, right from processing to delivery was a challenging task," he says.

Balaji has a career that spans 12 years, and he has grown rapidly up the ranks at Polaris. "There's always been an immense amount of challenging work and project opportunities at Polaris", he says. "And hard work and dedication are appreciated here, I used to be an engineer." But now he has moved into another area of operation. Balaji has been part of the senior management of Polaris since 1999 and is currently busy building a team that should help to take it to new heights.

A married man of simple tastes, Balaji spends his spare time either reading a Sidney Sheldon fiction novel or books on management. But given a choice he would go for music for he believes that nothing beats listening to old classical music.

Growth Control

Nisha Ninan, human resources director of Apex Technologies, Bangalore, enjoys the challenge of working with start-ups and small companies. "It gives me the opportunity to work in the building of a company," says this 33-year-old.

She joined Apex Technologies five months ago and is responsible for managing the overall human resources and training functions at the company. The IT firm provides packaged software solutions to the insurance sector and has a 60 per cent market share in the Asia-Pacific region.

Ninan has great faith in the role that HRD plays in the success of a company. She is confident the five-man band at Apex will contribute significantly to the growth of Apex. Ninan enjoys the fact that she is involved in the production and planning of the organisation. "You can influence the direction of their growth ," she says. "It gives me the opportunity to strategise to build competitiveness." In her short stint at Apex she has already played a pivotal role in recruiting senior personnel such as vice-presidents of marking and production.

Ninan, who got her management degree in Xavier's Labour Relations Institute in Jamshedpur, specialised in personnel management and industrial relations. She has had considerable experience in the software industry in the field. Before she joined Apex she was assistant manager at SAP India Private Ltd., where she was responsible for the entire HR functions of the Indian operations. Earlier she had worked at IB, Wipro and GE medical systems where her responsibilities included recruitment, HR policies and procedures, training development.

While studying for her B.A. Psychology at Delhi University she was involved in dramatics, debating and singing. "I am an outdoors person and enjoy sports also", she says. But for now, when she is not busy building the skills of the people at Apex, she prefers to spend time with her two children.

Growth of Entrepreneurs

In terms of benefiting the people, the development of small and medium-scale industries and businesses offered many advantages. Most important perhaps, amid the mounting unemployment, are the small and medium enterprises which generate more jobs and often use labour-intensive methods of production. Industries and business of smaller size also promote better income distribution and development of entrepreneurship and general skills, in addition to such broader benefits such as rural industrialisation and increased export earnings.

One of the most potentially fruitful areas of human resources development for small and medium-sized enterprises is the training of entrepreneurs and managers. Such training programmes should be as well rounded as possible, covering not only the basis of business, technology and so forth but also helping the trainees to identify their aptitudes, motivating them, encouraging innovative thinking and helping to develop personalities and attitudes geared for success. Indeed, small industries and businesses are ideally suited for capitalising on entrepreneurial skill, initiative and talent and thus assisting in building as dynamic private sector in the developing countries.

The growth of entrepreneurship in the post-planning period has been significant. For example, between 1960 and 1989, the number of private companies went up from 26,000 to nearly 1,05,200. It will be seen that the maximum increase in the number of factories was in the case of industries which by virtue of their being in the small/medium-scale sector are less regulated than others. The increases in the number of factories in industries like tobacco and related products, wood and wood products, rubber and rubber products, jewelry, photographic and optical goods, watches and clothes, medical, surgical and scientific equipments, sport equipments, cold storage, etc. was more than thirty times during the period 1959-1989.

The growth in the number of small entrepreneurs has been encouraging. The small-scale sector has grown in volume from 16,00 units in 1950 to over 18 lakh units by the end of 1989. The range of items produced by the small-scale sector ranges from consumer goods to high perecision items.

Not only has the number of entrepreneurs grown over a period of time but the scope of entrepreneurship is also getting broad-based. Earlier, for a large proportion of firms in India, the basic unit of entrepreurship was the extended family. This tendency is now getting diluted. A study conducted a few years back by the Economic and scientific Research foundation (ESRF) indicates that out of a sample of entrepreneurs studied by them, around 1/5 were managers and engineers before they turned entrepreneurs. It was found that around 57 per cent of the new entrepreneurs in starting small-scale units were motivated by the experience that they had gained from the previous employment. Entrepreneurship in these cases was not necessarily in-born but largely acquired.

Though impressive in certain ways, the development accomplished so far, as indicated before, is inadequate and far from satisfactory when set against the needs, as also the existing vast potential. In fact, according to Prof. Herbert Giersh, a noted economist, there is no shortage of entrepreneurial talent anywhere in the world, but the actual numbers depend on the demand conditions, i.e., the demand permitted, induced or actively provoked by the socio-economic structure and the politico-economic environment. According to him, a mixed capitalistic economy such as ours offers scope for development of entrepreneurial talent not only in the private sector but also in the government sector. The main disadvantage is that bureaucracy tends to limit the scope for entrepreneurial activity in the private sector.

Environment for Entrepreneurship

The entrepreneurs do not appear spontaneously. While the other factors of production are at last, in principle, available for hire but enterprise is not. It has to come from different vocations. Even the educational system in most of the developing countries is designed in such a way as to create more job-seekers. To sum up, entrepreneurs appear to have been motivated by a combination and interaction of the following factors of environment:

1. Socio-economic environment;
2. Family background;
3. Standard of education and technical knowledge;
4. Financial stability;
5. Political stability and government policy;
6. Caste and religious affiliation;
7. Availability of supporting facilities;
8. Achievement motivation; and
9. Personality and personal skill.

The environmental factors may be summarised as follows:

1. Enrepreneurship is not influenced by single factor but is the outcome of the interaction and combination of various environmental factors.
2. By changing the environment, society can be recreated.
3. It is the 'desire to make money' that drives one to start an industry rather than the amount of money one possesses and
4. Encouraging government policy and social recognition influence a person to become an entrepreneur. Educationist must think of modifying the educational system so as to produce more job-creators rather than just job-seekers.

Work Cultures of the Past and the Future

Work Culture of the Past	Work Culture of the Future
= individualism	= communitarianism
= independence	= interdependence
= autocracy	= democracy
= humanity against nature	= humanity part of nature
= unsustainable production	= sustainable production
= unsustainable consumption	= sustainable consumption
= patriarchy	= gender equality
= intercultural intolerance	= intercultural tolerance
= interreligious intolerance	= interreligious tolerance
= conflict resolution by confrontation	= conflict resolution by negotiation
= reliance on defence	= reliance on security
= reliance on rational intelligence	= reliance on emotional intelligence

Entrepreneurial Initiative

Recent data on entrepreneurial initiative and self-employment reflect a few problems. These problem must be overcome to develop entrepreneurial skills, more importantly, the entrepreneur has to initiate the process of development overcoming the barriers. This is itself a challenging task. This unprecedented, perpetual change with unlimited barriers will make entrepreneurial initiative in the future more significant and ifinitely, more dynamic.

The message is that stimulating entrepreneurial initiative is the strategic process that embodies calculated strategic choices. There are strategies open to the entrepreneur himself in terms of industry choice and individual and resource-tasks fit and there are strategies open to the regulators and support agencies in terms of use of industrial policy tools and incentives and explicit stimulation of industrial sectors or branches. A conceptual frame that contains both dimensions could provide a convenient base for analysis and possible policy action.

Encouraging entrepreneurial initiative is an issue common to both developed and developing countries and the search for effective means is proceeding in earnest. The analysis had dealt with a way of viewing the constraints embodied in the process of creating a new business or manufacturing operation.

The slow pace of the propensity to enterprise is mainly due to the existence of a tangible set of barriers prohibiting the process of entry into, continuity in and an eventual exit from a business venture of a would-be entrepreneur. This is a function of forces that one may view as barriers limiting a fully-fledged business performance. There may be entry barriers, survival barriers and exit barriers.

Importance of an Entrepreneur

The entrepreneur is one of the most important input in to the economic development of a country or of regions within the country. Entrepreneurial competence makes all the difference in the rate of economic growth. In India, state and private entrepreneurship co-exist. The small-scale industrial sector and business are left completely to private entrepreneurs. It is, therefore, in this context that an increasingly important role has been assigned to the identification and promotion of entrepreneurs for this sector.

The need for a broad-based entrepreneurial class in India arises from the need to speed up the process of activating the factors of production, leading to a higher rate of economy growth, dispersal of economic activities, development of backward and tribal areas, creation of employment opportunities, improvement in the standard of living of the weaker sections of society and involvement of all sections of society in the process of growth.

Several factors go into the making of an entrepreneur. Individuals who initiate, establish, maintain and expand new enterprises constitute the entrepreneurial class. The socio-political and economic conditions, the availability of industrial technology and know-how, state of art and culture, of business and trading, existence of markets for products and service and the incentives and facilities available for starting an industry or business, all have a bearing on the growth of entrepreneurship. A conducive environment is created through the policies and interest of the government in economic and industrial development.

It is now well recognised that entrepreneurs can be developed through appropriately designed entrepreneurship development programmes. These programmes broadly envisage a three-tiered approach: developing achievement motivation and sharpening of entrepreneurial traits and behaviour, project planning and development and guidance on industrial opportunities, incentives and facilities and rules and regulations and developing managerial and operational capabilities. Various techniques and approaches have been developed and adopted to achieve these objectives, keeping in view the target-groups and /or target areas. The structuring of the programmes and training methodology also necessitate consideration of the specific target-groups and target areas. Methodology for selection of the prospective entrepreneurs as well as support service after training have a significant impact on the success of the entrepreneurs' development programmes.

Entrepreneur and Entrepreneurship

Entrepreneur and entrepreneurship are co-related.

The entrepreneur is the person who bears risks, unites various factors of production and carries out creative innovations. He is an individual or one of a group of individuals who tries to create something new. He always attempts to bring about change in terms of factor proportions which is known as innovation.

Y.C. Deveshwar
ITC

D.S. Brar
RANBAXY

On the contrary, entrepreneurship is the set of activities performed by an entrepreneur. It is the process of identifying opportunities in the market place and marshalling the resources required to pursue these opportunities for long-term gains. It is the attempt to create value.

The relationship between an entrepreneur and entrepreneurship is given in table.

The Relation between Entrepreneur and Entrepreneurship

Entrepreneur	*Entrepreneurship*
Visualiser	Vision
Initiator	Initiative
Able	Ability
Innovator	Innovation
Skilled	Skills

Organiser	Organisation
Designer	Design
Leader	Leadership
Risk-bearer	Risk
Motivation	Motivation
Builder	Team
Director	Direction
Imitator	Imitation
Creator	Creativity
Planner	Planning
Decisions-maker	Decision-making
Goal-setter	Goal
Inspirer	Inspiring
Excellor	Work Culture
Character	Values
Integrator	Integrity
Character	Fair-Play
Balanced	Patience
Striver	Persistence
Re-inventor	Re-invent
Foresighter	Foresight
Dreamer	Dreams
Talented	Talent
Player	Fair play

The Single-Most Critical Ingredient that makes a successful entrepreneur is passion. Without passion, entrepreneur might succeed in managing an organisation but he can never succeed in inspiring his people. Unlike in art, where intense individual passion is enough to attain excellence, managing an organisation requires the leader to be able to infuse his whole team with that same passion.

An entrepreneur shares his passion with his term by translating it into a vision for the organisation. He needs to coax, cajole and inspire his people into sharing his vision. Alexander's soldiers grew tired and weary on more than one occasion, but were driven to great achievements by his passionate leadership. On the eve of each charge, Alexander used his communication skills to psyche up his army.

The entrepreneur must also evoke trust among his followers. He should communicate with empathy and yet not deviate from his mission.

Passion also generates courage of conviction, which acts as a source of strength in times of adversity. Mahatma Gandhi was convinced that the British rule in India was unjust and it was his moral duty to fight it. It was this conviction that gave him the courage to take on the might of the Empire.

Organisations need leaders who are passionate institution-builders, institutions survive their builders and contribute enormously to the society. Dr. Vikram Sarabhai, the man behind the setting up of India's space research program, IIM Ahmedabad, the Physical Research Laboratory, and many other institutions, might not be around today, but his institutions continue to remind us of his contributions to the nation's progress.

Entrepreneurship is about understanding that an organisation will function effectively when it has the right mix of people, backgrounds, and experiences. This entails radical changes in recruitment policies. Entrepreneurship is a long journey and not a destination. It presupposes and presumes great preparation. To be an entrepreneur one must have a sound grounding in preparation. It is the art of human relationships (ability to interact with other people). It also calls for growing mastery over the work and long hours of hard work. The status and quality of entrepreneurship directly depends on these ingredient characteristics.

Above all, the entrepreneur should strive at all times to attain transparency in his organisation. Information should be freely given to those who need it. The entrepreneur should send out a message that information is not a source of power for an individual, but a power that contributes to the growth of an organisation.

Entrepreneurship management is basically concerned with the development and co-ordination of entrepreneurial functions. In a way, an entrepreneur precedes entrepreneurship.

Experience shows that entrepreneurship as an economic function is not a single point but rather a varied range of behaviour. There are six critical dimensions that distinguish entrepreneurial behaviour from more administratively-oriented behaviour: (i) strategic orientation; (ii) commitment to opportunity; (iii) the resource commitment process; (iv) the concept of control over resources; (v) the concept of management and (vi) compensation policy.

		Desired future state involves growth or change: Yes	Desired future state involves growth or change: No
Sell-perceived Power to Achieve Goals	Yes	Entrepreneurs	Satisfied Manager
	No	Frustrated Potential Entrepreneurs	Bureaucratic Functionary

Fig. 4.3 : Manager's Opportunity Matrix

A matrix defining entrepreneurship is shown in Fig.4.3. One can see how the present position influences whether one has entrepreneurial potential or not. It also clearly states that the particular skills, talents and attitudes towards risk influence the perception as to whether an outcome is feasible. Training, knowledge and self-confidence contribute to such perceptions.

The importance of this figure cannot be overemphasized since individuals place themselves in their particular box for rational reasons relating to their own lives; however, for the firms desiring to build the entrepreneurial spirit, action is required.

Creation of a Dream

Azim Premji
WIPRO

Creating a dream gives entrepreneurs the energy and desire to become involved in its implementation and to be willing to change. During the formulation of the dream, everyone participates (including the leaders), and this allows people to start seeing each other in a different light. How long they will maintain their commitment depends upon (i) how well the organisation's leaders function in their new role of facilitating resolution of the needs or issues that are at variance with the dream, (ii) how clearly the leaders articulate and share information about the business needs and (iii) how well the leaders openly acknowledge their willingness to change, in whatever fashion, to attain the dreams.

The process of creating dreams should be tailored to the situation with the objective of having the entire organisation ultimately share the dream. In a large organisation, there will be many dreams formulated by interdependent parts of the organisation. At some point, these should be integrated into a total organisational dream. We have found that creating a dream in a bottoms-up manner where all organisational levels participate in some fashion is better than a tiered, top-down approach.

Box 4.5

Dreams Unlimited

For industries a change in the environment does not change the basic task. The challenge is two-fold—build a range of services and a truly global workforce. The basic task is really five-fold :

- Execution excellence is everything
- Rally the organisation around a powerful vision
- Do not let the enthusing culture binding the organisation get diluted as we grow rapidly
- Continuously enhance value for our customers
- Continuously enhance value of the people who have chosen to work with us.

The vision articulated by the entrepreneurs is :

Business leadership

Customer leadership

People leadership, and

Brand leadership.

Towards this end, create a work place culture which is open, apolitical and rooted in values.

Dreams are unlimited. Opportunities are plenty and only really great people will build great organisations.

To illustrate the content of a typical dream, let us look at the leadership portion of one from a Honeywell factory, which evolved as follows:

Leadership should be the ability of those leading work units (managers, supervisors, engineers, technical support and group leaders) to create an atmosphere of acceptance, openness and trust that will properly motivate members of the work units.

Interpersonal competence should be the ability to relate to people in a considerate and effective way.

Brijmohan Lal Munjal
HERO HONDA

This means that the leader:

1. Cares —
   (a) Gives positive feedback for a well done job.
   (b) Shows confidence in employees.

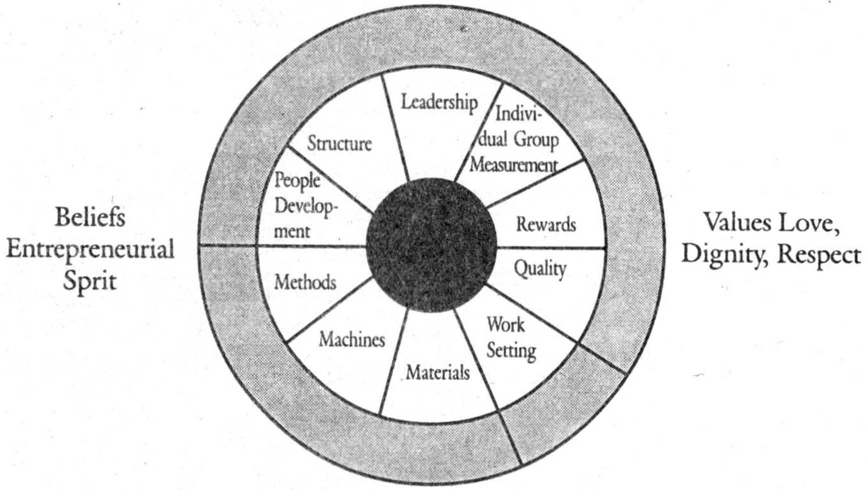

Fig. 4.4 : Basic Elements—Entrepreneurial Involvement

   (c) Is fair and objective, not vindictive.
   (d) Practices what is preached; does not ask for something that he or she would not be willing to do.
   (e) Has a down-to-earth, person-to-person approach; acts as part of a team and
   (f) Is compassionate and understanding; creates an atmosphere of acceptance and trust.
2. Skillfully communicates—
   (a) Listens actively.
   (b) Clarifies priorities.
   (c) Is available.
   (d) Links management with employees, employees with management, and employees with each other. Communicates effectively with all people on all shifts through all levels of the organisation.

(e) Provides feedback for both good and bad work.
(f) Talks openly and gives straight answers about what is happening.

3. Guides, inspires—
   (a) Encourages advancement.
   (b) Gives direction to the work unit.
   (c) Is proud of loyal and supportive of employees.
   (d) Has a sense of vision—a dream that is blend with employees' dream.
   (e) Projects a positive attitude.
   (f) Is courageous.
   (g) Sets a good example; is friendly, not moody.
   (h) Enjoys his or her work and
   (i) Keeps promises, plows through red tape.

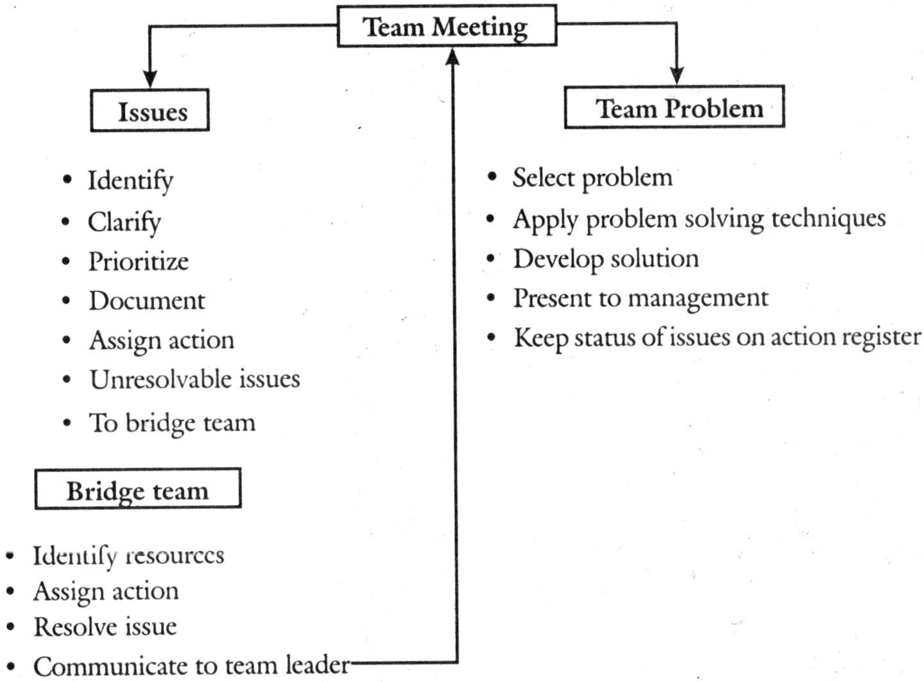

Fig. 4.5 : Team Process

Administrative competence should be the ability to achieve organisational goals within the bound of the business constraints and policies and procedures. This means that the leader :

1. Understands his or her job.
2. Understands employees' jobs:
   (a) Utilises people's skills effectively.
   (b) Is concerned with employees' work and the workflow.
   (c) Stands up for and shows confidence in employees.

N.R. Narayana Murthy
INFOSYS

3. Takes immediate action:
   (a) Does not ignore problems.
   (b) Follows up on promises.
   (c) Gets tough when necessary.
   (d) Takes action to remove poor performers.
   (e) Assures that the next in command knows his role and has authority to act and
   (f) Provides proper human resources for all shifts and all levels of an organisation.

Change for present life style	↔	*Form new enterprise*
Work environment		Desirable
Disruption		1. Cultural
		2. Subculture
		3. Family
		4. Teachers
		5. Peers
		Possible
		1. Government
		2. Background
		3. Marketing
		4. Financing
		5. Role models

Fig. 4.6 : Decision for a Potential Entrepreneur

Entrepreneurial Decision

Entrepreneurial decisions occur despite recession, inflation, high interest rates, lack of infrastructure, economic uncertainty etc. Each of these decisions is a personal human process that, although unique, have some common characteristics. The impulse to change his/her life style and create something new and an inner urge to do something worthy, are the forces behind these decisions. At times, perhaps even more stimulation for change comes from a negative force-disruption. At times, the available opportunities force a decision in individuals to take up entrepreneurial work like all process it entails movement from something to new something.

Karshanbhai Patel
NIRMA

What causes this change due to the work environment or disruption to result in a new company being formed instead of something else? The decision to start a new company occurs when an individual perceives that it is both desirable and possible.

The perception that starting a new company is desirable results from an individual's culture, sub-culture, teachers, family and peers. A culture that values an individual who successfully creates a new business will spawn more company formations than one that does not. For example, India places a high value on being your own boss, individual opportunity, being a success and making money—all aspects of entrepreneurship. What is more, many different sub-cultures that shape value systems are operating within a cultural framework. More importantly, these sub-cultures support and even promote entrepreneurship. Thus entrepreneurial decision making has more bearing on the sociological, cultural, sub-cultural, psychological and political environment, while satisfaction and adequate rewards are the optimistic goals.

Entrepreneurial Skills

To deal with entrepreneurial skills is to concern oneself with a wide coverage of aspects of setting up an enterprise and its management. It is not confined to visualisations, planning, setting-up and risk-taking. The skill which an entrepreneur possesses include his ability to deal with new situation organisations and social and economic forces as they emerge from time to time. The skills to deal with a situation, anticipated or suddenly emerging, must be an essential characteristic of an entrepreneur.

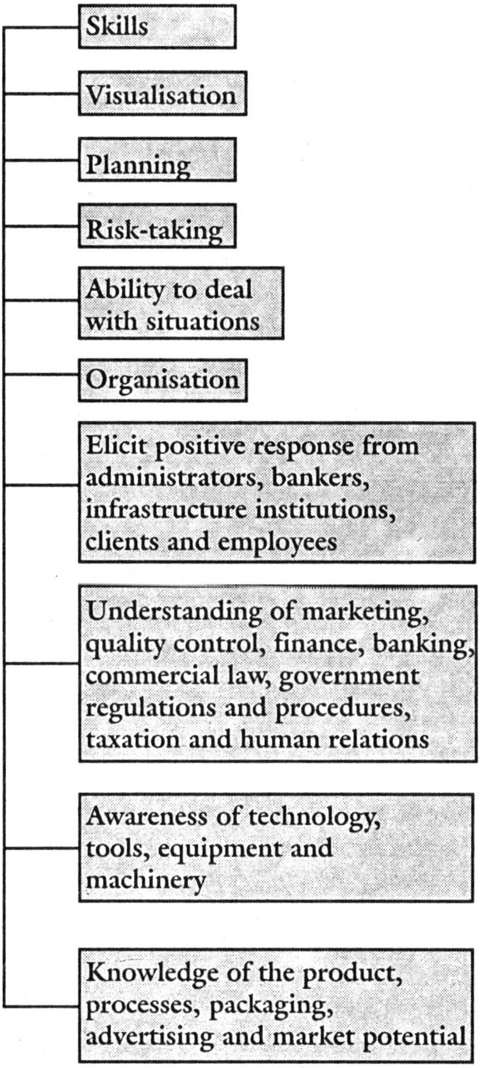

Fig. 4.7: Entrepreneurial Skills

The small entrepreneur must have the skill to elicit positive responses from administrators, bankers, infrastructure institutions, clients and employees.

The entrepreneur is rarely a master of all management skills, and yet is usually directly responsible for all aspects of business. Often he or she has to be the general manager, production manager, purchasing manager, personnel manager, controller and research organiser for the business, all rolled into one, at least during its early years. The entrepreneur has, therefore, to have an understanding of marketing, quality control, finance, banking, commercial law, government regulations and procedures, and human relations as each of them has a vital bearing on the health of the enterprise.

Need for Skills

We often talk of transfer of technology. As a matter of fact, the whole world is talking about it. There is hardly any international event whether at the global or regional level where this subject does not come up for discussion. The poor nations demand technology and resources from industrialised and rich countries and rightly so. The developing countries would rather export semi-finished and finished products which are value added than export raw materials. The development of entrepreneurial skills must precede transfer of technology, if we do not desire to keep such technologies and equipment serving such technologies idle. One has also to realise that technologies are developing very fast and skills also match this dynamic growth. The entrepreneur has to be made aware of the imperative needs of updated technologies, modern tools and equipments, processes and systems and skills. In this task, his whole organisation, however small it may be, has to join the exercise.

It is observed that in many least developed countries, sophisticated equipment and machinery imported at heavy cost, often under pressure of international financial institutions or aid agreements, are lying unutilised for want of efficiently trained hands. It is obvious that the accelerated development of human resources and appropriate training of manpower must be concurrent with the transfer of technologies which are relevant to the needs of each developing country. This will call for an inventory of existing manpower, degree of their present skills, arrangements for proper imparting and skills needed. This should have a relation to natural endowment and resources and their optimum utilisation.

Types of Skills

Types of skills will vary according to location, products, clientele etc. In the rural areas, a small enterprise making goods for local consumption. Based on local raw materials, would need relatively simpler skills. In urban areas, the product, processes, packaging and advertising have to match with the growing sophistication of consumer goods, preference of needs etc. They call for an intensification of efforts to develop matched skills in all areas of entrepreneurial activity.

Skills for New Class of Entrepreneurs

As stated earlier, entrepreneurship in most developing countries has been confined to person coming from the traditionally trade oriented families. Now, there is an emphasis on new classes of entrepreneurs. These would include women, tribals and young men from non-traditional families. For women entrepreneurs, special training facilities have to be provided owing to the special difficulties faced by them as compared to men. For tribal entrepreneurs, care will have to be taken that their basic culture, crafts and skills are not materially affected and lost following the emergence of competitive entrepreneurships.

Attributes of Entrepreneurs

The attempts to discover the secret of entrepreneurial success has preoccupied writers and analysts from a variety of disciplines. Biographies of successful entrepreneurs and businessmen, for example, frequently reflect the tendencies of the subject of such studies in terms of simple virtues of thrift, hard work and clean living. As an alternative to the biographical models are those studies that turn the entrepreneur into a superman, manipulating the complexities of an uncertain world with a sure and omnipotent touch. Thus, emerges the notion of the 'genius entrepreneur' whose success is in large measure caused by his unswerving dedication to achieving high goals. He has vision on which he badges his own objectives and set his own goals. And he does this not simply on the basis of last year's results plus some growth factor, but on the basis of his own perception, of his capabilities and to satisfy his own needs.

Perceptions
Dedication
Vision
High Goals / Objectives
Thrift
Vigorous Energy
Hard Work
Clean Living
Quest for New Ideas
Willingness to Assume Risks
Unceasing Curiosity
Restless Urge to Get Going
Sense of Acquisitiveness to Get Things Done
Insight
Gambler's Instinct
Initiative
Creativity
Zest to Explore the Unexplored
Problem-Solving Ability
Ability to Marshall Resources
To Achieve One's Objectives and Goals
Administrative Ability

Fig. 4.8: Attributes of an Entrepreneur

Among other distinguishing attributes of entreprener are a willingness to assume risks; a sense of acquisitiveness or unceasing curiosity; insight into the relationship between concepts, objectives, needs, and of needs satisfaction; sound judgement as to what is central and peripheral to attaining his objectives; initiative and creativity; problem-solving ability; ability to marshall resources needed to achieve his objectives and goals; and the administrative ability to organise those resources to accomplish his goals and satisfy his minor needs.

A good entrepreneur should act with self confidence, avoid anger, take prompt and timely decisions on a rational basis, think clearly with maturity.

He should have adequate knowledge of human relation at all levels, objective analysis, ability to communicate effectively with passion and belief.

He is also capable to set challenging yet realistic and achievable goals and a passion to achieve such goals and have technical competence. Other important traits are :

- Emulative
- Conceptual skills
- High integrity and honesty
- Flexibility of mind, and
- Ability to establish proper priorities.

A good entrepreneur must above all be a role model who can be emulated by the workers (employees).

Conclusion

Entrepreneurs play an important role in the development of society. For example, the use of Jeans in America has created the demand for them throughout the world. Similarly, Coca Cola has been accepted as a social drink. The introduction of colour T.V. has provided society with a means of information and entertainment. The society has accepted the innovations of such entrepreneurs as Gillet, the Wright Brothers and Henry Ford. The inventions of these great entrepreneurs of the history has revolutionized the life styles of men in society today.

The role of entrepreneurs in economic development varies from economy to economy, country to country, depending upon its material resources, industrial climate and more importantly, the responsiveness of the political system to the growth of entrepreneurs. By and large, the entrepreneurs' contribution to development and growth is relatively higher in favourable opportunity conditions than in less favourable situation. The growth of an entrepreneurial society will bear fruitful results in a short-span.

Entrepreneurship, the *de facto* barometer of overall economic, social and industrial growth, has brought about revolutionary changes in society. It is the *sine quo non* of a nation's progress. It has facilitated large-scale production and distribution. It has widened the area and scope of the marketing of goods and services. Perhaps it is for these reasons that the small business sector has been given priority in our national development programmes, for entrepreneurship flourishes when the size of business remains relatively small and viable.

Modern business studies have a distinct entrepreneurial discipline. The approach to the study of entrepreneurship is multi-disciplinary. It impinges on such areas as demography, economic anthropology, business history, politics, sociology, psychology, marketing and finance. That is why entrepreneurship development becomes an integral part of the overall economic, social and industrial development of a country. This is what makes the identification and management of entrepreneurial functions a highly complex exercise.

THE IDEAL ENTREPRENEUR

Not a workaholic. Sure, you should be prepared to work long—and irregular—hours, but the freedom to choose and prioritize free time is always at hand. If you cannot sleep at night, as long as there is a single file left unperused, a memo unread, a number uncrunched, back off right now. Entrepreneurship isn't a one-dayer. You must have the self-control to play for a long innings instead of burning yourself out.

Be warned, therefore, even when you are your own boss, long-term sustainability demands that you balance your professional and personal life. Only then can you truly make your own business sustainable in the long-term.

To Morph into an Entrepreneur

- Managers must be able to translate their career ambitions into specific business goals.
- They must use their people management skills to motivate and inspire their employees.
- Managers must capitalize on their skills to manage the financial aspects personally.
- They must turn their aggression in the workplace into a risk-taking approach.
- They must leverage their functional expertise when choosing their line of business.
- Managers must develop leadership qualities on the job before venturing out on their own.

Prepare, therefore, a mental checklist of the other side to the entrepreneur's job. Sure, your once-in-a-life-time innovative idea will convert customers immediately, but have you the prudence of a penny-pinching CFO? The diplomacy of the personnel manager? The doggedness of the door-to-door salesman? You will need them all, in addition to that gem of an idea.

The entrepreneurship audit will judge an individual's capabilities, be it an entrepreneur or not. Just try it.

THE ENTREPRENEURSHIP AUDIT

Do you measure upto the tough task of being your own boss? Assess impartially and objectively your positive and negative points in becoming your own boss. If need be, negative points might be corrected by training and education. Take this test to find out:

		Yes	No
1.	Do you enjoy taking big, even unwarranted risks?	❑	❑
2.	Do you plan ahead on most things you do?	❑	❑
3.	Do you have a head for numbers and finances?	❑	❑
4.	Do you make it a point to complete what you start?	❑	❑
5.	Can you survive a drop in your standard of living?	❑	❑
6.	Are you able to take decisions without dithering?	❑	❑
7.	Are you free of major financial commitments?	❑	❑
8.	Can you get along with different kinds of people?	❑	❑
9.	Is your career path in your company flattening out?	❑	❑
10.	Do you enjoy travelling on work?	❑	❑
11.	Are you capable of leading people?	❑	❑
12.	Do you have a clear vision about your dreams?	❑	❑
13.	Do you have innovative ideas about projects and services?	❑	❑
14.	Have you acquired specific skills to run a new venture?	❑	❑
15.	Do you plan your work methodically?	❑	❑
16.	Are you adaptable and flexible?	❑	❑
17.	Do you prefer working alone to working in a team?	❑	❑
18.	Do you find your self envying entrepreneurs?	❑	❑
19.	Can you cope with punishing work schedules?	❑	❑
20.	Does your spouse support your plans?	❑	❑

The Scoring

Give yourself 5 points for every YES, and 0 for every No.

Total ☐

The Rating

0-35	You won't get far with I Inc. Be satisfied with what you already have in hand.
40-60	The passion as a self-starter is weak. You seek the status quo rather than a crisis.
65-100	All systems go. Greener pastures and challenges await you.

Chapter - 5

THE ENTREPRENEUR AND THE LAW

Introduction

Regulations are the basis of steady growth. In a society, regulations are the governing factors, ensuring that everything occurs in conformity with the plans and policy adopted, the instructions issued and the principles established. They pinpoint the weaknesses and errors so that they may be rectified and their recurrence may be prevented. They operate on everything—people, objects and actions. Thus, a regulation is a process by which we may check whether or not plans are being adhered to, whether or not a proper progress is being made towards the objectives, whether the environment is saved from pollution whether law and order is maintained or not, whether the interests of the workers are safeguarded or not, whether the small entrepreneurs are getting the raw materials or not, and whether there are any deviations against which a corrective action needs to be taken.

Objective

The basic objective behind the whole process of regulations is to ensure that the results of operations conform as closely as possible to established standards of goods, specified procedures or instructions. Small-scale industry has to develop as an important segment of society; as such it has to adhere to the rules of the land, i.e., it has to be subject to the various regulations. Regulations governing Small-scale industry are of two types: (i) protective and (ii) promotional. Protective regulations are by way of various safeguards, while promotional regulations are in the nature of giving a push to the small-scale industry, i.e., they are growth-oriented.

There are various rules and regulations applicable to different group of industries for various purposes. Some of these are described below:

(i) Registration/Licensing : Industries with an investment of less than Rs. 75 lakh in plant and machinery are small-scale industries. They may be registered with G.M. District Industries Centres of the district concerned to get benefits.

An ancillary unit (SSI) is defined as one having capital investment in plant and machinery not exceeding Rs. 75 lakh which produces parts, components, subassemblies and makes supplies against known or anticipated demand of one or more large units manufacturing/assembling complete product and which is not a subsidiary or controlled by any large unit in regard to the negotiation of contract for supply of its goods to any large unit. This will not however, preclude an ancillary unit from entering into agreement with a large unit, giving it the first option to take the former's output.

The unit set-up primarily for the replacement market falls within its scope. Manufacture of tools, dies, jigs and fixtures is also recognised as an ancillary industry. These ancillary unit (SSI) can also get themselves registered with G.M. District Industries Centres of the district concerned.

Regulations

Right from the beginning, a small-scale industry is regulated and governed by the following regulations: (a) State Industries Acts; (b) The Factories Act, 1948; (c) The Shops & Establishment Act, 1948; (d) The Indian Boiler Act (if applicable); (e) The Payment of Wages Act, 1936; (f) The Minimum Wages Act, 1948; (g) The Workmen's Compensation Act, 1923; (h) The Employees Provident Fund Act, 1952; (i) The Employees State Insurance Act, 1948; (j) The Income Tax Act, 1961; (k) The Central Sales Tax Act and State Sales Tax Act; (l) The Drugs Control Act; (m) The Payment of Bonus Act, 1978; (n) The Industrial Employment (Standing Orders) Act, 1926 and (o) The Industrial Disputes Act, 1947.

In addition, the small-scale entrepreneur has to be well versed in excise, customs procedures and export and import regulations and procedures. He should always seek assistance from the following professionals: (a) Inspecting Staff of Government; (b) Labour Consultants (c) Financial Consultants.

The salient features of the regulations governing the small-scale industries are summarised below:

Industrial Development (Regulation) Act (IDRA)

The IDRA is an instrument in the hands of the Government for the control and direction of private sector industrial investment through the mechanism of the industrial licensing system, which enables it to exert pressure on the applicants in a variety of ways. Conceptually, the government ought to direct further industrial investment in such product lines as would better serve the overall national interest and in such geographical areas which need it the most.

It is a complicated, time-consuming and costly exercise to acquire an industrial licence. Sometimes, it takes years before it can be obtained. Obviously, it cannot be the intention of the Government to extend this procedure to the small-scale sector because it would be impossible to work towards implementation. A small unit cannot even prepare an application for an industrial licence; and there is nobody to help it in preparing it. There is no agency which is capable of checking the veracity of what the applicant says in his application, much less comment thereon.

In recent years, there has been quite a clamour from various associations of small-scale industries for their legislative protection. In August 1971, the Small-Scale Industries Board, at its 29th meeting, had recommended to the Government to set up a committee to examine the feasibility of enacting suitable legislations for the development of small-scale industries. Always eager to form committees, the Government speedily acceded to the recommendation of the Board and constituted a committee in January 1972 under the chairmanship of Mr. A. R. Bhat to draft legislation for the small-scale sector. It was, moreover, required to identify specific areas where legislation was considered necessary and to submit drafts for the purpose.

Factories Act, 1948

(i) Definition of a Factory : Section 2 (m) defines a factory as any place wherein ten or more persons are working and in which a manufacturing process is carried on with the aid of motive power supplied by steam, oil or electricity. Premises in which power is not used come under the defienition of a factory if twenty or more persons are working in them. This definition brings a greater number of places under the purview of this Act than was the case under the Act of 1934.

(ii) Employment of Children : The Act fixes the minimum age of persons who can enter a factory for work at 14 years. It prohibits the employment of children upto the age of 13.

The Act further lays down that a qualified surgeon must certify that a person has completed the age of 14. Such certificates must be obtained by a factory manager and must be available for inspection by factory inspector.

(iii) Hours of Work for Children : The Act reduces the hours of work for children between the ages of 14-17 from 5 hours a day to 4½ hours a day. It also prohibits work at night for such persons.

(iv) Hours of Work for Adult Female and Male Workers : The Act prohibits employment of women in factories between 6 P.M. and 7 A.M. It reduces the hours of work for adult men and women workers from 54 to 48 per week and from 9 hours to 8 hours a day.

The Act also lays down that the eight hours of work will be spread over a period of not more that 10½ hours. Further it provides that no worker shall work for more than 5 hours before he has had an interval or rest of at least half an hour. Lastly, the Act lays down that those workers who are made to work for more than 8 hours a day or 48 hours a week shall be paid for the extra hours at the rate of twice their ordinary rates of wages.

(v) Cleanliness : The Act lays down that every factory shall be kept clean and free from effluvia arising from any drain, privy or other nuisance. Accumulation of dirt and refuse shall be removed daily from the floor and the benches of work-rooms, from staircases and passages, and disposed of in the suitable manner.

The floor of every work-room in a factory shall be cleaned once a week.

All inside walls, ceilings and partition shall be white-washed at least once in fourteen months; if they are painted or varnished, they shall be re-painted or revarnished once in five years.

Effective arrangements shall be made in every factory for the disposal of wastes arising out of the manufacturing process carried on therein.

(vi) Ventilation and Temperature : Effective and suitable provision shall be made in every factory for securing and maintaining in every work-room adequate ventilation by the circulation of fresh air and the maintenance of such temperature as will secure therein reasonable conditions of comfort for those working there. Where excessively high temperatures are necessary for technical reasons, adequate measures shall be taken by the management to protect the workers from such temperatures.

The State Government may prescribe a standard of adequate ventilation and reasonable temperature for any factory or class of factories and can suggest ways and means for reducing excessively high temperatures.

In any factory, where dust or fumes injurious to the health of workers arise in any manufacturing process, effective measures shall be taken to prevent their inhalation or accumulation in any work room.

(vii) Artificial Humidification : In factories where humidity is artificially increased, the State Government may make rules:

(a) Prescribing standards of humidification;

(b) Regulating methods used for humidification;

(c) Directing prescribed tests for determining humidity, and directing that such tests are carried out—their results recorded and

(d) Prescribing methods to be adopted for securing adequate ventilation and cooling of the air in those rooms where artificial humidity is introduced.

Water used for the purpose of humidification shall be such as has been certified by the municipal authorities as fit for drinking.

(viii) Overcrowding : To prevent overcrowding in a factory, the Act lays down that, in factories built before the passing of this Act, there shall be space of at least 350 cubic feet per worker and in factories built after the Act came into force, it shall be at least 500 cubic feet. To arrive at these figures, a height above 14 feet shall not be taken into consideration. In accordance with this rule, the Chief Inspector of Factories will communicate to each factory manager the maximum number of workers that may be employed on any premises. He has, however, the power to exempt any factory or work-room from this rule, if he is satisfied that its observance of this rule is not necessary in the interest of the workers employed therein.

(ix) Lighting : It is the duty of the management of a factory to maintain sufficient and suitable lighting, natural or artificial or both, in factory and in all the work-rooms.

All glazed windows and sky-lights shall be kept clean on both the inner and outer surfaces, and effective measures shall be taken for the prevention of glare and formation of any shadows which may cause eye-strain or create a risk of accidents.

The State Government may make rules as to what is sufficient and suitable lighting, for a factory or a class of factories.

(x) Drinking Water : In every factory, effective arrangements shall be made to provide, suitable points conveniently situated for all workers employed therein, a sufficient supply of wholesome drinking water.

In every factory, where more than 253 workers are ordinarily employed, provision shall be made for cool drinking water during the hot weather.

(xi) Toilets : In every factory, sufficient toilet facilities of the prescribed types, shall be provided at places which are conveniently situated and are easily accessible to workers at all times while they are at the factory.

The State Government may prescribe the number of public toilet services to be provided in any factory in proportion to the number of male and female workers ordinarily employed therein.

(xii) Provision of Spittoons : In every factory, there shall be a sufficient number of spittoons in convenient places and they shall be maintained in a clean and hygienic condition.

(xiii) Safety provisions : According to the Act of 1934, a factory manager could afford to wait till an Inspector of Factories gave instructions as to what ought to be done to ensure the safety of workers. The Act of 1948 has placed the responsibility for safety matters on the shoulders of the occupier or the manager of a factory. He must comply with all the safety provisions without waiting for the inspector's instructions.

Secondly, the Act places legal responsibility on the management for the maintenance and use of safety guard. It is its duty to supervise the use of these guards by the workers.

The specific provisions for safety are as follows: in every factory all dangerous parts of tall machines, such as the moving parts of prime movers, flywheels, electric generators, motors, rotary converters, etc. shall be securely fenced by safety guards of substantial construction which shall be kept in position while the parts of machinery they fence are in motion.

(xiv) Dangerous Fumes : Adequate provision shall be made in a factory where dangerous fumes are present in any chamber, tank, pipe, etc., for the egress of such fumes.

(xv) Explosive Gases, Dust, Fume : If, in any factory, the manufacturing process raises dust, gas, fume or vapour which is likely to explode on ignition, all measures shall be taken to prevent any such explosion by —

(a) Providing an effective enclosure of the plant or machinery used in the process or

(b) The removal or prevention of accumulation of such dust, gas or fumes.

(xvi) Safety of Factory Building and Machinery : If it appears to the Inspector that any building or part of factory is in such a condition that it is dangerous to human life or safety, he may serve on the managers of the factory an order in writing specifying the measure that should be adopted and the specific date by which they should be carried out to ensure the safety of the building or factory. He may also serve an order on the manager, prohibiting its use until proper repairs or alterations have been carried out.

(xvii) Welfare Provisions : ***(a) Facilities for Washing :*** In every factory, adequate and suitable facilities for washing shall be provided and maintained for the workers. Adequately screened facilities for washing shall be provided for male and female workers separately. Such facilities shall be conveniently accessible and shall be kept clean.

(b) Storing and Drying Clothes : The State Government may require any factory or class of factories to make provision therein of suitable places for keeping clothes not worn during working hours and for drying wet clothing.

(c) Facilities for Sitting : In every factory, suitable arrangements for sitting shall be provided and maintained for all workers obliged to working a standing position in order that they may take advantage of any opportunity for rest which may occur in the course of their work.

(d) First-Aid Appliances : First-aid boxes, equipped with the prescribed contents, which will be really accessible during all working hours, shall be provided and maintained in every factory. The number of such boxes shall not be less than one for every one hundred and fifty workers.

(xviii) Penalties for Breach of Provision of the Act : For any contravention of the provisions of the Act, the occupier and the manager of a factory shall each be guilty of an offence and be punishable with imprisonment for a term not exceeding three months or with a fine up to Rs. 500 or with both.

If any person, who has been convicted of any offence punishable under the provisions of this Act, is again found to be guilty of an offence involving contravention of the same provision within a period of two years from the date of conviction with imprisonment upto six months or with a fine up to Rs. 1,000 or with both. This Act, for the time, provides that if any worker contravenes any provision of this Act or any rules or orders, such as the use of safety guards, spitting only in spittoons provided for the purpose, he shall be punishable with fine upto Rs. 20.

India's ratification of International Labour Convention No. 90 prohibiting the employment of young persons in factories at night necessitated an amendment of the relevant sections of the Factories Act, 1948. This was achieved by passing an Amendment Act in April 1954. This Act added a new chapter on "Annual Leave with Wages" to the Factories Act, 1948. It lays down a period of 240 days as the minimum attendance necessary during a calendar year to qualify for leave with wages. It also prohibits employment of young persons on cleaning, lubricating or adjusting any prime mover or transmission machinery while it is in motion, if such work exposes them to a risk of injury.

Income-Tax Act

The tax concessions provided in the Income-tax Act for small-scale industries are of minor significance. Under section 80 HHA, which came into effect from the assessment year 1978-79, an assessee is entitled to a deduction in respect of profit and gains derived from new small-scale industrial undertaking set up in any rural area at the rate of 20 per cent for the first ten assessment years. One of the conditions is that the unit should have commenced its manufacturing activity after September 30, 1977. This concession is discriminatory, for there is no justification for denying the benefit to those units which commenced manufacturing activity before September 30, 1977. Moreover, the units in urban areas have been neglected. Unless we have correct statistics of the proportion of small-scale units in rural areas to those in urban areas and the proportion of the tax collected from rural units to the tax collected from urban ones, the significance of such a discriminatory tax concession cannot be evaluated.

Another incentive is the investment allowance under section 32A of the Act, under which a small-scale unit is entailed to a deduction at the rate of 25 per cent of the cost of plant and machinery installed after March 31,1976. This allowance is capital-oriented whereas most of the small-scale units are capital-saving and labour-oriented.

At present, there is no Central Government definition of the term *small-scale industrial undertaking* — a fact which indicates how unimportant these undertakings are in the eyes of the tax department. According to the definitions given under sections 32 A & 80 HHA, the term is used to mean an industrial undertaking whose aggregate value of machinery and plant — other than tools, jigs, dies and moulds — installed on the last day of the previous year for the purpose of the business of the undertaking, does not exceed Rs. 10 lakh. In Section 58 A of the Companies Act, however, the term is defined as any industrial undertaking registered with the Directorate of Industries or the Directorate of Small-Scale Industries.

The Industrial Employment (Standing Orders) Act, 1946

The absence of standing order clearly defining the rights and obligations of the employer and the workers in respect of recruitment, discharge, disciplinary action, holidays, leave etc. was one of the most frequent causes of friction between management and workers. On the recommendations of the Tripartite labour conferences held in 1943, 1944, 1945, the Government of India passed the Industrial Employment (standing orders) Act in 1946. This Act provides for the framing of standing orders in all establishment employing 100 or more persons. It requires employers to submit, within six months of the enactment of the law, standing orders covering the classification of workmen (permanent, temporary, etc.), the manner of intimating to them their hours of work, holidays, pay days and wage rates, the procedure to be followed while applying for leave and holidays the termination of employment for notice of discharge and for disciplinary action. In pursuance of this Act, the Central Government published the central rules in 1946 which were applicable to the Commissioner's provinces and to the undertaking under the Central Government. Its lead was promptly followed by all State Governments. In Maharashtra state, it has been made applicable to establishments in which fifty or more persons are employed.

The Indian Trade Unions Act, 1926

The experience of the working of the system of free enterprise in the industrial field revealed that, though theoretically both the employers and workers were free to enter into a contract and to agree upon the wages to be paid and received, in point of fact, for various reasons, this freedom did not benefit the workers in any way. Firstly, the commodity that a worker has to sell is highly perishable in the sense that if he refuses to work on a particular day because the wages offered are low, he cannot store up his labour of that day to be used the next day. This compels him to accept work even if the wages offered are unsatisfactory. Secondly, as his income is very low, he is not able to accumulate any savings which he can fall back upon if and when he refuses to work. The only alternative to refusal to work because of low wages is, therefore, starvation. These two factors compel a worker to accept low wages and so the theoretical freedom of contract is not of much use to him. Lastly, the fact that a worker is a small-scale seller and the employer is a large-scale buyer reduces his bargaining power to a very great extent. It is possible for the employer to refuse the wage which a worker demands because it is possible for him to engage somebody else who is willing to work at a lower wage. It is, however, relatively difficult for a worker to find an alternative employer who would pay in the wage he demands. His weak bargaining position thus compels him to accept whatever wages are offered to him.

Rules of a Trade Union : The rules of a union must contain the following provisions: (a) the name, (b) the objects for which it has been established, (c) the purpose for which its general funds will be applicable, (d) maintenance of the list of members for inspection by officers and members of the Union, (e) the admission of ordinary members who shall be persons engaged in the industry with which the Union is connected and also the admission of honorary members to form the executive of the union, (f) the conditions under which members are entitled to the benefits ensured by the rules and under which fines or forfeiture may be imposed on them, (g) the manner in which any rule shall be amended, altered or rescinded, (h) the manner in which the members of the executive and other officers of the Union shall be appointed and removed, (i) the safe custody of the funds of the Union, the audit of accounts and inspection of the account books by the officers and members, and lastly (j) the manner in which the Union will be dissolved.

Right of Registered Trade Unions: A registered trade union has a right:

(a) To collect membership fees on the premises of the factory without interference from the management;

(b) To put up notices of the meetings of the union and of other activities of the Union on the premises of the factory;

(c) To use the general funds for specific purposes;

(d) To raise funds for political purposes at the option of the members;

(e) To conduct a strike by peaceful methods;

(f) To be exempted from the provisions of Section 120B, subsection (2) of the Indian Penal Code if the members conduct a peaceful strike;

(g) To appoint outsiders in a number which is not more than one-half of the total number of office-bearers to the executive of the Union and

(h) To send to the Registrar, every year, an audited statement of receipts and expenditure.

The Payment of Wages Act, 1936

The payment of wages to factory workers in a particular form and at regular intervals without any unauthorized deductions is the objective of this Act.

Scope of the Act: The provisions of the Act are applicable to workers engaged in factories as defined by the Factories Act of 1948, and to persons employed on any railway by contractor or sub-contractor. The State Government may, after giving three months' notice of its intention of doing so by a notification in the Official Gazette, extend the provisions of this Act to any class of persons employed in any industrial establishment. The provisions of this Act are applicable to those persons whose wages do not exceed Rs. 400 per month.

The date of payment of wages: The wages of every person employed in a factory, industrial establishment or a railway, where less than 1,000 persons are employed, shall be paid before the expiry of the seventh day after the completion of the wage period, generally a month; the wages for a month, for example, shall be paid before the seventh day of the next month. In the factories in which more than a thousand persons are employed, the wages shall be paid before the expiry of the tenth day of the next month. The wages of a persons whose services have been terminated shall be paid on the next working day after such termination.

The payment of wages shall be made on a working day.

Authorised deductions: The Act authorises an employer to make deductions from wages for the following purposes only: (a) fines, (b) absence from duty, (c) damage to or loss of goods or money, where such damage or loss is due to the negligence or default on the part of the employee, (d) housing accommodation supplied by the employer and (e) such amenities and services supplied by the employer as the State Government may authorise.

(i) Fines shall be imposed for those acts of commission and omission which the employer, with the approval of the State Government, may have specified by notice to his employees.

(ii) Fines shall not be imposed on any employee unless he has been given an opportunity to show cause why the fine should not be imposed.

(iii) No fine shall be imposed on persons below the age of fifteen.

(iv) The fine so imposed shall be recovered in instalments or after the expiry of sixty days from the day on which it was imposed.

(v) The fine and the actual amount recovered shall be recorded in a separate register in the prescribed form and all amounts of fines realised shall be utilised only for such purposes as are beneficial to the employees and as are approved by the prescribed authority. Applications for the recovery of fines, or of deductions not authorised under the Act, for delay in payment of wages shall be presented within six months of the date on which such fines were imposed or deductions were made or wages were due.

The Workmen's Compensation Act, 1923

Within the installation of machinery operated by motive power, the number of accidents in factories have increased considerably. Many times, workers lost their fingers, sometimes their hands and feet and in some cases even their lives while working on machines in factories. This meant the loss of earnings for those who were involved in accidents and, in cases where a worker died, his dependants were left to starve. From a purely humanitarian point of view, it would be natural to expect that employers should give some compensation to such workers or their dependants. Further, even on economic grounds, it could be argued that the amount of compensation is a legitimate element of the cost of production under the factory system and, therefore, neither society nor employers should grudge paying it whenever workers were involved in accidents. Some enlightened employers did pay compensation to their employees when they suffered accidents; but a large majority was not willing to accept this responsibility. The workers, however, could not claim compensation as a matter of right; and even when compensation was paid, there was bound to be an honest difference of opinion between an employer and an employee as regards the fairness of the amount paid to the disabled factory worker. Workmen's Compensation Acts have been passed in almost all countries.

The following are the provisions of the Indian Workmen's Compensation Act:

Employer's Liability for Compensation: If a personal injury is caused to a worker by an accident arising out of and in the course of his employment, his employer shall be liable to pay compensation in accordance with the provisions of this Act.

When Employer is not Liable: The employer, however, shall not be liable if (a) the injury results in a partial or total disablement of the worker for less than three days; (b) if the injury can be directly attributed to the worker having been under the influence of drink or drugs; (c) if the injury can be directly attributed to the wilful disobedience by the worker of an order expressly given or (d) to the wilful removal or disregard by the worker of any safety guard or other device which he knew has been provided for the purpose of securing his safety.

Occupational Diseases: If a worker engaged in any employment which involves the handling of wool, hair bristles or animal carcasses or loading or unloading of such merchandise, or in processes carried on in compressed air, or in processes which involve the use of lead or tetraethyl or in process involving exposure to nitrous fumes, contracts diseases like anthrax, compressed-air illness, led poisoning by nitrous fumes respectively; or when engaged continuously for not less than six months in any employment specified in Part B of Schedule III, contracts any disease specified in this schedule as an occupational disease, the contacting of such a disease shall be regarded as an injury by accident and shall be deemed to have arisen out of and in employment. The State Governments in the case of employments specified in Part C of the schedule may make additions to the list of employments in Schedule II and specify the corresponding diseases after giving three months' notice in the Gazette.

Types of Injuries : Injuries for the purposes of this act have been classified into the following categories: (i) death, (ii) permanent total disablement, (iii) permanent partial disablement and (iv) temporary disablement, partial or total.

Amount of Compensation : The Act provides for Compensation for these categories of injuries in Schedules I to IV.

Medical Examination: A worker who has given notice of an accident shall submit himself to a medical examination, if the employer insists on it, by a qualified medical practitioner and free of charge. Similarly, a worker who is in receipt of half-monthly payments under this Act shall submit himself to such medical examination from time to time.

If a worker refuses to submit himself to such a medical examination without sufficient cause, his right to compensation shall be suspended.

The Employees State Insurance Act, 1948

Experience in the working of the Workmen's Compensate Act of 1923 revealed that the benefits conferred by it upon factory workers in many cases, did not reach them, this was due to various reasons. Firstly, a claim for compensation for injury has to be filed in an ordinary court of law and the lack of finance often made it impossible for a worker to file such a suit and fight it out. Secondly, for an employer armed with expert legal advice, it was often possible to prove that the accident either did not arise out of and in the course of employment, or that it was due to the worker concerned being under the influence of drink or drug at the time of the accident, or that it was due to his negligence or his disobedience of safety rules. In such conditions, workers were generally unwilling to go to a court of law, and preferred to accept whatever compensation employers chose to pay out of a sense of pity or charity. The Employees' State Insurance Act 1948 was framed to prevent such victimization of the worker by the employer.

Contributions: Every person, who is employed for wages in or in connection with the work of a factory or establishment to which this Act applies, shall be insured. All the insured workers, except those who earn wages of less than one rupee per day, shall pay their contribution to the Employees' State Insurance Corporation at the rates specified in the First Schedule to the Act. The employers shall pay their contributions at the rates specified in the above schedule.

Distribution of Benefits under the Act: The insured persons, or as the case may be, their dependants, shall be entitled to the following benefits, namely:

(a) **Sickness Benefits :** Periodical payments, to any insured person in case of his sickness certified by a duly appointed medical practitioner;

(b) **Maternity Benefits :** Periodical payments, in case of confinement, to an insured woman certified to be eligible for such payments, by an authority specified in this behalf by the regulations;

(c) **Disablement Benefits :** Periodical payment to an insured person suffering from disablement as a result of an injury sustained in the course of his employment;

(d) **Dependants' Benefits :** Periodical payments to such dependants of an insured person who dies as a result of an injury sustained in the course of his employment and

(e) **Medical Benefits :** Medical treatment for and attendance on an insured person.

The Corporation may at the request of the government of India, extend medical benefits to the family of the insured person. Accordingly, these benefits have been so extended from 1st January 1962.

A person who is in receipt of sickness or disablement benefit, must observe the following conditions:

(a) He shall remain under medical treatment at dispensary, hospital, clinic or any other institution provided under this Act and shall carry out the instructions of the medical officer or medical attendant in charge thereof;

(b) He shall not, while under treatment, do anything which might retard or prejudice his chances of recovery;

(c) He shall not leave the area in which medical treatment provided under this Act is being given without the permission of the medical officer or such other authority as may be specified in this behalf under the rules framed for this purpose and

(d) He shall allow himself to be examined by any duly appointed medical officer or any other person authorised by the corporation in this behalf.

Penalties : If a person makes a false statement for the purpose of causing any increase in payment or benefit, or for the purpose of causing any payment or benefit to be made where no payment or benefit is authorised, or for the purpose of avoiding any payment to be made by himself, he shall be punishable with imprisonment for a term upto three months or with fine up to Rs. 500 or with both.

If any person fails to pay any contribution which he is liable to pay, or deducts from the wages of an employee the whole or any part of the employee's contribution or reduce the wages or any privileges or benefits admissible to an employee, dismisses, discharges, reduces or otherwise punishes an employee in contravention of Section 73, or fails or refuses to submit any return required by the regulations or makes a false return, or obstructs any Inspector or the official of the Corporation in the discharge of his duties, or is guilty of contravention of, and non-compliance with any of the requirements of this Act, he shall be punishable with imprisonment upto a period of three months or with fine up to Rs. 500 or with both.

Industrial Disputes Act 1947

Industrial disputes, strikes and lock-outs were not very common occurrences in India till 1914. It was, however, during the Great War of 1914-18 that the strike came to be regarded as an ordinary weapon of industrial warfare. During the War, while the cost of living went on rising, the wages did not keep pace with it. This gave rise to serious discontent among industrial workers and led to a series of strikes, notably in the textile industry in Mumbai, in the post-war period. In addition to low wages, there were many other causes which were partly responsible for the outbreak of strikes during this period. The more important of these were long hours of work, bad conditions, insanitary housing conditions, absence of any provision till 1922 for compensation for injuries sustained in the course of employment, absence, till 1925, of the right to form a trade union, ill-treatment of workmen by foremen or other mill officials etc.

The important provisions of the Industrial Disputes Act of 1947 are:

(i) If any industrial dispute exists or is apprehended, the appropriate Government may, by order in writing, (a) refer the dispute to a Board for promoting a settlement thereof; or (b) refer any matter appearing to be connected with or relevant to the dispute to a Court of Inquiry or (c) refer the dispute to a Tribune for arbitration.

(ii) If either of the parties to a dispute or both of them apply to the Government to refer a dispute to a Board, Court or Tribunal, the appropriate Government, if satisfied that the person applying represents the majority of each party, shall make the reference accordingly.

(iii) If a dispute has been referred to a Board or a tribunal, the government may prohibit the continuance of any strike or lock-out in connection with such a dispute.

(iv) A Settlement arrived at in the course of conciliation proceedings under the Act, or an award which is declared by the Government as binding on all the parities to the dispute for at least six months.

(v) An award declared by a Government shall come into operation on such date as may be specified by the government and shall remain in operation for a period of one year, or a shorter period, if so fixed by the Government.

(vi) Workers employed in public utility industries shall not go on a strike and the employers in such industries shall not resort to lock-outs —

(a) without giving a fourteen days' notice and before the period of notice expires or

(b) during the tendency of conciliation proceedings.

(vii) Workers employed in any industrial establishment shall not go on strike—

(a) during the tendency of conciliation proceeding; or

(b) during the tendency of proceeding before a Labour Court, Tribunal or National Tribunal or

(c) during a period in which a settlement or award is in operation.

A strike or a lock-out, in contravention of any of these provisions shall be illegal.

No person shall knowingly expend or apply any money in direct furtherance or support of any illegal strike or lock-out.

Penalties : Any worker who commences, continues or acts in furtherance of an illegal strike shall be punishable with imprisonment up to one month or with fine up to Rs. 50 or both.

The Employees Provident Fund Act, 1952

The Act provides for the institution of a contributory provident fund in establishment in which 20 or more persons are employed. The contribution, which shall be paid by the employer to the fund, shall be $8\,^1/_3$ per cent of the basic wage and the dearness allowance payable to each employee, while the employee's contribution shall be equal to the contribution payable by the employer.

The Indian Boilers Act, 1923

An owner of a boiler shall not use it or permit to be used,

(a) Unless it has been registered in accordance with the provisions of this Act;

(b) In the case of a boiler transferred from one state to another, until the transfer has been reported in the prescribed manner;

(c) Unless certificate or provisional order authorising the use of the boiler is obtained under this Act;

(d) At a pressure higher than the maximum pressure recorded in such certificate or provisional order:

(e) Unless the boiler is in charge of a person holding a certificate of competency.

Procedure: The owner of a boiler may apply to the Inspector to have the boiler registered. Every such application shall be accompanied by the prescribed fee. The Inspector shall examine the boiler and submit a report to the Chief Inspector in the prescribed form.

The permit is a 'must' for boilers.

The Indian Electricity Act, 1910

The act relates to the supply and use of electricity energy.

Issue of Licence : A State Government may, on an application made in the prescribed form and on the payment of the prescribed fee, grant a licence to supply energy in any specified area and also to lay electric supply lines for the transmission of energy.

Intellectual Property Rights

Intellectual Property (IP) comprises legally protected rights in products of the mind, including useful inventions, novel designs, creative works, symbols of origin or sponsorship, non-public business information, and the like. (Abstract ideas, however, are generally not protected as IP). Intellectual property includes patents, copyrights, trademarks and trade dress, and trade secrets. In the industrial countries and in increasing number of developing nations, owners of IP rights of different kinds receive limited, defined exclusive rights to make, use, sell, copy, distribute, and/or license their inventions or creations.

International Law on Intellectual Property Protection

- *Paris Convention* (1883, revised most recently in 1979) : 128 countries are signatories; a landmark agreement on patents, trademarks, and industrial designs.
- *Berne Convention* (1886, revised most recently in 1971) : 111 countries are signatories; an agreement on copyrights encompassing literary and artistic works.
- *Patent Cooperation Treaty* (1970, revised most recently in 1985) : 79 countries are signatories; created a union for cooperation in filing, searching, and examining patent applications; facilitates filing of separate applications in member countries.
- *General Agreement of Tariffs and Trade Agreement on Trade-Related Aspects of Intellectual Property Rights* (GATT/TRIPS, 1994) : establishes minimum universal standards on patents, copyrights, trademarks, industrial designs, geographical indications, integrated circuits, and trade secrets; includes transitional arrangements.
- *World Intellectual Property Organisation* (WIPO, 1967) : a Geneva based agency of the United Nations created to encourage participation of developing countries in the international patent system.
- *Madrid Agreement and Protocol* : provides for international registration of trademarks with WIPO; 35 countries are signatories; the US is not yet a member.
- *Trademark Law-Treaty (1994)* : 35 countries are signatories; established maximum formal requirements that may be imposed on trademark applicants and registrants by member countries.
- *Some regional intellectual property agreements* : regional agreements with intellectual-property provisions include European Patent Convention, African Regional Intellectual Property Organization, Organisation Africaine de la Propriete

Intellectually, Pan American Trade Mark Convention, NAFTA, ANCOM, and Caricom.

Four Ways of Going Global

There are four entry level options for Indian players seeking a global market. The first route which is the most basic, and followed by the majority of Indian players, entails a local manufacturer serving as a *sourcing agent* for local distributors in that country. However, this is at best a short—term strategy susceptible to the whims of distributors.

The second entry option is a collaborative effort wherein local agents provide the distribution and marketing input to the Indian company. This is a route followed by many Indian players including Titan, Balsara, Maruti Udyog and Bajaj Auto.

The Indian company retains control over key marketing and branding issues. Clearly a long-term entry option, the arrangement gives the marketer a controlling interest and an assurance of commonality of product messaging and packaging, irrespective of the country the brand is being sold in. In such an arrangement, the Indian marketer provides development material and business promotion options to local distributors, and media costs are shared jointly by the two parties involved.

Marketers opting to follow the third route make a solo entry through independent distributors, in a manner similar to the route followed in India. However, this route is usually followed only in countries that offer a consumer profile closest to India, since it is a highly expensive route and open to failure.

The fourth more convenient and easily accessible alternative is to start as a private label supplier at the lower price end through the mass merchandising outlets of foreign buyers. Balasara is probably the best example of an Indian company taking the private label route articulately in the North American and European tooth paste markets. Of late, however, market analysts claim that this route is no longer as viable as it once was with private label marketing wars rampant in the US. Moreover, private lable manufacturers can at best be called global suppliers.

Conclusion

Rules and regulations governing small-scale industries act as a governor ensuring steady growth of the industry as well as the environment (ecosystem) and the labour force. It not only ensured healthy growth but also rapid growth. The basic objective of rules and regulations governing small-scale industries is to ensure that the results of operation confirm as closely as possible to established standards of goods, specified procedures or instructions. Rules and regulations are meant to put small-scale industries, enabling them to move on the successful track.

They are the directions, for excellence, growth and development and regulations is a monitoring mechanism of rules. Since the small-scale enterprise is concerned with land, environment, goods, people and consumers, rules and regulations have been formulated to safeguard these varied interests. If there is greater awareness among the entrepreneurs, these rules and regulations have minimum effect and disturbance. Thus, rules and regulations ensure steady and rapid growth of small-scale industries, develop new products and markets, produce quality goods and promote healthy development of human resources. More importantly, small industries are located nearer to the natural resources and human resources, do not pollute or degrade the ecosystem, intimidate and exploit layout and cheat the consumer on all counts. Rules and regulations are, therefore, the basic component of small-scale industries. They are like the lamp post directing the growth of this sector on a firm ground.

Inspector Raj: The Great Survivor

The licence-quota raj may be over but the inspector raj still reigns supreme. Industry may have been delicensed in 1991 but is still highly regulated. Each industrial unit is visited by between 40 and 60 inspectors in the course of a month. The following is an illustrative, and not an exhaustive, list of inspectors. There maybe several more inspectors depending on the kind of manufacturing activity. As a result, small and medium enterprises are forced to shell out bribes to these officers. Or else face harassment.

Ministry	No. of Inspectors	Work Done
Industry	5	Check registration, inventories, tax payment quality control, safety Equipment
Home	2	Check fire protection facilities and compliance with Explosives Act
Planning & Statistics	1	Collect data on production, manpower, man-hours utilised and lost
Finance	12	Five for income tax (three of them checking the same records for three different departments): seven from excise department
Separate Revenue	5	Enforcement, verification and recovery of sales tax enrolment of professional tax; weights and measures
Revenue Department (State government) tax	1	Registration of professional
Labour	8	Checking compliance with different labour laws, checking the same records
Municipal Corporations	2	Municipal byelaws
Power & Energy	1	Electricity connections
Health & Family Welfare	2	Hygiene and occupational health
Urban Affairs & Employment	1	Sanitation
Environment & Forests	2	Pollution control
Communications	1	Telecom facilities
Local Self-government	2	Octroi and mass raids
Food & Drug Administration	1	Safety standards

ANNEXURE

A. ACTS AFFECTING AN INDUSTRIAL UNIT

1. The Agricultural Produce (Grading & Marketing) Act, 1937
2. The Aluminum (Control) Order
3. The Arms Act, 1959
4. The Art-Silk Textiles (Production & Distribution) Order, 1962
5. The Beer and Wine Prohibition Act, 1956
6. The Central Excise and Salt Act, 1944
7. The Cigarette (Regulation of Production & Distribution) Act, 1975
8. The Cinema Carbons (Control) Order, 1961
9. The Coffee Act, 1942
10. The Choir Reeling (Licensing) Order, 1968
11. The Cold Storage Order, 1980
12. The Commercial Vehicles/Tractors/Motor Cars (Distribution & Sales) Control Order, 1971
13. The Cooper (Prohibitions of use in Manufacture of Electric Cables and Wires) Order, 1970
14. The Cotton Textiles (Control) Order, 1948
15. The Dangerous Drugs Act, 1983
16. The Drugs and Cosmetics Act, 1940
17. The Drugs and Magic Remedies (Objectionable Advertisement) Act, 1954
18. The Drugs (Price Control) Order, 1979
19. The Essential Commodities Act, 1946
20. The Ethyl Alcohol (Price Control) Order, 1966
21. The Fertilizer Control Order, 1957
22. The Foodgrains (Prohibition of Use in Manufacture of Starch) Order, 1966
23. The Fruit Products Order, 1955
24. The Gold (Control) Act, 1968
25. The Household Electrical Appliances (Quality Control) Order, 1976
26. The Indian Boilers Act, 1923
27. The Indian Explosive Act, 1884
28. The Indian Forest Act, 1927
29. The Indian Standard Institute (Certificate Mark) Act, 1952
30. The Insecticides Act, 1968
31. The Iron and Steel (Control) Order, 1956
32. The Jute Textiles (Control) Order, 1961
33. The Kerosene/Light Diesel Oil/ Furnace Oil (Fixation of Selling Prices) Order, 1973

34. The Meat Food Products Order, 1973
35. The Medical and Toilet Preparations (Excise Duties) Act, 1956
36. The Minerals (Regulation and Development) Act, 1957
37. The Molasses (Control) Order, 1961
38. The Non-Ferrous Metals (Control) Order, 1958
39. The Packaged Commodities (Regulation) Order, 1975
40. The Paper (Control of Production) Order, 1974
41. The Paraffin Wax (Supply, Distribution and Price Fixation) Order, 1972
42. The Press and Registration of Books Act, 1971
43. The Prevention of Food Adulteration Act, 1954
44. The Rice Milling Industry (Regulation) Act, 1958
45. The Rubber Act, 1947
46. The Solvent Extracted Oil, Deoiled Meal and Edible Flour (Control) Order, 1967
47. The Sugar (Control) Order, 1966
48. The Sugar (Price Determination) Order, 1972
49. The Sugarcane Press Mud (Control) Order, 1961
50. The Textile Machinery (Production and Distribution) Control Order, 1962
51. The Textiles (Production by Knitting, Embroidery, Lacemaking & Printing Machines) Order, 1962
52. The Textiles (Development and Regulation) Order, 1992
53. The Textiles (Production by Handlooms) Control Order, 1956
54. The Tobacco Act, 1978
55. The Vegetable Oil Products (Control) Order, 1947
56. The Weights and Measures Act, 1958
57. The Wheat Roller Flour Milling (Licensing and Control) Order, 1957
58. The Woolen Textiles (Production and Distribution) Act, 1962

B. LABOUR LEGISLATION

1. The Apprenticeship Act, 1961
2. The Contract Labour Act, 1970
3. The Employees' Provident Funds and Family Pension Fund Act, 1952
4. The Employees' State Insurance Act, 1948
5. The Employment Exchange (Compulsory Notification of Vacancies) Act, 1959
6. The Employment of Children's Act, 1938
7. The Equal Remuneration Act, 1976
8. The Factories Act, 1948

9. The Industrial Disputes Act, 1947
10. The Industrial Disputes (Amendment) Act, 1956
11. The Industrial Employment Act, 1946
12. The Industrial Relations Act, 1946
13. The Maternity Benefit Act, 1961
14. The minimum Wages Act, 1948
15. The Payment of Bonus Act, 1978
16. The Payment of Gratuity Act, 1972
17. The Payment of Wages, 1936
18. The Sales Promotion Employees Act, 1976
19. The Shops and Establishment Act & Rules, 1948
20. The Trade Unions Act, 1926
21. The Workmen's Compensation Act, 1923

C. OTHER ACTS MEANT FOR SPECIFIC INDUSTRIES

1. The Beedi and Cigar (Conditions of Employment) Act, 1966
2. The Coal Mines Labour Welfare Fund Act, 1947
3. The Coal Mines Provident Fund and Bonus Scheme Act, 1948
4. The Dock Workers (Regulation of Employment) Act, 1948
5. The Indian Dock Labourers Act, 1934
6. The Indian Ores Mines Labour Welfare Cess Act, 1961
7. The Industrial Disputes (Banking and Insurance Companies) Act, 1949
8. The Industrial Disputes (Banking Companies) Decision Act, 1955
9. The Limestone and Dolomite Mines Welfare Fund Act, 1972
10. The Mica Mines Labour Welfare Fund Act, 1946
11. The Motor Transport Workers Act, 1961
12. The Plantation Labour Act, 1951
13. The Working Journalists (Conditions of Services) and Miscellaneous Act, 1955

D. TAXATION

1. The Central Sales Tax Act, 1956
2. The Profession Tax Act, 1959
3. The Gift Tax Act, 1958
4. The Income-tax Act, 1961
5. The State Sales Tax Act, 1956
6. The Wealth Tax Act, 1957

E. REGULATION OF INDUSTRIES

1. The Indian Partnership Act, 1932
2. The Indian Companies Act, 1956
3. The Industries (Development and Regulation) Act, 1951
4. The Emblems and Name (Prevention of Improper Use) Act, 1950
5. The Companies (Acceptance of Deposits) Rules, 1975
6. The Capital Issue (Control) Act, 1947
7. The Monopolies and Restrictive Trade Practices Act, 1969
8. The Land Acquisition Act, 1894
9. The Urban Land (Ceiling and Regulation) Act, 1976
10. The Water (Prevention and Control of Pollution) Act, 1974
11. The Prevention of Black Marketing and Maintenance of Supplies of Essential Commodities Act, 1980
12. The Conservation of Foreign Exchange and Prevention of Smuggling Activities Act, 1947
13. The Imports and Exports Control Act, 1947
14. The Securities Contracts (Regulation) Act,1956
15. The Foreign Exchange Regulation Act, 1973
16. The State Aid to Industries Act, 1973
17. The Sick Industrial Combines (Special Provisions) Act, 1985
18. The Shops and Establishment Act, 1948
19. The Cement Control Order, 1967
20. The Jute Packing Materials Act, 1987
21. The Explosives Act, 1884
22. The Petroleum Act, 1934
23. The Inflammable Substances Act, 1952
24. The Patents Act, 1970
25. The Designs Act, 1911
26. The Trade and Merchandise Marks Act, 1958
27. The Smoke Nuisance Act, 1963

F. GENERAL LEGISLATIONS

1. The Banking Regulation Act, 1949
2. The Negotiable Instruments Act, 1881
3. The Indian Stamp Act, 1899
4. The Indian Evidence Act

5. The Companies Law, 1956
6. The Indian Companies Act, 1956
7. The Indian Registration Act, 1908
8. The Limitation Act, 1963

Summary

Sr. No.	*Type of Legislations*	*No. of Legislations*
A	Acts Affecting Industrial Units	58
B	Labour Legislations	21
C	Other Acts (Specific)	13
D	Taxation	6
E	Regulation of Industries	27
F	General	8
	Total	133

Note : There are about 133 Acts and Orders about which the entrepreneur or his legal advisor should have some knowledge. The list is not exhaustive, but covers a good ground. For details, references may be made to the undated Acts/Orders in original wherever applicable.

Chapter - 6

PROMOTION OF A VENTURE

Introduction

A small-scale industrialist has to be conversant with the varied regulations governing the small-scale industry and the procedures to be followed in order to acquire the necessary assistance and incentives offered by the Government from time to time.

The procedural aspects of the small-scale industry are quite formidable. Each and every entrepreneur is often overwhelmed by the multitude of procedures which have to be faced at every stage of the development of a small-scale industry. It is therefore, necessary to emphasise here that the student should concentrate more on the purpose and the principle underlying the various procedural formalities, than on such routine formalities as filling in various forms, applications etc.

Box 6.1

Are You Ready for Business?

Some questions to ask yourself before you take the entrepreneurial leap.

– Udayan Ray (30 Apr 2001)

Bitten by the business bug? Remember, it's not easy to shake off the soporific security of a 9-to-5 job and perks to adopt a career that promises huge rewards but is rife with uncertainties. Ask yourself these questions before you make the leap.

Have the personality? You have to have passion but equally, you have to be a good general. You must attract great talent, and later get the best out of your team and motivate it.

Can you persevere? There will be setbacks: finance, labour, market downturns. You must have tremendous faith in yourself and your idea to weather these.

Have the big idea? First, evaluate your business idea. Is it unique or is it better/cheaper than the rest? It's a good idea to use informal market research to get feedback on the idea's viability.

What's your gameplan? Figure out your scale of operations: will you cater to a niche segment? Chart a road map of your business goals and time frames.

Is it on paper? Make a sound business plan. This process will help you spot planning oversights early. If you're looking for loans, a business plan is mandatory.

Where is the money? Figure out how much you can raise from personal and other sources. Money from the wrong investors can be source of conflict.

Is cash flow in place? Cash flows must see you through contingencies and hidden costs, and help you stay afloat for at least six months after start-off. Don't make optimistic revenue projections.

Will revenues be stable? Get at least one or two anchor clients, the ones who will provide large, regular orders.

How lean can you get? Keep a tight leash on expenses till operations stabilise. Cut down on fixed costs, like high rentals, till your venture finds its feet.

Then act.

1. Evaluate your business idea and ensure your product/service is superior to what's available in the market.
2. Making a sound business plan will help you spot planning oversights early. Also essential if you want a loan.
3. How much money can you raise from personal sources? Will your cash flows see you through the initial period?
4. Attract talent and make the most of your team. And have enough faith in yourself, your idea and your team to weather initial setbacks.
5. Get at least two anchor clients who can provide large, regular orders. This should keep revenues stable.

Right Thing at the Right Time

In this chapter, the treatment of procedures-right from conceiving a small-scale industry until the repayment of creditors and ploughing back of profits-is based on the personal and practical experience of a small industrialist. In the latter part of the discussion, a reference has been made to the varied regulations mentioned later that a small-scale industrialist has to abide by. They are:

The relevant procedures to be followed when setting up a small-scale industry have been covered with, reference to various phases of its development. These phases are:

1. Selection of a small industry and preparation of feasibility and project reports;
2. Accommodation, power and other infrastructural facilities;
3. Machinery;
4. Raw materials;
5. Finance;
6. Marketing and
7. Securing various incentives offered for the development of the small-scale industry.

1. Selection of a Small-scale Industry

The process of setting up a small-scale industry has been indicated in Fig. 6.1, which has been drawn on the basis of practical experience gained in its promotion. It indicates all the important stages in setting up of a small-scale industry.

The objectives of the promotional regulations are to provide an impetus to the growth of a small-scale industry and regulate the supply of machinery, electricity, water, premises, finance, raw materials and markets. The process of production and marketing is governed by set rules and regulations. In a way, these regulations are a boon to the small entrepreneur.

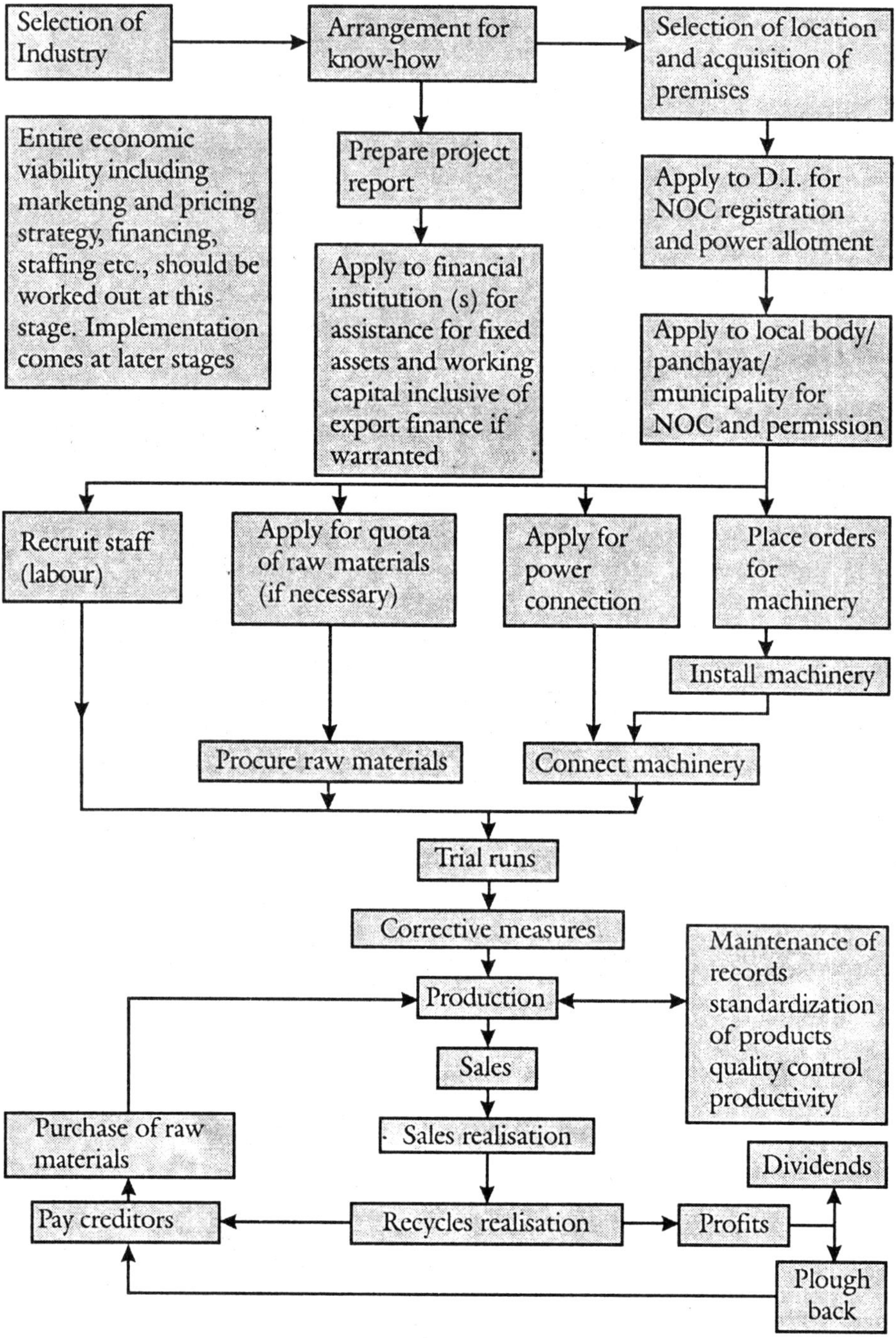

Fig. 6.1 : Process of setting up a small-scale industry

Starting a Small-scale Industry

A small entrepreneur is the chief executive of his unit, its floor supervisor, accounts clerk, purchase manager, salesman, legal and economic adviser, planner and visionary — all in one.

Every now and then, you will come across advertisements and announcements in the newspapers, enticing you to set up small industries under the aegis of the State Small Industries Corporations, which promise you the world : a fully developed industrial shed with power and water, assistance in getting you raw materials, machinery on hire-purchase basis, common services facilities, training facilities and facilities in the marketing of your product. You are assured of term loans on attractive terms and working capital in time and at concessional rate. In backward areas, a number of additional subsidies are available.

PHASES | *OBJECTIVES*

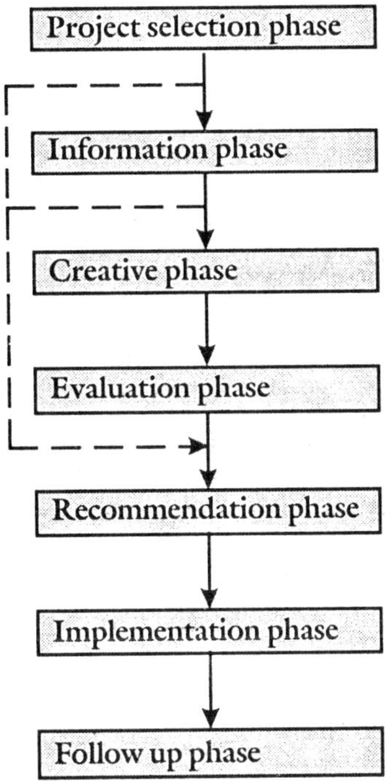

To select those products, process or systems in an organisation where the value and cost ratio is low and where analysis will lead to increased benefits

(a) To gather, organise and analyse data
(b) To define functions
(c) To establish a functional monetary value

To generate alternate methods for providing necessary functions

(a) To develop, refine and evaluate alternate methods generated during the creative phase
(b) To determine the cost
(c) To select feasible method offering best value

To prepare and present a report containing recommendation along with benefits

(a) To establish a plan to action for implementation of the selected method
(b) To obtain approval
(c) To perform all other actions necessary to put the proposal into effect

(a) To follow-up and audit actual results
(b) To resolve problems, if any, during proposal implementation.

Fig. 6.2 : Project Objectives

An entrepreneur may be a qualified engineer. Even so, he should not dream of becoming a small entrepreneur unless he is confident of meeting the following twelve essential requirements:

(i) The entrepreneur should be fully conversant with the product line. It is not enough that he knows the method of manufacture; he has to know how to operate the machines etc.

(ii) He should have adequate shop floor experience to guide the machine operators in tool-setting techniques or the die-maker on the specific needs of his press tools.

(iii) He should be familiar with the raw materials he requires, their specifications, how to ensure their quality and where to get them at reasonable prices.

(iv) He should know how to keep accounts, how to maintain stores, how to prepare the balance sheet etc.

(v) He should have knowledge of marketing channels, distribution network, agency practices, transport intricacies and the economics of packaging.

(vi) He should know how to ensure the stipulated quality of his product.

(vii) He should be well versed in taxation and other laws governing small-scale industries.

(viii) He should be willing to put up with polluted environments and small inconveniences.

(ix) He should be willing to put up with bureaucratic regulations and insults, and move with the wind.

(x) He should know how to avail himself of the various benefits available for the small-scale industry.

(xi) He should possess the following qualities—expertise, shrewdness, resourcefulness and most important, perseverance. There is no substitute for hard work.

(xii) He should have the guts to withstand the polluted climate in which he has to build his unit.

Objectives: Any entrepreneur desirous of starting a small-scale industry should have a clear picture of the objective of his project. It is advisable to prepare a comprehensive check list. Such a list, embracing all the important factors, has been given below for the guidance of prospective entrepreneurs. Students will get an insight into the various processes of a small-scale industry.

CHECK LIST

Does your industry have scope for development?	Yes-No
(Consult Director of Industries)	
Is there enough demand for the item you propose to manufacture?	Yes-No
Do you have some experience of	
(a) Manufacturing	Yes-No
(b) Marketing?	Yes-No
Have you studied the viability of your scheme?	Yes-No
(Consult the Small Industries Service Institute)	
Is factory space available:	
(a) In an Industrial Estate	Yes-No
(b) In an Industrial Area or	Yes-No
(c) In some other approved place?	Yes-No
Have you obtained the necessary licence from the municipality or the local body?	Yes-No
Are the necessary raw materials available:	
(a) Indigenously	Yes-No
(b) Are they to be imported?	Yes-No

Are facilities available for:	
(a) Tooling	Yes-No
(b) Quality Control?	Yes-No
Is necessary labour available:	
(a) Of skilled Workers	Yes-No
(b) Of semi-skilled workers?	Yes-No
Have you the necessary technical background for:	
(a) The manufacture of the various parts	Yes-No
(b) Operations?	Yes-No
Have you studied your product in resect of:	
(a) The manufacture of the various parts	Yes-No
(b) Production planning	Yes-No
(c) Inspection and quality control	Yes-No
(d) Assembly	Yes-No
(e) Packing	Yes-No
(f) Diversification?	Yes-No
Have you the necessary finance:	
(a) Are you a client of any bank?	Yes-No
(b) Has any bank offered you	
(i) Short-term loans?	Yes-No
(ii) Long-term loans?	Yes-No
(c) Have you any assets?	Yes-No
(d) Are your assets adequate for obtaining the necessary funds?	Yes-No
(e) Have you other sources/ways of raising money?	Yes-No
(f) Have you approached the Director of Industries/State Financial Corporation for financial help?	Yes-No
(g) Do you propose to approach the NSIC/SSIC for machinery on hire-purchase basis?	Yes-No
(h) Have you adequate cash/bank arrangement to furnish the earnest money required by the NSIC ?	Yes-No
What are your markets?	
(a) Local	Yes-No
(b) Country-wide	Yes-No
(c) Export?	Yes-No
How would you market your products(s)? Through	
(a) Retailers	Yes-No
(b) Wholesalers or	Yes-No
(c) Agents?	Yes-No

Are necessary transportation facilities available by	
(a) Road	Yes-No
(b) Rail?	Yes-No
Have you attended a course on	
(a) Production, Planning and Control	Yes-No
(b) Purchasing and Marketing	Yes-No
(c) Finance and cost control	Yes-No
(d) Personnel Management	Yes-No
(e) General Industrial Management?	Yes-No
Have you entered into a foreign collaboration agreement for	
(a) Technical know-how	Yes-No
(b) Royalty/commission on sales?	Yes-No
(c) Has your agreement been approved by the Government?	Yes-No

Feasibility Report

Before starting a small-scale industry, one should consult the Director of Industries and the Small Industries Service Institute (SISI) located in one's State. The SISI guides entrepreneurs as to the type of industry to start, where to start and how to start it. The SISI helps them to select the various items of manufacture which have scope for development in different areas. It suggests the lines on which a project report for the proposed units should be prepared for the consideration of various financial institutions, with a view to securing financial assistance. Similarly, technical help in the selection of proper raw materials and type of machinery is also provided. Apart from this, the SISI gives valuable information of the various incentives available to small-scale industries from various organisations.

Project Feasibility Analysis

A project feasibility analysis includes market analysis, technical analysis, financial analysis and social profitability analysis. Although each feasibility analysis is different and is tailored to the product, its goal is to identify the strengths and weaknesses of the project.

The starting point of a project analysis is the establishment of the objectives to be attained. The next stage is the pre-selection stage—the advisability of having an indepth study. The analysis stage consists mainly of three factors—market, technical and financial analysis. A market analysis is a method of screening project ideas as well as a means of evaluating a project's feasibility in terms of the market. A market analysis should cover the following areas:

(i) A brief description of the market including the market areas, methods of transportation and existing rates of transportation, channels of distribution and general trade practices are also included.

(ii) An analysis of past and present demands, including the determination of quantity and the value of consumption and identification of major consumers of the product.

(iii) An analysis of past and present supply, broken down as to source (whether imported or domestic) as well as information which will assist in determining the competitive position of the product such as selling prices, quality and marketing practices of the competitors.

The technical analysis of a project feasibility study establishes whether the project is technically feasible or not, and whether it offers a basis for the estimation of costs. Moreover, it provides an opportunity for a consideration of the effect of various technical alternatives on employment, ecology, infrastructure demands, capital services, support or other industries, balance of payments and other factors. A technical analysis should contain a review of the techniques or processes to be applied and should incorporate:

(i) A description of the product, including specification relating to its physical, mechanical and chemical properties, as well as the uses of the product.

(ii) A description of the selected manufacturing process, showing detailed flow charts and presenting the alternative process which may have been considered and the justification for the adoption of the selected process.

(iii) A determination of the plant size and production schedule, which includes the expected volume for a given time period on the basis of start-up and technical factors.

(iv) Selection of machinery and equipment, including specifications, equipment to be purchased and its origin, quotations from suppliers, delivery dates, terms of payment and a comparative analysis of alternatives in terms of cost, reliability, performance and spare parts availability.

(v) An identification of the plant's location and an assessment of its desirability in terms of its distance from raw material sources and markets. For a new project, this part may include a comparative study of different sites, indicating the advantages and disadvantages of each.

(vi) A design of the plant lay-out and an estimate of the cost of the erection of the proposed buildings and land improvements.

(vii) A study of the availability of raw materials and liabilities and utilities, including a description of physical and chemical properties, quantities needed, current and prospective costs, terms of payment, locations of sources of supply and continuity of supply.

(viii) An estimate of labour requirements, including a detailed breakdown of direct and indirect labour requirements, and the supervision required for the manufacture of the product.

(ix) A determination of the type and quantity of waste to be disposed of together with a description of the waste disposal method, its costs and the necessary clearance from proper authorities and

(x) An estimate of the production cost of the product.

In the financial analysis of a project feasibility study, the emphasis is on the preparation of financial statements, so that the project may be evaluated in terms of the different measures of commercial profitability and the magnitude of financing required may be determined. The financial analysis requires the assembly of the market and technical costs estimated into various proforma statements. If it is necessary to have more information on which to base an investment decision, a sensitivity analysis or possibly, a risk analysis may be conducted. The financial analysis should include:

(i) For projects that involve new companies, statements of total project cost, initial capital requirements and cash flows relative to the project time-table.

For all projects, financial projections for future time periods including income statements, cash flows and balance sheets are inoperative.

(ii) For all projects, supporting schedules for financial projection, stating the assumption made as to the collection period of sales, inventory levels, payment period of purchases and expenses, and the element of production cost, selling, administrative and financial expenses.

(iii) For all projects, a financial analysis showing returns on investments, returns on equity, break-even volume and price analysis.

(iv) For all projects, if necessary, a sensitivity analysis to identify items which have a substantial impact on profitability, or possibly a risk analysis.

For the small entrepreneur, the studies conducted during the analysis stage of the project provide the material for an assessment. If positive results are obtained, the entrepreneur, in seeking finance will want to prepare an investment proposal. The planners or government officials, however, having obtained positive conclusions from the economic feasibility study, will want to evaluate the element of social profitability.

The purpose of the investment or loan application is to convince a lender (financial institution) that the project is a desirable investment; that it not only possesses the potential for profit but that the proposed management team has the capability to achieve the potential. The investment proposal normally contains:

(i) General information on the product, company history, the nature of the industry and the reputation and qualifications of the existing or proposed management.

(ii) A description of the period, which usually consists of extracts from economic feasibility studies and includes information on such items as market, production, selected manufacturing methods (with detailed indication of the cost of equipment and operational expenses) and a financial statement and

(iii) Miscellaneous information, such as the steps taken for the implementation of the project and the qualifications of the technical partners envisaged or selected.

Once the industry is identified, the SISI prepares a feasibility report and project report, giving one a comprehensive idea of an industry's prospects and profitability.

Licences: An impression seems to have gained round among some people that there are some restrictions on the setting up of small-scale industrial units and that licences from either the Central or State Governments have to be taken out before an entrepreneur can take steps to start a small-scale industrial units. This impression is not correct. It is open to any entrepreneur to set up an industrial unit in the small-scale sector; no formal permission from the State or Central Government is necessary for this purpose. Also, industries employing less than 100 workers and having fixed assets of less then Rs. 10 lakh need not obtain any licence under the industries (Development and Regulation) Act.

Small-scale units have, however, to conform to the rules and regulations prescribed by the State or local authority under the factories act, the Commercial Establishment Act, the Town Planning Rules and made for the issue of quotas of raw materials etc.

However, powerlooms do not come under the purview of the small-scale industries programme. For installing powerlooms, the prior permission of the Textile Commissioner, Government of India, Mumbai, is required.

(1) Registration of Small-scale Industries

In their own interest, all existing small-scale units or intending entrepreneurs employing more than 10 workers should get themselves registered with the Director of Industries in their State. A coy of this application for registration should be sent to the Director of small Industries Service Institute in the concerned State. Such registration with the Director of Industries and the Small Industries Services Institute will be of considerable help to the small-scale unit in obtaining financial assistance from the government and for obtaining machinery on hire-purchase basis from the national Small Industries Corporation. Assistance in the supply of controlled raw materials, essentiality certificate for imported raw materials and components and facilities for export promotion, would then be made available easily to small-scale units registered with the State Director of Industries. The registration number is now required to be quoted while submitting import applications. The registration number is now required to be quoted while submitting import applications. Registration procedures have been substantially simplified. Revised forms of SSI have been introduced from 1.1.1994.

(2) Infrastructure

This pertains to approaching the Director of Industries and/or the SISI in the State to provide you with built-up factory space in an industrial estate or develop the factory site, power etc. After the initial clearance from the State Director of Industries, the municipality or the Panchayat issues a 'No Objection Certificate.' The procedure for obtaining the basic infrastructure facilities is given below.

The mechanics of establishing a new factory in Greater Mumbai are:

(i) Apply to the Industries Commissioner, Industries and Labour Department, Government of Maharashtra, and obtain a 'No Objection Certificate.'

(ii) With a copy of the above NOC, apply, in Factory Form 'A' to the Ward Engineer of B.M.C.

(iii) Clarification and submission of further details on the information supplied in Form 'A' may, follow.

(iv) The sub-Engineer will inspect the premises and submit Form No. '2' to his Assistant Engineer.

(v) The Sub-Engineer will scrutinise and confirm if the applicant's activity conforms to the Zone and will intimate to the applicant in form No. '3' if there is no objection or in From No. '4' if there is any objection.

(vi) Form 'B' will be received by the applicant if Form No. '3' is issued to him. This form should be filled in and submitted.

(vii) Within 21 days after the submission of Forms 'A', 'B' and the factory plans in triplicate, the Assistant Engineer will issue Form Nos. '5' and '6' in which he will specify:

(a) The electric power sanctioned (thereafter the BEST provides electricity);

(b) Adequate water facilities provided;

(c) The various requirements, requisitions and conditions for operating the factory, including those required by the Chief Inspector of Factories.

Form 'C' will also be issued along with these forms. (Upon complying with the stipulation in Form 'B', the BMC should be informed thereof in writing.)

Thereafter, permission to commence production will be given.

(3) Machinery

The small entrepreneur needs the requisite type of machines for production. He can get the necessary machinery from the National Small Industries Corporation under a hire-purchase scheme.

The scheme for the supply of indigenous and imported machines on hire-purchase basis was launched in March 1956 to enable small entrepreneurs without substantial means to avail themselves of assistance. The scheme is different from the credit operations scheme for entrepreneurs. The NSIC has acquired the necessary experience and expertise in the procurement of machines from the right sources. It also takes care of problems upto the stage of delivery of machinery to the entrepreneurs. Also, while financial institutions look mainly to the creditworthiness of entrepreneurs, the NSIC would look primarily to the motivation of the individual applicant, his capacity, his technical competence and his managerial ability to run the enterprise.

The small entrepreneur should enlist himself as a member with the NSIC. His application form should be accompanied with the Registration Certificate and report of the Director of Industries. The application for obtaining machines under the hire-purchase scheme of the NSIC is quite comprehensive. The small entrepreneur has to provide full details, along with the relevant documents.

The application form for hire-purchase machinery calls for information regarding the organisational set-up of a unit, its programme of production and the marketability and profitability of the enterprise. It also calls for additional information regarding the cost of production, the infrastructure facilities available for the unit, the technical capability of the entrepreneur etc. The details in the application are self-explanatory.

(4) Raw Materials

The raw materials required by small-scale units may broadly be classified as under:

(i) Raw material components and spares—both indigenous and imported;

(ii) Non-ferrous materials—both indigenous and imported;

(iii) Iron and steel—both indigenous and imported and

(iv) Chemicals—indigenous and imported.

Under the liberalised scheme, the actual users are provided with adequate foreign exchange to meet their justifiable requirements of imported items of industrial materials. The 'priority' industries are assured of an adequate supply to the extent of their requirements by way of grant of rotational licences.

Small-scale units should apply directly to the Regional Licensing Authority, and not through the sponsoring authority, for import license for raw materials, components and spares after utilising the previous set of licences to the extent of 90 per cent by way of opening their own credit, or 60 per cent by way of actual import, covering six months' requirements of the unit. New units should submit their applications through their respective sponsoring authority.

The State Director of Industries allocates indigenous non-ferrous metals. Some of the non ferrous items are canalised through the State Trading Corporation of India (STC). The raw materials imported by the STC are given to the SSI units in accordance with the recommendations of the Director of Industries concerned.

Iron and steel raw materials are canalised through the MMTC in accordance with the recommendations of the Director of Industries.

In times of difficulties, the decontrolled chemical raw materials are canalised through the DGTD in accordance with the recommendation of State Director of Industries. Indigenous controlled chemicals are allocated through the State DIS/SICs. Imported raw materials are canalised through the STC.

In short, controlled and imported raw materials are to be obtained through the State DIS, SICs (SSI).

(5) Finance

The financial function in a small-scale industry is similar to the financial function in any other organisation, but with this essential difference—that there are a host of banking and insurance regulations to be strictly adhered to and quite a few precautions to be taken.

The areas where finance would be needed, after the small-scale industrialist fixes the land accommodation are:

(i) Purchase and installation of machinery;

(ii) Procurement of raw materials and components and the manufacture of products;

(iii) Working funds and

(iv) Availability of funds until the realisation of sales.

The State Director of industries provides loans for block capital under the Industries Act. One should apply through the sponsoring authority. State Financial Corporations provide long-term credit for the purchase of fixed assets. The application should be submitted to the SFCs along with the following documents: (i) Project report; (ii) Copy of registration; (iii) Cashflow statement and (iv) Stock statement.

In some States, the SFCs and the banks have agreed to process the common application for loans. For an amount of Rs. 2 lakh the commercial bank provides medium-term installment credit. It also provides loans for meeting needs for working capital for the purchase of raw materials, as also for day-to-day requirements.

In order to get a loan from a commercial bank, the entrepreneur has to fill in an application form as per the specimen (Annexure VIII) and submit it to the bank along with the following documents:

(i) Authentic copies of balance sheets and profit and loss accounts (if the industrial concern is a limited company or an industrial co-operative society).

(ii) A statement of assets and liabilities in the prescribed form (Appendix I of Annexure VIII) in the case of partnership and proprietary concerns.

(iii) Proforma statements in all other cases.

(iv) Copies of the affidavit in regard to the size of the unit.

(v) Technical feasibility report from the Small Industries Service Institute, the Director of Industries, if obtained, may also be enclosed.

Box 6.2

To take or not to take

Indians are known to be entrepreneurs. But to be one needs funds. A guide to bank funding for 'wanna-be' entrepreneurs...

Munira Mohta is an Architect cum interior designer who works for a famous Architect firm. She has had a good stint of three years at the same job and is itching to strike out on her own. But the big question that looms large in her head is how to fund for the office space and expenses till plum projects fall on her lap.

Sudenshu Gupta wants to start an auto ancillary unit. He has done his homework on the manufacturing side of the business as well as built report with a number of Auto Manufacturers who have assured him of regular orders.... He knows his idea is sure fire if only....

If wishes were horses all of the above would have been riding them as CEOs. But the biggest thorn on their future bed of roses is MONEY... or rather a lack of it.

FOCAL POINT

- Individuals wish to start off businesses but cannot due to lack of funds.
- Banks provide finance to entrepreneurs under many schemes.
- If your papers are in order it is safe and fast to avail credit from a bank.
- Till you pay off the loan, banks are owners of your property.
- You have to be psychologically strong to be an entrepreneur.

In an ideal world, all of them would have Sugar Daddies to fund their dreams, If they decide to wait and save up till they shore up all the capital they require the business opportunity may no longer be a viable option. The only other option is of course a rich father in law or the Bank. Banks have lots of schemes for schemes for such entrepreneurs.

TERM LOANS : Normally these loans are given to fund property and immovable assets like plant and machinery. The repayment is 3 to 5 years and the interest is in the range of 11% to 14%.

Working Capital Loans/Cash Credit : Simplistically this loan would finance the day-to-day running of your business. The interest charged is on the actual amount used and falls within the band of 10.5% to 12%.

Bill Discounting Facility : Say, you sell goods to X & Co. You raise a bill but give them credit for three months. If you want the money right away, the bank shall deduct some charges, pay you the bill amount and levy interest. After 3 months the bank collects directly from X & Co.

Apart from the above there are many schemes floated by the banks like Small Scale liberalized schemes, Entrepreneur's Scheme, Schemes for Women Entrepreneurs etc.

A composite, tailor-made package can also be devised for suitable customers. What are the pros and cons for availing this kind of a loan?

Pros :

- If you have a dream, this is most certainly the safest way to finance it.

  Alternatively, you can find people who also believe in you and finance you in terms of equity or extend a loan to you. In that case you make partners in your business or pay them interest just like a bank. The only hitch is that individuals can decide to pull out of your business at will, which just might leave you in the lurch.
- Banks will clear repayment and interest schedules making cash flow planning easy.
- Banks have technical teams that sometimes help you in assessing the viability of your projects.

Cons :

- There will be tons of administrative work, scores of forms to be filled.
- Normally, banks require the entrepreneur to bring in his own money into the business. This is called margin money.
- Banks will have a first charge on your assets. This means that till you pay the bank off completely, they are the owners of the property they have given a loan for.
- Banks ask for personal guarantee and/or Guarantors. This means that if your business fails, your personal assets like house etc. can be attached and/or your Guarantors will be made to repay your loan.

If you can sleep peacefully at night after taking on a debt and you are sure your business will generate at least that much money to take care of the interest and loan repayment, you have the stomach of an entrepreneur. Go for it.

(6) Marketing

The rationale of the Government Purchases Scheme of the Corporation lies in the fact that the Government of India is the largest single buyer; and by channelising these purchases in favour of small-scale units, it gives a tremendous boost to the marketing of their products.

The salient features of the scheme are:

(a) The small-scale units, desiring to avail themselves of assistance, have to enlist themselves with the NSIC;

(b) Instead of purchasing tender sets from the DGS & D, the small units enlisted with the NSIC automatically gets them from it and its branches free of cost;

(c) If their prices are acceptable to the authorities, they are not required to pay a security deposit on the issue of a competency certificate by the NSIC;

(d) Price preference upto 15 per cent over the quotations of large-scale units is considered by the purchasing agency, depending on the merits of each case;

(e) Wherever they feel that injustice has been done to them, the NSIC takes up their cases with the DGS and D and other government departments such as Defence, the Railways and the P&T Department in order to find out the reasons for non-placement of the contract with the units, and tries to redress their grievances.

In the beginning, purchases in respect of only 16 items were reserved exclusively for the small-scale sector; the number of such items has steadily increased, and at present is estimated to be at 379.

Marketing of Products of Small-Scale Industries

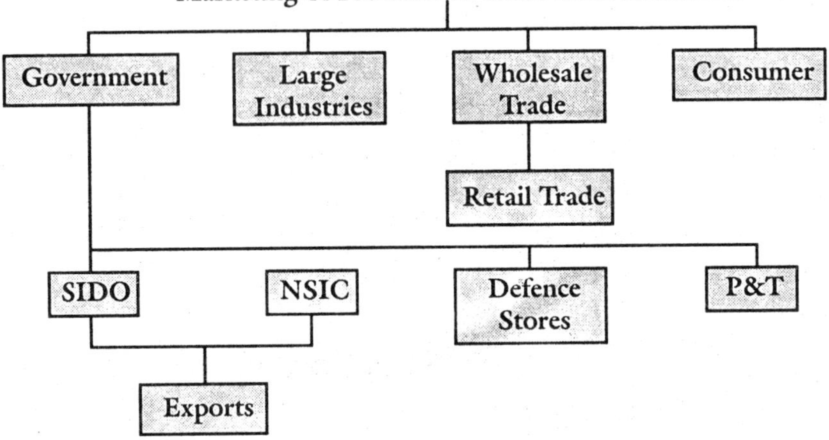

Fig. 6.3 : Marketing of Products of SSIs

The Corporation also helps small-scale industries in securing contracts from other government departments such as Railways, Posts and Telegraphs etc.

Hitherto, the purchase programme has been restricted purely to Central purchase houses like DGS & D, the P&T and the Railways. It is proposed to extend the base further to cover state government departments such as the State Electricity Boards, PWDs etc. and provide liaison offices at each of the principal purchase centres of the State.

(7) Incentives

For availing oneself of the various incentives, it is advisable to seek the help of the SISI and/or the Director of Industries.

The Small Industries Development Organisation (SIDO), Ministry of Industry, Nirman Bhavan, New Delhi, co-ordinates policies and programmes at the national level and provides a comprehensive range of extension services through its network of sixteen Small Industries Service Institutes, nineteen Branch Institutes and forty-five Extension Centres.

At the State level, organisations like State Directorates of Industries, Small Industries Development Corporations and Finance Corporations cater to the need of small industries; these needs include land, sheds, credit, power, raw materials etc.

The National Small Industries Corporation (NSIC), Okhla, New Delhi, provides machines and equipment on hire-purchase basis to entrepreneurs, assists units to participate in stores purchase programmes and provides training and prototype development facilities.

Registration with the NSIC entitles the units to obtain facilities from central or State Government organisations. New units have to apply to the respective State Directors of Industries for provisional registration, which is given within a week. It enables the party to take the necessary steps to bring the unit into existence, i.e., apply for sheds in industrial estates or on developed sites for water and power connections and for credit facilities. After the party has taken all the steps, it can apply for registration.

SIDO provides technical consultancy on improved technical processes, use of modern machines and equipment and technical assistance on all aspects of production. Each SISI has attached workshops for common facility services, training of workers, demonstration of modern machines and processes, making of tools and dies etc.

The Winning Edge

The opening up of the Indian small industry sector to competition as well as the increase in the need to cater to the global market demands fresh perception of the radical changes in the 90s. Consequently, the Indian small industry sector must change first to survive, as well as restructure itself, to meet the new challenges through a critical evaluation of the forces of free global trade and increased competition. These events demand quantum strategic changes in terms of industry culture, flattening of the organisation structure, employee empowerment as well as team building. Only those organisations which can respond to these changes will be able to survive and retain a winning edge.

Some of the important characteristics that differentiate the successful organisations from the unsuccessful ones are:

1. The most important aspect of successful business is leadership. It calls for clear vision, goals and objectives, well defined mission, dash and employees' participation.
2. Adequate but well-orchestrated control. Constant feedback of results, as well as setting up and adherence to high standards, gives an organisation a cutting edge over others. Planning, foresight and analysis are also important qualities.
3. To be able to extract the best from its employees through total involvement, the organisations put a lot of emphasis on proper internal communication and on training employees.
4. The successful organisation is one which is very close to the market place. The process of systematic market research is used to develop products or process and to provide value for money to the customers. This helps to gain a market share.
5. The next most important characteristic of a wining business organisation is 'Zero Basing' or sticking to the last—knowing what business the company is in and swiftly recognising when it has diverted into an unsuitable path.

Fig. 6.4

6. Another important characteristic for success is commitment to innovation which is vital in keeping ahead of the competition and perhaps the most difficult one to achieve. Yet, most of the organisations just pay lip service to creativity and innovation. They ask for new ideas and then quickly reject them and even when a new idea is accepted, the employee rarely gets a reward proportionate to the idea's worth.

Successful business organisations create a climate that encourages new ideas as a part of the employee's job. Anything that helps create an innovative culture and a natural curiosity, about how things are done in other companies will add value to the organisation.

Vision

To be self-employed one has to be a vision. To entrepreneurs who has it as one of their fundamental characteristics, vision is a vivid, dramatic and complete picture of what the company wants to be, and do. Crucially, this future is not one that can be reached in normal course; it needs a quantum leap.

Vision has been defined as the power of perceiving by imagination or by clear thinking. In the organisational context, vision is a picture of the future of the organisation. Vision is the hallmark of a forward looking organisation. It provides the motivation needed to get the best out of an organisation—enterprise and people. Vision inspires one to strive for better.

The founder of an organisation needs to paint a picture of the organisation as he sees it in the future. This encompasses primarily its scope as an organisation in terms of areas of business or products; the geographic boundaries and the value system by which it desires to attain the same, and a clarity of the relationships that it will develop with various members associated with the organisation.

It is important for an enterprise to have clarity of vision primarily because the organisation can stay focused, and not wander off into any unrelated areas that arise as a result of opportunities or apparent synergies. For instance, a company may feel that it can get into situations of vertical integration to optimise cost/returns, profitability, etc. While it may be profitable in the short run or may appear to be a strategically good move, it may not be optimal in the long term if it is not in keeping with the corporate vision.

Similarly, a firm's long-term interests in terms of developing a well-integrated organisation may not be served if it considers unrelated diversification just because an opportunity comes its way, or because the officials have specific contact with certain officials in the government.

The second important reason why clarity of vision is needed is because it develops a culture of learning within the organisation, in order to fulfill the clarified and stated vision. For instance, if an organisation's vision is to expand and become a global player in the market of the developing world, then the entire organisation could develop an interest in the specific industry sector and the geographic area and would, over a period of time, gain the knowledge to fulfill that vision.

Clarity of vision also enables the entire organisation to develop an inspirational force towards attaining a common goal, thus enhancing the team building process in an organisation since the entire organisation as the team will perform even a simple task.

An organisation (entrepreneur) must develop its vision statement based on where it is today via a thorough analysis of swot.

BUILDING A VISION : STAGE-I

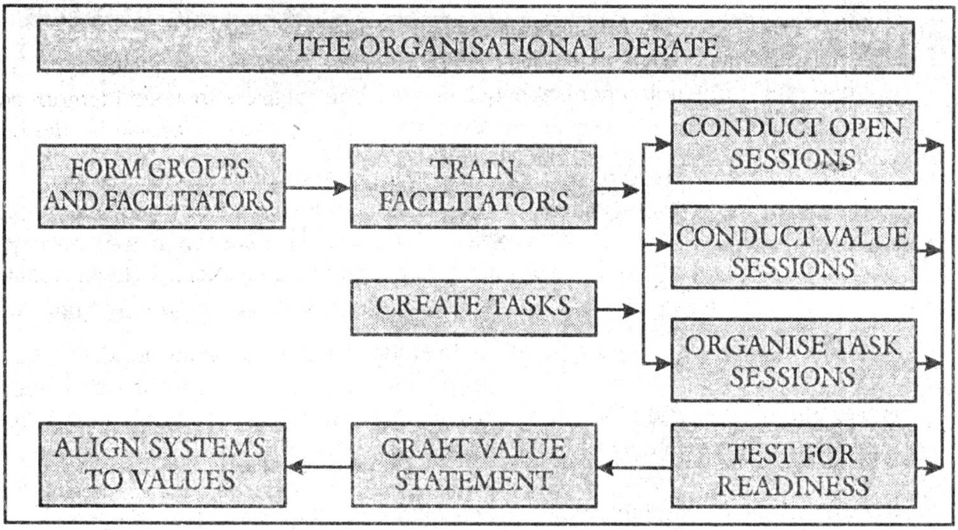

Increased Innovation

Innovation will provide the basis for the sustainability of an organisation. Richard Foster in his book *Innovation* has sketched the curve of performance versus effort for technological progress. The result is an S-shaped curve that moves from infancy to explosion and then a gradual maturation. The key to sustainability is the ability to glide through successive such S curves, in other words, the ability to continually innovate. 3M, on account of its constant innovation (it has something like 60,000 products in its stable) has been able to glide smoothly through many successive S-curves and thus has built an incredible amount of staying power in the market.

Implicit in continuous innovation is the importance of cannibalisation. Intel is one of the few organisations that has perfected the art of cannibalisation. As the market of a processor begins to mature, Intel launches a superior processor, and tries to make the market graduate to its new offering. This not only pre-empts imitators, but also keeps margins high for Intel. In fact, with its continual innovation and cannibalisation, Intel has been able to create an artificial monopoly for itself.

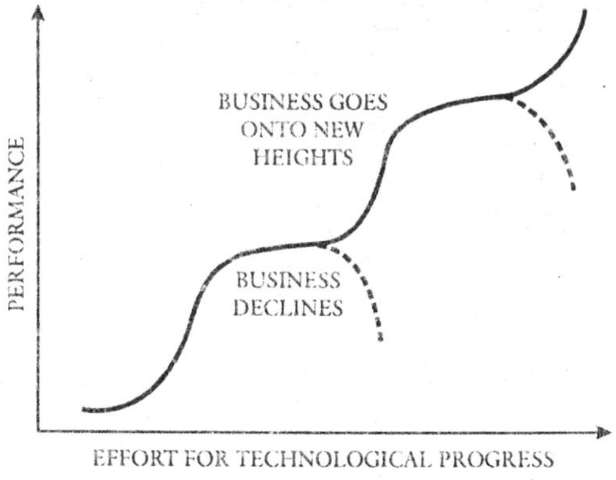

Fig. 6.5 : The Successive S-Curve

New Business Concept Generation and Gestation Process

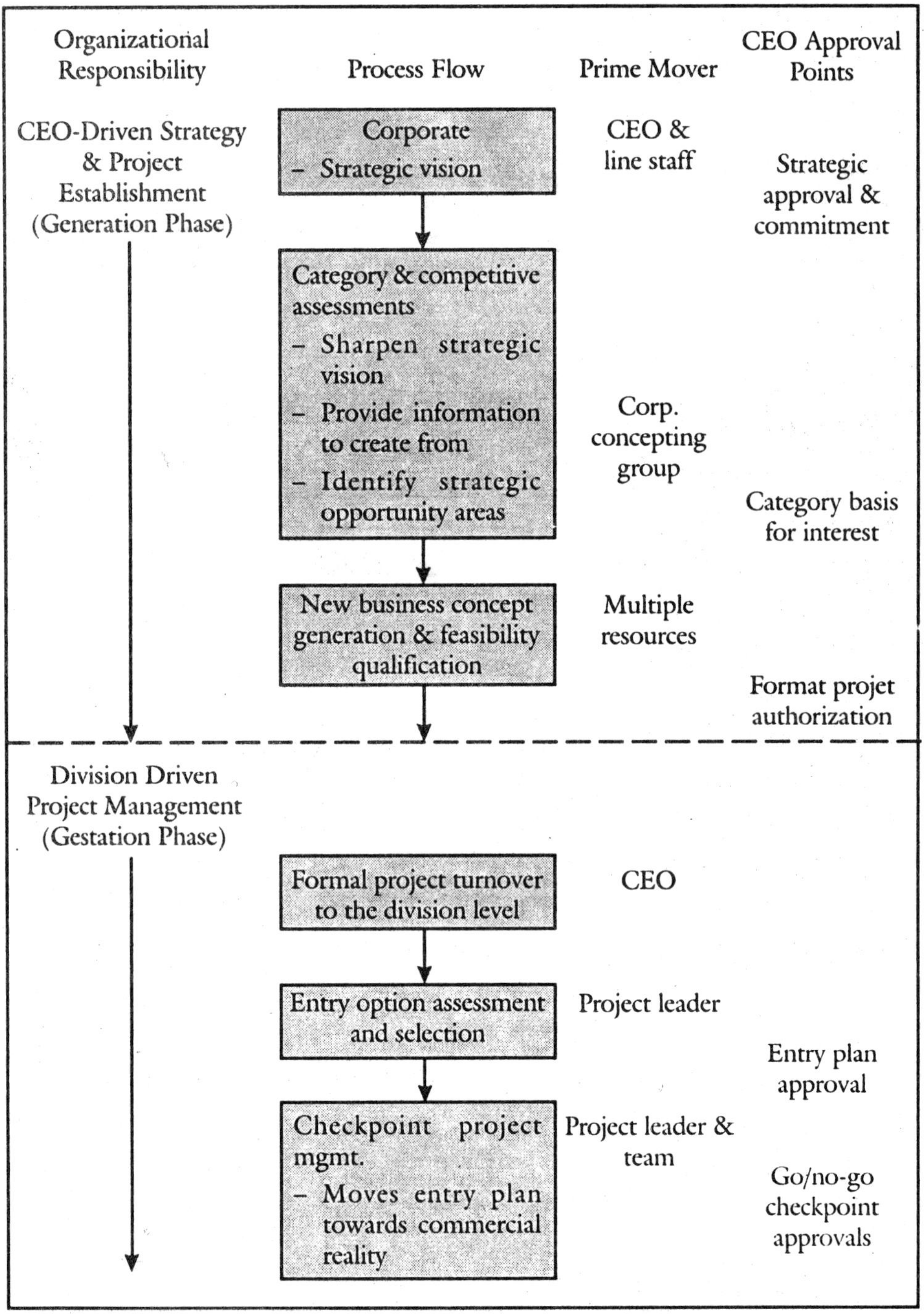

Though there are no set rules, Rosebeth Moss Kanter, a Professor at Harvard University has suggested six characteristics of innovation:

- Uncertain
- Knowledge intensive
- Controversial
- Crosses boundaries
- Changes work relationships and hierarchical arrangements
- Conditions for organisation and innovation are different from those of adoption and diffusion.

Thus, "if innovation is uncertain, fragile, political and imperialistic (reaching out to other territories)," she adds, "then it is most likely to flourish where conditions allow flexibility, feedback, quick action and intensive care, coalition formation, and connectedness." Here Kanter also hints at the organisational environment that surrounds the entire process.

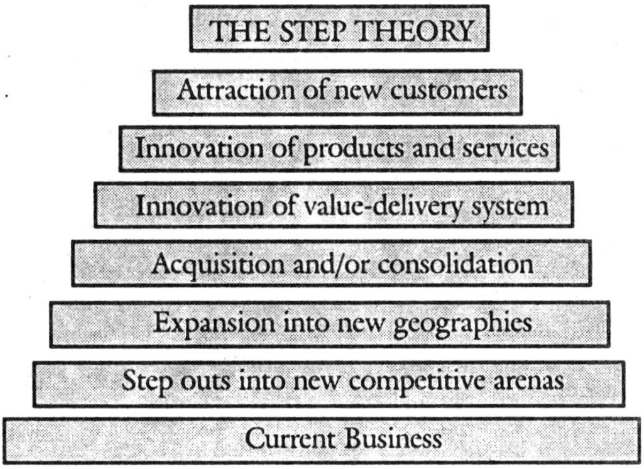

The innovation process involves at least five generic stages:

- Idea generation and concept definition
- Model development
- Limited/test production
- Full production and growth
- Diffusion and adoption

Innovation cannot be divorced from change. A technological innovation may bring a change in the materials, manufacturing process, stop-floor management, product packing and marketing strategies too. This change may be opposed by the people affected by it and this could initiate a debate or opposition which is seldom objective. Often restructuring in an organisation follows a major innovation or break through. It is important to ensure that a minor innovation that could possibly take place at such a time is not ignored.

Peaks of Success

Fuelling ambitions and dreams. Breathing life into promising business ventures. Charting the course of incisive business ideas. Providing foresight with a fine sense of direction. Helping insightful, imaginative business ideas glide smoothly over rough passages. Helping vision and enterprise sight the target and achieve it with pin-point accuracy. Complementing acumen and enterprise with a steady flow of resources. Partnering enterprises on the move, till they reach the Peaks of success.

SUCCESS FACTORS FOR TODAY

- Total quality in manufacture, design, & delivery
- Lean organisation
- Focus on core competence (market segments)
- Productivity (new product development)
- Global player
- Total customer satisfaction

SUCCESS FACTORS FOR TOMORROW

- More of all the above
- Risk management
- Survival skills
- New organisation
- Learning organisation
- Creativity

Steps of the Ladder

For starting an enterprise, an entrepreneur will have to climb the steps narrated on the next page, one by one; and for doing so, he would do well to give careful thought to the following considerations. This thought in advance may help him to avoid some mistakes. So many things must be considered that unless some kind of a check list is followed seriously, there is the danger of important matters being overlooked. And, once the entrepreneur has started the business, his getting busy with the urgency of the day-to-day details reduces the opportunity of thoughtful consideration to important questions.

Obviously, this list does not cover everything. It should be used as a starter. The list is designed with the object of focusing the entrepreneur's thought, on the different steps of the ladder he would have to climb. Carefully consider each one as it applies to your particular problem. Before deciding to ignore any question, completely satisfy yourself that it does not apply to your particular operation.

Although the ladder of success an entrepreneur has to climb in setting up an enterprise and run it consists of 34 steps, the ladder may undergo a change with the change in the environment and entrepreneurial climate. For an entrepreneur, work is worship. Leisure is a luxury. There is nothing like hard work. A 14 to 18 hour work is the norm. He should have a killer instinct to push ahead in the competitive environment.

Steps of the Ladder the Entrepreneur has to Climb :

It is a continuous process of industrialisation.

34. ANCILLARY DEVELOPMENT
33. GROW BIGGER
32. COMPETE WITH OTHERS
31. MODERNISATION
30. DIVERSIFIACATION
29. PLOUGH BACK PROFITS
28. KEEP UP-TO-DATE
27. SELL
26. PRODUCE
25. PLAN OUT RECORD-KEEPING
24. ORGANISE MARKETING
23. DECIDE ON PRICING POLICY
22. TRIAL RUN
21. RECRUIT PERSONNEL
20. PROCURE MATERIALS
19. INSTAL MACHINERY
18. PLAN BUYING
17. APPLY FOR MATERIALS (IF IMPORTED OR CONTROLLED)
16. PLACE ORDER FOR MACHINERY (PREFERABLY ON HIRE-PURCHASE)
15. PLAN SOURCES OF MACHINERY
14. PLAN FINANCE
13. OBTAIN CLEARANCE FROM CENTRAL, STATE & LOCAL AUTHORITIES AND SSI REGN. NO.
12. MAKE SURE WHAT LAWS WILL PARTICULARLY AFFECT YOU
11. ARRANGE THE WORKSHED WITH FACILITIES (PREFERABLY ON RENT)
10. DECIDE ON LOCATION AND SITE
9. OBTAIN THE PROJECT REPORT FROM SISI OR ELSEWHERE OR PREPARE IT YOURSELF
8. DECIDE WHETHER TO PURCHASE A GOING CONCERN OR TO START A NEW ONE
7. DECIDE ON FORM OF OWNERSHIP [SOLE-PROPRIETARY/ PARTNERSHIP/CO-OPERATIVE/COMPANY (PRIVATE/PUBLIC)]
6. CHOOSE A LINE
5. DATE WITH YOURSELF FOR A DECISION
4. DISCUSS WITH ALL AROUND YOU AND WITH SISI & D.I. OFFICE
3. CONSULT PUBLICATIONS AND AGENCIES
2. DATE WITH YOURSELF FOR NEWER IDEAS
1. ANALYSE YOURSELF AND YOUR OBJECTIVES

Conclusion

As an entrepreneur you have the pleasure of being in charge of your own business. And it is possible for you to exercise your individuality.

Employment generation, dispersal of industries in rural and semi-urban areas, utilisation of local resources and skills and development and widening of entrepreneurial base figure prominently in our plan priorities. Similarly, maximisation of exports has assumed added importance in the context of current balance of payments position. The prospects for export of non-traditional items such as readymade garments, leather and marine products, processed food, plastics and engineering goods etc. have improved.

As the main thrust of the new economic policy is to encourage competitiveness, characteristic of market-driven economy, small-scale units have to increasingly equip themselves to be on their own. Technology, together with quality promotion measures, holds the key to improved factor productivity and strengthening of competitiveness. An enlightened entrepreneurial class, fully conscious of the directions in which changes are taking place, can look forward with confidence to improve its market share, both within and in a global setting in recognition of the opportunities available for further growth.

But you may have to face some problems too. Raw materials may be scarce. Finding a market for your products may not always be easy. Procuring or executing really large orders may be virtually possible.

You would need assistance in such circumstances. And this can best come from oganisations that are specially geared to assist small-scale units.

Primarily, it is necessary to decide on what to manufacture, where and how. Then follows the process of establishing a small-scale industry. But, till the dream is realised, there are a number of hurdles, which could be crossed over, if one takes care. Herein, one's perseverance is at least. Let us start the hurdle race. No, before participation in this hurdle as well as marathon race, let us prepare ourselves or be fit for the race.

If you are a novice in the field, the first exercise you should concentrate on is what items you can market either on your own or through a reliable selling agency. Once a product is decided, you can then take up for examination their manufacture, marketing, viability and profitability in the small-scale sector. You are just a pin a small pin in the huge machine of industry. While exploring the market, please assess the element of competition. Please do not overlook competition to your products as well as the capacity of the competitors to outwit you by underselling. Bear always that the road is not smooth. Even the hurdles are of uneven nature, competition is taken for granted. Even the special institution will suggest to you to manufacture only such item which you can successfully market.

The age of continuous change has finally arrived. The choice is between two positions; either we can influence the same to the advantage of the firm, or end up as victims of the onslaught caused by the change. Accepting the status quo will directly lead to competitive decline. A better approach would be to shift the managerial and organisational mind-set to the new paradigm stated above and thereby increase the overall capabilities of the firm to take charge of its own destiny.

ANNEXURE 1

PROCESS OF SETTING UP A SMALL-SCALE INDUSTRY—GUIDELINES

1. *Selection of Industry*	
Small Industries Service Institutes	They guide entrepreneurs in the selection of industries, areas, suitable raw materials and machinery.
Indian Investment Centre, Parliament Street, New Delhi-1.	It advises on foreign capital participation and technical collaboration. Provides guidance to entrepreneurs regarding government policies, procedures, available incentives and facilities for investment, economic size of unit and magnitude of investments required demand forecast, availability of raw materials etc.
Ministry of Industrial Development and Company Affairs, New Delhi.	It approves the cases of foreign collaboration.
2. *District Industries Centres*	In each district, there would be one agency to deal with all requirements of small and village industries, which would be called the Districts Industries Centre. Under the single roof of the centre, all the services and support required by small and village entrepreneurs would be provided. The centre would have a separate wing for looking after the special needs of cottage and household industries, as distinct from the small industry. The Rural Industries Project and Rural Artisans programme would be merged with the programme of the District Industries Centre. Each DIC would have a General manager and seven managers of different disciplines for looking after planning and economic investigation, credit, marketing etc.
3. *Factory Accommodation*	
Directors of Industries	They provide built-up factory space in industrial estates or developed factory sites, power, water etc.(The building designs have to be approved by Municipalities or Corporations while power and water connections are sanctioned by State Governments/ undertakings.)

4. *Industrial Estates*	There are more than 600 industrial estates in India which provide constructed accommodation in developed areas. Main facilities include common facility service, workshops, allotment of sheds on hire purchase, confessional charges on water and power, exemption from octroi duty on building materials etc.
5. *Registration*	Although it is not mandatory, it is certainly helpful to obtain the SSI Registration Number from the Director of Industries.
6. *Machinery* Small Industries Service Institutes	They advise about the kind of machinery and equipment needed for the manufacture of different products.
National Small Industries Corporation,	It supplies indigenous as well as imported machinery on hire-purchase basis.
New Delhi State Small Industries Corporations	They provide indigenous machinery on deferred credit basis.
Chief Controller of imports and Exports, New Delhi	He issues import licences for machinery of foreign origin on the recommendation of the Directors of Industries.
Consultants	Install machinery as per the layout drawn by them.
7. *Raw Materials* Development Commissioner, Small-Scale Industries, New Delhi	He procures raw materials for the small industry and distributes them among state governments. He also arranges imports of raw materials through the Minerals and Metals Trading Corporation and the State Trading Corporation of India.
Directors of Industries	They allot quotas of scarce raw materials.
State Small Industries Corporations	They supply raw materials.
Chief Controller of Imports and Exports and his Port Offices	They issue licences for the import of raw materials.
8. *Finance* Small industries Development Bank of India, Lucknow, 1989	Small Industries Development Bank of India (SIDBI) has started operations through its 25 offices located in different states of the country. The SIDBI has been set up under an Act of Parliament as the principal financial institution for

	promotion, financing and development of industry in the tiny and the small-scale sector. The SIDBI is also expected to coordinate the functions of the institutions engaged in similar activities. The SIDBI is a wholly-owned subsidiary of the Industrial Development Bank of India (IDBI). It has taken over IDBI's financing activities relating to the small-scale sector.
State Financial Corporations	They provide long-term credit for the purchase of fixed assets.
State Directors of Industries	They provide loans under State Aid to Industries Act/Rules for block capital.
State Bank of India and its subsidiaries	They sanction medium-term and instalment credit loans for the purchase of machinery and the construction of factory buildings. They also provide working capital for the purchase of raw materials and meeting other day-to-day requirements.
Commercial Banks	They sanction loans for working capital needs.
Small Industrial Service Institutes	They furnish technical reports to Institutes, the State Bank of India on the applicant units.
9. *Technical know-how*	
Small Industries Service Institutes	They prepare improved designs and Institutes drawing for products. They assist in making tools, dies, jigs and fixtures. They help in the optimum utilisation of men, materials and machinery. They prepare management control charts for the maximisation of profits. They train managers and supervisors in industrial management. They train workers to upgrade their skills. They demonstrate modern technical processes.
National Small Industries Corporation, New Delhi	They give advanced training in their Prototype Production-cum-training Centres in the operation of modern machiners.
Council of Scientific and Industrial Research, New Delhi	It develops new technological processes and disseminates the same to the industry.
Productivity Councils	Train factory-owners to increase Productivity.

Small Industry Extension Training Institute, Hyderabad	It gives full-time and management training to managers/proprietors in the small industry sector.
Central institute of Tools Designs, Hyderabad	Specialises in provision of technical consultancy and tool facilities, training in design and manufacture of tools.
Institute for design of Electrical Measuring Instruments, Mumbai	Provides technical know-how and testing, calibration laboratory, workshop and training facilities to electrical measuring instrument manufacturers.
10. *Standardisation* Small Industries Service Institutes	They provide technical guidance in the production of goods according to prescribed standards.
Indian Standards Institution	It prescribes specifications for the products and issues ISI certification.
Directors of Industries	They prescribe standards and give 'Q' Mark to the small industry's products.
Quality Control	Those in charge provide technical guidance in maintaing the quality of products.
11. *Marketing* Small Industries Service Institutes	They conduct distribution and surveys for the benefit of small industrialists. They enlist the units for participation in the Central Government Stores/Purchase Programme. They issue competency certificates to the units receiving government orders. They promote ancillary relationships with large and medium-scale units in public and private sectors.
National Small Industries Corporation, New Delhi	It secures contracts from the Director General of Supplies and Disposals, Railways, and Defence Departments for supply of manufactured goods by small-scale units.
State Small Industries Corporations	They secure orders from the State Government and other semi-government organisations for the supply of stores.
12. *Export* Small Industries Service Institutes	They enlist small units for participation under the Export Aid to Small Industry Scheme of the State Trading Corporation of India. They render technical counselling services for a satisfactory execution of export orders.

	They disseminate information about the items having export markets.
	They maintain a close liaison with specialised agencies like the Export Promotion Councils to have up-to-date knowledge about the products having export markets.
Chief Controller of Imports and Exports, New Delhi	He issues licences for the export of products to foreign countries.
Directorate of Export Promotion, Udyog Bhavan, New Delhi	It collects and supplies information on foreign markets.
	It carries out market studies for particular products.
	It publishes Trade Directories, Brochures and Bulletins.
Export Promotion Councils	They organise exhibitions and show-rooms.
	They maintain a close liaison between Indian exporters and foreign buyers. They settle commercial disputes.
	They frame special export promotion schemes.
State Trading Corporation of India, New Delhi	It registers units for participation under Export Aid to Small Industry Scheme. It helps the small-scale units in the preparation of sales leaflets, price lists etc. It secures export orders for small industries.
Trade Fair Authority of India, New Delhi	Organises National Small Scale Industries Fairs.
	Conducts publicity work, projects image of the industry and assists in finding potential markets.
13. *Inventions*	
The Inventions Promotion Board, 39 Ring Road, Lajpat Nagar IV, New Delhi-110 014	It promotes workable inventions of practical utility through financial assistance and other incentives.
The Central Institute of Tools Design, Hyderabad	It produces tools, jigs, fixtures, dies and moulds.
	It trains practicing personnel in the design and manufacture of tools etc.
14. *Training*	
Small-Scale Industries Development Organisation	It trains practicing managers and technologists.
Small Industries Service Institutes	They conduct management courses for senior managerial personnel.

Extension Centres	They conduct regular and ad hoc training courses in various technological trades for skilled and semi-skilled workers.
Indian Investment Centre	Conducts regular entrepreneurial development programme courses. Assistance is given to the trainees in the identification of project reports. They are also helped in obtaining the necessary financial assistance from the financial institutions and guidance is also provided up to the stage of trial production.
Small Industry Extension Training Institute	Offers training in industrial management and other aspects of small industries development; undertakes feasibility and research studies and collects and disseminates technical information through its Documentation Centre.
	Under assistance to Young Engineers Program, training is provided through specified agencies and interest subsidy, i.e., difference between interest rate of 7% per annum and the normal rate charged by the financial institutions is provided subject to a maximum of Rs. 20,000 per annum for a period of five years in backward areas and three years in other areas.
National Institute for Entrepreneurship and Small Business Development	NIESBUD is an apex body established in 1983 for coordinating and overseeing the activities of various institutes/agencies engaged in entrepreneurship development in the small industry and small business.
15. *Problems*	
The Federation of Associations of Small Industries of India, Rohtak Road, New Delhi, Chambers of Commerce and Industry.	They represent the problems faced by the small industries to the Government. They discuss problems and represent them to the appropriate authorities
16. *Monitoring*	
The national Alliance of Young Entrepreneurs	It is a national level apex organisation of entrepreneurs. It assists promoting new enterprises through first-generation entrepreneurs. It also monitors the programmes of entrepreneurial development in India.
17. Other Voluntary Organisations	AWAKE, WIMA, SEWA, WASME, etc.

CASE STUDIES

A STUDY IN SUCCESS

Murudeshwar Ceramics Forays into New Areas

Inspiration and Early Beginning

Rama Nagappa Shetty would have been ploughing in his ancestral fields but for his father's inspiration. Today, he heads a multicrore empire, whose flagship company Murudeshwar Ceramics Ltd. is a study in success.

Shetty started off in the late fifties with some money loaned by his father. He ventured into construction and took up minor jobs like metalling and asphalting of roads. By 1961, he had become big enough to undertake construction of three major bridges on the Honnavar-Gerusoppa road in North Kanara district. In 1996, he moved his operating base to Hubli and switched over to irrigation power works. Since then, Shetty has not looked back.

He has, over the years, executed major irrigation works like the Malaprabha, Ghataprabha and Upper Krishna projects. He has even completed the prestigious Varahi hydel power project, the first underground power house in Karnataka. Currently, Shetty has his hand full. He is also involved in the upper Krishna canal work and the Gerusoppa dam for the Sharavathi project—both financed by the World Bank.

Diversification

A natural offshoot of all this construction activity was the Murudeshwar Tile Factory, set up at Murudeshwar in 1977. Explains Shetty, "In North Kanara, we get a lot of clay suitable for manufacturing Mangalore tiles." Now, this is the biggest Mangalore tile factory in North Kanara district. A decade late, Shetty set up Murudeshwar Ceramics Ltd., a joint-sector undertaking with the Karnataka State Industrial Investment & Development Corporation, for the manufacture of ceramic glazed tiles. "In 1985, the KSIIDC was looking for a partner for a ceramic tile venture and my father, who showed an interest, was awarded the project."

Ceramics

A Rs.13.45 crores project to manufacture 12,500 tonnes per annum of ceramic tiles, the MCL project was financed by an equity capital of Rs. 4.50 crores and loans of Rs. 8.80 crores. The plant was completed in a record 14 months times. MCL is one of the major industries to have come up in the backward North Karnataka region. He selected Hubli for MCL because of its proximity to raw material sources and to the major consuming centres like Mumbai, Bangalore, Pune and Goa.

Turnover

In the first year itself, for a 11-month period in 1988-89, MCL achieved a turnover of Rs. 9.64 crores and posted a net profit of Rs. 42 lakhs. In 1991-92, its sales moved to Rs. 29.66 crores, while the net profit reached Rs. 4.79 crores. The EPS also moved from Rs. 0.94 in 1988-89 to Rs. 9.53 in 1991-92.

Over the years, MCL ceramic tiles marketed under the brand name "Naveen" have been well accepted in the ceramic tile market in spite of the tough competition from established players like Johnson Tiles, Somany, Pilkington and Spartek. Compared to Spartek, MCL has an edge in quality. It also enjoys an advantage in price since it enjoys a tax holiday between 1990 and 1993. And in spite of a large number of entrants in the market, MCL has managed to survive because of its higher capacity utilisation and cost control measures. Today, "Naveen" ceramic tiles are available in over 40 colours and shades.

Capacity Utilisation

In 1990 MCL doubled its capacity to 25,000 tpa. By January 1993, this will go up to 40,000 tpa at a cost of Rs. 17 crores. This should help them reach a turnover of Rs. 37 crores in 1992-93. Since the domestic market was growing slowly, MCL decided to concentrate on exports as well. In 1991-92, MCL exported Rs. 45 lakh worth of ceramic tiles to the Middle East. This year, it has so far exported tiles worth Rs. 60 lakhs against a target of Rs. 1 crore.

Marketing

The domestic market has improved this year. And they are tapping the market aggressively with the help of 160 dealers most of whom sell only "Naveen" ceramic tiles. They have eight marketing offices and they will soon set up marketing offices in Pune, Vizag and Ahmedabad as well.

But it has not always been smooth sailing for MCL. The government has labelled ceramic tiles as a luxury item and clamped a 57.5 per cent excise duty on them. MCL's cost of production is less than mosaic tiles. But then they are bogged down with the excise duty.

In four years, MCL has notched up 9.3 per cent of the market share in ceramic tiles. It has recorded an impressive growth in the net sales (26.8 per cent), gross profit (31.3 per cent) and net profit (45 per cent). Its dividend went up, thanks to its excellent performance, from 16 per cent in 1990-91 to 20 per cent in 1991-92.

New Avenues

During 1971-72, Mr. R.N. Shetty promoted Seshank Sea Foods Ltd. at Bhatkal in North Karnataka for processing and export of sea foods. This year it hopes to achieve an export turnover of Rs. 25 crores. It exports to Japan (which is the major buyer), the US and France.

Mr. Shetty now plans to go in for aquaculture in a big way. For this purpose, he has already acquired 40 hectares of land near Kumta in North Karnataka and negotiations are on for another 60 hectares. This will be a Rs. 10 crore project.

TRANSFORMING DREAMS

Early Beginning

In 1966, a young electrical engineer, R.K. Parasuram, returned to his hometown Madras after working for General Electric Company, U.K., for 10 years. He dreamt of manufacturing world-class electrical transformers and selling them all over the world. Three decades later, his dream is coming true.

The Kappa group of companies (named after his wife Kamala Parasuram) — a bunchy of tiny private limited companies and proprietary firms with a turnover of Rs. 16 crores and an export turnover of Rs. 9 crores—manufacture almost the entire range of transformers. These are low-tech but essential items which require a lot of manual labour.

Having established his products successfully in the domestic market, Parasuram decided to go global. Exports in the early seventies really meant the rupee market. It was not easy to penetrate the European and American markets. So he looked towards South-East Asia which was a relatively easier hard-currency area.

No one had previously attempted to export products like transformers. Right from the outset, Parasuram's emphasis was on quality. The export products were produced to conform to the international standards prescribed by British Standards and International Electro-technical Commission. Due to the availability of cheap skilled labour, the cost of Kappa's transformers was very competitive.

First Order

In 1973, the company got its first export order from Dickson Primer, an engineering firm in Singapore, for 300 pieces of transformers worth Rs. 20,000. Singapore and Malaysia were the major markets then. By late 70s, Kappa decided to expand its activities to the Middle East. The focus was on Beirut. However, when the militarisation of Lebanon became complete in the early 80s exports to Beirut came to a grinding halt.

Parasuram was on the constant lookout of a big deal. Kappa's ability to produce transformers as custom-built original equipment fetched its first order from Siemens, Australia, in 1980. Siemens and Email-Westinghouse became their major buyers in Australia and New Zealand. A bulk of the company's international sales is to Asea Brown Boveri. Worth just Rs. 20,000 in the 80s, business with the Swedish-Swiss giant has now grown to Rs. 60 lakhs annually. Says Kamala, "With more and more enquiries from abroad, we opened an export office at Singapore in 1983."

In order to broad base exports, it was decided to trade in a wide range of current technology products not necessarily produced by the group. The relays produced by English Electric, semiconductor fuse and voltage transformer fuse links manufactured by S & S Power Switchgear Ltd. are some of the well-known products trade by Kappa Exports. Says T.V.G. Menon, general manager, relay division, English Electric, "We cannot export directly because of our agreement with our parent company. So we make our sales to Kappa who are doing a splendid job." Kappa has merged as the biggest exporter of electrical goods from South India. Today 60 per cent of Kappa's export turnover is from trading.

Kappa's exports reached Rs. 1 crore in 1987. Since then, the annual growth rate has been phenomenal, around 40 per cent now. The main reason for this, according to Kamala, was Kappa's strategic move to become a single-window export house for all electrical engineering equipment. Parasuram is convinced that constant upgradation of technology is the only way for survival. Five per cent of the total turnover is being spent on R & D and another five per cent on technological upgradation. According to Kamala, the neglected but important area in exports is packaging. Says she, "Our special packaging efforts to withstand the wear and tear of the transit costs an additional three per cent."

To ensure quality, Kappa has invested about Rs. 1 crore in various imported testing equipment and this has now proved to be a great advantage as the group is gearing to enter the European market in a big way. Says the founder's daughter Mira Parasuram, an electrical engineer, "We are working with the Indian Statistical Institute to get the ISO 9000 accreditation. Our production systems already seem to conform to international standards. We have to only effect changes in areas like inventory, billing and accounting. We will get our accredition in the middle of 1993." Kappa wants to reach an export figure of Rs. 100 crores by the turn of the century and hence it is seriously studying the Middle East and African markets.

Chapter - 7

FINANCING OF NEW VENTURES

Introduction

During the pre-independence period, financial constraints had hampered the rapid development of industries in the country. After independence, the Government built up a network of specialised financial institutions with a fairly big capital base to provide financial assistance to all types to industries, including small-scale industries.

A growing economy needs the support of a financial structure which is responsive to the needs of development. In India, in the process of financial deepening, commercial banks had to shoulder special responsibilities to meet the financial needs of diverse sectors of the economy, at various stages of development. In the process, they have evolved various modes and instruments of financing, fashioned various organisational innovations, moved away from traditional commercial banking and evolved into development banks, responsive to socio-economic needs.

Finance is now made available to entrepreneurs on a totality basis by commercial banks, except in cases where the State Financial Corporations and other similar financing agencies step in to meet their medium-term requirements. An appropriate type of credit is granted for the construction of the factory building, the purchase of plant, machinery and equipment, and for working capital requirements. In deserving cases, loans are advanced for the expansion, renovation and modernisation of plant and machinery. Banks and financial institutions provide the export finance needed by small industries for letters of credit, issuance of guarantees and extension of pre-shipment on a slab basis, with a favourable bias towards the smaller loans. Institutional support and economic factors are stimulating entrepreneurial activity and thus generating more robust economic development.

Types of Industrial Finance

Depending upon the nature of the activity, entrepreneurs require three types of finances, viz., *short-term, medium-term* and *long-term* finances. The distinctive features of these are emulated below :

Short-term Finance

Short-term finance usually refers to funds required for a period of less than one year. These funds usually required to meet variable, seasonal or temporary working capital requirements.

Borrowing from banks is a very important source of short-term finance. Other important sources of short-term finance are trade credit, instalment credit and customer advances.

Medium-term Finance

The period of one year to five years may be regarded as medium-term. Medium-term finance is usually required for permanent working capital, small expansions, replacements, modifications, etc.

Medium-term finance may be raised by (i) issue of shares; issue of debentures; borrowing from banks and other financial institutions; and ploughing back of profits (by existing concerns).

Long-term Finance

The period exceeding 5 years is regarded as long-term. Long-term finance is required for procuring fixed assets, for the establishment of a new business, for substantial expansion of existing business, modernisation etc.

The important sources of long-term finance are similar to the medium-term finance to industry.

Types of Finance

Short-Term	*Medium-Term*	*Long-Term*
(i) Bank credit	(i) Issue of shares	(i) Issue of shares
(ii) Trade credit	(ii) Issue of debentures	(ii) Issue of debentures
(iii) Instalment credit	(iii) Loans from banks and other financial institutions	(iii) Loans from financial institutions
(iv) Customer	(iv) Public deposits (for existing concerns)	(iv) Ploughing back of profits (for existing concerns)
	(v) Ploughing back of profits (for existing concerns)	

Sources of Finance

A characteristic feature of small-scale units is that the personal funds of entrepreneurs form a substantial proportion of the total assets. Most of the units are not corporate entities. The owners of small units, therefore, run a considerably higher risk than those of corporate units. The sources that usually provide the working capital requirements are commercial banks, special agencies like SIICOM, GIIC, and co-operative banks. Indigenous bankers, and moneylenders also advance loans for working capital needs. The fixed capital needs are usually met by State Governments (under the State Aid to Industries Acts/Rules), SFCs, NSI finance which finance machinery on hire-purchase basis, Corporations (SSICs), (SIDCs), the State Bank of India and subsidiaries, and other commercial banks.

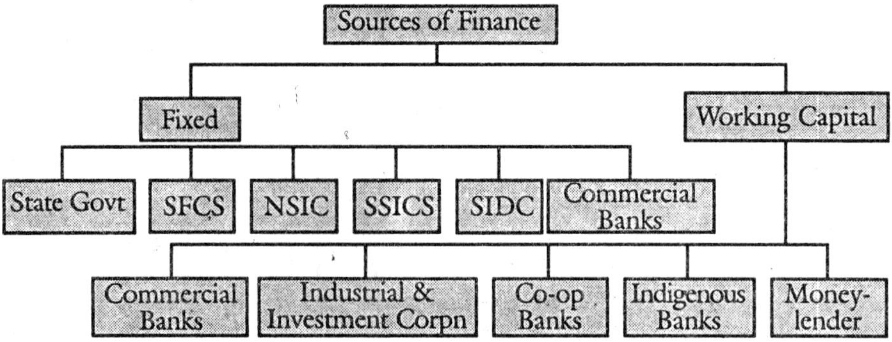

Fig. 7.1 : Sources of Finance for Small-Scale Sector

Broadly speaking, the various sources from which an entrepreneur can raise funds are enumerated in its balance sheet. These sources may generally be grouped under the following heads:

I. Internal

A. Paid-up Capital

(i) Ordinary shares

(ii) Preference shares

(iii) Deferred shares

(iv) Forfeited shares

B. Reserve Surplus

(i) Capital reserve

(ii) Development rebate reserves

(iii) Others

C. Provisions

(i) Taxation (net on advance of income-tax)

(ii) Depreciation

II. External

D. Borrowings

(i) From banks

(ii) From term-lending institutions like IDBI, IFCI, ICICI, Industrial Development Corporations, etc.

(iii) From government and semi-government agencies

(iv) Others

E. Trade Dues and Other Current Liabilities

(i) Sundry creditors

(ii) Others

The share distribution of source and of all companies and profit-making companies is as follows :

Table 7.1

Sources of Finance

Sources	*All Companies (505) %*	*Profit-making Companies (450 %)*
A. ***Internal Sources***	34.2	35.5
1. Paid-up capital	0.5	0.5
2. Reserves and surplus	17.2	18.9
3. Depreciation	16.5	16.1
B. ***External***	65.8	64.5
4. Paid-up capital	2.1	1.8
5. Long-term Borrowings	31.0	31.1
(a) Debentures	9.6	9.8
(b) From Financial	14.8	14.6
(c) Banks	–	–
(d) Others	6.6	6.7
6. Bank borrowings for working capital	7.7	7.3
7. Trade dues and other current liabilities	21.3	20.4
8. Non-current liabilities	3.7	3.9
Total A & B	100.0	100.0

Table 7.1 indicates that the companies' dependence on financial institutions and banks is to the extent of 40 per cent of its total funds for development. Even to some extent companies depend heavily on banks to recover their trade dues for development. Thus, financial institutions' involvement is nearly 60 per cent as far as finance alone is concerned. This apart, their promotional consultancy and other related services go a long way towards the process of economic development. It is true that industrial development or even the entire process of economic development, is dependent on the financial institutions and their innovative assistance on an ongoing basis.

The funds which an industry can raise depend on its productive activity and the uses to which these funds are put:

(i) *Gross Fixed Assets :* Land, building, plant and machinery — these are, by and large, met out of market borrowings or term loans from financial institutions, including banks.

(ii) *Working Capital* : This includes inventories — raw materials, components, finished goods, work in progress and operating expenses — wages, salaries, lighting and other running expenses. All these expenses are met out of commercial bank loans in the form by hypothecation credit or pledge loans.

(iii) Funds are also required for (a) making loans and advances in the course of day-to-day purchase-and-sale operations; (b) sundry debtors — that is, for sale on credit basis; (c) investments; and (d) building up other assets.

F. Miscellaneous

All these sources of finance are not available to all the small units. Much would depend on the status, character and period of time the units have been in operation. For example, a new small unit has no reserves to provide for depreciation. These are built up in gradual stages out of the funds set apart in the course of current operations.

Moreover, the funds a small-scale industry can raise depend upon the character of the company, its productive activity and the substantial uses to which these funds are put — irrespective of it being a private limited or a proprietary concern.

Analysis of Financial Ratios

The financial data of small units are usually worked out in terms of some of the important conventional ratios. Most of the ratios, however, do not indicate any definite relationship with credit facilities. A detailed discussion of this aspect has been undertaken in the technical volume. It will be sufficient to mention here that comparatively high inventory-to-sales ratios were recorded by units which received institutional credit facilities. The average net working capital needs of small units, which are also given, show that the units which received credit facilities need a comparatively high average working capital. A major proportion of the net working capital, however, was accounted for by inventories. The figures in the statement do not, by themselves, point to any firm conclusions regarding the place of inventories among the factors to be taken into account by banks while examining the credit proposals of small-scale units.

Balance Sheet of Institutional and Non-Institutional Borrowings

The survey also gives information on the balance sheet of both institutional and non-institutional borrowings of small units. It shows that institutional borrowings per unit varied from one unit to another, and were the highest in the case of the following categories of units :

(i) Units whose assets exceeded Rs. 10 lakhs;

(ii) Units which manufactured electronic and electrical goods;

(iii) Units of 6 to 10 years standing;

(iv) Units which employed 101 and more persons;

(v) Public limited companies;

(vi) Units which were registered; and

(vii) Units located in industrial estates.

It may be pointed out here that those units which had high savings per unit institutional borrowings recorded high inventory ratios. The average non-institutional borrowings per unit in respect of respective classifications were the highest in the case of units which —

(a) Borrowed from banks/co-operatives;

(b) Whose assets were above Rs. 10 lakh and which employed 101 or more persons;

(c) Were private limited companies, registered units and located in industrial estates; and

(d) Belonged to the manufacturing group, including chemicals, dyes, etc.

It is also known that both large and small units borrow from institutional and non-institutional sources. However, the extent of reliance on non-institutional sources was lower in the case of large units than in that of small units. At the same time, even the smaller units obtained a major portion of their credit needs from institutional lenders. Further, the average non-institutional borrowings formed a major proportion of average borrowings (institutional and non-institutional) on the part of units which did not approach any commercial bank/co-operative for credit or which did not get any institutional credit even though they asked for it. It has been mentioned above. Clearly, the reliance on institutional sources was relatively high on the part of modern younger and larger small-scale industrial units.

Table 7.2

Sources and Uses of Funds of

1,125 Selected Small Private Limited Companies

	(Rs. Crores)	*% share in the total*
(1)	*(2)*	*(3)*
Sources of Funds		
Internal Sources	468	22.52
A. 1. *Paid-up capital*	9	0.43
B. Reserves and surplus	13	0.58
2. Capital reserve	5	
3. Development rebate reserve	16.	
4. Others	2	
C. Provisions	446	21.46
5. Depreciation	408	19.63
6. Taxation (net of advance of income-tax)	17	0.82
7. Other current	10	0.48
8. Non-current	11	0.53
External Sources	1,610	77.48
D. Paid-up capital	100	4.81
9. Net issues	100	4.81
10. Premium on shares	–	–
E. Borrowings	898	43.21
11. From banks	543	26.13

12. From Industrial Finance Corporation and State Financial Corporations	–	–
13. From other institutional agencies	27	1.30
14. From Government and semi-Government agencies	5	0.24
15. From others	323	15.54
F. Trade dues and other current liabilities	611	29.40
16. Sundry creditors	575	27.67
17. Others	36	1.73
G. 18. *Miscellaneous non-current liabilities*	–	–
19. Total	2.078	100.00
Uses of Funds		
H. Gross fixed assets	710	34.17
20. Land	31	1.49
21. Buildings	140	6.74
22. Plant and machinery	420	20.21
23. Capital works in progress	2	0.10
24. Others	116	5.58
I. Inventories	514	24.73
25. Raw materials, components, etc.	290	13.96
26. Finished goods	193	9.29
27. Works in progress	27	1.30
28. Others	59	2.84
J. Loans and other advances and other debtor balances	744	35.80
29. Sundry debtors	598	28.77
30. Others	146	7.02
K. 31. *Investments*	37	1.78
L. 32. *Other assets*	7	0.34
M. 33. *Cash and bank Balances*	80	3.85
34. Total	2,078	100.00

According to a study of small private limited companies, conducted by the Reserve Bank of India some time back, these companies relied on external sources for financing assets. Of the total resources of Rs. 2,078 crores, external sources contributed as much as Rs. 1,610 crore (77.5 per cent) to asset formation. Of this amount, borrowings constituted more than 55.8 per cent, while trade dues and other current liabilities contributed about 38.0 per cent. Bank borrowings, in particular, accounted for more than one-third of the total external resources. Among the internal resources, depreciation provision amounting to Rs. 408 crore constituted the main source. It represented 87.18% of total internal resources.

While assessing the resources of a concern, we have to bear in mind whether it is a new concern or a long-established concern; whether it is a private company or a proprietary concern; the nature of activity—whether manufacturing or trading; whether the purpose of raising resources is modernisation and expansion of business, or the establishment of a new concern, or increase in turnover.

The expansion or diversification of business involving an addition to plant and machinery should be met out of owned funds—that is, out of depreciation and provisions– or out of increase in capital, out of term loans. The ability of a concern to raise resources from all or some of these sources depends upon its strength, character and standing in the market. If the purpose is a mere increase in the turnover of the business which involves a larger inventory and increased operating expenses, the additional funds should be raised by way of bank loans.

From a banker's point of view, there are well-established guidelines for assessing the credit requirements of a concern. A banker analyses the balance sheet and evaluates the turnover of funds, sales and other operating results in assessing the viability of a unit.

There are certain established ratios. For example:

(a) The debt equity ratio;

(b) Turnover to net worth;

(c) Return on capital employed;

(d) Net profit as a percentage of net worth;

(e) Dividend paid to shareholders;

(f) Ratio of current assets to current liabilities.

A banker has to look behind these figures and assess the technical and managerial competence of a management, and the integrity of the men running a concern, in order to decide whether credit should or should not be advanced.

Credit is a very important element in the process of economic development. It stimulates economic activity, particularly in countries which are short of capital and entrepreneurial talent. Because of the dearth of these two basic elements in the process of development, bankers who create credit have been assigned a vital role in stimulating the process of development.

Norms for Inventory and Receivables

For an efficient management of assets, the Tandon Committee suggested norms for raw materials, stack-in-process, finished goods and receivables. These norms represent the maximum levels of holding inventory and receivables in each industry.

Coverage : These norms are made applicable to all industrial borrowers, including small-scale industries, with aggregate limits from the banking system in excess of Rs. 10 lakhs and extended progressively to small borrowers.

Objective : The norms for the four kinds of current assets are related to consumption/cost of production/cost of sales/sales, respectively. If the carryover of any one kind of asset is higher than the relative norm level, the surplus is treated as "excess" carryover to be shed off, failing which an amount equivalent to the value thereof would be treated as excess borrowing. Again, such excess holding cannot be set off against any shortfall in the holding of other assets, for the norms represent the maximum permissible levels of holding; and they are not entitlements. Lending banks are expected to scrutinise the periodic stock and receive statements to determine whether the borrowers comply with the aforesaid stipulation.

Experience shows that while norms are reckoned in sanctioning credit limits, these are not uniformly complied with subsequently, through the medium of monthly stock statements. Although both Tandon Committee and the RBI had hoped, while introducing the report, that excess current asset holdings would be adjusted in two months, this has not happened. In fact, RBI itself has had to adopt a flexible approach by permitting, *inter se*, adjustments of norm levels of different assets, raising norm levels, etc.

Given the manufacturing cycle of a borrower, starting with raw materials to stocks-in-process, and further to finished goods, it is only logical to think of a combined norm for all the three items in relation to the value of output. A lending bank ought to scrutinise the levels of each kind of current assets in the ordinary course of its vigil on the borrower's operations; but to treat any of them as excess holding, even as the overall level is considered reasonable and consistent with production, is to make things unnecessarily complicated; and this serves no worthwhile purpose. It is said that combined norms may be developed for different industries from the RBI studies on company finances. These may be revised, from time to time, to meet the objectives of national economic policies and/or bring them in tune with the policy by individual industry groupings. Thus, the suggested modification of laying down a combined norm for inventories in relation to the value of output, and receivables to sales as at present, would make things pragmatic, without jeopardising the interests of the lending bank and without hurting any macro economic objectives.

The suggested norms are as follows:

Table 7.3

Suggested Norms for Inventory and Receivables

Indu-stry	*Raw materials (including stores and other items used in the pro-cess of manu-facture)*	*Stocks-in-process*	*Finished goods*	*Receiv-ables* and bills purchased and discounted*
(1)	*(2)*	*(3)*	*(4)*	*(5)*
(i) Cotton and Synthetic Textiles	Cotton 2 (Bombay and Ahmedabad areas) 2 Eastern areas (Bihar, Orissa, West Bengal and Assam) 2½ (Other than the above areas) 2 Other raw materials	¾ (Composite textile mills) ½ (Other mills)	- 2¼-	

Table 7.3 (Contd.)

(1)	(2)	(3)	(4)	(5)
(ii) Man made Fibre	½	½	-1¾-	
(iii) Jute Texbiles	2½	¼	1 (For domestic sales) and 1½ (For exports)	1½
(iv) Rubber Products	2	¼		-1¾-
(v) Fertilisers (a) For nitrogenous plants	¾ (Units near refinery) ½ (Units away from refinery)	Negligible	1(where stocks are in plant site) ½ (Where stocks are also in upcountry centres)	1¼
(b) For phosphatic plants	2 (Units in port areas) 3 (Units away from port areas)	Negligible	1 (Where stocks are in plant site) 1½ (Where stocks are also in upcountry centres)	1¼
(vi) Phamaceuticals	2¾	½	2	1¼
(vii) Dyes and Dystuffs	2¼	1	¾	2¼
(viii) Basic Industrial Chemicals	2¾	¼	1	1¾
(ix) Vegetable and Hydrogenated Oil	1	Negligible	¾	
(x) Paper	2-6 Bamboo and Wood (to be built up in stages from November to May and thereafter to be brought down 2¼ Chemicals		1 (For controlled sales) and 3/4 (for free sales)	¾
(xi) Cement	2¼ Gypsum ¼ Limestone ¾ Coal ½ packing material	½	-1-	
(xii) Engineering Automobiles & ancillaries	2¼	¾	-2½-	

Table 7.3 (Contd.)

(1)	*(2)*	*(3)*	*(4)*	*(5)*
(xiii) Engineering Consumer Durables	2	¾	-2½-	
(xiv) Engineering Ancillaries (other than Automobile ancillaries) and Component Suppliers	2	¼	-2½-	
(xv) Engineering machinery manufactures Capital Equipment Suppliers (Other than Heavy Engineering)**	2¾	1¼	-3½-	

Notes :

(i) Raw materials are used in so many months.

(ii) (a) Stock-in process expressed as to many months' cost of production.

(b) In individual cases, the bank may deviate from the norm for Stock-in-process if it is satisfied that the actual process time involved in any particular unit, say, in view of the nature of production, past experience and technology employed, is more than the suggested norm.

(iii) (a) Finished goods and receivables are expressed as so many months' cost of sales and sales respectively. These figures represent only the average levels. Individual items of finished goods and receivables may be for different periods, which may exceed the indicated norms so long as the overall average level of finished goods and receivables does not exceed the amounts as determined in terms of the norm.

*(b) The norm prescribed for receivables relates only to inland sales on short-term basis (i.e., excluding receivables arising out of deferred payment sales and exports.)

(iv) Stocks of spares are not included for norms, since in financial terms they are not significant in many industries. Banks will ascertain the requirements of spares for individual units. They should, however, keep an eye open to ensure that spares do not exceed 5% of the total inventories.

(v) Heavy Engineering will include the supply of whole or substantial plants involving a long manufacturing period, i.e., sugar, cement, steel and textile plants.

Source : Report of the Study Group, RBI, 1975, pp. 20 & 21.

Illustration

ABC Industry

Estd. 1969	
Manufacturer of automobile spare parts & nuts & bolts	
Investment in Plant & Machinery	Rs. 15 lakhs
Bankers	Bank of Bombay
Capital	Rs. 5 lakhs
Reserves	Rs. 3 lakhs
Net Worth	Rs. 8 lakhs

(Rs. in lakhs)

Current Liabilities		*Current Assets*	
Creditors for Purchase	55	Raw Materials	120
Other Current Liabilities	25	Stock-in-progress	20
		Receivables	30
	80	Finished goods	40
		Other current assets	10
Borrowings	120		
(i) Long-term	50		
(ii) Short-term	70		
	200		220

1st Method		*2nd Method*		*3rd Method*	
Total Current assets	220	Total Current assets	220	Total Current assets	220
Less: Current Liabilities other than bank borrowing	80	25% from long-term sources	55	Less: Core current assets	55
Working capital gap	140		165		165
25% of above form long-term sources	35	*Less:* current liabilities other than bank	80	25% of above from long-term sources	41
Maximum bank borrowing permissible	105	Working capital gap	85	*Less:* current liabilities	80
			140	Other than bank borrowing	44
		Maximum bank borrowing permissible	85	Working capital gap	140
				Maximum bank borrowing permissible	44
Excess Borrowings	15	Excess Borrowings	35	Excess Borrowings	96
Current ratio 1.19:1		Current ratio 1.33:1		Current ratio 2.12:1	

Scientific Approach to Working Capital

A scientific approach to working capital involves a study of the factors which affect the need for working capital — the terms offered by suppliers, the terms offered to customers, the average period of lead time for various inventory items, the seasonal fluctuations in sales, the production cycle, the level of stock and other influential factors. These factors may be used to relate balance sheet items to sales volumes. The relationships yield measures which may serve, among other things, as tools for the prediction of future working capital needs.

For scientific study of the working capital problem, a mathematical model may be developed to state the important quantitative relationships among different variables. In order to construct such a model, it is necessary to make an objective study of the situation. In the case of working capital, the relevant factors which should be studied are the relationship that exist between the amounts of the current assets and current liabilities, and the volume of sales.

In developing the model, the first step is to analyse the relevant factors of a company's situation. This involves an examination of the records, a study of actual procedures and a consultation with company officials.

The suggested method of forecasting working capital needs is an improvement on the methods which are currently employed by companies. The use of the model would result in a more accurate forecast, allow for improvement through observation and experience, and act as a useful tool for the assessment of the size of the working capital.

The use of the working capital model is appropriate for many types of businesses. In companies which manufacture different types of products involving varied materials or processes, separate sub-models may be constructed, and these may be combined in the final analysis. Where conditions are changing rapidly, the effects of the changes can be estimated objectively.

As long as the general pattern of the production and financial process does not change substantially, the model will hold good. When any change occurs, fresh study of the pertinent items would be sufficient.

In most cases, this type of working capital model can be developed easily. It would enable managers to forecast the level for each working capital item and ensure that the necessary resources are available. In addition, the model could establish working capital standards. A comparison of the actual with the standards would provide a measure of the efficiency of financial management.

Management

Effective financial management is based on three factors: analysis of past performance; planning for future activities; and control of current activity. Control is achieved by implementing decisions in accordance with agreed plans. Accordingly, financial planning is of crucial importance in a small unit.

Effective working capital management calls for an understanding of cash requirements at varying stages of design, development, production and marketing. The overall efficiency of the working capital is judged by the annual result it produces.

Working capital management is an integral part of the overall management of small-scale industries. Here is need for greater co-ordination between small-scale industries and financial institutions. Towards this direction, the Small Industries Development Bank of India (SIDBI) has been set up to provide strong support to small-scale industries.

It is essential that financial institutions should safeguard their interests with adequate security. At the same time, small industrial concerns should not, as far as possible, be denied the assistance they deserve or need. Lack of finance is often not the cause, but the result, of difficulties in other areas. In such cases, what is needed are measures to set right those factors which would render financial assistance, good returns. It is common knowledge that the small-scale sector needs non-financial assistance — marketing assistance, technical guidance and training in management, etc. It has also arranged training programmes for small entrepreneurs; but the scope of operation of these needs to be expanded. Above all, there is need for greater co-ordination at all levels between the financial and non-financial institutions and agencies engaged in the promotion of small-scale industries.

In the present Indian context, the socio-economic obligations of a banker include identification of project ideas, project formulation, managerial talent and provision of technical and managerial guidance to new ventures, with a view to broad-basing entrepreneurial talent and assisting in the creation of more employment opportunities in the country. The banker who controls credit is a "supply leader", as opposed to his erstwhile role of a "demand follower." He is no longer a "wholesale" banker sitting in an ivory tower. His new role as an agent of economic development is to assist in the development and growth of economic activities.

Planning and control of working capital centres round sound cash planning which includes setting of cash policies and procedures and the control over cash and credit. Cash is of course a very sensitive component of working capital. The working capital has, therefore, to be managed properly, especially by the SSIs, because over or under circulation may create volatile problems.

Financing of Industrial Estates

Financial institutions have commenced extending estimated direct assistance for financing of industrial estates. Such ventures estimated at Rs. 300 lakhs are covered under the IDBI's re-finance scheme where primary lending is effected through the SFCs, SIDCs and commercial banks. Industrial estates costing beyond Rs. 300 lakhs are extended direct financial assistance by the all-India financial institutions.

The main aspects considered in proposals for setting up of industrial estates are the suitability of the location, availability of power, water, raw materials, skilled and unskilled labour, transport and communication facilities, market for the products of industries to be set up in the estate and the potential for overall economic growth. Significant emphasis initially is, therefore laid on physical survey of the site and its proper designing.

Size of Industrial Estate

The size of the estate should preferably be not less than 15 acres of land where the cost is up to Rs. 300 lakhs and not less than 25 acres of land where the cost is more than Rs. 300 lakhs. This size results in individual units driving the advantage of some economy in overhead expenses and sharing of some common facilities. However, it may not always be practical to insist on the minimum size of land and the financial institutions may, under such circumstances, relax the minimum area where the estate is in urban areas or if the estate is proposed in a multi-storeyed building.

The institutions also desire that the project acquires adequate reserve land at the beginning itself as the cost of acquiring adjacent land at a later date might become prohibitive. Twice the estimated initial capacity for sheds booked/expected to be booked is considered a fair reserve area over the present requirements. This is not, however, taken as an inflexible norm and for large estates, particularly in urban and semi-urban areas, the reserve may be less, say equal to the area initially required.

Capital Needs

A business enterprise requires capital or finance for the following purposes :

1. Fixed Capital : It is long-term or permanent finance. It is required to acquire or create fixed assets such as land, buildings, construction of plant or factory, installation of machinery, procuring tools and accessories, purchase of furniture and fixtures, and any other fixed property or durable asset. Fixed capital is permanently sunk in business. It represents permanent investment. Initial fixed capital is usually raised through equity capital and for specialised financial institutions in the form of long-term loans.

2. Working Capital : It is short-term finance. It is required for financing day-to-day manufacturing and marketing operations. It represents current finance or financing current assets. A business must have necessary cash flow to meet day-to-day expenses and current liabilities. It assures the liquidity and solvency of a business. The minimum or regular working capital is also raised through equity capital or ownership resources. However, additional and seasonal needs of current finance are always met by short-term borrowing in the form of bank credit and trade credit. Fund-flow or cash-flow statements indicate the needs of current finance and a business must maintain adequate cash resources to meet current liabilities.

3. Capital for Growth, Modernisation, Mergers, Amalgamation, etc. : Every business enterprise has two main objectives, viz., survival and growth. Growth may take place through expansion, diversification, mergers, amalgamation, etc. We need additional fixed as well as working capital to finance our plans of growth. It is raised partly through internal sources of finance, such as depreciation and retained profits and partly through share capital or debenture capital. Long-term loans from capital market institutions can also be raised for financing expansion. Many companies have financed growth through self-financing or retained profits.

Types of Capital

Capital is classified into four categories :

- Equity Shares
- Preference Shares
- Debenture Shares
- Reserves (retained profit as a source of internal finance to expand both fixed capital as well as working capital)
- Creditorship securities which consist of debentures and bonds are credit instruments which are widely used to raise funds by companies. Capital raised through creditorship securities is known as borrowed capital or debt capital.

Equity Financing

Equity share capital is the backbone of any company's financial structure. The word 'equity' means ownership interest or the interest of shareholders as measured by capital

Chart
Capital Structure

Ownership Securities (Share Capital)

Equity Shares

Features:

1. Risk Capital
2. Fluctuating Dividend
3. Changing market price (Par or paid-up Value fixed)
4. Growth prosepct, i.e., capital appreciation in future
5. Protection against inflation, i.e., rising price level
6. Normal voting rights

Features of Deferred Shares:

(a) Last claim in profit-sharing
(b) Last claim in return of capital
(c) Widely changing dividends
(d) Extraordinary voting rights
(e) Only for private companies

Preference Shares

1. Cumulative/non-cumulative
2. Redeemable/non-redeemable
3. Participating/non-participating
4. Convertible/non-convertible

Features:

(a) Fixed return of income, i.e., Dividend
(b) First preference in profit-sharing
(c) First preference in repayment of capital
(d) No chance to share the fruits of prosperity
(e) No normal voting rights

Creditorship Securities (Debenture Capital)

(A) On the basis of Redemption
  1. Redeemable
  2. Perpetual

(B) On the basis of Security
  1. Secured or Mortgage
  2. Simple or Naked

(C) On the basis of Transferability
  1. Registered
  2. Bearer

(D) On the bais of Convertibility
  1. convertible/non-convertible

Features:

(a) Loan of Borrowed capital
(b) Fixed income or fixed interest
(c) Right of priority in return of capital
(d) No voting rights
(e) May involve mortgage of Co.'s property
(f) Usually redeemable after certain period

and reserves. The term is also used to refer to the unlimited interest of ordinary shareholders. Hence, ordinary shares are often called 'equities.' Business enterprises, large, medium, small, must have capital to start operations and to continue in business.

Function of Equity

In most enterprises, the primary function of equity capital is to finance the purchase of buildings, machinery and equipment. Its secondary function is to protect long and short-term creditors, who make funds available to the business. Its third function is to serve as a cushion to absorb losses that may occur.

Debentures

A debenture is defined as "as a document under the company's seal which provides for the payment of a principal sum and interest thereon at regular intervals which is usually secured by a fixed or floating charge on the company's property or undertaking which acknowledges a loan to the company."

COMPARATIVE STUDY : PREFERENCE VS. EQUITY SHARES

	Points of Difference	*Preference Shares*	*Equity Shares*
1.	Right of receiving Dividend	They enjoy first preference to get dividend.	Second claim to receive dividends, if there is balance or surplus profit.
2.	Right of receiving back their capital	They enjoy first right of priority even in this respect.	They rank next to preference share in the return of capital.
3.	Rate and Magnitude of dividend	Dividend fixed by Articles, e.g., 8 per cent per annum. It is usually subject to income tax. No rise in the dividend when the company is prosperous, except when shares are participating preference shares. Unpaid dividends can accumulate if they are cumulative preference shares.	Dividend fluctuating according to asset value, earning power and stability of the company. Rising dividends when the company is prosperous. Equity Shares have no sub-divisions. They are always non-cumulative.
4.	Voting Rights	They are entitled to enjoy voting rights only under exceptional circumstances, e.g., dividends unpaid for 2 years or resolution affecting their rights is to be passed.	They enjoy normal voting rights. They are the real risk bearers. Voting rights shall be in proportion to the paid up amount in shares.

5.	Face Value	Relatively higher. Usually Rs. 100.	Neither too high nor too low. Usually Rs. 50.
6.	Redeemability during lifetime of the company.	They can be redeemable at the end of a certain period (e.g., 10 years). They are very useful for raising temporary additional finance for further expansion.	Equity shares are always irredeemable and they constitute a permanent share capital of the company, not subject to redemption during the lifetime of the company.
7.	Appeal to Investors	They involve a small risk. Their rights are secured and stable. The cumulative type has practically no risk. Hence, they appeal to cautious investors, who prefer stable and regular dividend.	The equity share capital, in the absence of deferred shares, is called the risk capital of the company. They have to bear the risk of loss in the expectation of higher and rising dividends. Hence, they appeal to ordinary investors, who prefer rising though unstable income.
8.	Capital	No capital appreciation as no chance to share in Co.'s prosperity.	Capital appreciation possible due to prospects of rising dividends.

COMPARATIVE STUDY : SHAREHOLDERS VS. DEBENTUREHOLDERS

	Points of Difference	*Shareholder*	*Debentureholder*
1.	Nature of Capital	Share capital is the owned capital, an external source of getting capital, generally non-repayable during the lifetime of the company. It is a permanent capital.	Debenture capital is loan capital, an external source for raising capital, usually repayable during the lifetime of the company, having a fixed period of maturity say, 20 or 30 years.
2.	Status	A shareholder is the proprietor or owner of the company—a registered member.	Debentureholder is the creditor of the company either secured or unsecured.
3.	Income	A shareholder may get a dividend fixed or variable depending on the distributable annual net profits. Dividends shall be payable only out of annual or undistributed profits.	Income on the debenture is a fixed rate of interest lower than the normal rate of dividend. Interest must be paid irrespective of annual profit, even out of capital when the company makes no profits.

4.	Repayment	No repayment possible except (1) under winding up, (2) when reduction of capital is approved by special resolution and confirmed by Court when shares are redeemable preference shares.	Can be paid-off as per agreement or at the option of the company. They can become payable automatically at the time of winding up or when the company makes a default.
5.	Position at winding up	They stand last as claimants for the return of capital. All creditors must be satisfied first and if there is a surplus or residue, it may be shared by them as per Article.	Debentureholders have a prior claim to the return of capital. If they are secured creditors, they can realise their security and prove for the balance at the time of company's liquidation.
6.	Rights and Privileges	They are governed by the Articles of Association Members are entitled to receive notices, annual accounts and report, attend general meetings, exercise their right of vote. In case of partly-paid shares, they are able to pay calls.	Debentureholders have no such rights and privileges enjoyed by shareholders. As per trust deed they may be entitled to get copies of annual accounts and appoint one or two directors as their representatives on the Board.
7.	Taxation	Dividend not deducted from profits for taxation on Co. income.	Interest deducted from profits of the Co. to arrive at the taxation base.
8.	Issues	Shares cannot be issued at a discount without fulfilling certain legal conditions.	Debentures can be issued at a premium or even at a discount without any legal restrictions.

Assistance in the form of *suppliers' line of credit* is provided to manufacturers for promoting sale of industrial equipment on deferred payment terms. This credit facility can be availed of by actual users for balancing equipment, replacement, or modernisation purposes only. Under this scheme, a non-revolving line of credit is extended to a seller to be utilised within a stipulated period. This facility is very much similar to the Bills Rediscounting Scheme, except that in this case, the payment is directly received by the supplier from the financial institution, as compared to an intermediary commercial bank in the earlier case.

Seed Capital Assistance is provided to encourage a new class of entrepreneurs so as to bring about wider dispersal of ownership and control of industrial undertakings. This special scheme has been introduced for the purposes of supplementing the resources of the entrepreneur. Assistance is provided in the form of interest-free loans to the extent of the deficit in the required promoters' contribution. Such assistance ranges from Rs. 15 lakhs to Rs. 40 lakhs per project, depending on the number of applicant promoters.

Equity and Preference Capital funds can be procured from the following sources :

- Promoter's quota :

  Inter-corporate investments.

  Promoters, directors, friends and relatives (including non-resident Indians)

  Foreign collaborators.

  Oil exporting developing countries.

  State Industrial Development Corporations.

  Shareholders of promoter companies.

  Internal accruals.

  Rights issue to existing shareholders.

- Non-promoter's quota :

  Public issue to Indian residents.

  Public issue to non-residents of Indian origin on a repatriable and non-repatriable basis.

Debenture Capital funds in the form of secured convertible or non-convertible debentures can be raised by listed public companies and public sector corporations with the objective of financing any expansion or diversification project or to augment the long-term resources of the company for working capital requirements.

The issue of debentures for financing working capital requirements cannot exceed 20 per cent of the gross current assets, loans and advances. The issue of debentures for project financing is considered on the basis of the approval of the scheme of finance by the financial institutions and the MRTP Commission (where applicable).

The debt-equity ratio after including the proposed debenture issue should not generally exceed 2:1. This norm is relaxed for capital-intensive projects.

The shares of the company proposing the issue of debentures must, however, have been listed in one or more stock exchanges and the market quotation of its equity shares must have been above par for at least six months prior to the date of application to the Controller of Capital Issues for permission to issue debentures.

Government Subsidies are extended by the Central and State Governments to projects being established in industrially backward areas.

For purposes of capital subsidy from Central Government, backward areas have been divided into three categories by the Ministry of Industries. Category 'A' comprising of 134 no-industry districts and special regions is eligible for subsidy at the rate of 25 per cent of the investment subject to a maximum of Rs. 25 lakhs. Category 'B' comprising of 54 districts is eligible for subsidy at the rate of 15 per cent of the investment subject to a maximum of Rs. 15 lakhs. Category 'C' comprising of 113 districts eligible for subsidy at the rate of 10 per cent of the investment subject to a maximum of Rs. 10 lakhs. Subsidy under Category 'C' is, however, not granted to MRTP/FERA companies.

In additional to the subsidy by the Central Government, State Governments operate the State Subsidy Scheme in order to achieve a wide dispersal of industrialisation within the state. The rate and amount of subsidy varies from state to state, with the upper ceiling generally remaining within a maximum of Rs. 25 lakhs.

The State Governments also operate the Sales Tax exemption and the Sales Tax Deferment Schemes. Under these schemes, industries being located in industrially backward areas get exemption/deferment of sales tax on purchases and sales for a period ranging between five to seven years. The quantum of benefit under these schemes is, however, restricted to a percentage of the fixed capital investment, subject to a maximum upper limit. These funds can be well used for augmenting margin money requirements for working capital or for phased capital expenditure.

Programme for the Advancement of Commercial Technology (PACT) is the outcome of an agreement between the Governments of India and U.S.A. signed in August 1985 under which the United States Agency for International Development is providing funds for promotion and financing of Indo-US joint ventures in research and development. The Industrial Credit and Investment Corporation of India Limited is managing and administering the entire operations of PACT.

PACT will support selected Indo-US joint ventures in research and development by offering need-based promotional assistance and conditional grants towards meeting part of the research cost which in turn, will provide an in-built protection against risks associated with market-oriented research and development. The assistance from PACT will normally be limited upto US $ 500,000 or 50 per cent of the total estimated cost, whichever is lower.

Public Subscription to Capital

Equity capital, after deducting the amount to be statutorily subscribed by the promoters, may be offered to the public for subscription in cash. The public may represent resident Indians or non-resident Indians or a combination of both, depending on the quantum and percentage of equity funds to be raised.

Assuming a representative project having a debt-equity ratio of 2:1, with promoters' contribution of 20 per cent, the promoters would be required to subscribe to 60 per cent of the equity capital and the balance of 40 per cent would be issued to the public for subscription. Generally, to become eligible for listing on a recognised stock exchange, companies are required to issue 60 per cent of their capital to the public for subscription through a prospectus. The public issue may, however, be reduced to a minimum of 20 per cent of the capital in certain cases, depending on the specific scheme of finance and its approval by the Government of India.

Deferred Payment Guarantee assistance is provided in rupee and foreign currencies. Guarantee is issued on behalf of the purchaser in favour of machinery suppliers offering the facility of deferred credits. A nominal guarantee commission fee is levied by the financial institution on the assisted concern. In case of default in payment of deferred instalments, the financial institution makes the payment to the machinery supplier and later recovers the amount from the assisted concern.

Guarantee Assistance is provided for foreign currency loans raised by industrial concerns from institutions and banks abroad. A nominal guarantee fee is levied on the assisted concern for the foreign currency loan guaranteed.

Underwriting Assistance for issue of shares and debentures is provided as a part of the overall financial package by the participating financial institutions. In respect of non-convertible debentures, the underwriting assistance is restricted to 50 per cent of the issue in respect of MRTP companies and 60 per cent of the issue in respect of non-MRTP companies.

Assistance by way of *direct subscription to shares* is extended to small issues which are not feasible for issue to the general public through prospectus. In respect of joint sector companies, capital is subscribed by the state level financial institutions as a part of the promoter's contribution.

Soft Loan Assistance is a special scheme operated through the Industrial Development Bank of India, the Industrial Fiance Corporation of India and the Industrial Credit and Investment Corporation of India Ltd., for modernisation and rehabilitation of industrial undertakings. The loans are extended on concessional terms in regard to the rate of interest, promoter's contribution, debt-equity ratio, initial moratorium and the repayment period. In pursuance of the decision taken by the Government of India, loans under this scheme have been exempted from convertibility stipulations.

Assistance through the Technical *Development Fund* was introduced in March 1976 for important of small value balancing equipment, technical know-how, foreign consultancy services and drawings and designs by industrial units to enable them to achieve fuller capacity utilisation, technological upgradation and higher exports. The limit for total imports under the scheme is restricted to the equivalent of Rs. 100 lakhs per undertaking per year. The Industrial Development Bank of India provides rupee loans upto a maximum of Rs. 125 lakhs at interest of 12.5 per cent per annum to enable the utilisation of import licences issued under the TDF scheme. The scheme covers all industries and permits import of any inputs needed for improving export capabilities.

Speed Capital Assistance

With a view to assisting entrepreneurs who have skills but lack finance to put in the requisite promoters' contribution, the IDBI has been operating two Seed Capital Schemes, viz.:

(i) SFCs' special share capital scheme under which the SFCs provide seed capital assistance to projects in the small scale sector from their special class of share capital contributed by the concerned State Government and the IDBI in agreed proportion; and

(ii) The IDBI's own scheme for such assistance to be operated mainly through the SIDCs/SIICs for medium-sized projects costing upto Rs. 1 crore.

The IDBI has been operating a special scheme of concessional assistance to small scale industrial units under the Credit Guarantee Scheme of the Government of India. The units located in specified backward areas are eligible for additional concessional facilities. As it will not be possible for the IDBI to reach a large number of small industrial units scattered all over the country, the flow of its assistance to this sector has necessarily to be direct in the form of refinancing of loans granted by banks and State Financial Corporations (SFCs). A small amount of assistance also flows through the rediscounting of the bills arising out of the sale of indigenous machinery on deferred credit basis. The main features of these schemes are given in the following paragraphs.

SFCs/Small SIDCs raise a special class of share capital contributed by the concerned State Government and IDBI with the object of proving equity type assistance on soft terms to small scale entrepreneurs who lack adequate financial resources to set up projects in the small scale and tiny sectors. The special capital assistance takes the form of subscription to share capital (equity or redeemable cumulative preference shares) or soft loans, or both, in the case of proprietary/partnership concerns or co-operative societies. Assistance is extended to bridge the gap between the minimum promoters' contribution and the amount actually brought in. The amount of assistance is limited to 20% of the project cost, subject to a maximum amount of Rs. 4 lakhs per project. Relaxation of the debt-equity norm of 2:1 will be considered in the case of units seeking special capital assistance.

Liberalisation of Seed Capital Scheme

Following a review of the operations of the Seed Capital Scheme, the IDBI introduced certain liberalisations/modifications therein, aimed at promoting new entrepreneurs and dispersing entrepreneurship. The liberalisation/modifications cover, *inter alia* :

(a) Broadening of the definition of the term "new entrepreneurs" to include entrepreneurs technically qualified or otherwise, who possess, acquire or secure technical know-how, who have a worthwhile project technically feasible and economically viable, and who possess the ability to set-up and run the enterprise, but who lack adequate resources to bring the required promoter's contribution;

(b) Extension of the scheme to successful entrepreneurs in the small sector who propose graduating to the medium-scale sector, whether by setting up a new enterprise or by undertaking expansion/diversification schemes;

(c) Extension of the scheme to all projects which are eligible for financial assistance from the IDBI, either directly or through refinance; and

(d) Reckoning for the contribution mobilised by the promoter from his relatives, associates and friends for the purpose of his matching contribution, to determine the quantum of eligible (seed capital) assistance.

The purpose of effecting these changes in the scheme is to make it more accessible to deserving promoters having the necessary entrepreneurial potential.

Venture capital is a new financial service, the emergence of which went towards developing strategies to help a new class of new entrepreneurs to translate their business ideas into reality. As the name suggests, it implies capital provided to start a new venture. The capital provided to start a venture is known as venture capital. In particular, for a small entrepreneur with zeal and dynamism but inadequate or lack of finance, venture capital or seed capital is boon making it a launching pad for financial growth.

Identifying Sources of Seed and Start-up Capital

In this era of change, the entrepreneur with a bright idea could get short-changed. Venture capital will no longer be about seed financing—a small amount of capital extended to an inventor to prove a concept-or start-up financing—funds given for product development and marketing provided the company has been in business for a short while. Instead, it will be about extending finance to firms that have already managed to reach a certain level of operations. Until the project breaks even a continuous stream of funds is required for working capital and expansion expenses.

Venture capital is invested usually in companies with very little trace-record. As a result, investment has to be based on insufficient past data. The investment is in new, small companies and the investor-investee relationship is more intimate than in the case of pure equity financing.

Over the years, venture capital has given birth to what are today mega corporations. Venture capital in most cases came in at the idea stage. Examples are many — Tandem Computers (non-stop computers), Genentech (bio-medical products), Apple Computers, Qume Corporation (computer printers).

The Paradigm Shift Venture Capital

	The Old	*The New*
See And Start-Up Capital	• Conditional Loans • Equity Support From Financial Institutions • Social Development Funds • Informal Sources	• Conditional Loans • Equity Support From Financial Institutions • Social Development Funds • Infomal Sources • Venture Leasing
Expansion	• Term Loans	• Equity Support From Financial Institutions • Private Equity • Convertible Debentures • Cumulative Preference Shares
Bridge Financing		• Bank Loans • Special Purpose Vehicles

Vision of Venture Capital

The vision of venture capital is focussed on new projects, seed capital, technology and innovation.

Venture Capital Aims to :

- Fuel ambitions and dreams
- Breathe life into promising business ventures
- Chart the course of incisive business ideas
- Provide foresight with a free sense of direction
- Help in building enterprise vision
- Smoothly glide over rough passages
- Partner enterprises on to script thrilling success
- Complement acumen and enterprise with a steady flow of resources
- Inspire enterprises to script thrilling success
- Plot finance on a firm life-cycle curve.

The Venture Capital Guide

	IDBI	TDICI	RCTC	SBI Caps	Grindlays	Canfina
Size of funds (Rs. crore)	NA	(a) Rs. 20 (b) Rs. 100	NA	NA	12	NA
Assistance per project (Rs. crore)	Rs. 2.50	Rs. 2	Needbase depending on merits of each case	upto	–	–
Nature of assistance	Conditional loan/Equity	Contitional loan/Equity	Loan/Equity	Equity	Equity	Equity/ Conditional loan
Promoter's contribution		(i) 10% of project cost if it is <50 (ii) 15% cost if it is < 50 lakhs	To be decided on likely risk, technology & resource capability	–	–	NA
Terms of assistance	(a) Initially @6% during development period and there after 17% pa. Royalty on sales in some cases (b) Equity subscription in exceptional cases	(a) If equity subscribed when disinvestment made, option given to promoters to buy back at negotiated price (b) No int; only a change on commercial implementation of the project	Initiallay @ 6% pa during development period and on commercialisation @ 14% Royalty in some cases. Repayment within 10/12 years. In case of equity participation buy back facility	Disinvestment after commercialisation of the project		
NA	NA					
No. of projects assisted	41	46	168 (Dec. 1988)	21	16	2
Amount sanctioned (Rs. crore)	31.44	23.17	2	10	9.6	0.34
Key industries		Medical applied research, polio vaccines, electronic equipment for defence applications, auto components, chemicals	Foodfeed tech, chemicals tech, chemicals and application software, biotech, diagnostics & vaccines, drug and plasma	Watches, seamless metal, ceramics, cement	MEG, colour picture tubes, drydock	NA

Note : Credit Capital Venture Fund, the other private sector fund, is not operational yet.

Salient Features of Venture Capital

(a) It is a high risk venture. The success rate in developed economies like USA is around 60% whereas in a developing country like ours, the success rate is expected to be around 20% - 30%.

(b) It finances high-tech projects.

(c) The gestation period is long. The benefit or profit from the venture capital investment will start accruing only after an average period of 4 to 5 years.

(d) The venture capitalist also makes available to the assisted units managerial and marketing assistance.

(e) When the assisted company has reached a certain stage of profitability, the venture capitalist sells his shares in the stock market at a hefty premium. He thus makes good profit as well as gets his locked up funds released for redeployment in some other ventures.

(f) It makes provision for conditional loans, which unlike the conventional loans, don't carry interest charge. Instead, it carries a royalty linked to sales generated by the company after commercialization. The rate of royalty is fixed depending on the profitability of the business and the fund's requirement of a reasonable return.

(g) The conditional loan is essentially a quasi-equity instrument which does not place a servicing burden on the company in the initial periods and seeks a return commensurate with the success of the ventures.

(h) It is a long-term investment and the returns are in the forms of capital gains.

(i) It is an active form of investment with a higher degree of involvement in the management of a venture.

Forms of Venture Capital

Based on the four stages of development of a business, venture capital financing may be classified as seed finance, start-up finance, beginner's finance and establishment finance. During the first stage of starting a business, i.e., at the formulation of an idea stage, the risk associated is very high. Here an idea needs to be translated into a business proposition. So the finance required at this stage is the seed finance from the venture capital fund. The second stage being the implementation phase, start-up finance from venture capital is required for the purpose of implementing the appropriate production processes. In the third stage, commercial production is to be started and beginners finance is required to develop the marketing and other infrastructures. In the fourth and the last stage, when the business is fully established, it requires finance for its growth and expansion so as to reap the economies of scale. Here establishment finance is sought from the venture capital fund. The degree of risk associated with a business gradually diminishes in every subsequent state of business development. Comprehensive venture capital financing may take all of the above forms.

Venture Capital : Stages of Financing

Seed Money Stage: Small amount of financing needed to prove a concept or develop a product. Marketing is not included in this stage

Start Up: Financing for a firm. That started up in the past one year. Funds are likely to pay for marketing and product development

First-Round Financing Additional Money to begin sales and manufacturing after a firm has spent its start-up capital

Second-Round Financing: Funds earmarked for working capital for a firm that is selling its product, but is still losing money

Third-Round Financing: Funds Financing for a firm that is breaking even and is contemplating an expansion project

Fourth-Round Financing : Money provided for firms that are likely to go public soon. Also known as bridge financing

Functions of Venture Capital

Venture capital plays a crucial role in fostering industrial development by exploring vast and untapped potentialities. The key functions of venture capital are :

(i) Venture capital provides finance as well as skills to new enterprises and new ventures of existing ones based on high technology innovations. It provides seed capital funds to finance innovations even in the pre-start stage. In the development stage that follows, the conceptual stage venture capitalist develops a business plan (in partnership with the entrepreneur) which will detail the market opportunity, the product, the development and financial needs. In this crucial stage, the venture capitalist has to assess the intrinsic merits of the technological innovation, ensure that the innovation is directed at a clearly defined market opportunity and satisfy himself that the management team at the helm of affairs is competent enough to achieve the targets of the business plan. Therefore, venture capitalist helps the firm to move to the exploitation stage, i.e., launching of the innovation. While launching the innovation the venture capitalist will seek to establish a time frame for achieving the pre-determined development marketing, sales and profit targets. In each investment, as the venture capitalist assumes absolute risk, his role is not restricted to that of a mere supplier of funds but that of an active partner with total investment in the assisted project. Thus, the venture capitalist is expected to perform not only the role of a financier but also skilled and multi-faceted intermediary supplying a broad spectrum of specialist services — technical, commercial, managerial, financial and entrepreneurial.

(ii) The venture capitalist fills the gap in the owner's funds in relation to the quantum of equity required to support the successful launching of a new business or the optimum scale of operations of an existing business. It acts as a trigger in launching new business and as a catalyst in stimulating existing firms to achieve optimum performance.

(iii) The venture capitalist's duty extends even as far as to see that the firm has proper and adequate commercial banking and receivable financing.

(iv) The venture capitalist assists the entrepreneurs in locating, interviewing and employing outstanding corporate achievers to professionalise the firm.

Venture capital assistance provided by the financial institution is in the form of project loans, equity, conditional loans (Quasi-equity), comprehensive techno-managerial support and guidance service including technology information.

The essential objective of venture capital is to achieve high returns on its investment. This makes 'cashing out' (i.e., withdrawing from the investments) imperative, unless further extraordinary returns are expected.

The role of the venture capital need not be restricted to manufacturing industries. Some of the ventures funded in the UK by venture capital funds included sale of antique remodelled jewelry, publishing of specialist books, the baby and health care market, retirement homes, distribution of indoor plants and plant arrangements to the major retail shops, and even small houses. In India, venture capital activity would play a catalytic role in encouraging the entrepreneurial process in the industrial scene. In encouraging a new class of promoters, viz., investors, innovators, professional executives and technocrats, it would lead to greater dispersion of economic power.

How do Venture Capital Funds Invest?

Typically VCFs enter a company at a very early stage (see graph). Angel investors are the highest risk takers as they enter the company at the concept or seed stage. The VCFs enter at the early growth stage, when the company management has identified the business prototype and customer base. The VCFs thus lead the company through its expansion, helping with back-end systems, sales and market share growth.

When considering an investment, venture capitalists carefully screen the technical and business merits of the proposed company. Given the nature of risks associated with the funding at such an early stage, most VCFs lay a lot of importance on the management quality. "A VCF manager does not take more than five minutes to decide if the management quality is not okay", explains an industry expert. The two key points that a VCF manager sees are whether the entrepreneur has a vision and whether the management team is cohesive. Here he looks out for various questions like:

- How do the entrepreneurs work together?
- How compatible is the VCF with the team?
- How do complete is the management expertise in the area of business? This means does the team have members with expertise in various aspects of business?
- How is the chemistry between the various members of team?

They also check on the softer issues like temperament of team members, past records and overall management competence. Thus, behind the financial and business analysis of the proposed business plan, it is these soft issues which finally lead to the VC funding a company.

Venture Capital Funds

The guidelines on 'venture capital' issued by the Reserve Bank of India towards the end of 1988, were a recognition of their role in Indian conditions. As the situation stood at the end of 1989, venture capital funds still had a long way to go. The Technology Development and Investment Corporation of India, a subsidiary of ICICI, Technology Development Fund set up by Industrial Development Bank of India (IDBI), the Equity

Development Scheme set up by SBI Capital Markets Limited and Canfina, which have been joined by India Investment Fund, promoted by Grindlays Bank, are some of the venture capital institutions set up in India. The Credit Capital Venture Fund is the first private sector venture capital company to go public. More companies are expected to enter the field soon, with the International Finance Corporation, Washington, and the World Bank both planning venture capital joint ventures in India. These ventures have been successful to a large extent.

Working of Venture Capital

A promoter comes forward with a new but as yet untried product or process. He needs a financial backer to help him to set up his plans or buy out a part or the whole of an existing enterprise. He may not be able to go to the regular banks or conventional financial institutions for one of the two reasons: the product may be untried and there may be teething problem to overcome in its design and marketing. Alternatively, their promoter may have no previous track record as an investor. In such cases, the financier (a venture capitalist) may come forward and lend him the money on the understanding that, if the enterprise proves successful, it will 'go public', i.e., it will make an initial public offer (IPO) of its share. The more successful the venture has been, the higher will be the profit made by both the promoter and financier through sale of shares.

The Difference Between Seed Capital and Venture Capital

Seed capital schemes, as these are understood in India are not the same as venture capital. The primary purpose of the former is to help the technocrat-entrepreneurs setting up manufacturing activities to meet the promoter's contributions and thus takes the form of 'gap-filling', whereas in the case of venture capital, the primary return sought by the venture capitalist is the eventual capital gain by investing in companies having attractive growth and earning potential, rather than a steady interest or dividend yield.

The Difference Between Venture Capital and Term Financing

The difference between venture capital and term financing lies in the preferred investment instrument, in the type of collateral accepted and in the magnitude of the risk involved. In the case of venture capital, the collateral often takes the form of intangible assets such as research results, innovative marketing ideas or managerial and technical skills. The cash flows of venture capital client generally start with a long period of negative results.

Schemes in Operation

It is intended that venture capital assistance should go mainly to schemes with the following objectives :

(a) To encourage indigenous technology and its commercial application.

(b) To adopt and modify the applications of imported technology in such a manner that it will be appropriate to the Indian environment.

The assistance is generally being provided for the purpose of—

(i) Setting up of pilot projects.

(ii) For technological innovations and modernisation.

(iii) For developing appropriate technology.

(iv) For meeting the cost of marking surveys and market promotion programmes. Of course, venture capital excludes financing of enterprises engaged in trading, brooking, investment or financial services, agencies or liaison work.

Venture capital in India is available mainly in three forms, equity, conditional loans and income notes. The income note is a novel way of financing, made by venture capital in India. It is a hybrid security, combining the features of conventional and conditional loans, where the entrepreneur has to pay the interest as well as the royalty. Some private sector venture capital companies have started region specific and industry specific venture funds. For example, Credit Capital Venture Fund (CCVF) of the Credit Capital group has started a region specific fund known as South Asian Regional Apex (SARA) fund to be invested in 10 specified states of the country. Similarly, it has also started an industry specific fund, such as Information Technology Fund and the Auto Ancillary Fund, its modus operandi being to focus on financing promising ventures in these industries. A novel security like 'participating debenture' has been introduced by the Twentieth Century Finance Corporation.

Advantages of Venture Capital

Venture capital has made significant contributions to technological innovations and promotion of entrepreneurship. Many of the path breaking technologies world over in the field of bio-technology, microelectronics, computers (e.g., Apple, Micro, Lotus, Intel Microsoft, etc.) have emerged from small businesses set up by people with ideas (but no financial resources) and supported by venture capital. Essentially, venture capital is:

1. *Economy oriented*
   (a) Helps in the industrialization of the country.
   (b) Helps in the technological development of the country.
   (c) Generates employment.
   (d) Helps in developing entrepreneurial skills.
2. *Investor oriented*
   (a) The benefit to the investors is that they are invited to invest only after the company starts earning profits, so the risk is less and the healthy growth of capital market is entrusted :
   (b) Profit to Venture Capital Companies/Venture Capital Funds.
3. *Entrepreneur oriented*
   (a) Helps small and medium first generation entrepreneurs to translate their ideas into reality.
   (b) Promotes and fosters entrepreneurship in the country.

VENTURE LEASING

A leasing arrangement in which the lessor provides both the asset and the equity capital to the lessee is venture leasing

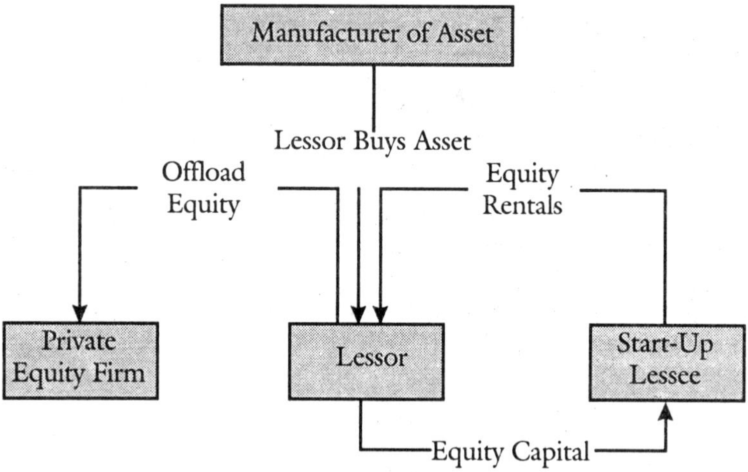

Fig. 7.2 : Venture Leasing

Advantages

- Minimises initial investments by start-ups
- Rentals can be tailored to the cash-flow profile
- Equity participation can lower lease rental
- Asset risk transferred to lessor

Disadvantages

- May be difficult to off-load equity stake
- Depreciation tax-shield transferred to the lessor
- High agency costs to prevent misuse of asset
- Lower debt capacity for lessee

India has all the main ingredients for venture capital business, viz., large investible funds with the public, a sound technological base, a large number of risk-takers, professional managers, entrepreneurs and scientists and a growing capital market. If the concept of venture capital is successfully implanted, it will not only provide the stimulus for an industrial leap but also pave the way for the private sector sharing the responsibility of industrial finance with the public sector. And, to that extent, there is a gradual loosening of the government's budgetary support for the *private sector's development through concessional long term credit from the public sector.* It will also bring a new deal for the fast growing numbers of technocrats, managers, and professionals in our country with an instinct for entrepreneurial risk taking. Thus, venture capital promotes entrepreneurships, accelerates the process of industrialisation, promotes new products and services and generates employment opportunities for skilled as well as unskilled workers. The economy receives a new boost.

Venture capital refers to financing of opportunities based on technological innovations in contrast to the conventional security used lending. No doubt, it is a late entrant in the field of industrial financing in India and is in its infancy. But it still has tremendous potential for growth. Its growth will provide a stimulus to the development of indigenous technology and a new generation of entrepreneurs in the country. Rapid industrialisation and the promotion of entrepreneurship will boost and consolidate the deepening of venture capital services.

Debt Financing

Factoring is a debt-collection service where the factor — usually a financial institution — buys out a client's (supplier's) book debts (accounts receivables). At present, only a part of the receivables are financed by banks and other financial institutions through bill discounting. Full service factoring also involves the factor taking over the administration of client's sales ledger, chasing debtors and evaluating credit risks.

Factoring is a financial service designed to help firms in better management of their receivables. Called a para-banking practice, it is widely used in the developed world. It has taken a root in India only recently. The Reserve Bank of India set up a study group to suggest a format for promotion of factoring services. Some guidelines have been announced.

In old-line factoring or full-factoring, the factor

(a) runs the sales ledger for clients,

(b) takes the responsibility for debt collection,

(c) provides cover against debt default, and

(d) makes available funds against debts assigned to it.

A factoring service is a continuing arrangement under which a financing institution takes on the credit and collection responsibilities of its client, purchases and recovers his trade dues. A factor smoothens the payment and mechanism for supplies. It involves an outright sale of the receivables of a firm to a financial institution, called the *factor*, specialising in management of trade credit. The factor collects the accounts on the due dates, makes payments to the firm and assumes the risks associated with the collection of accounts. The fee charged is usually a percentage of the value of the receivables factored.

Factoring basically means purchase of book-debts of clients. If working capital funds could be recycled with greater velocity through better management of credit extended to buyers and collection of their dues, industrial units could improve their profitability considerably. It is this factor which can help factoring services to emerge as a new financial service. In order to be an economically viable proposition, a factoring agency has to build up a suitable infrastructure so as to ensure optimum efficiency in the working of credit and collection departments, so that the fixed costs are absorbed at low unit costs.

Profile of a good factoring candidate:

- Rapid growth in its present start-up phase, with a good sales niche and satisfied customers;
- Product permits mark-ups to cover factoring costs and does not require substantial after-sales service or involve long-term progress payments;
- Inventory (such as imports) must be purchased well before sales;

- Accounts receivables are reliable and unencumbered;
- The company may also be one that's in its mature stage in the business cycle, using factoring to supplement other forms of longer-term financing.

Mechanics of Factoring

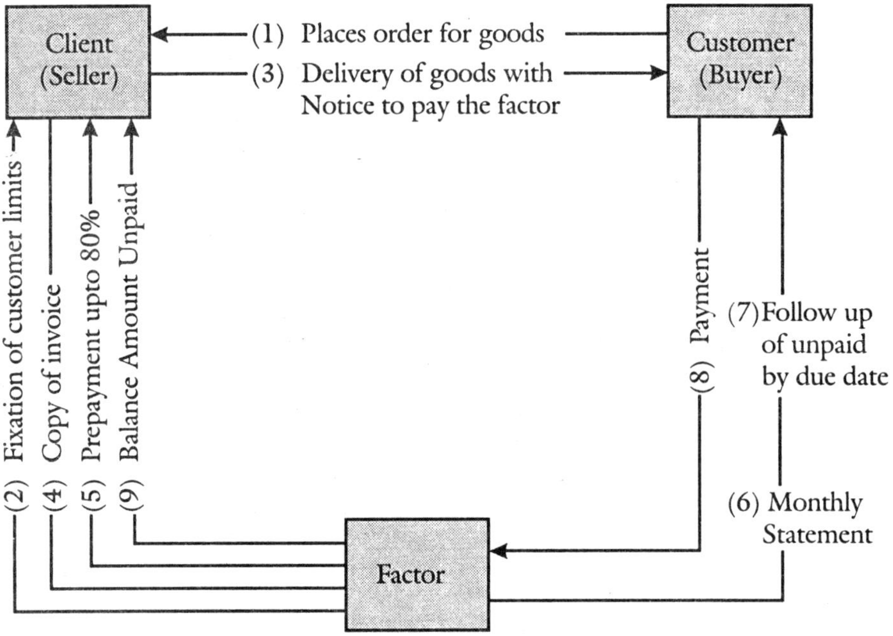

Fig. 7.3 : Mechanics of Factoring

The steps involved in factoring are enumerated below:

Step I: The customer places an order with the seller (the client).

Step II : The factor and the seller enter into a factoring agreement about the various terms of factoring.

Step III : Sale contract is entered into with the buyer and the goods are delivered. The invoice with the notice to pay the factor is sent along with it.

Step IV : The copy of the invoice covering the above sale is given to the factor, who maintains the sale ledger.

Step V : The factor prepays 80% of the invoice value.

Step VI & VII : Monthly statements are sent by the factor to the buyer. If there are any unpaid invoices, follow up action is initiated.

Step VIII : The buyer settles the invoices on expiry of credit period allowed.

Step IX : The balance 20% less the cost of factoring is paid by the factor to the client.

How it Works?

A factor purchases the receivables of a client, maintains a separate sales ledger and attends to the client's book keeping work relating to the accounts receivable. The mechanics is simple: the seller of a product negotiates with the factor to set up a factoring relationship. The latter does a credit check on the buyer and, if he is found creditworthy, gives its approval and sets a credit limit and period for the latter. The client then sells the goods to the buyer and sends the invoices to the factor. The factor, in turn, hands over the invoices to the buyer and pays the seller after retaining a margin. The retained amount is paid to the seller after the factor recovers the dues from the buyer.

Factoring helps the seller by putting hard cash in his hands faster. The main problem sellers face relates to delay in payments, particularly when the buyers are public sector giants like the Railways, State Electricity Boards and the P.W.D.s. Faced with this tight-fisted lot and many large private sector companies which cause hardship to suppliers by delaying payments, it is not surprising that the RBI study group has identified the numerous small and medium scale units as the potential users of factoring services.

Types of Service

Factoring agreements can be classified into two: recourse factoring and non-recourse factoring. Based on the nature of finance offered by the factor, arrangements can also be classified into advance and maturity factoring. There are again special types of arrangements such as bank participation, supplier guarantee, confidential and international factoring.

Thus, the various services fall under one of the following six main types: full factoring (also called old-line factoring), recourse factoring, maturity factoring, advance factoring, undisclosed factoring (also called confidential factoring) and invoice discounting.

In non-recourse service, the factor has no recourse to the firm in the event of a customer defaulting on payments. Thus, it assumes the risk of bad debts. Even under this arrangement, the factor retains the right recourse, if the customer falls to pay for any reason other than financial distress. In recourse factoring, the firm bears the credit risk inherent in the receivables assigned to the factor.

(a) Where the *factor* provides an advance against the uncontrolled and *'not due'* receivables of a firm, it is known as advance factoring arrangement.

(b) Mature factoring is where assistance is provided against collections and possible insurance against bad debts.

(c) Under bank participation factoring, the firm creates a floating charge on the factor reserves in favour of commercial banks and borrows against these reserves.

(d) Under supplier guarantee factoring, the arrangement is designed to help a firm which acts as an intermediary between the supplier and the customer. Under this arrangement, the factor provides a guarantee to the supplier against the invoices raised by him on the firm. The firm raises the bills on the ultimate customers and assigns them to the factor. This arrangement is advantageous to both because the factor takes care of collection of bills for both the parties. The intermediary is also able to earn a gross profit with no financial commitment on its part.

(e) International factoring generally refers to the factoring of export sales. In addition, an international factoring house also undertakes completion of all legal and procedural formalities connected with the export sale.

Factoring has many similarities with bill discounting. Both make available to the supplier finance against invoices. Both discount (purchase at a price lower than the face value) invoices which the buyer would have otherwise paid to the supplier at the end of the credit period. It is here, however that the similarities end.

The discounted bills may be rediscounted several times before they mature for payment. The last holder of the bill receives the full amount of the bill. Debt purchased under factoring cannot be rediscounted, at least as of now. It can only be refinanced.

The factor buys the book debt of the client at a discount, normally 20 per cent, giving 80 per cent of the invoice value to the client. The factor pays back the discounted 20 per cent to the client when the latter's customer makes payment.

Box 7.1

Types of Factoring

(i) Notified Factoring

Here, the customer is intimated about the assignment of debt to a factor and also directed to make payments to the factor instead of to the firm. This is invariably done by a legend on the invoice which states that the receivables arising out from the invoice has been assigned to or sold to the factor.

(ii) Non-notified or Confidential Factoring

Under this facility, the supplier / factor arrangement is not declared to the customer unless or until there is a breach of the agrement on the part of the client, or exceptionally, where the factor considers himself to be at risk.

(iii) With Recourse/without Recourse Factoring

Under a *'with recourse'* arrangement, the client will carry the credit risk in respect of debts sold to the factor. In *'withough recourse'* factoring, the bad debts are borne by the factor.

(iv) Bank Participation Factoring

The client creates a floating charge on the factoring reserves in favour of banks and borrows against these reserves.

(v) Export Factoring

There is usually the presence of 2 factors : an export factor and an import factor. The former buys the invoices of a (local) client exporter and assumes the risk in case of default by the overseas customer. Because of distance, different conditions or lack of information, the export factor usually farms out to an agent (or affiliate company), known as the import factor, the administrative job of servicing the debts owed to its exporting client.

The commission and fees received in the course of providing his service is what the factor earns. These earnings are higher than the earnings from bill discounting. With the discounting rate at a minimum of 16.5 per cent (bank rate), the minimum cost of factoring works out to about 19 per cent. The responsibility for collecting debts rests with the factor, who must ensure that customers pay on time, until in bills finance.

Advantages

- Management adds cash to the bottom line and improves the debt-to-equity ratio. No long-term negative implications to the balance sheet are recorded.
- Advance inventories can be purchased despite cash flow shortages. Temporary reversals need not have a negative effect.

- Slow-paying customers can be carried at little or no charge.
- High-growth start-up can finance growth on a current basis.
- A seed company can, in effect, *"borrow"* money with no credit rating. The cost of money is low or non-existent if the unit sales price of products can be marked up.
- Many factor companies require no minimum volume of amount. Factoring can be a one-time-only strategy, although infrequent factoring results in higher rates and / or deeper discounts on the asset.
- *Prompt Payment and Reduction in Debt :* Capital locked up in the form of outstanding sundry debtors is available for use within the business, as all sales becomes cash sales.
- *Improves Current Ratio :* Improvement in the current ratio, an indication of improved liquidity, enables better working capital management.

Disadvantages

- Unless the company can mark up the sale price of its products, the cost of short-term money can be high.
- Relations with customers might be jeopardized by the loss of personal contact — especially so if the factor company is not tactful in collecting the amounts owing.
- A bad credit rating can result in additional factor fees and less favourable contract terms.
- Factoring can reduce revenue, earnings or accounts receivables unless there is a matching increase in cash.

Future Prospects

With the advent of globalisation and opening up of the Indian economy, financial sector is set to play a pivotal role in the overall economic development of the country. Mergers and acquisitions are the need of the hour and corporate giants are taking birth to derive the maximum advantage of optimum size and economies of scale of production. Syndication of loans is to replace consortium advances. Securitisation of assets is the new mantra heard recently. Assessed bank finance has replaced the old MPBF concept. Big corporates are able to raise ECBs at cheaper rates. In the process, weaker and smaller SSI sector will suffer from the competition posed by the big corporates. To enable the SSI sector to withstand such competition they should manage their affairs efficiently and professionally. As the banks and financial institutions are moving away from the traditional lending activity to new profitable services, the SSI sector is looking for an agency which can fill the gap created by this situation. In the light of the above, factoring is going to play an important role in filling the gap and enable the SSI sector to become competitive and profitable. Export factoring services are being extended by HSBC and Foremost Factors in small volumes. Factoring companies are not in a position to extend this facility to the exporters on open account sales, as they cannot offer competitive rates at par with banks, since they are not eligible for refinance, being registered as NBFCs. They have been requesting for FI status to become eligible for refinance. A factoring law, which would address the present inadequacies and impediments stalling the growth of factoring business, is also likely to be passed shortly.

Factoring is likely to help in systematising trade credit in India. During the past two decades and more, the Reserve Bank of India has been trying to systematically develop a bill market in this country. Reluctance of the trade and industry to accept the rigorous discipline of the bill culture has been one of the reasons why the bill market scheme failed to operate as an effective economic activity in India. Stamp duty on bills and the reluctance of the Government departments and public sector industrial units to abide by the bill discipline also contributed to the different success of the bill market scheme. Factoring would relieve businesses, particularly the small industry and trade, of the burden of collecting their dues from their trade debtors. In fact, inability to recover the receivables in time is one of the major factors responsible for the cash-flow problems of a large number of manufacturing units, particularly in the small and medium-scale sectors. If a factoring institution takes over this responsibility and computerises its operations, it can generate enough data on the payment behaviour of a large number of firms and companies in the country. If this information can be supplied to the rating agencies, it can make or mar the business reputation of firms, who are lax in honouring their commitments on trade dues. As the economy becomes diversified and the number of units increases, manual control over trade dues will become progressively difficult and factoring, with the support of computerised accounting, can be a great help. An efficient financial system like factoring can sustain itself on a viable basis only if a conducive environment is created and fostered.

Government Support

Entrepreneurs in India are offered a number of incentives because they fulfil two important objectives of economic development. Firstly, they facilitate the decentralisation of economic power by encouraging prospective entrepreneurs to take up industrial ventures and assist in the dispersal of industries over the entire geographical area of the country. Secondly, they facilitate the transformation of the traditional technology, which is characterised by low skill, low productivity and low wages, into a modern technology, which is characterised by improved skills, high productivity, rising wages and a higher standard of living. Incentives and subsidies serve as a catalyst to start a dynamic process of development. They also influence the location of enterprises and contribute to regional distribution and development.

The Ford Foundation Team, which visited India in 1953-54, suggested a positive programme for the development of modern small-scale industries. Based on the recommendations of this team, the Government provided a broad based infrastructural and institutional set-up for the accelerated growth of small-scale industries.

In the present chapter, an attempt has been made to indicate the assistance and the incentives which are available from the Government.

Incentives

The term 'incentive' means encouraging action. It is a motivational force which makes an entrepreneur take a right decision and act upon it. Broadly, incentives include concessions, subsidies and bounties. Economic incentives — both financial and non-financial — push an entrepreneur towards decision and action.

'Subsidy' denotes a single lump-sum which is given by a government to an entrepreneur to cover the cost. The term 'bounty' denotes a bonus or financial aid which is given to industry to help it to compete with other units in the country or in a foreign market. The objective of incentives is to motivate an entrepreneur to set up a new venture in the larger interest of the nation and the society.

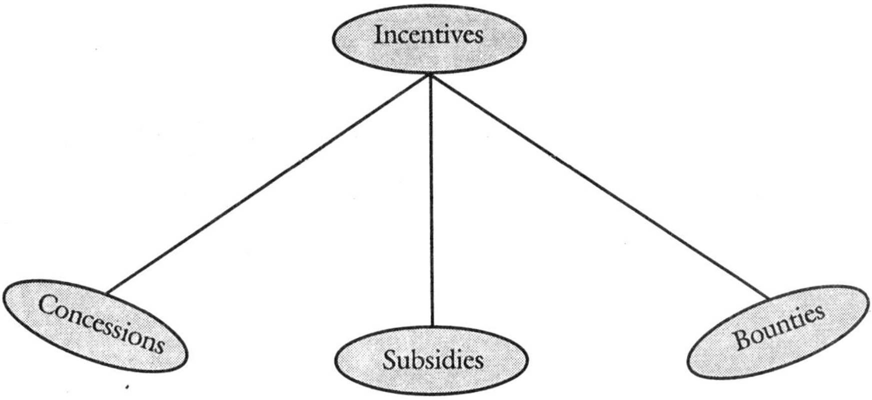

Fig. 7.4 : Pattern of Incentives

Controversies on the Efficacy of Incentives and Subsidies

Often one comes across an intellectual controversy over the good or evil or nil effect of incentive programmes. According to one criticism, the argument proceeds, of course, with empirical evidence and other pure measurement approaches, that incentive schemes would ultimately deteriorate into useless tax give-aways, would only cause other States to reciprocate with the result that industry locations would be affected by those lures and would leave the financial position of the exchequer seriously impaired. While this argument may be true, the industrial development schemes have been with us for more than three decades. As against this view, there are study result establishing the economic significance of the impact of incentive programmes. We also find, to our surprise, the fast-growing literature on the reappraisal of the 'legitimacy' of the regional economic/industrial policy with incentive schemes.

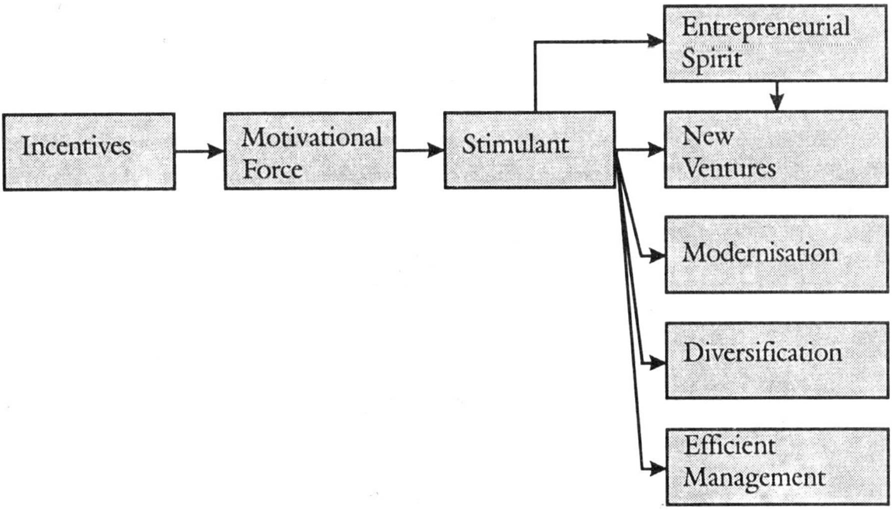

Fig. 7.5 : Incentives as a Motivational Force

Need for Incentives

The need for incentives and subsidies arises for the following reasons:

1. To correct regional imbalances in development : The usual package of incentives and concessions has been available in backward as well as developed districts. It has been, however, the experience of industrial administration, department of industries, district level officers, development corporations, etc., that what is lacking in the backward districts is overall environmental growth. One of the ways is to identify pockets of savings of different activity groups like traders, businessmen, agriculturists, professionals, etc., and provide them with relevant information, as well as suitable incentives, to offset the disadvantages prevailing in such places. Industrial policy uses incentives both to correct the market imperfections and to accelerate the process of industrialisation so as to drive the forces of supply and demand to reach the eqilibrium level. Such a policy then aims at inducing some entrepreneurs or sections of the community (e.g., technicians) to locate their industrial units in areas selected by Government, rather than those of their own choice. Regional balance can also lead to effective utilisation of regional resources, disparities in income and levels of living and contribute to a more integrated society.

2. To promote entrepreneurship by removing economic constraints : As for the economic constraints, the new entrants in the field face many impediments on account of inadequate infrastructure. The new entrepreneur suffers because of the distance separating central administrative organs from entrepreneurs and their projects, deficiency of various supporting services such as market intelligence, entrepreneurial guidance, entrepreneurial training, technical consultancy and merchant banking facilities, lack of an institutional mechanism to provide full-time management personnel complementary to the new entrepreneurs, and finally, from insufficient orientation of the promotional institutions, barring a few exceptions, at the State level to the needs of new entrepreneurs.

The various incentives normally aim at mitigating some or all of the problems by several means. Industrial estates, industrial complexes, industrial nucleus etc., availability of power, concessional finance, capital investment subsidy, transport subsidy, etc., are all but a few examples of incentives to solve the constraints impeding the emergence of entrepreneurs in industry.

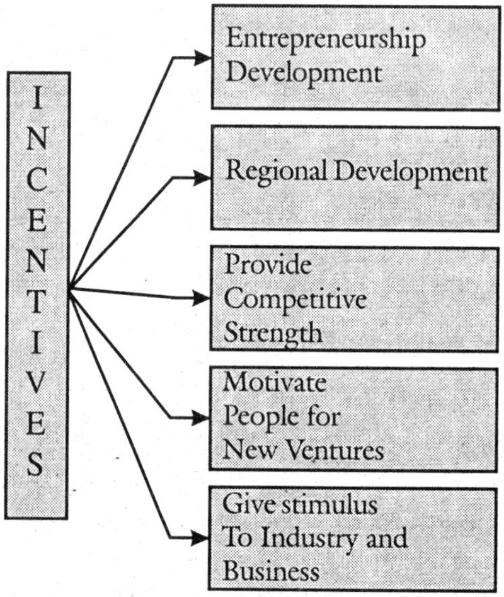

Fig. 7.6 : Objectives of Incentives

3. *To provide competitive strength, survival and growth :* Some of the incentives are concerned with the establishment of industries while others are concerned with the survival and growth of industries. Several incentives are confined to the first few years of the establishment of the unit while a few of them are made available over a long period. Instances may be cited for the reservation policy for small-scale industry due to which a small firm can hope to compete in the market to which entry by larger units is barred. If a small-scale unit is already established and is brought under the reservation policy later, it will be a case of incentive to support its competitive strength. For a newcomer, the reservation is an incentive to enter the industry itself. A price preference improves its competitive strength.

Schemes of Incentives in Operation

Different incentive schemes applicable to the industrial sector in India are in operation. These schemes are offered by the Central and State Governments including Union Territories. The list of incentives offered by either or both Governments are listed below :

(i) Export/Import subsidies and bounties,
(ii) Interest free loans,
(iii) Subsidy for R & D works,
(iv) Capital Investment subsidy,
(v) Transport subsidy,
(vi) Interest subsidy,
(vii) Subsidy for power generators,
(viii) Exemption from property tax,
(ix) Subsidies to artisans and traditional industries including handlooms,
(x) Incentives to non-resident Indians,
(xi) Special incentives to women entrepreneurs,
(xii) Exemption from income-tax,
(xiii) Interest-free sales tax loans,
(xiv) Sales Tax exemptions,
(xv) Subsidy for buying test equipment,
(xvi) Subsidy for industrial housing,
(xvii) Land and building at concessional rates,
(xviii) Price preference to SSI Units,
(xix) Subsidy/assistance for technical consultancy,
(xx) Exemption from stamp duty,
(xxi) Concessional water,
(xxii) Provision of seed capital,
(xxiii) Allotment of developed/constructed sheds,
(xxiv) Allotment of controlled or subsidised raw material, and
(xxv) Subsidising the cost of market studies/feasibility studies or reports.

The Assistance Programme

Some of the important measure of assistance now available for entrepreneurs in the industrial sector are :

(i) Technical assistance through industrial extension service;
(ii) Assistance for obtaining raw materials;
(iii) Cash assistance;
(iv) Supply of machinery on hire-purchase basis;
(v) Marketing assistance;
(vi) Assistance to small entrepreneurs;
(vii) Rural Industries Projects.

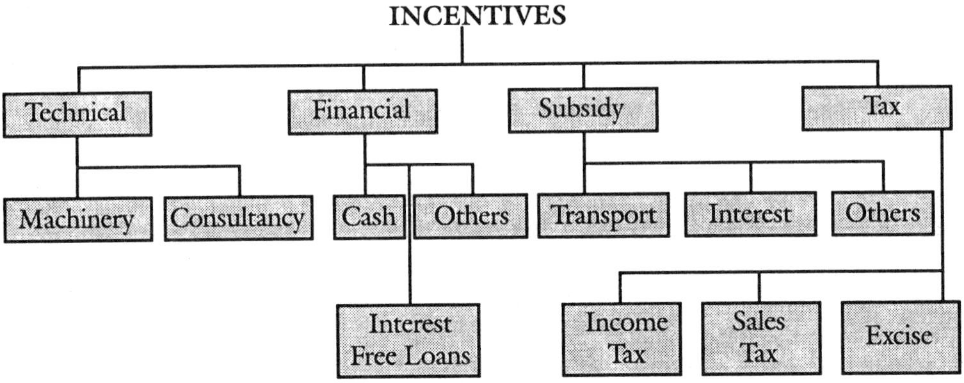

Fig. 7.7 : Types of Incentives

In order to promote industrialisation of the country as a whole and to remove disparities in levels of development between different regions, the Central Government is operating three major schemes, viz., Central Investment Subsidy Scheme, Transport Subsidy Scheme and Central Assistance Scheme for Infrastructural Development in No-Industry Districts.

Central Investment Subsidy Scheme

This was introduced in 1971, and has been modified from time to time. The Scheme is for encouraging setting up of industries in centrally notified backward areas. For setting up industries in Category "A" backward areas, subsidy is allowed at the rate of 25% subject to a maximum of Rs. 25 lakhs (enhanced to Rs. 50 lakhs for setting up electronics industry in hilly districts). It is 15% and 10% subject to a maximum of Rs. 15 lakhs and Rs. 10 lakhs for category 'B' & 'C' districts respectively. MRTP / FERA companies are not eligible for subsidy in Category 'C' areas. Entrepreneurs who set up nucleus plant in Category 'B' and 'C' districts / areas are eligible for 20% and 15% subsidy, subject to a maximum of Rs. 20 lakhs and Rs. 15 lakhs respectively. Since the inception of the Scheme and upto December, 1989, a total sum of Rs. 855.46 crores has been reimbursed to States/Union Territories excluding Delhi and Chandigarh.

Transport Subsidy Scheme

The Scheme was introduced in 1971 and is applicable to hilly, remote and inaccessible areas. It covers the entire North Eastern Region including Sikkim, Jammu & Kashmir, Himachal Pradesh, hill districts of Uttar Pradesh, Lakshadweep and Andaman & Nicobar Islands and Darjeeling District of West Bengal. Identified promotional institutions which transact business on behalf of small, village and cottage industries are also eligible for Transport Subsidy. Transport Subsidy is paid on the transport costs of industrial raw materials which are brought into and finished goods which are taken out of these areas to identified rail heads / ports. In the North Eastern Region including Sikkim, Jammu & Kashmir, Lakshadweep, Andaman & Nicobar Islands, subsidy is available at the rate of 90% for movement of raw materials within the North Eastern region and at the rate of 50% for movement of finished goods within the North Eastern Region from one state to another state. For airlifting of electronic components/products from Calcutta airport to the airport nearest to the locations of the industrial units in North Eastern Region and Sikkim, subsidy is allowed at the rate of 75% and *vice versa*.

Central Assistance for Infrastructural Development in No-Industry Districts under the Old Scheme

To assist the State Governments in taking up infrastructural development in one or two identified growth centres in each No-Industry District, the Central Government gives financial assistance which is limited to one-third of the total cost of infrastructural development, subject to maximum of Rs. 2 crores per district. Two types of patterns have been laid down for the purpose:

Pattern I

Rs. 2 crores as subsidy from the Central Government.

Rs. 2 crores as share of the State Government.

Rs. 2 crores as loan from I.D.B.I. on concessional terms.

Pattern II

Rs. 2 crores as subsidy from the Central Government.

Rs. 4 crores as share of the State Government.

Rs. 5 crores as loan from I.D.B.I. on concessional terms, after the shares of State and Centre are spent.

For States in the North Eastern Region, the Scheme has been further liberalised. In a total project of Rs. 4 crores, the Central Government's shares would be 50%, i.e., Rs. 2 crores per district and the State Governments have the option to fund the balance of Rs. 2 crores either from their own funds or by raising a loan from I.D.B.I. Construction of sheds, subject to a ceiling of 25% of the total cost, has been allowed in the case of the North Eastern region only.

So far 51 growth centres in 44 districts of the States of Rajasthan, Orissa, Uttar Pradesh, Karnataka, Madhya Pradesh, Bihar, Maharashtra, West Bengal, Tripura, Nagaland, Arunachal Pradesh and Mizoram have been approved by the Government for development of infrastructural facilities.

Scheme for Growth Centres

The Government announced on June 3, 1988, the decision to set up 100 growth centres throughout the country over the next five years or so. These growth centres, which would act as magnets for attracting industries to backward areas, would be endowed with infrastructural facilities on par with the best available in the country, particularly in respect of power, water, telecommunication and banking. Each growth centre would be provided with funds of the order of Rs. 25-30 crores in order to create infrastructural facilities of a high order.

In the first phase, it was decided to take up 61 growth centres, allocated to various States/Union Territories as indicated below :

	State	*No. of Growth Centres*
1.	Andhra Pradesh	4
2.	Assam	2
3.	Bihar	5
4.	Gujarat	2
5.	Haryana	2
6.	Jammu & Kashmir	2
7.	Karnataka	3
8.	Kerala	2
9.	Madhya Pradesh	5
10.	Maharashtra	4
11.	Orissa	3
12.	Punjab	2
13.	Rajasthan	4
14.	Tamil Nadu	3
15.	Uttar Pradesh	6
16.	West Bengal	3
17.	Arunachal pradesh	1
18.	Goa	1
19.	Himadhal Pradesh	1
20.	Manipur	1
21.	Meghalaya	1
22.	Mizoram	1
23.	Nagaland	1
24.	Pondicherry	1
25.	Tripura	1
	Total	61

The States/Union Territories were asked to identify double the number of growth centres allocated to them but the final selection of these was to be done by the Central Government. The State Governments also free to include any of the growth centres already approved under the erstwhile Scheme for developing such centres in the 'No-Industry Districts.'

The growth centres were not to be located within 50 Kms of the boundary of 7 cities with a population of above 25 lakhs, 30 Kms from the boundary of 2 cities with a population of above 15 lakhs but below 25 lakhs and 15 Kms from the boundary of 12 cities with a population of 7.5 lakhs but below 15 lakshs.

The growth centres were located close to District/Sub-Divisional/Block/Taluk/ Headquarters or developing urban centres.

The board financing pattern for development of infrastructure in selected growth centres was as follows:

1.	Central Government (Equity)	Rs. 10 crores
2.	State Government (Equity)	Rs. 5 crores
3.	All India Financial Institutions (including Rs. 2 crores as equity)	Rs. 4 crores
4.	Nationalised Banks	Rs. 1 crore
		Rs. 20 crores
5.	Market borrowings	Rs. 10 crores
	Total	Rs. 30 crores

The growth centres selected under this Scheme were included in Category 'B' (unless they were already included in Category 'A') of the list of Backward Areas and were entitled to all incentives available from time to time for Category 'B' areas. The State Governments were requested to make suitable provisions in their States / Union Territories Plan for 1989-90 for the development of these growth centres.

Technology Policy

Over the years, a diversified and sophisticated industrial base has been built up in the country along with technological skills and capabilities. The requirements of the industrial field are now vastly different from those in the early stages of industrialisation. The Government's basic policy towards import of technology is aimed at reducing unnecessary dependence on external resources and achieving self-reliance through optimum utilisation of indigenous resources. It is, however, recognised by the Government that it is equally necessary to update production technology continuously to keep pace with the rapid technological advances taking place in the developed countries. The import of technology is, therefore, selective, and is ordinarily permitted in high technology areas, in export-oriented or import substitutions manufacture or for enabling indigenous industry to upgrade its existing technology to attain efficiency and competitive strength. Government has also laid emphasis on the need to ensure efficient absorption and adaptation of the imported technology through adequate investment in research, engineering and development.

The objectives of the technology policy as embodied in the Statement issued in January 1983, are the development of indigenous technology and efficient absorption and adaptation of imported technology appropriate to national priorities and resources.

It has been recognised that in-house Research and Development units in industry provide a desirable and essential interface between efforts within national laboratories as well as production in industry. Encouragement is, accordingly, given to individual units for setting up in-house R & D units with a view to absorbing, assimilating and adapting imported technology as well as development of advanced technology.

Foreign Investment

Government's foreign investment policy is selective and is designed to channelise such investment into areas which require sophisticated technology, or where critical production gaps exist, or which would help increase the country's export potential. Foreign investment is regarded as a vehicle for transfer of technology that is needed by the country. The normal ceiling for foreign investment is 40% of the paid-up equity capital of the company, but a higher percentage of foreign equity may be considered in priority industries if the technology is sophisticated and closely held or if the venture is largely export-oriented. For wholly export-oriented units even 100% foreign equity can be considered. The foreign share capital should be contributed by way of cash and not by way of supply of machinery and equipment or remuneration for know-how and technical assistance. However, the Government of India, in 1980, relaxed the policy in respect of investors from the Oil Exporting Developing (OED) countries. Accordingly, investment upto 40% in the equity of new ventures without being linked with technology transfer can be made by investors from OED countries in specified industries. A second exception to the general policy is investment by Non-Residents of Indian origin who are allowed to invest in Indian industrial units under certain schemes and subject to certain conditions even if there is no transfer of technology along with the investment.

Payment for technology and know-how can be made either in the form of annual royalty or as lumpsum payment or a mixture of both. The rete or royalty depends on the nature of technology and is normally limited to 5% for a period of 5 years. Where both lumpsum and royalty payments are involved, the maximum payment is restricted to 8% of the net ex-factory value of production calculated for a period of 10 years. It has recently been decided that while the existing norms regarding royalty and lumpsum payments should continue, these norms can be relaxed so that the existing ceiling on royalty / lumpsum payments does not come in the way of obtaining sophisticated and closely-held technologies.

Technical Assistance

The industrial extension service, which is the most important item in the programme for the development of small industries, aims at providing complete technical, economic and managerial consultancy services to small-scale industries in order to upgrade the skills of workers, increase their productivity and wages, reduce the cost of production, improve the quality of the goods produced, and strengthen competitive position of the small units.

The industrial extension service is provided through the SSIs and Industrial Extension Centres located in different parts of the country. The SISIs are State-level agencies which render co-ordinated industrial extension services, while the Extension Centres are miniature institutes in the sense that their activities are limited to one or more specific industries and restricted to a smaller area. The Extension Centres, like the Small Industries Service Institutes, assist individual entrepreneurs to solve common technical problems, suggest improved designs and more up-to-date techniques of manufacture, train workers in improved techniques of production, management, marketing, etc., and serve as common service facilities centres. These services are now offered by 16 small Industries Services Institutes, 5 Branch Institutes and 64 Extension Centres dispersed all over the country.

Broadly speaking, the industrial extension service provides technical assistance, economic service, and management consultancy services. The technical assistance includes:

(a) Advice on improved technical process and the use of modern machines and equipment;

(b) Preparation of drawings and machines and machine parts, equipment, dies, tools and fixtures ;

(c) Demonstration of the use of modern technical processes through workshops and mobile workshops mounted on trucks;

(d) Research on proper use of equipment and improved designs of machinery;

(e) Training classes in various technical trades like foundry, heat treatment, machine shop and blueprint reading for the benefit of small industrialists and artisans ;

(f) Assistance in the development of ancillary units ;

(g) Information which is made available to small industries on all technical matters.

Technical assistance is rendered in co-ordination with economic services and management consultancy services, and the whole programme has been widened to embrace all the small units. The quality of this programme, too, has been improved over the years.

Technical advice is rendered in various forms and includes (i) on the-spot advice in the factory to solve technical problems and (ii) advice at Small Industries Service Institute's office on technical problems, including advice on when, how and where to start small industries.

Besides incentives and subsidies given by the Centre, the State Governments too offer fiscal and monetary incentives and subsidies help entrepreneurs setting up their industries in the States to overcome certain disadvantages. The entrepreneurs are attracted to some State for their package of incentives and subsidies. The foremost incentive is a stable government with an excellent law and order situation followed by availability of disciplined, dedicated and skilled labour force. However, states do attract industries by giving incentives in regard to sales tax, octroi, and subsidised loan. These incentives have helped in large measure in attracting entrepreneurs to set up industries — and accelerate the process of industrialisation. State incentives and subsidies have helped entrepreneurs to locate their projects and industrialise the State on a firm foundation. The innovations of these incentives and subsidies indicate their adaptability and the vital role they have been playing in the process of industrial development, spanning rural and urban, backward and non-backward and organised and unorganised, large, medium and small sectors of the economy — each sector needing different approaches, strategies, skills and techniques.

Institutional Credit

Broadly, entrepreneurs requires finance for six types of its activities at different phases.

Firstly, for consultancy, research and development, feasibility study etc. (pre-operative expenses).

Secondly, for the purchase of land, developing the area, construction of factory premises, developing other basic infrastructure, purchase or machinery and its installation.

Thirdly, a small enterprise requires money to purchase raw materials for its manufacturing process, spares and a spare parts for its machinery.

Fourthly, finance is required to hold the stock in process but also finished goods pending sale.

Fifthly, the unit requires money to pay wages and salary, fuel, power, water, selling expenses, interest on funds borrowed, etc. This apart, the enterprise requires to pay bonus to employees, taxes and duties, etc.

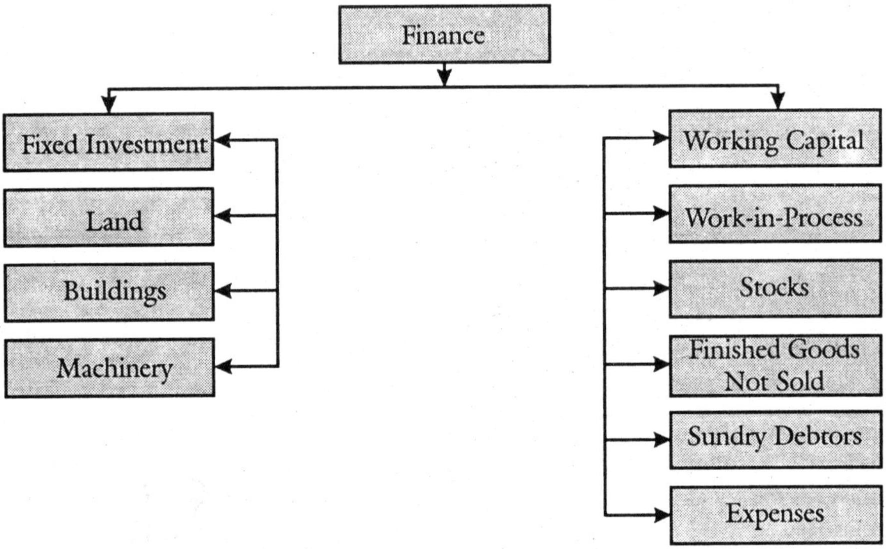

Fig. 7.7 : Financial Requirements of Small Enterprises

Box 7.2

Charter for Small Scale Industries (SSIs)

1. Simplified & bilingual applications for credit facilities to SSI units are available at all our branches.
2. Acknowledgments are issued to SSI units immediately on receipt of loan application by branches.
3. SSI loan applications/credit proposals are disposed off within the stipulated Time Norms from the date of receipt of application completed in all respects.

(a) Upto Rs. 25000/-	2 Weeks
(b) Over Rs. 25000/- & up to Rs. 5 lakhs	4 Weeks
(c) Over Rs. 5 lakhs	8 to 9 Weeks

4. Margin :

Upto Rs. 25,000/-	Nil
Over Rs. 25,000/-	15% to 25% as determined by Bank

5. Rate of Interest :

Upto Rs. 50,000/-	9.00% p.a. For Working Capital Loans. 9.50% p.a. For Term Loans.
Above Rs. 50,000/- & Upto Rs. 2 lakhs	PLR for Working Capital limits (Presently 11.00%) PTLR for Term loans (Presently 11.50%)
Over Rs. 2 lakhs	ROI not exceeding the cap of 2% over PLR/PTLR as the case may be WEF 01.04.2003

6. Collateral-free loans upto Rs. 5 lakhs.
7. Collateral-free loans over Rs. 5 lakhs & upto Rs. 15 lakhs based on good track record and financial position of the borrowing unit.
8. Collateral/Third Party Guarantee free credit limits (Fund Based) upto Rs. 25 lakhs if covered under Credit Guarantee Fund Scheme for Small Industries (CGFSI).
9. Composite Loans under Single Window concept of RBI upto Rs. 50 lakhs.
10. Loans under Margin Money Scheme of Khadi & Village Industries Commission under their Rural Employment Generation Programme (REGP) for setting up industrial/service units in Rural/Semi Urban areas focussing on employment generation.
11. Equity type Soft Loans under National Equity Fund (NEF)/Mahila Udyam Nidhi (MUN) Schemes of SIDBI and Special Assistance to Women Entrepreneurs through CED for Women/Mahila Banking Branches.
12. Loans under Technology Upgradation Fund Scheme (TUFS) for Textile & Jute industrial units in SSI sector AND to 21 Specified Industries in SSI sector for Technology Upgradation under Credit Linked Capital Subsidy Scheme (CLCSS).
13. Term Loans for Acquisition of ISO 9000 Series certification by SSI units.
14. Standby Credit for Capital Expenditure upto Rs. 5 lakhs along with renewal of working capital facilities for making small additions to fixed assets.
15. Laghu Udyami Credit Cards/Artisan Credit Cards up to a limit of Rs. 2 lakhs.
16. Focussed attention at our 37 Specialized branches located in different parts of the country.

Assistance Schemes of Various Agencies

State Financial Corporation (SFCs), grant term loans for the purchase of land construction of factory premises and purchase of machinery and equipment for the setting up of new industries or for expansion or modernisation of the existing ones. SFCs generally prescribe a margin of 25 per cent and allow an initial holiday of two years for loan repayment (this period can be increased to five years in backward districts). The usual repayment period varies from 7 years to 10 years (to 12 years in backward districts). All fixed assets are charged to the SFCs as security for these advances.

The National Small Industries Corporation (NSIC) and State Small Industries Corporations (SSICs) supply machinery on a hire-purchase basis to small-scale and ancillary industries, inclusive of the value of machinery and equipment already installed. The payment for the machinery and equipment is made directly to the suppliers. The hire purchase value is generally recovered in 13 half-yearly instalments are paid before the due date. While NSIC supplies both imported and indigenous machinery, SSICs supply only indigenous machinery.

State Directorates of Industries extend assistance ranging between Rs. 10,000 and Rs. 50,000 for the construction of factory premises, purchase of machinery and equipment and working capital. A margin of 25 to 50 per cent is retained on the value of assets, including those created out of the loan. These loans are repayable in five to seven years.

Commercial banks provide short-term and medium-term financial assistance. The short-term credit facilities are granted for working capital requirements of units like those for raw materials, goods-in-process, finished products, bill receivable and book debts. The medium-term loans are granted for the acquisition of land, construction of factory premises, purchase of machinery and equipment and pre-operative expenses. These loans are generally granted for periods for 5 to 7 years. They also establish letters of credit on behalf of their clients favouring suppliers of raw material/machinery (both Indian and foreign) which extend the bankers' assurance for payment and thus help their delivery. Certain transactions, particularly those in contracts of sale to government departments, may require guarantees, being issued in lieu of security earnest money deposits for release of advance money, supply of raw materials for processing, full payment of bills on assurance of performance etc. Commercial banks issue such guarantee also.

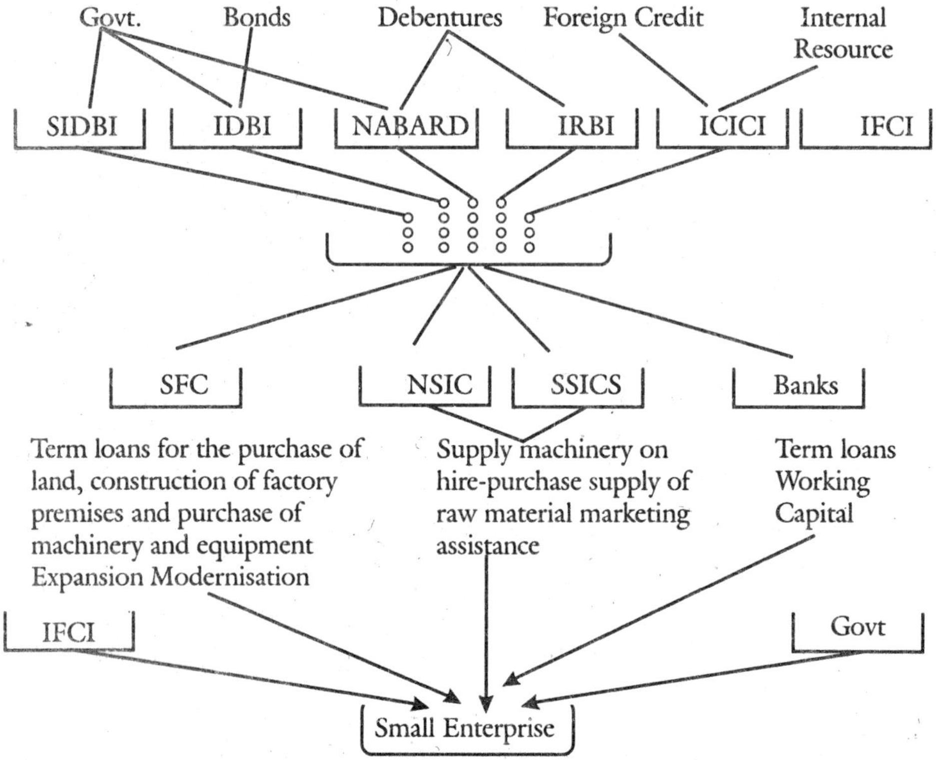

Fig. 7.8 : Types of Assistance Extended by Banks

The Small Industries Development Bank of India (SIDBI), The Industrial Development Bank of India (IDBI), the National Bank for Agriculture and Rural Development (NABARD) and the Industrial Reconstruction Bank of India (IRBI) and the Industrial Credit and Investment Corporation of India (ICICI) provide refinance facilities to banks and financial corporations for financing the small-scale industrial sector. The credit provided by banks to small-scale industrial sector is treated as credit to the 'priority sector.'

The Small Industrial Development Bank of India (SIDBI), the appex developmental body for small, tiny and village industries extend assistance to SSI units through two major schemes:

(a) *The Bills Rediscounting Scheme :* Under this Scheme, the manufacturers of indigenous machinery / capital equipment can offer deferred payment facilities to their buyers (the period of such payment being not less than six months and not more than five/ seven years), the relative bills, accepted/guaranteed by the buyer and/or his bankers, can be discounted by the manufacturer with his own bank to realise the cost of machinery immediately. The latter, in turn, rediscounts the bills with the SIDBI and obtains the amount paid; subsequently, he takes them back before their due dates and presents them for payment before the buyer/his guarantor.

(b) The Refinance Scheme under which SIDBI refinance eligible term loans granted by banks to the SSI borrower.

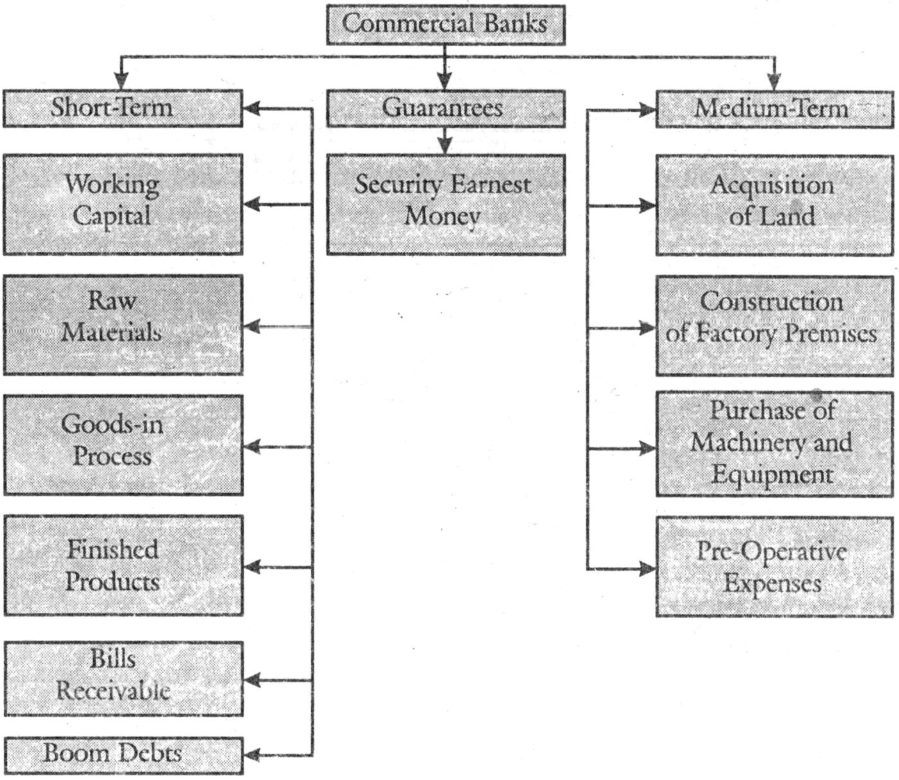

Fig. 7.9 : Types of Assistance Extended by Banks

Commercial banks provide finance both for medium-term as well as working capital. More than 25 lakh accounts are in operation. Banks provide finance through varied tailor-made schemes to foster the development of small-scale industries in consonance with national objectives. A schematic financial outlet of banks is presented in Fig. 3 and Fig. 4.

The industrial development banks in India do not merely extend term loans to qualifying entrepreneurs for their viable projects but look on themselves "as companies in the business of enterprise-creation, and towards that end, they are prepared to provide all assistance at the stages of project conception, formulation, presentation for assistance and for successful implementation." They even provide information on marketing, technology and other related fields. There is a lot of "project counselling" and "financial counselling" also so that the projects are not only successfully commissioned and their loans recovered but also that the projects are efficiently managed and grow on long-term basis. Thus, the commitment of the development banks to the sources of the enterprises is "total encompassing each stage of the project cycle." The development banks have also been able to guide the Indian promoters to professionalise management.

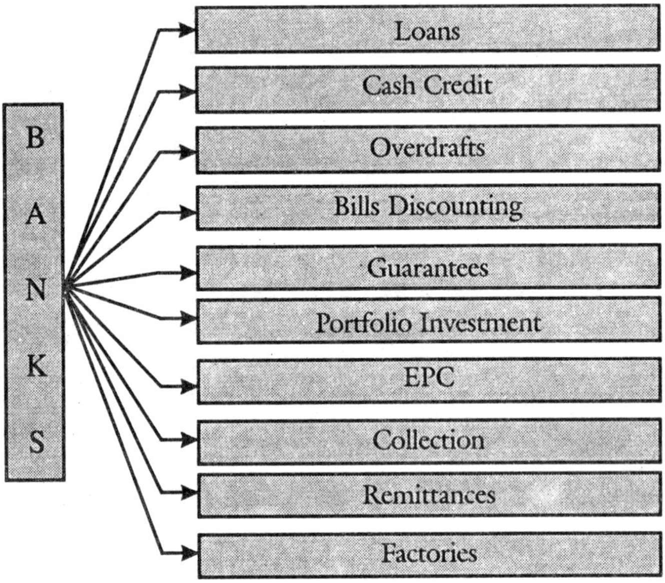

Fig. 7.10 : Finance by Commercial Banks

SSI FINANCING
BANK'S COMMITMENT

1. Acknowledgment of loan applications by branches.
2. To issue applications accompanied by checklists.
3. To comply with time norms for disposal of applications, received complete in all respects.

   2 weeks for loan upto Rs. 25,000/-

   4 weeks for loan upto Rs. 5 lakhs.

   8-9 weeks for loan over Rs. 5 lakhs.

4. No collateral security for loans upto Rs. 5 lakhs.
5. No collateral for loans over Rs. 5 lakhs and upto Rs. 15 lakhs subject to good track record and financial position.
6. To consider composite loan upto Rs. 50 lakhs.
7. To compute working capital requirements based on Nayak Committee norms. Loan quantum: Minimum 20% of anticipated annual turnover.
8. To cover loan accounts with limits upto Rs. 25 lakhs without collateral security/ third party guarantee under CGFTSI, if eligible.
9. To offer concession in interest rates upto 1% under "Priyadarshini Scheme" (Scheme for Women Entrepreneurs).
10. To consider short-term loan facility at Sub-PLR rates to meet temporary liquidity requirements of eligible credit worthy existing borrowers with good track record under "Star SSI Suprime Scheme."

These financial institutions have been endeavouring to give a qualitative thrust to industrial change in India, particularly in the field of : (a) The Industrial development of backward regions; (b) The promotion of small scale industrial units ; (c) The prevention of concentration of economic power through regulating assistance to MRTP houses; and (d) The rehabilitation of sick units.

However, this is not to say that all that can be done for a rapid and balanced regional industrial development in India has been done, or that finance alone can solve all the problems of industrial development. The problems of industrial development are multi-dimensional, and making finance available does not ensure industrial development. The growing industrial sickness and technological obsolescence have become major problems and have retarded progress. In addition to devoting more attention to these problems, term-lending institutions have to see to it that their various activities promote and spread the spirit of entrepreneurship and develop a healthy industrial culture, which will ultimately help in accelerating the industrial growth of the country.

New or existing SSI (Small Scale Industry) units whether or not assisted by SIDBI including units graduating to medium scale are eligible for the working capital term loans from SIDBI. They are aimed to help SSI units in starting their commercial production without difficulty and funding the up scaling of their operations.

All the assisted units of SIDBI covered under the proposed scheme are required to eventually switch over to commercial banks within a reasonable time frame (3-5 years) for meeting their regular working capital requirements. The venture outlay (i.e., project cost + working capital) should be beyond Rs. 1 crore and upto Rs. 3 crores.

Lower ceiling may be considered by SIDBI in respect of units assisted under SIDBI's schemes, viz., ancillary, TDMFS, ISO 9000, Vendor Development, Marketing Equipment, Finance Scheme etc. The Debt Equity Ratio should not exceed 2:1 for total venture outlay.

Channels of Assistance by SIDBI

SIDBI's financial assistance to small scale sector have three major dimensions :

(i) Indirect assistance to primary lending institutions (PLIs)
(ii) Direct assistance to small units
(iii) Development and Support Services

Indirect Assistance

SIDBI's schemes of indirect assistance envisage credit to SSIs through a large network of 913 PLIs spread across the country with a branch network of over 65000. The assistance is provided by way of refinance, bills rediscounting and resource support in the form of short term loans / line of credit in lieu of refinance, etc.

Refinance

- The main objective of SIDBI's refinance schemes being enhancement of flow of credit to the SSI sector and augmenting the resources of PLIs, the Bank provides refinance to PLIs against the term loans granted by them for:
  - Setting up of new SSI projects and for expansion, technology upgradation, modernisation, quality promotion, diversification by existing units and rehabilitation of sick SSI units.
  - Small road transport operators, qualified professionals for self-employment, small hospitals and nursing homes, cyber cafes, marketing, industrial infrastructure and to promote hotels and tourism-related activities.
- SIDBI extends Financial Support (Short Term Loans) to scheduled banks in respect of their outstanding portfolio relating to SSI sector against which no financial support has been availed of from other institutions.

Rediscounting

- In order to help the machinery manufactures in the SSI sector and to maximise their sales by offering deferred payment credit to the prospective purchaser users, the Bank operates a Bills discounting Scheme where bills arising out of sale/purchase of machinery discounted by scheduled commercial banks are re-discounted by SIDBI. Facilities under the Scheme are also extended to cover purchases of machinery by Small Scale Industries.

Direct Assistance

The objective behind SIDBI's direct assistance schemes has been to supplement the efforts of PLIs by identifying the gaps in the existing credit delivery mechanism for Small Scale Industries, Direct assistance is provided under several tailor-made schemes through SIDBI's 41 Regional/Branch Offices spread across the country.

Assistance is provided directly for

- Setting up of new SSI units, small hotels, hospitals / nursing homes
- Technology upgradation and modernisation, expansion, diversification
- Quality upgradation / acquiring of ISO 9000 series certification
- Development of markets for SSI products
- Development of infrastructure for SSI sector
- Pre-Shipment and Post-Shipment Credit & Export Bill Finance
- Discounting of bills of manufacturer-seller in SSI sector, selling either equipments or components
- Factoring services.

SIDBI offers

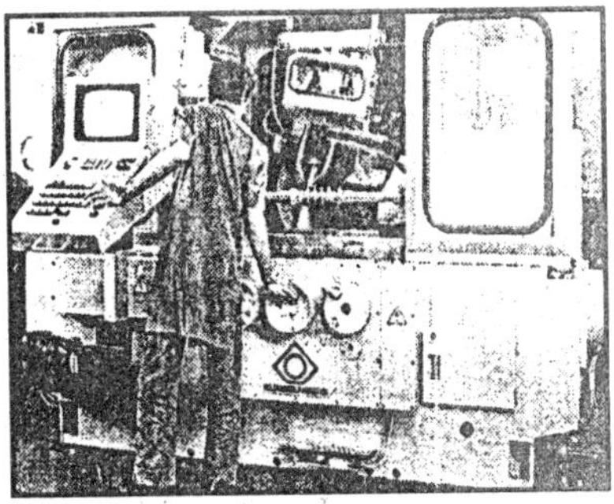

- Financial assistance to SSI units under Technology Development and Modernisation Fund (TDMF) Scheme
- Financial assistance to SSI units in the textile and cotton ginning and pressing sectors for taking up technology upgradation and modernisation under Technology Upgradation Funds Scheme (TUFS)
- Financial assistance to tanneries for taking up modernisation under the Tannery Modernisation Scheme (TMS)
- Twelve percent capital subsidy on loans advanced to SSI units engaged in select product sub-sectors for technology upgradation by scheduled commercial banks, SFCs and NSIC under Credit Linked Capital Subsidy Scheme
- Short-term loans to Stated Electricity Boards to facilitate their purchases from SSIs and effect payment in time. Discounting of invoices of SSIs supplying their products to large purchaser companies in the public/private sector
- Interest subsidy in respect of certain hotel projects under one, two and three star and heritage category, where loans are sanctioned after approval of projects from the Department of Tourism
- Support to obtain credit rating from accredited rating agencies.

SIDBI's Foreign Currency Assistance Includes

- Foreign currency loans to import equipment by existing export-oriented SSI units and new units having definite plans for entering export markets
- Foreign currency loans to execute confirmed export orders by way of pre-shipment credit/letter of credit and post-shipment credit facilities
- Pre-shipment and Post-shipment Credit in Rupees terms to exporting SSIs for greater flexibility
- Export bills financing in foreign currency.

SIDBI's Venture Capital Includes

- Assistance to small scale entrepreneurs using innovative indigenous technology and expertise
- Contribution to corpus of other venture funds
- Promotion of State level venture capital funds and a National Venture Fund for Software and IT Industry dedicated to small scale units in Software/IT industry
- SIDBI has entered into a Memorandum of Understanding with Small Enterprise Assistance Funds of United States of America.

Lines of Credit are Established by SIDBI in Favour of

- State Financial Corporations
- State Industrial Development Corporations

- State Small Industries Development Corporations (for supplying raw material and extending marketing support to SSI units)
- Factoring Companies (to factor receivables of SSIs)
- National Small Industries Corporation Ltd.

Development and Support Services

- The bank extends development and support services in the form of loans and grants to different agencies working for the promotion and development of SSIs and tiny industries. Over the years, the initiatives of SIDBI under promotional and developmental activities have crystallised into the following important areas:
- Enterprise Promotion with emphasis on Rural Industrialisation
- Human Resource Development to suit the SSI sector needs
- Technology Upgradation
- Quality and Environment Management
- Marketing Promotion, and
- Information Dissemination.

Enterprise Promotion is Supported Through

- **Micro Credit Scheme**

  Having encouraged by the result and to accord focused attention for increasing flow of funds to the poor through sustainable micro finance institutions (MFIs), SIDBI launched a SIDBI Foundation for Micro Credit on November 27, 1998. The foundation presently functioning as a department of the Bank commenced its operations in January 1999 with an initial corpus of Re. 1 billion. The mission of the Foundation is "to create a national network of strong, viable and sustainable micro finance institutions from the informal and formal sectors to provide micro finance services to the poor, especially women." The new approach not only envisages financial assistance but also strives to build and strengthen the management capabilities of the micro finance practitioners and related institutions through customised capacity building inputs for achieving sustainability, economies of scale, desired outreach, etc. SIDBI Foundation has taken a lead in the country by initiating a pioneering effort for 'capacity assessment rating' of NGOs/MFIs.
- The foundation has entered into an agreement with International Fund for Agricultural Development (IFAD), Rome for upscaling its operations. Earlier, SFMC had signed a MoU with Department for International Development (DFID), UK for grant support for financing various capacity building initiatives of the Foundation as well as MFIs. The Foundation has drawn up a comprehensive action plan with a view to mainstreaming the micro finance and providing capacity building support to the micro finance institutions.
- **Rural Industries Programme**

  Rural Industries Programme (RIP) has been designed to provide a cohesive and integrated package of basic inputs like information, motivation, training and credit, backed by appropriate technology and market linkages. The programme is executed through Non Governmental Organisations, Technical Consultancy Organisations and development professionals.

- **Mahila Vikas Nidhi**

  Mahila Vikas Nidhi Scheme is aimed at the economic empowerment of women, especially from the weaker strata in rural areas by providing them with avenues for training and employment by creation of infrastructure in the form of Training-cum-Production Centres. The Projects are implemented through accredited NGOs with good track record in the field of enterprise development for women.

- **Entrepreneurship Development Programmes**

  The programmes aim at training various target groups with entrepreneurial traits so that they obtain necessary information, motivation and guidance in setting up their own enterprises. Specialised Entrepreneurship Development Agencies are supported to conduct programmes for specific target groups such as rural youth, women, SC/ST, ex-servicemen, etc.

Human Resources Development of the SSIs is Pursued Through

- Small Industries Management Programme (SAMAP), and
- Skill-cum-Technology Upgradation Programme (STUP).

While SIMAP is designed to develop a cadre of second line industrial managers, specifically trained to assist SSI entrepreneurs in discharging multiple responsibilities, STUP has been formulated to improve the performance of existing SSI units by developing/strengthening managerial skills and technical competence of entrepreneurs and senior executives. The reputed management/technical institutes are provided grant/corpus support to conduct these programmes.

Programmes for Technology Upgradation Include

- Technology upgradation in identified industry clusters
- Technology transfer
- Quality improvement.

Quality and Environment Management Programmes Aim At

- making the SSI units aware of the importance of environmental issues and providing them with necessary technical support to implement projects which can provide relative social and environmental benefit as compared to financial cost incurred, and
- educating the SSI units about environmental regulations, which need to be adhered to and the steps required to operate within prescribed norms.

Marketing Promotion Initiatives Include

- Sponsoring / organising exhibitions in India and abroad with intention of subsidising participation costs for SSIs
- Typing up with renowned organisation to provide market information at concessional rates
- Rating services to export-oriented SSI units, and
- Sponsoring market studies.

Information Dissemination Initiatives Include

- Promoting new units by identification and publicity of viable project ideas and business opportunities through project profiles, Udyog Sadhana Radio Programme and Udyog Sadhana Television Series
- Publication of "SIDBI Report on Small Scale Industries Sector" on an annual basis
- Publication of theme-based Reports for SSI sector such as "Technology for Small Scale Industries—Current Status and Emerging Needs"
- Product specific sectoral studies to assess the impact of policy changes
- WTO impact studies.

Conclusion

Finance is one of the basic requirements of a project which an entrepreneur needs to start with at every stage of the project. Project finance is both short-term and long-term. The sources from which entrepreneurs can meet their financial needs for their projects are: *Internal source* and *external sources*. Besides, the entrepreneur raises his finance by availing of available subsidies, state aid to industries, etc. Project finance, therefore, is very crucial to the success of a project. In this chapter, the various facets of project financing have been discussed.

The concept of '*feasibility*' covers the following areas:

(a) Is the idea technologically sound? — Technical feasibility.

(b) Would it be commercially viable? — Commercial viability.

(c) What would its economic dimensions be? — Economic viability.

(d) What financial demands would it make on the promoters, the company and outside creditors? To put it differently, what is the size of funds required — cost of the project.

Finance is available for a project. But there is need for prudent financial management. All along, there is need for planning the flow of funds for the smooth functioning of a project. A successful project is one which generates its own finances to a greater extent and finances its diversified activities. Internal resources will serve as a backbone of a project.

The generation of internal resources not only benefit the enterprise, but also the entrepreneur, shareholders and the society. Above all, a prudent of internal resources may also assist the natural growth of the capital market.

For a small-scale enterprise, internal generation of funds is a boon. These resources will net fixed capital requirements and short finance requirements to some extent. It helps modernisation, diversification and expansion of an enterprise. Besides, meeting financial requirements, retained earnings (Internal resources) reflect the solvency and the sound health of an enterprise.

Finance, which has been aptly described as the "life-blood" of industry, is a prerequisite for the mobilisation of real resources to organise production and marketing. Depending upon the nature of the activity to be financed, business requires short-term, medium-term and long-term finance.

Financial management is an integral part of industry and ranks equally in importance with other key components like production and marketing. Capital and finance form the bed rock foundation of industrial development. They are provided by a number of financial institutions. The saga of industrial development in the post-independence period is the story of these core institutions.

ANNEXURE I

FACILITIES FOR AND INCENTIVES TO SMALL-SCALE INDUSTRIES

Land	States develop industrial areas with infrastructure facilities and allot, sell or lease on a no-profit-no-loss basis with 10 per cent to 12 per cent down payment and the balance in instalments at low rates of interest.
Investment Subsidy	Investment subsidy, ranging between 10 per cent to 15 per cent, subject to a ceiling is granted to industries to be set in backward and tribal areas.
Interest Subsidy	Interest subsidy at different rates is granted to industrial units set up by educated self-employed, technocrats, engineers, craftsmen and artisans, subject to the capital investment not exceeding the limit set by the different States.
Power Tariff	A subsidy on electricity tariff for a period of 3 to 5 years is granted according to use and on certain terms and conditions. This is made available for certain types of units whose power constitutes a major item of production cost. The type of product produced is also taken into consideration while granting this subsidy.
Financial Assistance	States grant financial assistance by way of interest-free loans, sales tax loans and loans from State Financial Corporations. The amount of assistance varies according to the type of industry and is given against immovable property and personal security. Assistance to artisans and craftsmen ranges between Rs. 3,000, Rs. 5,000 and for others between Rs. 10,000 and Rs. 25,000 at an interest ranging between 7.5 per cent and 13.5 per cent. The repayment period is between 5 and 10 years or more. The grant of financial assistance depends on the type of industry, products produced and on merit.
Technical Assistance	The State's Directorate of Industries and the Industries Department provide technical guidance for the setting up and erection of machinery and also expansion. All possible technical assistance is given to new entrepreneurs.
Feasibility Study	For industries having definite prospects, State Governments, through their own agencies conduct feasibility studies free of cost up to Rs. 1000 or grant 50 per cent to 75 per cent subsidy for the preparation of feasibility reports. This cost is converted into the share capital of the Government.
Price Preference	State Government and Local Boards give a price preference of 15 per cent to 20 per cent over the prices offered for the products of large and medium industries in all government purchases and on products for a certain period provided the quality is on par with that of similar products of bigger units.

Others Octroi is exempted on capital equipment and raw materials for different periods for industries. Property tax is exempted for new industries for a certain period. Subsidy on transport cost and supply of water on a no-profit-no-loss basis. Housing schemes get 50 per cent loan and 25 per cent subsidy. Royalties on raw materials to Government considered on merit on an economic basis. Assistance to educated unemployed, engineers, technically qualified persons, etc., to set up own units.

QUICK GUIDE TO SOURCES OF FINANCE

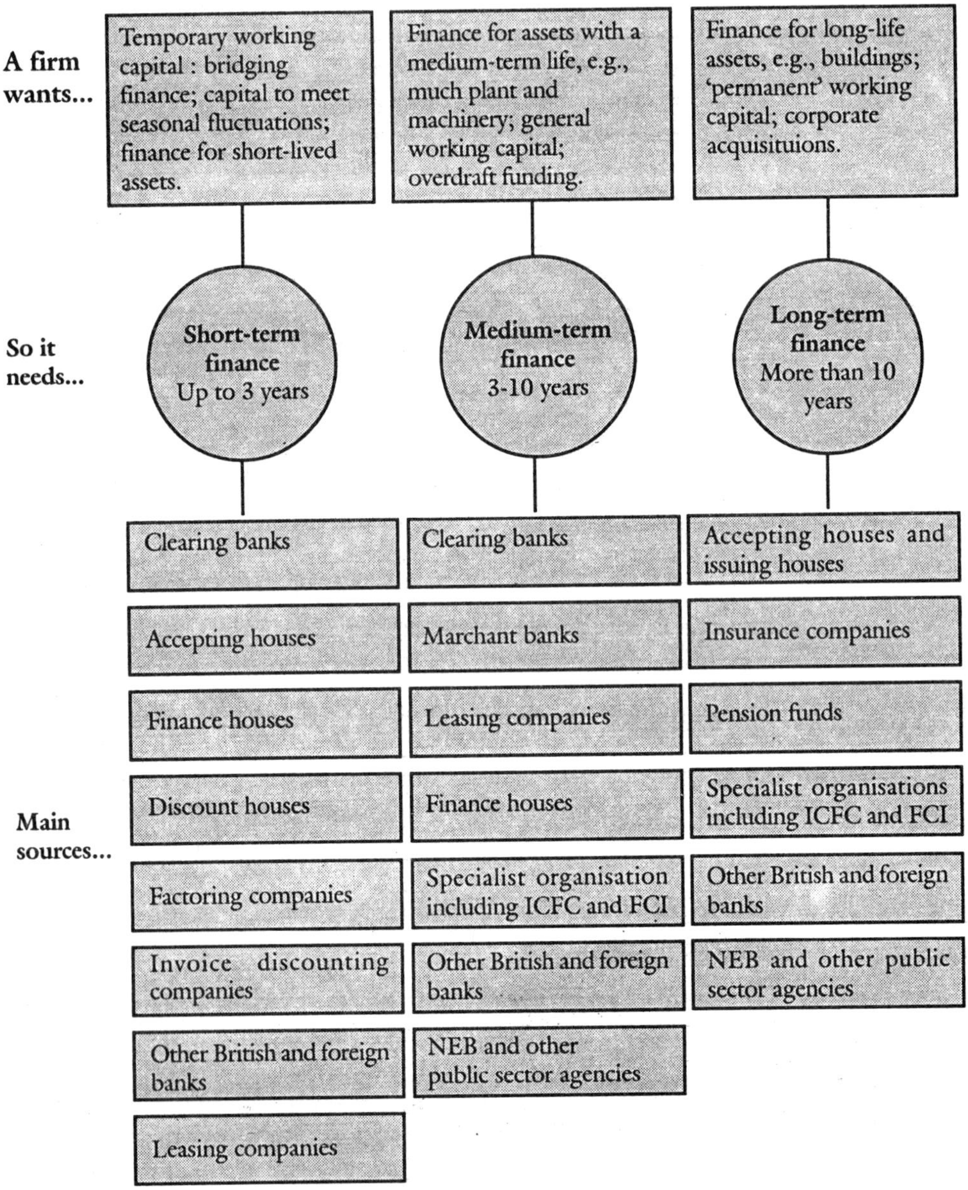

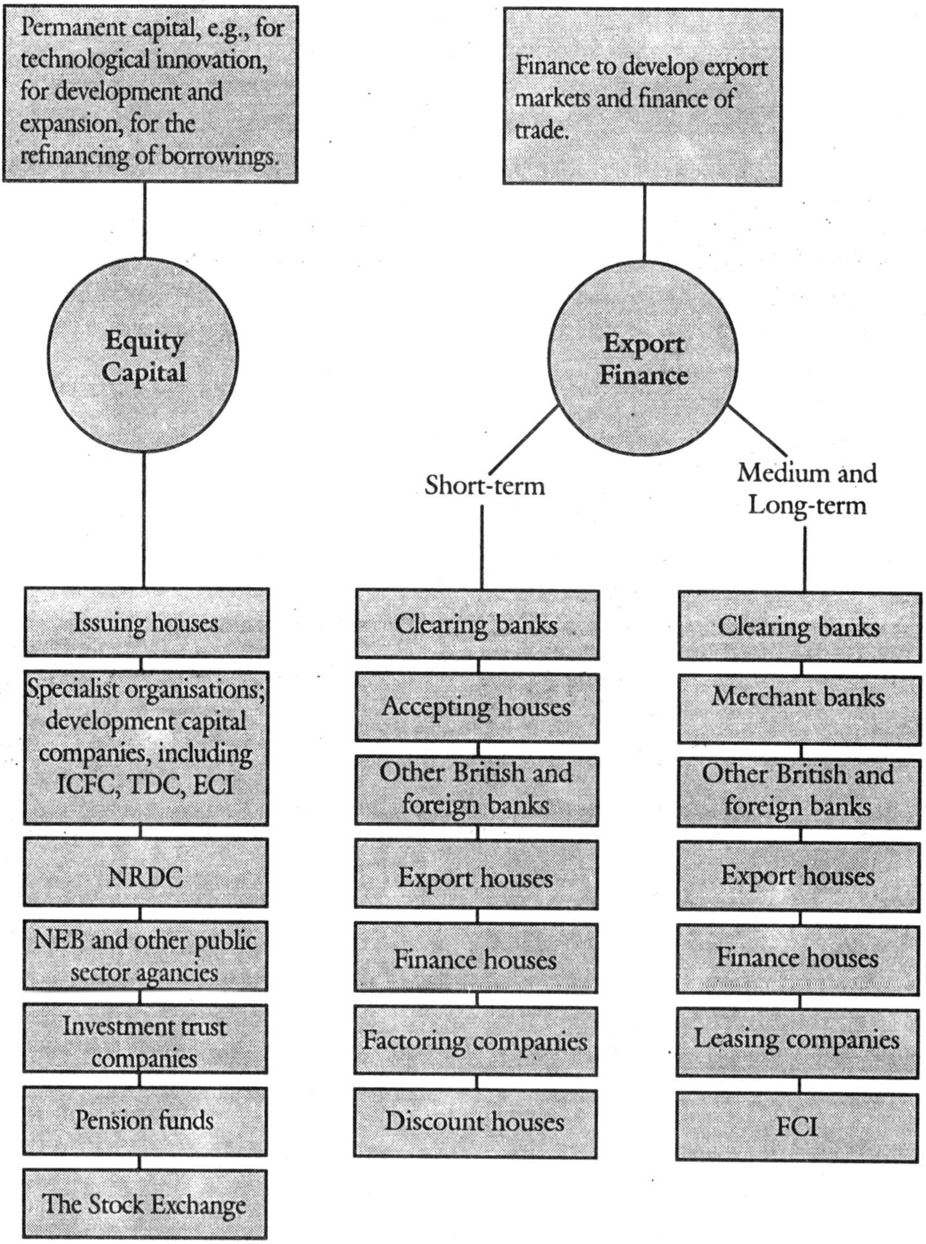
Permanent capital, e.g., for technological innovation, for development and expansion, for the refinancing of borrowings.
Equity Capital
Issuing houses
Specialist organisations; development capital companies, including ICFC, TDC, ECI
NRDC
NEB and other public sector agancies
Investment trust companies
Pension funds
The Stock Exchange
Finance to develop export markets and finance of trade.
Export Finance
Short-term
Clearing banks
Accepting houses
Other British and foreign banks
Export houses
Finance houses
Factoring companies
Discount houses
Medium and Long-term
Clearing banks
Merchant banks
Other British and foreign banks
Export houses
Finance houses
Leasing companies
FCI

Chapter - 8

PROJECT PLANNING

Introduction

Project planning is emerging as an important area of project management. Project planning will cover all aspects relating to an enterprise—a project. Broadly, planning implies comprehensive and co-ordinated activities in all facets of an enterprise and is aimed at the acceleration of development. Herein macro-and micro-planning are blended to ensure the success of the project. It, therefore, involve commitment at all levels to the development ideal. Project planning is a process involving the joint effort of a team of entrepreneurs, technicians and skilled workers. A planned project is a tool to achieve the objective of the project at a minimum cost.

Planning is essentially an intellectual process of careful thinking and analysis of facts, future trends and other related factors that go into the enterprise. The Haimann rightly observes, "Planning is the function that determines in advance what should be done. It consists of selecting the enterprise objective, policies, programmes, procedures and other means to achieve the enterprise objectives. It is looking ahead and preparing for the future."

Clearly, change can no longer be considered as an aberration.

In an age of perpetual change, planning presents a special problem for business. For example, how do you plan a product with a five-year lead time? And with markets changing and competition intensifying almost daily, how do you plan and develop systems to guide your company through the present and on to the 21st century?

Business's only answer is to plan for change as a way of life. Rather than making only occasional and drastic course corrections, business must now getout in front of the change curve and lead change rather than follow it. Business must invent a whole concept of itself. It must see itself not land bound by tradition and predetermined plans but rather flowing along with the river of change. It must work with nature, not against it. It must make progress by changing the very essence of the enterprise, by creating new opportunities and by creating its own future.

Having an effective plan for crisis is usually about 90 per cent of the solution to that crisis. But getting ahead of the change curve doesn't mean that business people must make advance plans for each an every contingency. You can go broke buying insurance. And you can paralyze an institution with too much planning.

Steps in Business Planning

The basic job of the entrepreneur is to conceive business visions and turn them into business realities. Vision has two parts. The first is the intuitive discovery of a potential business pattern—involving so called "right brain" activities. The second part of building a vision is the often tedious yet crucial work of business planning. In business planning, you convert your intuitive vision into an action plan. The two parts of vision cannot be done sequentially. The task alternates rapidly between the creative—thinking up ways the business could unfold—and the analytical—figuring out the concrete implication of the intuitive vision.

Business planning documenting as best as you can everything that is important to the business such as:

- Your destination.
- The strategies for getting there.
- Where you would like to be at specific times.
- The obstacles you may encounter.
- The approaches you plan to use in overcoming these obstacles.

Uses of a Business Plan

Many people think of a business plan as a tool for raising money or getting corporate approvals. Actually, its value as selling tool is a small part of the value of business planning. The benefits of the planning process include training yourself to become more entrepreneurial, screening your ideas, attracting a venture team, building team consensus as well as getting the money and permission to proceed.

BUSINESS PLAN OUTLINE

Cover Sheet

Name of business

Names of Principals

Address and telephone number of business

Statement of Purpose (Executive Summary)

Description of business—product of service

Business structure

Description of :

Amount of money being requested

How funds will be used

How funds will be repaid

Marketing Plan

The industry

Competition

Market size and opportunity

Market segments served

Marketing mix

Key factors to success in market

Financial Plan

Sources and application of funds

Capital equipment list

Balance sheet

Break-even analysis

Income statements

Pro-forma cash flow statements

Organizational Plan

Location of business

Organizational structure

Management

Non-management personnel

Summary

Application and expected effect of loans on business

Supporting Documents (as required)

Personnel resumes

Job descriptions

Credit reports

Letters of reference copies of contracts

Copies of leases

Copies of letters of intent

Legal documents

Production requirements

Source : Reprinted by permission of the publisher, from Robert D. Hisrich and Candida G. Brush, *The Women Entrepreneur: Starting, Financing, and Managing a Successful New Business* (Lexington, Mass: Lexington Books, D.C. Heath and Company, Copyright 1986), 64.

Right Thing at the Right Time

The Success of a small-scale industry solely depends upon one's doing the right thing at the right time. In other words, a small-scale industrialist has to be conversant with the varied regulations governing the small-scale industry and the procedures to be followed in order to acquire the necessary assistance and incentives offered by the government from time to time.

The procedural aspects of small-scale industry are quite formidable. Each and every entrepreneur is often overwhelmed by the multitude of procedures he has to face at every stage of the development of a small-scale industry. It is, therefore, necessary to emphasise here that the student should concentrate more on the purpose and the principles underlying the various forms, applications, etc.

In this chapter, the treatment of procedures—right from conceiving a small-scale industry until the repayments of creditors and ploughing back of profits—is based on the personal and practical experience of a small industrialist. In the latter part of the discussion, a reference has been made to the varied regulations that a small-scale industrialist has to abide by.

A discussion of the relevant procedures to be followed when setting up a small-scale industry has been dealt with reference to the various phases of its development. these phases are:

1. Selection of a small industry and preparation of feasibility and project reports;
2. Accommodation, power and other infrastructural facilities;
3. Machinery;
4. Raw Materials;
5. Finance;
6. Marketing; and
7. Securing various incentives offered for the establishment of small-scale industry.

Stated in simple terms, planning is a technique of organising, developing and controlling business activity in a systematic manner. But, surprisingly enough, we more often hear of conscious planning in social activities rather than in business life. In business/ industries, people are, by and large, hesitant to plan because of:

(a) The uncertainties inherent in the ever-changing economic environment which very often renders planning hazardous, if not meaningless;
(b) The lack of professional management;
(c) The tendency of businessmen to follow the rule-of-thumb methods; and
(d) The absence of a comprehensive and reliable management information system;

However, these are precisely the reasons which make the use of this technique imperative. Indeed, the greater the uncertainty, the greater is the need for planning and the benefits from planning would be extensive because an entrepreneur's response to change can be quicker. It is said: "today is the product of yesterday's decisions: and the future that we plan today affects the present."

Conscious planning is necessary for survival in industries in which capital commitments are heavy and financial risks high, and which necessitates heavy research and development expenditure in an environment of acute competition and fast changing market preferences and consumer tastes.

Technique of Planning

The technique of planning was first introduced by the multinational corporations as an instrument of management control and business development. As long as a business enterprise is small and manufactures only a few products for the limited and compact market with which it is familiar, it is possible for it to adapt itself to a change without much attention to planning, provided that the change is gradual. But when an institution grows into a multinational organisation, it is compelled to decentralise and delegate authority to branches and subsidiaries, and to operate on a system of remote control. With the rapid widening of the area of operations sectorally and spatially, in an ever-changing political, economic and social environment, intractable issues arise of co-ordination, control, decision-making and management.

What is Planning?

What, then, is planning? It is not an effort to predict results or to eliminate uncertainty. Broadly specking, it is an effort to develop and allocate financial and manpower resources as soundly as possible under certain conditions, and to be as well prepared as possible for the future. From this it is evident that planning must not be confused with prophecy or forecasting. Plans are certainly made in advance of an anticipated result. The fact that results cannot be guaranteed does not condemn planning or condone the failure of a plan. It is much more comprehensive than specific project planning. It involves nothing less than the total resources—financial and manpower of the small industries so that they may attain both short-term and long-term objectives. It involves a proper selection of objectives, strategies, policies, programmes and procedures. Above all it entails a consideration of the alternative to achieve the desired results. And this endevour becomes meaningful only if the planning and control processes are delegated downwards through all the levels of management to secure not only greater accuracy but, more importantly, personnel involvement and commitment all down the line.

In other words, a lack of understanding of, and confidence in plan among the line staff who are not closely associated with its preparation is bound to seal its fate in that it may not get off the ground. In such cases, pressures from top are of little avail. Planning is, therefore, much more than a mathematical exercise. It is a blueprint for action. It is a new technique of management, known as management by objectives, which calls for a complete change in the style of management, in the organisation structure and in information flow, combined with a complete change of attitude to people, to tasks, communications and control.

Types of Planning

Managerial plans are classified as follows:

1. *Objectives :* The objectives which an enterprise intends to achieve. Objectives are necessary for improving performance and to achieve good results.
2. *Policies :* Policies are a basic statement serving as a guide for planned action and implementation. They bring uniformity in decision-making.
3. *Procedures :* Procedures involve the selection of a course of action. They streamline of a course of action. They streamline activities and also help in control and co-ordination.
4. *Rules :* Rules are specific guideline for the enterprise. They also regulate and help in controlling the varied activities of the firm.
5. *Budgets :* Budget is a plan of action. It facilitates division of work and fixation of individual and divisional responsibilities. It also exercises economies of scale of operation of an enterprise.

6. *Programmes :* Programmes weld together different plans for implementing them into a complete and orderly course of action.
7. *Strategies :* Strategies may be regarded as a specific plan programme adopted in a competitive environment.

Phases of Planning

Corporate planning involves four main phases:

(i) Choice of definition of objectives and goals;

(ii) Preparation of operating plans for budgets to achieve these objectives, choice of a criterion that should be used for selecting a course of action in view of the significant, uncertain and multidimensional consequences;

(iii) Evolving strategies and taking strategic decisions in order to integrate these plans; and

(iv) Implementation.

The objective should preferably be measurable in value and time and described in terms of output—such as the expected rate of growth, profitability, return on investment, share of market and involvement in the socio-economic issues in accordance with public policy.

In arriving at a set of desired objectives a small-scale industry has to take into account several internal and external factors, to begin with, it must first decide where it is going; for unless it knows this , it cannot very well decide how to get there and know or evaluate the difficulties it is likely to encounter in reading its goal.

Situation Appraisal

A situation appraisal is concerned with an evaluation of the ability of a small-scale unit to perform the essential tasks of the business in which it wishes to specialise. It searches the whole spectrum of the small-scale industry to identify its strength and weakness in terms of opportunities and threats indicated by environmental analyses. Some major areas to be examined include management, organisation, lines of service, production schedules, geographic presence, pricing strategy, sales promotion and management, human resources and systems support. Each of these areas can be examined for efficiency, effectiveness, integration within the organisation, and the external image it would project of the unit.

A second aspect of a situation appraisal is an examination of the current financial performance of small industries. Each department and division must determine where it stands and how its position has been achieved. Data should first be collected on major categories of assets and liabilities, such as loans, deposits, total assets, earning assets and equity. The collection of data then leads to simple analytical measures, such as the rate of growth and stability to be achieved.

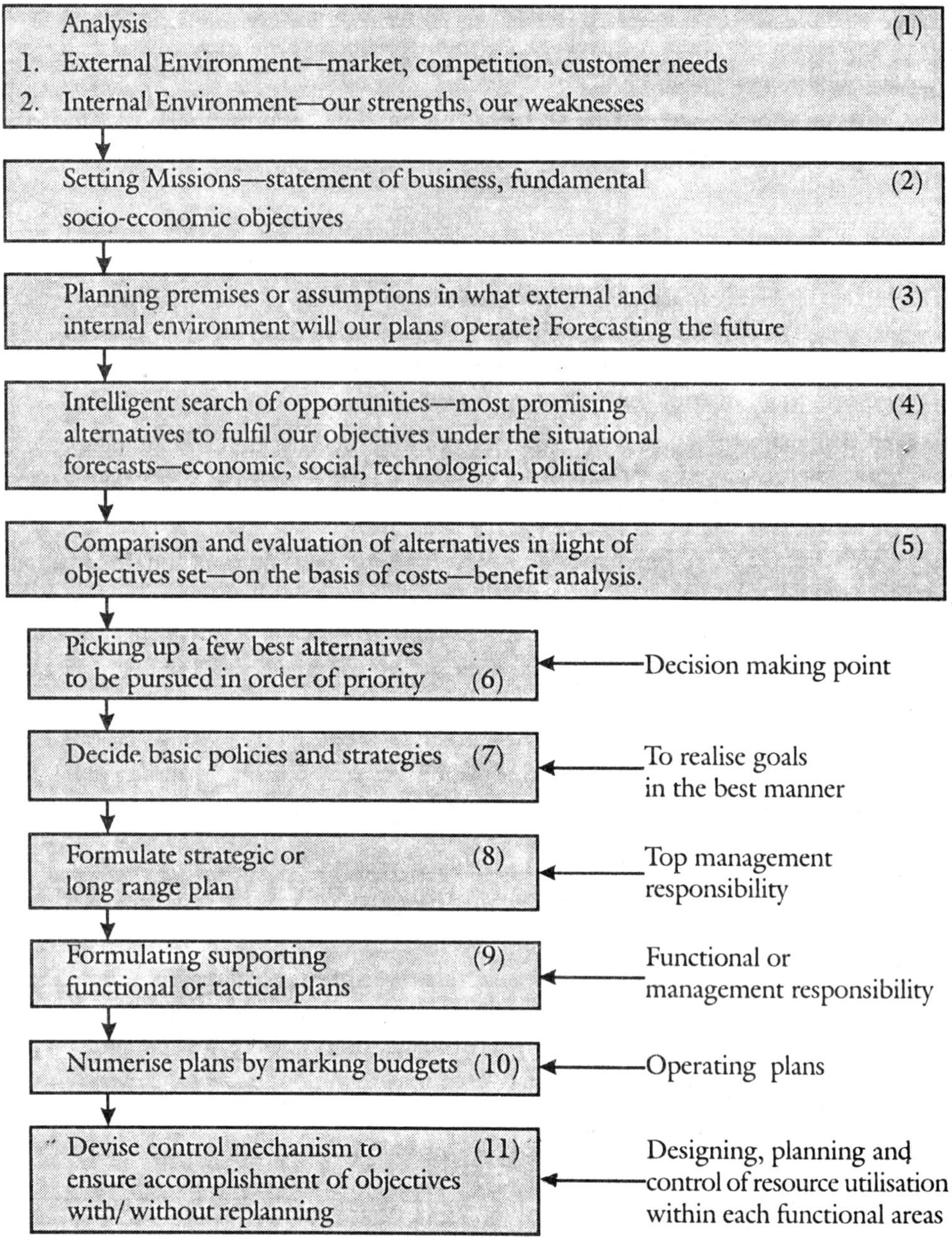

Fig. 8.1 : Steps in Project Planning Process.

(Planning is intelligent cooperation with the inevitable)

The next step is to develop market share for this purpose; it would be useful to build a comparative data base from a panel of small-scale industries considered to be competitive in various markets and products. The position of the small-sale industry in each major area for which financial objective have been stated is then compared with that of the small-scale industries in the panel for compound growth rates over the past five years. Such comparisons will indicate whether others in similar circumstances have been able to achieve the desired results, and whether the objectives are realistic.

On the completion of the environmental analysis and situation appraisal, the results should be assembled into a set of statements which describe the current position of a small-scale industry. It is now possible to study today's objectives and strategies as a major step in the process of translating the objectives and strategies which will guide the future development of small-scale industry.

Objectives and Strategies

The most critical and difficult task in planning is to establish objectives and strategies for the future. Strategic management, managing towards and by objectives, and strategies of the organisation—these are the new and dramatic developments in management and planning.

The establishment of objectives begins with an examination of the organisation as it exists, a statement identifying each major business and major market served, and a statement of the current objective and strategies of each unit. There is a natural tendency to follow organisational lines when working on this part of the task. Many a time, however an entirely different and revealing view results from stepping back and asking: How does the user of our services view us?

The basic value of management—how it views its customers, the competition it faces, Government regulations, how it deals with its employees, suppliers and others—determine the character and image of a small-scale industrial project. To the extent possible, the philosophy of management ought to be stated explicitly and incorporated in the internal planning literature at this point.

A capsule statement of current corporate strategies for each of the major business should be prepared for the guidance of executive management. It is important that members of the management agree on major thrusts of policy. For example, if executive management has not agreed on a location strategy, every proposal for a new location must be examined and evaluated as an entirely new decision.

An examination of its strengths and weaknesses, its opportunities and the threats it faces would probably uncover some core problems which need to be attacked by the management—for example, the need to establish a consistent pricing policy for all the customers or the means of payment for services rendered.

The identification of these core problems and the assignment of responsibilities for their solution are important at this point in the planning process. The next step in establishing objectives and strategies is to formulate existing objectives into a concise and consistent set of statements covering at least the financial and market position and public responsibility. These statements, communicated to every executive in the organisation and applied to daily activities, become powerful guiding forces for the small-scale industrial unit.

The time has now come to assemble the statement of the environmental analysis and situation appraisal as well as statements of current objectives, strategies and categories of corporate objectives for the future.

The statement of objectives for the future begins with a statement of mission, which provides a most important guidance mechanism, clearly delineating the fundamental business and thrust of the small-scale industry relating to the various stages of production and aspects of marketing.

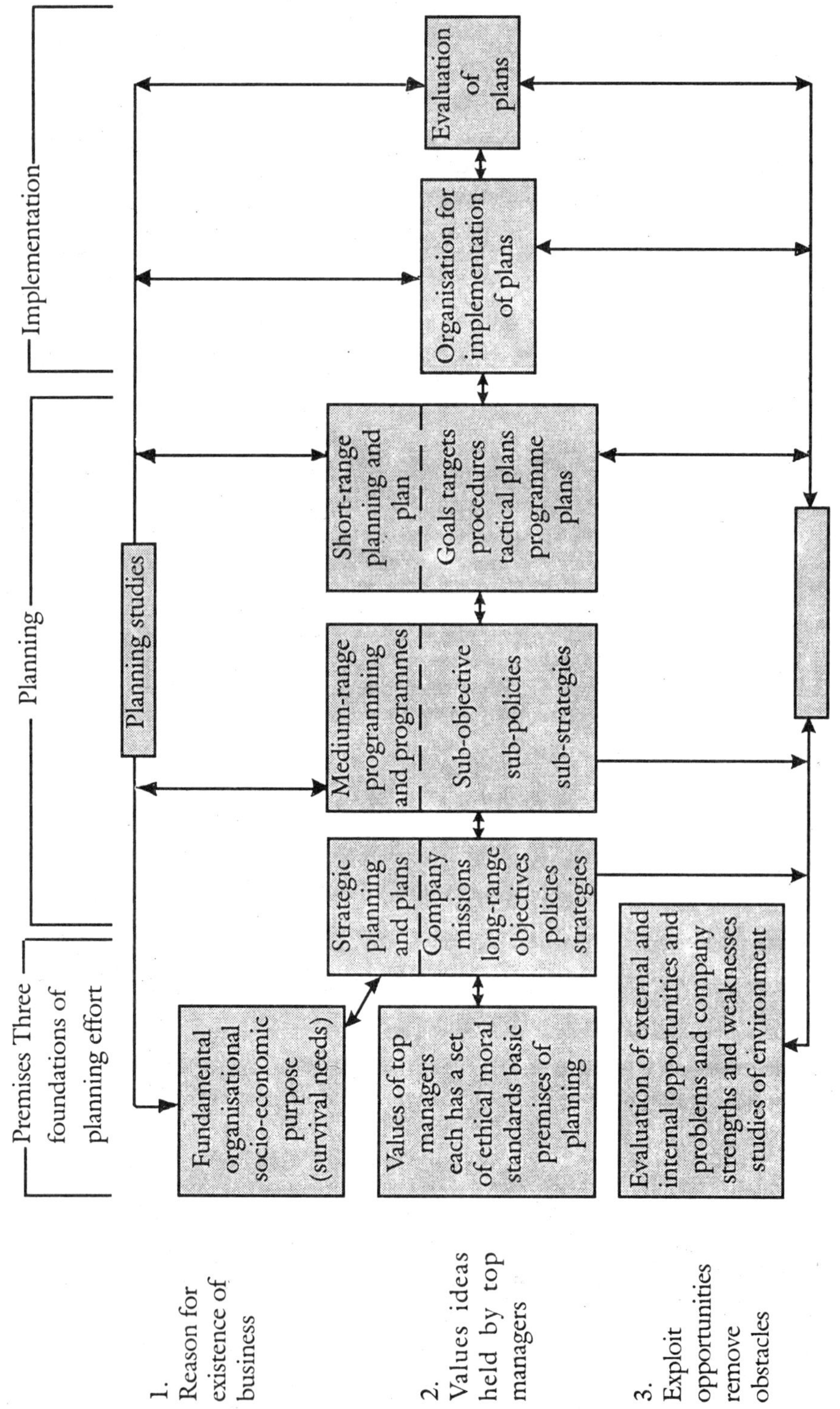

Fig. 8.2 : Structure and Process of Business Planning

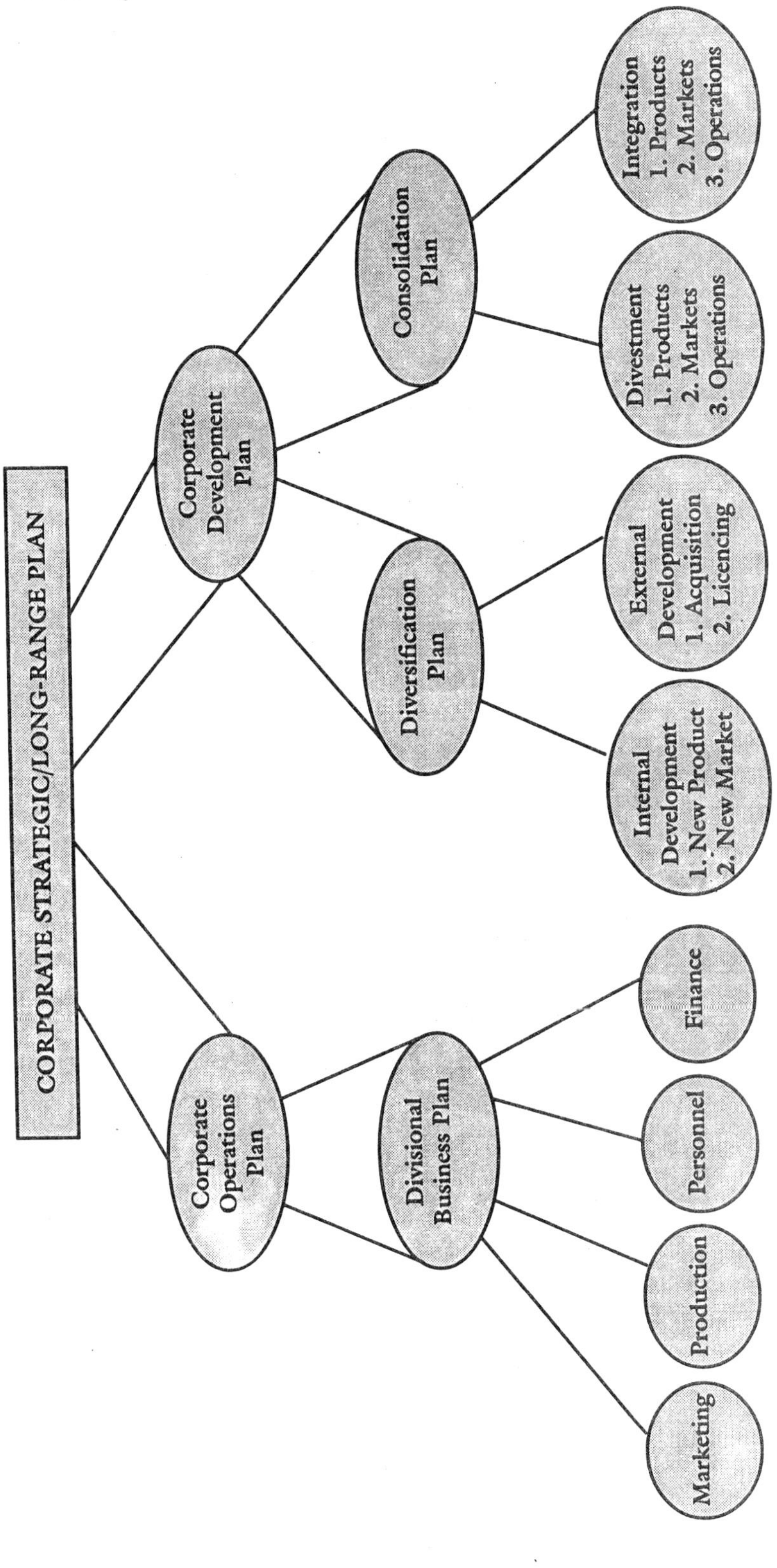

Fig. 8.3 : Structure of Corporate Planning

Each time the planning process is undertaken, important business, principle markets and management philosophy should be re-examined in detail and restated. This exercise provides an opportunity for the management to reevaluate its position and achieve a new commitment to principles. In addition, the new members of the management will want to approve these statements or suggest modifications in emphasis.

The new statement of objectives identifies the goal of the corporation and embodies the design and ambitions of the executive management. As such, the management notifies everyone of its members of the kind of corporate performance it expects of them.

Action Plans

The final step is to convert strategies into action plans, to be undertaken by the line organisation. The action plans should be communicated to the organisation through assignments that identify specific projects, short-term goals, requirements and time or period of their accomplishment.

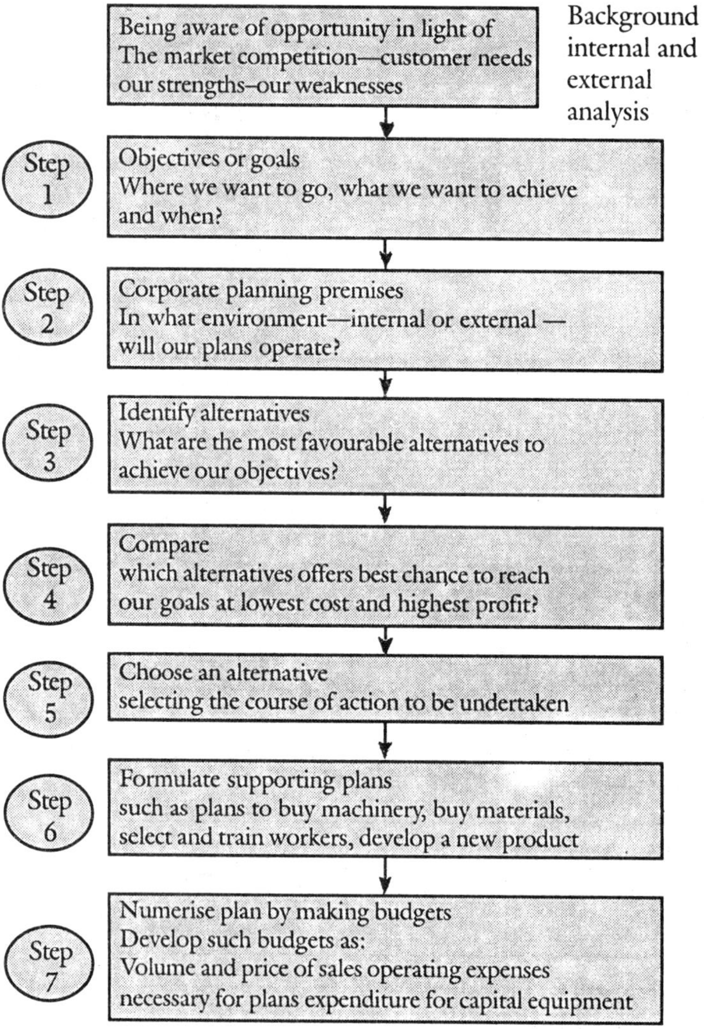

Fig. 8.4 : Steps in Planning (Kontz and O' Donnell: Management).

Note :

1. Planning is simply a rational approach to the accomplishment of an objective.
2. The planning process is similar to the procedure of decision-making through scientific analysis and investigation of problems and/or opportunities.
3. Planning is fundamentally choosing, and in this sense, it is essentially decision-making.
4. Planning is deciding in advance what to do, how to do it, when to do it and who is to it.
5. Planning bridges the gap between where we are and where we want to go.

Action plans result in very specific resource allocations, which may be quantified through a budget. A budget is detailed schedule of expected income and expenses and expresses financial and profitability goals for the first year of an action plan. It is prepared by profit and cost centres, the lowest organisation level in planning. The budget that flows from an action plan provides the link between the long-tern, strategic, managerial type of planning and the specific quantitative budgeting or profit planning for the year ahead.

In addition to management direction, action plans and budgets provide specific emphasis on activities that can be used to monitor performance. The measurement of variance from the budget provides the basis for a periodic review of progress towards goals and objectives.

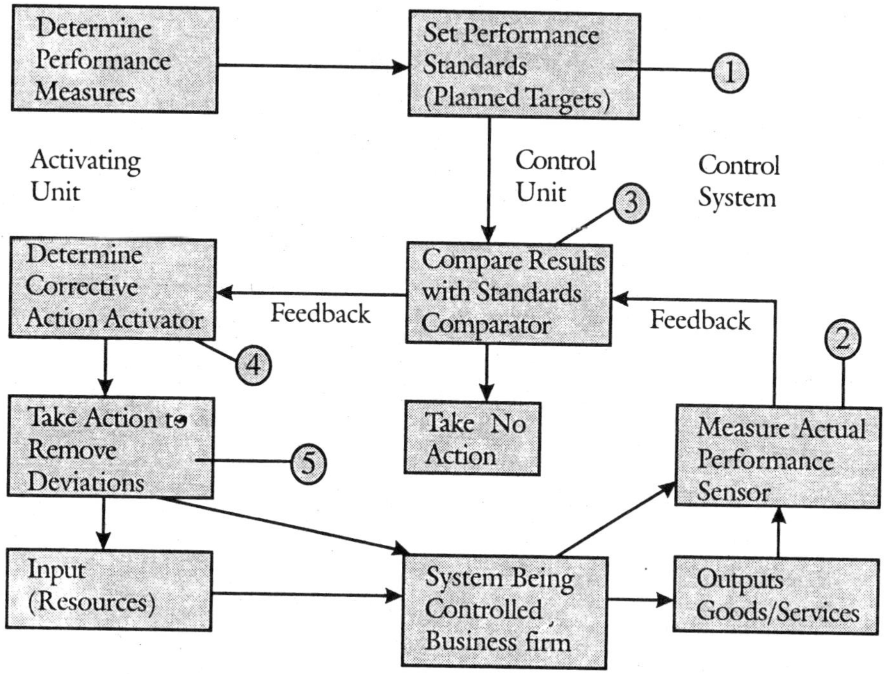

Fig. 8.5: Operating System

The essence of control is the ability to establish standards of performance for each organisational unit. Standards are developed from the sequential steps stated as part of the action plan and from the quarterly and annual targets in budgets and strategies. Performance can be measured against these standards and corrective action undertaken.

Tracking the performance is difficult because of the assumed condition underlying the action plan budget changes, and because the manager adjusts himself to match current conditions. Sometimes, organisational changes cause difficulties, when new managers are assigned to problems or reaping benefits not of their planning. To track the performance accurately, a sophisticated, flexible accounting system is needed to keep up with all the changes in plans.

First, control calls for the setting up of a plan, budget, a target, an objective, a standard—an aim to be achieved. You cannot have control without having a plan. That target may be the given of sales or production, a cost standard, a defined level of quality, or any other measurable attribute. Control implies measurement; you cannot control that which cannot be measured.

The second essential feature is communicating the plan to those concerned with implementing it or initiating the necessary action on it. It is self-evident that if the members of the team don't know where the goalposts are, they cannot be blamed for not scoring the goals. Yet this aspect of control is probably the most neglected in practice.

Third, there must be a means of monitoring the actual achievement, quantified in apportpiate units, whether these are monetary values or physical quantities.

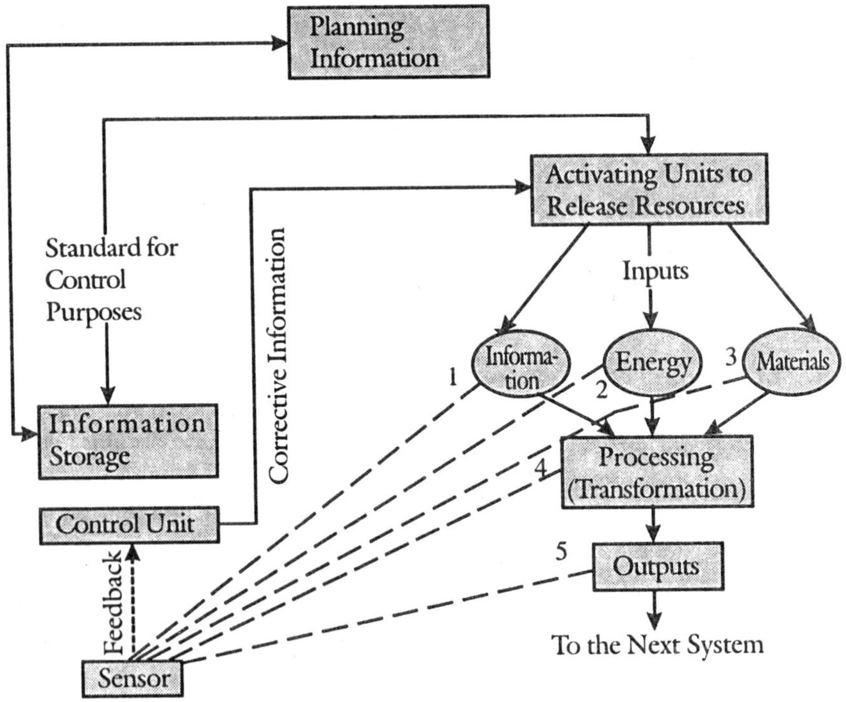

Fig. 8.6 : Flow of Planning and Controlling Information in a System

Note: Sensory devices to measure performance output are placed at five strategic points in the system flow to measure performance or output. The sensor date from these five points as shown by the five doted lines. The control unit, on the basis of feedback compares the actual performance with the standards laid down. Information to correct deviations is given to the activating units which make corrections.

In operation and control, input are inputs of information (for example, customer data, prices, discounts, delivery dates), inputs of energy (energy exerted by workers or energy used to operate machines), or inputs or materials (raw materials, invoice forms).

A computer is at present looking after the management information system. Management can now get a great deal of information very quickly.

The fourth essential stage of control consists in comparing the actual achievement with the target, uncovering any variances and identifying their cause or causes.

Finally, control implies that, in the light of the information uncovered, appropriate action is taken to rectify the situation or to adjust the standard, if necessary.

This simple, five-step procedures is widely accepted by many managers and has become most second nature with the management of progressive firms.

There are many managers, however, particularly in small firms, who have no inkling of the nature and purpose of control. In principle, there is much in common between management control and servocontrol mechanism in engineering, or a control device such as a thermostat. The function of a thermostat is to maintain the temperature at a predetermined level—the target. It monitors the actual temperature, compares this information with the standard taken, then takes an appropriate action by switching the source of health on or off. However, a big difference between the thermostat and the management control system is that the latter is prone to human error at all stages. The target may be ill-defined; communication may be imperfect or even omitted; the measurement of actual achievement may be inaccurate; the causes of the variance may be wrongly defined; or the management may take in appropriate action or no action at all.

The Enterprise Development Centre

The integrated method for facilitating the formation of new enterprises is known as the enterprise development centre. This brings together the key input face to face with the new generation entrepreneurs. It comprises four principal components, viz.: (1) the intrapreneurship centre; (2) the venture capital exchange; (3) the innovation centre; and (4) the incubation centre.

The intrepreneurship centre researches, creates skills, environment to facilitate the setting up of new enterprises.

The venture capital exchange provides the needed seed capital for new enterprises.

The innovation centre provides technological evaluation, entrepreneurial assessment, project planning, evaluation, commercial feasibility studies, the product development assistance to entrepreneurs.

There are five control points in the diagram, the final one measuring the output itself. Other control points measure resources and processing. A sensor is a unit for measuring performance or result.

The incubation centre provides the needed impetus to new enterprises to succeed and grow.

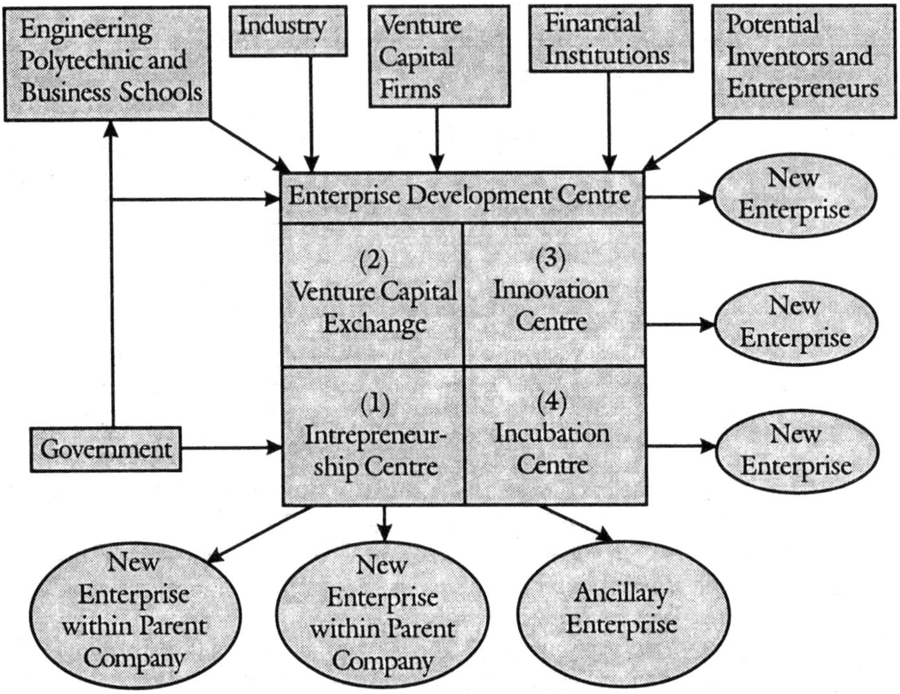

Fig. 8.7 : The Enterprise Development Centre

Feasibility Report

Before starting a small-scale industry, one should consult the Director of Industries and the Small Industries Service Institute (SISI) located in one's State. The SISI guides entrepreneurs as to the type of industry to start, where to start and how to start it. The SISI helps them to select the various items of manufacture which have scope for development in difference areas. It suggests the lines on which project reports for the purposed units should be prepared for the consideration of various financial institutions with a view to securing financial assistance. Similarly, technical guidance in the selection of proper raw materials and type of machinery is also provided. Apart from this, the SISI gives valuable information on the various incentives available to the small-scale industries from various organisations.

Project Feasibility Analysis

A project feasibility analysis includes market analysis, technical analysis, financial analysis and social profitability analysis. Although every feasibility analysis is different and is tailored to suit the product, its goal is to identify the strengths and weaknesses of the project.

The starting point of a project analysis is the establishment of the objectives to be attained. The next stage is the preselection stage—the advisability of having an in-depth study. The analysis stage consists mainly of three factors—market, technical and financial analysis: A market analysis is a method of screening project ideas as well as a means of evaluating a project feasibility in terms of the market. A market analysis should cover the following areas:

(i) A brief description of the market, including the market area, methods of transportation, existing rates of transport, channels of distribution, and general trade practices.

(ii) An analysis of past and present demand, including the determination of quantity and the value of consumption, and identification of the major consumers of the product.

(iii) An analysis of past and present supply, broken down as to the source (whether imported or domestic), as well as information which will assist in determining the competitive position of the product, such as the selling prices, quality and marketing practices of the competitors.

The technical analysis of a project feasibility study establishes whether the project is technically feasible or not, and whether it offers a basis for the estimation of costs. Moreover, it provides an opportunity for the consideration of the effect of various technical alternatives on employment, ecology, infrastructure demands, capital services, support of other industries, balance of payments, and other factors. A technical analysis should contain a review of the techniques or processes to be applied and should incorporate:

(i) A description of the product, including specifications relating to its physical, mechanical and chemical properties, as well as the uses of the product.

(ii) A description of the selected manufacturing process, showing detailed flow charts and presenting the alternative processes which may have been considered and the justification for the adotion of the selected process.

(iii) A determination of the plant size and production, schedule, which includes the expected volume for a given time period on the basis of start-up and technical factors.

(iv) Selection of a machinery and equipment including specifications, equipment to the purchases and its origins, quotations from suppliers, delivery dates, terms of payment, and a comparative analysis of alternatives in terms of cost, reliability, performance, and spare parts availability.

(v) An identification of plant's location and an assessment of its desirability in terms of its distance from raw material sources and markets. For a new project, this part may include a comparative study of different sites, indicating the advantages and disadvantages of each.

(vi) A design of the plant layout and an estimate of the cost of the erection of the proposed buildings and land improvements.

(vii) A study of the availability of raw materials and utilities, including a description of physical and chemical properties, quantities needed, current and prospective costs, terms of payment, location of sources of supply, and continuity of supply.

(viii) An estimate of labour requirements, including a detailed breakdown of direct and indirect labour requirements, and the supervision required for the manufacture of the product.

(ix) A determination of the type and quantity of waste to be disposed of, together with a description of the waste disposal method, its costs, and the necessary clearance from proper authorities.

(x) An estimate of the production cost of the product.

In the financial analysis of a project feasibility study, the emphasis is on the preparation of financial statements, so that the project may be evaluated in terms of the different measures of commercial profitability and the magnitude of financing required may be determined. The financial analysis required the assembly of the market and technical cost estimated in various performa statements. If it is necessary to have more information on which to base an investment decision, a sensitivity analysis or, possibly, a risk analysis may be conducted. The financial analysis should include:

(i) For all projects that involve new companies, statements of total project cost, initial capital requirements, and cash flows reactive to the projet time-table.

For all projects, financial projections for future time periods, including income statements, cash flow, and balance sheets.

(ii) For all projects, supporting schedules for financial projection, stating the assumption made as to the collection period of sales, inventory levels, payment period of purchases and expenses, and the element of production cost, selling, administrative and financial expenses.

(iii) For all projects, a financial analysis showing returns on investments, returns on equity, break-even volume, and precise analysis.

(iv) For all projects, if necessary, a sensitivity analysis to identify items which have a substantial impact on profitability or possibly a risk analysis.

For the small entrepreneur, the studies conducted during the analysis stage of the project provide the material for an assessment. If positive results are obtained, the entrepreneur, in seeking finance, will want to prepare an investment proposal. The planners or government officials, however, having obtained positive conclusions from the economic feasibility study, will want to evaluate the element of social profitability.

The purpose of the investment or loan application is to convince a lender (financial institution) that the project is a desirable investment; that it not only possesses the potential for profit but that the proposed management team has the capability to achieve the potential. The investment proposal normally contains:

(i) General information on the product, company history, the nature of the industry and the reputation and qalitifications of the existing or proposed management.

(ii) A description of the project, which usually consists of extracts from economic feasibility studies and includes information on such items as market, production, selected manufacturing methods (with detailed indication of the cost of equipment and operational expenses), and a financial statement.

(iii) Miscellaneous information, such as the steps taken for the implantation of the project and the qualifications of the technical partners envisaged or selected.

Once the industry is identified, the SISI prepares a feasibility report and project report, giving one a comprehensive idea of an industry's prospects and productivity.

Profiteering

Profiteering as an economic function, has to be understood as a concept distinct from profit. Profit, as enunciated by Pigou, is a particular species of monetary gain—a monetary gain secured in a particular way. To make a profit, in the sense relevant here—implies performing a middleman's or an entrepreneur's function, hiring the services of other men or buying goods from other men, and selling the products or the goods and obtaining, as a reward, the difference between outlay and receipt.

If the difference exceeds a socially acceptable limit, and that by questionable methods, it is a case of profiteering.

For the purpose of a realistic economic analysis we have to shelve the principle governing perfect market competition, and have to reckon with the forces of imperfect competition, duopoly, monosony and oligopoly, monopolistic competition and black market.

Before we analyse the economic process of profit-making and, in that context, the theory of maximisation, and finally of profiteering, it is necessary to appreciate that it would no longer suffice to assume merely that the demand and supply curves exist, and that some are elastic and some inelastic, or that some rise and some fall. If we do not so appreciate it, we shall reduce the study of economic phenomena of today's market situation to the simplicity of the concept of bilateral trade.

The assumption of perfect competition on which much of the supply and demand analysis is based must also be scrutinised. Perfect competitions is rare—and, in a real sense, does not exist anywhere outside the imagination of the economists. Over large areas of economic life, other systems of market relationships are of great importance.

Let us first indicate the principle of the profit-making process in a market of imperfect competition, as was done by the post-Chamberlain economists. Very briefly, the profit-making under imperfect market conditions is determined by what is called the dynamics of a marketer.

In the marketing of a product or a service, the larger the savings in a profitable succession of transformations of the product or the service (or in short, the investment), the greater the total profit.

But this is not all. The play of these savings is restricted, or even determined, by the nature and extent of market imperfection and the presence and delineation of risks and uncertainty.

According to the theory of profit optimisation, marginal conditions in the market will lead to optimisation of production in relation to its total marketable cost components, so that the maximum average revenue for minimum average cost is achieved. In any case, this will be one of the ends of the economic functions of a marketer under imperfect competition in his endeavour to optimise profit.

Profit maximisation, or profiteering, is conditioned by the "principle of increasing risk and uncertainty", as Kalechi calls it. With an increase in the potential of risks on the investment co-efficient, profits will increase or decrease to the extent of the risk that is taken.

In the long run, a small industry can survive only if it can make enough profit to pay a return on the capital after making adequate and necessary provisions. Profit, is the outcome of the operations of all small-scale industries and, in the ultimate analysis, of profit planning. Profit can be expressed as an earning per share, a return on the capital employed or a return on a shareholder's capital. There are difficulties in expressing all the three and in making comparison with the competitors in the field.

It has now been recognized that the old theory of profit maximisation is not strictly valid in the resent-day Indian context because of the developmental role which the small-scale industry is called upon to play in the context of its socio-economic obligations, although in the long run it has to be a profitable proposition if it has to survive in the fiercely competitive world of today. The central objective, therefore, should be a judicious combination of profit with achievements on the socio-economic front. Some economists refer to this as profit with growth. For our purpose, we shall assume that what small-scale industries are primarily striving for is improved profitability rather than maximisation of profit as an end in judicious combination of profit with achievements on the socio-economic front. Some economists refer to this as profit with growth. For our purpose, we shall assume that what small-scale industries are primarily striving for is improved profitability rather than maximisation of profit as an end in itself.

Operational guidelines form the basis or the cornerstone of an operational plan to be formulated at the branch level, or what is known as the performance budget. The final operational plan that emerges from the aggregation of the performance budgets of the various branches should give a clear picture of what the small-scale industry is expected to become in terms of assets and liabilities, revenue and expense, at the end of the period under review, supplemented by a statement of cash flow.

Implementation of Plans

Plans have no meaning if they are not implemented. Control, therefore, becomes an integral part of the planning process; and for control to be effective, the management should constantly know in an organised and systematic manner, how closely the action follows the plan, and to do whatever is needed to bring performance in line and with the plan. It is the variance from the plan which signals the need for corrective action; and this ought to be achieved through an efficient system of management information and monitoring of feedback information.

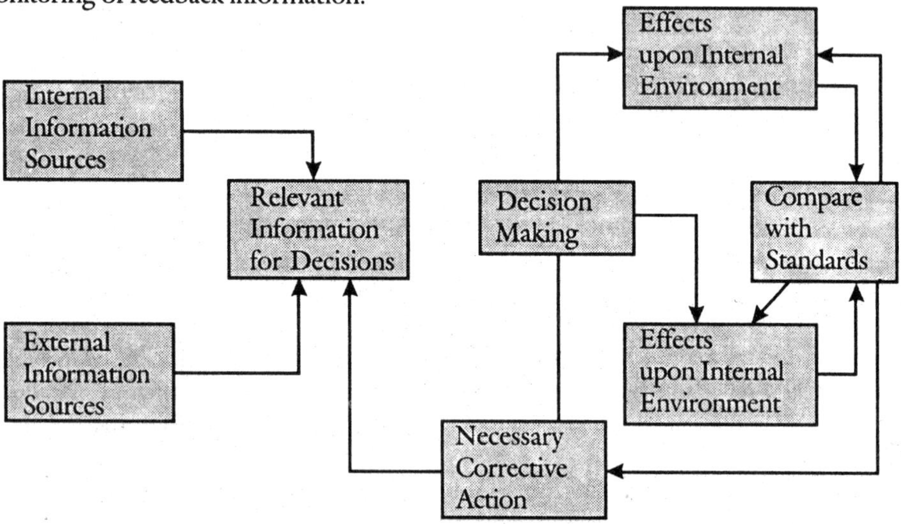

Fig. 8.8 : Basic Components of Management Information Systems

Notes :

1. Management Information System (MIS) is federation of sub-systems whatever is needed to bring performance in line and with the plan. It is the variance from the plan which signals the need for corrective action; and this ought to be achieved through an efficient system of management information and monitoring of feedback information.

In other words, corporate planning combines in the systematic, integrated and formal way, strategic, technical operational and projects planning over a period of years. It has often been described as a co-ordinated and cohesive set of strategic, technical and operational guidelines" or decision rules, quantified, as far as possible, in financial tems, by which an organisation seeks to attain its short and long-term objectives within the limits of its available and, one might add, "attainable" resources. Corporate planning is scientific because it defines and quantifies objectives. The results are reviewed periodically, and timely remedial action is taken if and when called for.

Management planning, on the other hand, falls into three distinct types of planning activities:

(a) Strategic planning for deciding long-term objectives—to be done by the corporate management (in the case of a small-scale industry, it is done by the entrepreneur or the proprietor);

(b) Action planning for achieving a qualified level of performance during the strategic plan period–to be done by the executive management (in the case of a small-scale industry, action plans are prepared for production, sales, finance and profitability);

(c) Operational planning for developing performance targets for a much shorter period, usually one year, in order to provide effective tools for management control–to be done in consultation with the operating management, i.e., the marketing department, the finance section, etc.

Here some very valid questions arise:

(i) How much do we change our style of management to enable every level of management—indeed, every member of the staff to contribute?

(ii) Is the organisational structure appropriate to the objectives? Will it stand the typical stresses and strains, and does it offer maximum freedom and flexibility in which one may perform? Are reponsibility areas clearly defined in realistic and workable manner in accordance with the need for the generation of revenue and/or expenses?

(iii) Is the formation structure appropriate, and does the revenue and/or expense reporting system follow responsibility areas so that managers may measure their performance and judge and control themselves?

(iv) Is there a fair basis for fixing the prices for the transfer of services and funds among the different responsibility areas?

These are vital matters involving a great deal of work, the implications of which cannot be considered here.

Planning Machinery

A word about the planning machinery. Planning is not the task of a functional department; it must be initiated at the top (small entrepreneur) and is an important part of every "line" manager's job. The planning staff is not paid to do the "line" manager's thinking; its function is advisory—analysing opportunities, studying the effects of environments, and coordinating. It may sometime be more important that they know a lot about planning than a lot about the technical aspects of a small-scale industry. They help to set up a decision-making process, but do not take the decisions. The planner is a kind of a pilot aboard a ship; he does not decide the destination; but he helps to set the course which the master of the vessel has decided upon.

Conclusion

Planning is a primary function of entrepreneurial management. It is a bridge between the present and the future. It gives entrepreneurs some purpose, objectives, programme direction towards the goals. Planning is deciding in advance what is to be done. It is primarily concerned with looking into the future, involving the selection of and the best alternative.

Planning is a best tool for small-scale enterprises to look into the future and meet the challenges and emerge victorious in milieu. Planning is, therefore, the first and primary function of small-scale entrepreneurs. Thus, planning logically precedes the execution of all other functions of an enterprise.

The process of planning helps the small-scale entrepreneur to regulate his production, sales and administrative cost, and to maximise his profit. The perspective outlook is a lever for efficient management and lays down a strong foundation for accelerated growth. Further, it enables the entrepreneur to plan for the expansion of his unit.

Chart
System of Policy Measures to Promote the Use of Information Systems

	(Survey-Studies)	Research on the development of new small and medium retail businesses Research on the wider use of microcomputers (Institute of the Japan Small Business Corporation).
	(Training-Activities) Preparations	Training activities on information processing and related matters (Institute of the Japan Small Business Cooperation) Facilities for training (Institute of the Japan Small Business Corporation)
1. Promotion of the use of computers by small and medium firms	(Consultation, Guidance)	Consultation to promote the introduction of computers OA System Center for Small and Medium Enterprises
	(Development of Technology)	Activities to promote the use of information systems in small and medium firms (Subsidies from the Information-Technology Promotion Agency, Japan)
		Research on the program of small and medium firms. Development of a general-purpose program for small and medium firms. Technology development for the uses of computers in small and medium firms.
	(Promotion of the introduction of equipment and programs)	Activities to lease computer equipment (Structural strengthening). System of program credit insurance. Loans for the modernization of equipment of smaller enterprises (Applied to the acquisitions of computers).

Chart (Contd.)

2. Establishment of an Information Service System	(Small Business Information Center) (Small and Medium Enterprise Regional Information Centers)	Collection and dissemination of information Establishment of information activity system of Regional Information Centers
	(Local Public bodies)	Research on regional information network systems of small and medium enterprises
	(Promotion Centers of Local Industries)	Activities to upgrade information functions Activities to Collect and disseminate information
3. Establishment of intensive information system in guidance organisations	(Small and Medium Enterprise Agency), Bureau of International Trade and Industry (Comprehensive Guidance Center) (Federations of Small Business Associations)	Commission on payment monitoring system to subcontractors Installation of Computers (15 Stations) Model Federation of intensive information operations (one federation)
	(Societies of Commerce and Industry, Chambers of Commerce and Industry) (Association for Subcontracting Enterprises Promotion)	Commission on research to develop an information processing system for the management of small-scale Firms Expenses to promote Computerisation of book-keeping. Rental fee of OA Equipment

Chapter - 9

FEASIBILITY STUDIES

Introduction

Some of the principal lessons that the World Bank has learned in assisting its member countries in managing their investment resources are offered not in the belief that they provide final answers to the formidable problems of development, but in the conviction that better national investment planning, macroeconomic and sector policies, and project work can ease the path of development, bring its benefits to people sooner, and distribute them more equitably.

Throughout the several stages of the project cycle, various dimensions of project work are addressed, both separately and in relation to each other, and in varying degrees of detail.

Technical Analysis

Of these dimensions, technical analysis is perhaps the most familiar. Among the issues of technical design are size, location, timing, and choice of a technology package. We have already alluded to the need to select a technology appropriate to the circumstances of the country and the requirements of the project. The point bears repeating in any list of lessons. "Appropriateness" is a relative concept. It generally means that the technology should be determined in relation to the objectives of the project, to the impact on intended beneficiaries, and to local conditions, including the availability and cost of capital, raw materials, and labour, the size of markets, and the present and potential capacity for planning and implementation.

Numerous tradeoffs are implicit in these considerations: for example, the technology may often have to be reduced in complexity to fit the capabilities of local institutions or the socio-cultural traditions of the beneficiaries. The range of choice is very wide, from sophisticated, high technology for long-distance telecommunications even in the least developed countries. Whatever the choice, it is important that it not be unduly biased by government interventions or price distortions of the kind referred to earlier.

Technical analysis also provides an opportunity to consider how a country can best take advantage of its investment plan, policy framework, and development projects to build a capacity to use science and technology effectively throughout the economy. Both trained people and institutions capable of utilizing their skills are required. In the early stages of a country's development, the emphasis should be on building local capacity to import technology from abroad knowledgeably and to adapt it to local conditions. At later stages, the emphasis should shift to the development of local technology and its integration with imported technology, and to the encouragement of local research and innovation.

Economic Analysis

The basic question that economic analysis addresses is how to allocate scarce resources among many competing uses. It seeks to determine not only whether a project can be expected to provide a satisfactory return to the economy, but also whether there is an alternative way of achieving the same objectives that would offer a higher return. The analysis entails a comparison of costs and benefits with and without the project, both discounted to present values, through the use of analytical techniques that by now are highly refined — though no more accurate than the underlying data. Its central concept — that, for purposes of economic analysis, resources should be valued in terms of their opportunity cost to the economy in their best alternative use — is applicable to all economic systems, whether market-oriented, centrally planned, or a combination of the two.

Most lending agencies use cost-benefit analysis to assess the projects they help finance, and many developing countries are applying this analysis in one form or another to projects that they fund from public resources. Private industrial enterprises also use cost-benefit analysis for major investments. If done properly, it can be a powerful tool for guiding investment choices.

Cost-benefit analysis encounters some practical problems, among them: how to define the situation "with" and "without" the project (which should not be confused with the situation "before" and "after" the project); how to handle sunk costs incurred before the analysis (the short answer is to disregard them); how to establish the shadow (that is, opportunity) prices for labour and capital, when market prices are distorted for various reasons; and how to deal with nonquantifiable benefits. For most of these problems of definition or measurement, reasonable approaches can be found that are consistent with the reliability of the available data. The results of the analysis can be presented as a measure of net present value, as an internal rate of return, or as a cost-benefit ratio; each has its particular uses.

Not all types of projects are amenable to cost-benefit analysis; it is not customarily used, for example, in evaluating education or health projects. Nor does it have the same meaning in different sectors. In power and water, for example, where prices are publicly administered rather than fixed by the marketplace, the economic rate of return is a minimum estimate, more indicative of the appropriateness of the regulated tariffs than of the real return to the economy. Cost-benefit analysis, therefore, is not very useful in comparing the merits or relative ranking of projects in different sectors. Much depends on the common sense, judgement, and even ingenuity of the analyst. Whim, bias, and intuition will also inevitably play a part. These caveats notwithstanding, economic evaluation can introduce rationality into the decision-making process, identify and measure risks, and avoid some of the more serious mistakes that can occur even in the best laid investment plans.

Financial Analysis

Financial analysis is a scientific tool. It has assumed an increasingly important role as a tool for appraising the real worth of an enterprise, its performance during a period of time and its pitfalls. Financial analysis helps in drawing out the complications of what it contained in the financial statements.

Financial analysis is defined as the process of discovering economic facts about an enterprise and / or a project on the basis of an interpretation of financial data. Financial analysis also seeks to look at the capital cost, operations cost and operating revenue. The analysis decisively established a relationship between the various factors of a project and helps in manoeuvring the project's activities. It also serves as a common measure of value for obtaining a clear-cut understanding about the project from the financial point of view.

An analysis of several financial tools provides an important basis for valuing securities and appraising managerial programmes. Financial analysis is a vital apparatus for the interpretation of financial statements. It can provide an insight into two important areas of management — return on investment and soundness of the company's financial position. David Hawkins observes that the analyst evaluates results against the particular characteristics of the company and its industry. He seldom expects answers from this process; but he hopes that it would provide him with clues as to where he should focus his subsequent analysis.

Internal management accounts provide information which is valuable for the purpose of control. The information is made available in the shape of accounting data, which may be in the form of statements — financial statements and accounting statements. A financial analysis reveals where the company stands with respect to profitability, liquidity, leverage and an efficient use of its assets. Financial reports provide the framework within which business planning takes place. They are the key through which an effective control of a business enterprise is exercised. A financial analysis is the process of determining the significant financial characteristics of a firm. It may be external or internal. The external analysis is performed by creditors, stockholders and investment analysts. The internal analysis is performed by the various departments of a firm.

Significance of Financial Analysis

Financial analysis primarily deals with the interpretation of the data incorporated in the proforma financial statements of a project and the presentation of the data in a form in which it can be utilised for a comparative appraisal of the projects. It is, in effect, concerned with the development of the financial profile of the project. Its purpose is to find out whether the project is attractive enough to secure funds needed for its various constituent activities and once having secured the funds, whether the project will be able to generate enough economic values to achieve the objectives for which it is sought to be implemented. Financial analysis deals not only with the financial aspects of a project but also with its operational aspects. As such it is necessary to undertake such an analysis not only in the case of industrial projects but also in the case of non-industrial projects.

Analysis of financial statements has become very significant due to the widespread interest of various parties in the financial result of a company. In recent years, the ownership of capital of most public companies has become broad-based. A number of parties and bodies, including creditors, potential suppliers, debenture-holders, credit institutions like banks, industrial suppliers, debenture-holders, credit institutions like banks, industrial finance corporations, etc., potential investors, employees, trade unions, important customers, economists, investment analysts, taxation authorities and Government have a stake in the financial results of a company. Various people look at the financial statements from various angles. A number of techniques have been developed to undertake analysis of financial statements in order to reach conclusions about the financial health, profitability and efficiency of an enterprise and also to compare an enterprise with other similar undertakings. The technique of ratio analysis is most important tool of financial analysis. It helps in comparing the performance of various companies and judge their financial soundness.

Issue of financial analysis arise in the course of project design in several ways. The first and most universal concern, applicable to all types of projects, is that there be sufficient funds both to complete the project and to operate and maintain it subsequently. This sounds obvious, but far too many development projects have been launched without adequate consideration of the future availability of funds. This is notably true for education projects, in which recurrent costs for teachers' salaries may quickly exceed the capital costs of the facilities; or for projects in irrigation, roads, health, water supply, and other infrastructure, in which facilities once completed may deteriorate rapidly for want of adequate maintenance. This reluctance to provide adequate recurrent expenditures reflects in part the greater political appeal of new investments and in part the unwillingness of most external leaders to finance such expenditures.

A second financial concern is to recover an appropriate portion of the costs from the beneficiaries or users. A cost recovery policy has three separate but related objectives:

- *Economic efficiency*: The resources provided under a project are used most efficiently when, they are priced in accordance with their marginal or opportunity cost. The extent to which efficiency prices can be applied, however, varies widely from sector to sector.
- *Income distribution:* In the interests of equity, the prices or other charges levied to recover costs should take into account differences in income levels (as affected by the project) and in ability to pay.
- *Revenue generation:* Governments in developing countries, being short of resources, need to generate revenue from projects. In addition, revenue-earning enterprises need to be made or kept financially viable. If rural and urban development, water supply, and other projects are to be replicable on the scale necessary to reach the large numbers of potential beneficiaries, a substantial contribution from the initial beneficiaries will often have to be secured.

Difficult tradeoffs may be required among these sometimes conflicting objectives, and the poorer the country the more painful the choices may be. Cost recovery for basic services can be an explosive political issue. This fact, together with administrative considerations, determines what can be accomplished and how quickly. Two important rules to follow are that new or increased levies should be related to benefits as they materalize and imposed in small but regular increments, and that similar situations should be treated similarly to avoid the appearance of discrimination.

The financial viability of revenue-earning enterprises — electric and water utilities, public and private industries, railways, telecommunication entities, and so on — can be translated into three subsidiary objectives or tests of performance:

- Will the enterprise have sufficient revenue to earn a reasonable return on its invested capital? As part of the test of "reasonableness," will it be able to generate enough funds internally from its operations to make a satisfactory contribution to its future capital requirements?
- Will the capital structure of the enterprise enable it to meet all of its capital obligations, including the service of its debt, in a timely manner?
- Will there be adequate liquidity, that is sufficient working capital, to cover all current operational requirements?

Insistence on financial viability is an important means of imposing discipline on an enterprise and encouraging efficient management and use of resources. There is almost always some scope for improving financial performance by raising operating standards and reducing waste. Achieving financial viability will, however, ultimately throw issues of tariff policy into bold relief. In many cases, increases in prices — often substantial — will be necessary to reach the financial objectives. To raise the price of a basic product or service that figures prominently in the cost of living is an act of political courage. But not to raise the price may, in the long run, have even more adverse economic, and therefore political, consequences. During an inflationary period, governments are especially reluctant to increase the cost of basic goods and services. This is understandable, but failure to raise prices may also have an inflationary impact if the government must borrow to cover the deficits.

One means of easing the bureaucratic and political pain of raising the price of public services, as we have noted, is to adjust prices in small increments and at regular intervals. Another is to make price increases automatic or quasi-automatic, as when fuel costs are passed on to users through equivalent increases in electricity prices without the need for government approval each time.

Social Analysis

Social analysis deals with the impact of projects on people. Its role is to consider the suitability of the proposed project design for the people it is intended to serve, to make proposals for improving the "fit" between the two, and to fashion strategies for project implementation that can be expected both to win and hold people's support and to achieve project goals by inducing changes in social attitudes and behaviour. Some projects — in such fields as rural developments, education, and health — are clearly oriented toward people. Infrastructure projects are less so, but even these may have to deal effectively with people, as workers or consumers, in order to achieve their objectives. A project that runs counter to or ignores the traditions, values, and social organization of the intended beneficiaries, or that is based on objectives which they do not share, has little prospect of success.

Social analysis is a relative newcomer among the dimensions of project analysis. It focuses on four principal areas:

- The socio-cultural and demographic characteristics of the project population.
- The way in which the project population is organized to carry out productive activities.
- The project's cultural acceptability, including its capacity for both adapting to people's behaviour and perceived needs and for bringing about changes in them.
- The strategy necessary to elicit commitment from the project population and to ensure their sustained participation throughout the project cycle.

Predicting social behaviour is even more uncertain than forecasting financial or economic behaviour. Project planners have often made unduly optimistic assumptions about local people's interest in and need for a project, the economic and social incentives for them to participate, and the rate at which change in their social condition can be brought about. Social analysis with professional training and broad experience can improve the projections. However, more importantly, they can make a significant contribution to a project's success by helping to design effective organizations and approaches to achieve desirable change in social behaviour.

Social analysis of projects has frequently failed to take adequate account of the particular interests and needs of women. Although they constitute half the world's population, women have reaped far less than their share of the benefits of development. Women tend to have less schooling than men, their mobility is constrained by economic and social considerations, and they often face legal barriers to their ownership of assets or access to credit. Yet women play a key role in the development process, both as producers and consumers; for example they provide most of the agricultural labour used in production, harvesting, marketing, and storage. Moreover, the central position of women in family life profoundly influences attitudes and decisions on education, nutrition, health, and family size. Thus, even if women never enter the formal labour market, ensuring that they receive an adequate education may be one of the best investments a country can make.

Failure to appreciate the role of women when projects are designed and implemented is not only inequitable but also retards the pace of economic growth. Decisions about which technologies to use and about how to provide a wide range of services must be made with full regard to women's needs and constraints; otherwise, project benefits will be reduced and the position of women made even worse. In many respects, women are the largest underutilized resource for development.

Institutional Analysis

In recent years, institutional analysis has become one of the important dimensions of project work. The outcome of development projects depends on the quality of the institutions responsible for them. Yet institutions in developing countries typically suffer from an acute shortage of experienced managers and staff, an excess of untrained staff, overstrained services and facilities, low wages and salaries, inadequate data and information system, and an inimical policy environment. There are no standard solutions and few readily transferable institutional models from either developed or other developing countries. Institutional development must be seen as a lengthy process of experiment and adaptation, subject to many reverses when political or economic fortunes change. Still, when strong institutions have been forged, they have played a key role in development.

The overall policy environment affects the performance not only of projects but also of the institutions responsible for them. If managers of these institutions are compelled to spend time and effort counteracting the impact of government economic policies (such as a critical shortage of foreign exhcange for spare parts, owing to an overvalued exchange rate), they cannot build long-term capacity effectively. Institutional problems multiply rapidly when government policies seriously distort the economic environment or when government regulations impose extraneous requirements, such as the employment of extra staff for political or social reasons.

Institutional problems have been compounded as more complex development objectives have been assigned to projects. Executing multicomponent projects or projects focused on alleviating poverty or upgrading social services has placed heavy demands on institutions. Knowledge of the economic, social, and behavioural characteristics of small farmers, urban squatters, or disadvantaged tribal people is still rudimentary. Understanding of the management and institutional techniques for dealing with such projects is also at an early stage.

Institutions in the public sector present a particular challenge, both because of their importance and because of the many problems they characteristically confront. A comprehensive reform of the public administration system — however badly needed — is a very ambitious undertaking. Few countries, developed or developing, have successfully carried out such a reform in the face of the strong resistance that these efforts generate. While careful diagnosis of the problem of the public service is a necessary first step in establishing an overall strategy for change, implementing the strategy will almost invariably call for a selective approach. The best results have been achieved by concentrating on a few of the more critical problems. The ones to tackle first are those that seriously constrain the performance of the public administration and that are within its capacity to solve; in addition, it should be possible to mobilize and maintain public support for the reform effort.

Parastatals and other forms of state-owned enterprise have proliferated in recent years. Their performance has at best been mixed, and concern has been growing about the need to increase their efficiency, reduce their deficits that burden the public budget, and avoid political interference in their affairs. Given the preponderance of public enterprises in the economies of many developing countries, reforming them has repercussions going far beyond improved project performance. Some governments, in fact, are beginning to devote considerable effort to limiting the spread of public enterprises and to transferring ownership of some of these enterprises to the private sector. The legitimate demands on the public sector are very large, and the capacity for public management is among the scarcest of development resources. This capacity should, therefore, be reserved for use where it is most needed and most likely to be efficacious; governments should exercise caution in deciding which fields are appropriate for public ownership.

For those agricultural and institutional parastatals carrying out processing, manufacturing or marketing operations that private producers and merchants can do efficiently, the simple answer may be to abolish them. For other parastatals, reducing the number of staff, rationalizing their structures, and appointing and promoting staff on the basis of merit are among the measures needed. In several countries, policy reforms are being tried that will improve the "rules of the game" under which the enterprises operate. This reform has two objectives: to give public enterprises greater authority and autonomy to carry out their activities in accordance with broad goals and specific performance targets agreed on with the government; and to hold the enterprises accountable for their results, while improving the flow of information to government about their performance.

A widespread weakness of development institutions, particularly but not exclusively in the public sector, is the shortage of qualified managers at the middle and upper echelons and of experienced specialists such as accountants and engineers. This is a basic characteristic of underdevelopment that can change only gradually. In the long run, the education through universities, vocational schools, and management institutes — must provide the solution. But some steps can be taken immediately. Expatriate managers and consultants can be used to free bottlenecks in the short run — as long as care is taken that this does not delay the development of local managerial capacity, but rather fosters it through counterpart and on-the-job training. Whatever the source of management, greater attention to organizational questions and improved management, accounting, and information systems and procedures can enhance effectiveness. Continuity of management is also important; frequent changes for political reasons are highly disruptive.

One fruitful approach to strengthening management in the public service is through improved incentives. Salary and other financial incentives for public officials cannot normally match those in the private sector, but disparities can be narrowed. In particular cases, elements of the financial package other than pay can also be improved without disturbing prevailing standards in the public service. Establishing "super-grades" outside the normal system may be a way to meet special needs, while making lateral entry and exit easier can encourage managers to view public service as a natural stage in a career.

Programs for training managers and staff also deserve much more attention. The potential contribution of such programs is very large, yet experience shows that too often they have little effect. Training programs cannot be added on to projects at the last moment, but must be planned carefully in advance and properly executed. Adequate resources, must be provided and skilled trainers recruited. As a general rule, the closer training is to the workplace in which it will be used, the more effective it is likely to be. This argues for on-the-job training when feasible.

Environmental Analysis

It is now widely recognized that environmental analysis is necessary for a country to ensure the sound management and use of its natural resources as an integral part of its strategy for economic growth. Desertification, deforestation, soil erosion, overexploitation of such renewable resources as fisheries, and air and water pollution are lowering the carrying capacity of the environment. Usually the poor are disproportionately affected by environmental degradation. The objective of environmental management should be to achieve a balance between human demands on the natural resource base and the ability of that resource base to meet these demands on a sustainable basis in the interests of future generations as well as those alive today.

With careful environmental management, the pace of economic and social progress need not be slowed. In environmental work, the "ounce of prevention" is almost always more important and less costly than the "pound of cure." Sometimes remedial action may not be feasible at all. All proposed development projects should be screened to detect those with a potentially harmful impact on the environment. Most environmental problems, if properly anticipated, can be dealt with at relatively small cost — usually less than 5 per cent of total project cost. Analysis of the tradeoffs between different design features and their environmental costs and benefits should be a routine part of project work; the analysis is complicated, however, by the fact that the standard time-discounting methodology, gives insufficient weight to environmental costs and benefits because of their long-term nature.

Procurement

Managing the procurement process is an important aspect of project implementation. Delays in acquiring the necessary goods and works are likely to be compounded into further delays and increased costs for the project as a whole. Procurement is therefore a process to be carefully planned, organized, and managed, the more so since the number of ways things can go wrong sometimes appears endless.

Procurement must serve three objectives. The first is to help ensure the efficient execution of the project by acquiring goods and works with the optimal combination of quality, price, and delivery time. The second is to promote such national goals as the development of local industry, the balanced regional development of industry, or the support of small-scale enterprises. The third is to comply with the procurement regulations of any external lending institutions helping to finance the project.

There are a wide variety of types and methods of procurement. Which is the most appropriate depends on the size and nature of the project, the particular goods or works to be procured, and the regulations of lending agencies. For large projects, international competitive bidding is generally the best way of ensuring efficient procurement, safeguarding against waste or corruption, and satisfying the interest of lending agencies that all qualified firms be permitted to bid. Local competitive bidding is more appropriate for small-scale procurement of goods and works in which foreign firms will not be interested: changes in procedures may be necessary to ensure effective competition among local firms.

Use of Consultants

Procurement of consulting services raises different issues. There is, first, the question of need. Most of the services for which consultants might be recruited can, in principle, be provided by local staff of the project agency if they are competent, experienced, and available. When such in-house capacity does not exist (as may often be the case) and cannot be put in place by additional training soon enough to meet the demands of the project, the next best choice is the use of local consulting firms. Establishing a local consulting industry is desirable both to provide some competition to stimulate agency staff and to supply more specialized skills or expert services. When local services are not available, firms from other developing countries may offer the dual advantages of better knowledge and understanding of comparable local conditions and relatively low costs. There will, however, remain some assignments — especially for large or complex projects and those requiring highly technical knowledge — for which only expatriate consultants from developed countries are qualified. Joint ventures between foreign and local consulting firms, if entered into voluntarily, are often a good way of developing local capacity.

The consultant-client relationship is a close, personal one; when a satisfactory partnership already exists with a particular firm, it may be eminently sensible to continue it. When no such relationship exists, or when for other reasons it is desirable to invite proposals from a short list of qualified firms, the selection process should ensure that price considerations are subordinated to a concern with quality. The cost of consulting services is usually only a small fraction of total project costs, but the quality of the work performed can have an impact on the final project out of all proportion to the cost.

Conclusion

Feasibility studies are the pre-requisites of a project, and it provides the much needed inputs to the entrepreneur in translating his dreams into a successful venture as per his vision and goals.

A project feasibility analysis includes market analysis, technical analysis, financial analysis and social profitability analysis. Although every feasibility analysis is different and is tailored to suit the product, its goal is to identify the strengths and weaknesses of the project.

The starting point of a project analysis is the establishment of the objectives to be attained. The next stage is the pre-selection stage — the advisability of having an in-depth study. The analysis stage consists mainly of three factors — market, technical and financial analysis. A market analysis is a method of screening project ideas as well as a means of evaluating a project's feasibility in terms of the market.

The technical analysis of a project feasibility study establishes whether the project is technically feasible or not, and whether it offers a basis for the estimation of costs. Moreover, it provides an opportunity for the consideration of the effect of various technical alternatives on employment, ecology, infrastructure demands, capital services, support of other industries, balance of payments, and other factors. Every entrepreneur should focus his attention on this important tool of management.

Chapter - 10

PROJECT APPRAISAL

Introduction

Project appraisal is an exercise whereby a lending financial institution makes an independent and objective assessment of various aspects of an investment proposition to arrive at the financing decision. Appraisal exercises are basically aimed at determining the viability of a project and sometimes, also in reshaping the project so as to upgrade its viability. This is done by allocating the term finance sought by a promoter.

The factors generally considered by institutions while appraising a project include technical, financial, commercial, economic, ecological, social and managerial aspects. This makes it necessary to recognise the inter-relationship underlying the various aspects of a project. For example, the size of the initial market and the estimates for demand build-up would determine the plant capacity and production phasing; these together would have a bearing on the profitability, which, in turn, would determine the means of financing. Location also has an important bearing on project cost and cost of production. Above all, the management behind the project has a decisive influence on most of these aspects. These considerations imply that project appraisal is viewed as a composite process as against the approach of viewing each aspect individually.

This chapter will focus on the appraiser's thinking process from the viewpoint of the lending financial institutions. This will help ensure necessary preparation on the part of the borrowers-entrepreneurs/businessmen/businesswomen.

Meaning

The exercise of project appraisal simply means the assessment of a project in terms of its economic, social, and financial viability.

This exercise is critical as it calls for a multi-dimensional analysis of the project that is, a complete scanning of the project.

Financial institutions and banks make a critical appraisal of projects which are submitted to them by the entrepreneurs for getting loans. They have traditionally been accepting the data provided by the entrepreneur as valid while assessing the project. In fact, the emphasis has largely been on the cash-flow and financial viability of a project in assessing their suitability for extending the loans.

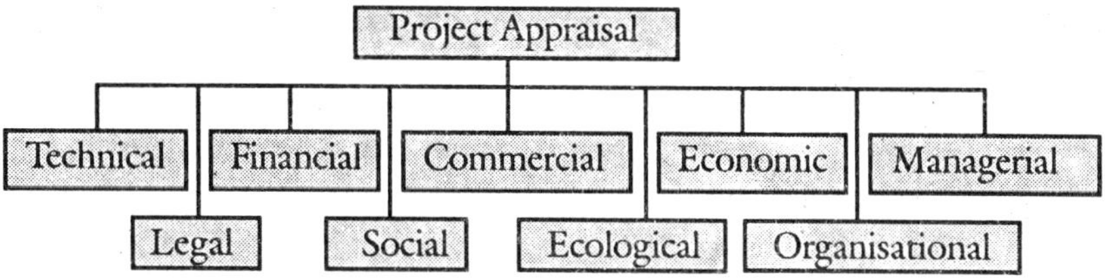

Fig. 10.1 : Aspects of Project Appraisal

Definition

Project appraisal can be defined as the promoter taking a second look critically and carefully at a project as presented by the promoter person who is in no way involved in or connected with its preparation and who is, as such, able to take an independent, dispassionate and objective view of the project in its totality, as also in respect of its various components. The person who carries out appraisal of a project is usually an official from the financial institutions or a team of institutional officials. Since all lending activities involve risk in a smaller or larger measure, project appraisal aims at sizing up the quality of projects and their long-term profitability aims at minimising the risk of lending by rectifying their weaknesses and improving their quality by incorporating into them features/ safeguards missed by the promoters, either because of lack of knowledge or information.

Scope of Appraisal

The appraisal of a project is undertaken by the financial institutions with the twin objectives of determining the market potential of a project and selecting an optimal strategy. The methods of analysis vary from project to project. Nevertheless, certain common aspects of study from the angle of technology and engineering are worth a mention:

— Choice of technical process and/or appropriate technology;
— Technical collaboration arrangements, if any;
— Size and scale of operations;
— Locational aspects of the project and availability of infrastructural facilities;
— Selection of plant, machinery and equipment together with background, competence and capability of machinery/equipment suppliers;
— Plant layout and factory buildings;
— Technical engineering services;
— Project design and network analysis for the assessment of project implementation schedule;
— Aspects relating to effluent disposal, management of entry, utilisation of by-products etc.
— Project cost and its comparison with other similar projects, based on technology, equipment, product mix and time spread;
— Determination of project cost estimates, profitability projections, etc.
— Sensitivity analysis.

It must be remembered that the different aspects of a project are not independent entities but are highly inter-related; and a meaningful project appraisal depends upon the appreciation of this fundamental fact. For example, the size of the total market for a product as it exists now and the year to year estimates of the future progressive call for expansion of demand would determine planned capacity of the proposed unit and the phasing of production over the years. These in turn would influence the project cost and profitability which would determine the means of financing. The cost of the project and profitability are influenced to a significant extent by its location. Over and above this, the management behind the project, has a decisive role to play in almost all aspects of the project.

Steps Followed in Project Appraisal

Project appraisal is a scientific tool. It follows a specific pattern. First and foremost, an analysis of a region's economy provides a general framework within which the assessment of any project is made. This analysis indicates whether the project is in a potential environment which enjoys priority for economic development of the region/state concerned. This exercise itself usually involves the investigation of six different aspects: economic, technical, organisational, managerial, operational, and financial. The relative importance of these different aspects can vary considerably according to circumstances and type of project. The main stages of the system of project appraisal are:

Step 1	—	Economic	Indicates priority use.
Step 2	—	Technical	Involves scale of the project and the process adopted.
Step 3	—	Organisational	Suitability is examined.
Step 4	—	Managerial	Adequacy and competence are critically scrutinised.
Step 5	—	Operational	Capability of the project.
Step 6	—	Financial	Determines the financial viability for sound implementation and efficient operation.

Project Appraisal Format

Criteria	*Project-I*	*Project-II*	*Project-III*	*Project-IV*
1. Investment size				
2. Location				
3. Technology				
4. Equipment				
5. Marketing				
6. Power & Water				
7. Others' performance				
8. Working capital needs				
9. Labour component				
10. Economic viability				
Total				

Point Scale: A = 5 points; B=4 points; C=3 points; D=2 points; E=1 point.

Fig. 10.2 : Steps of Project Appraisal

Economic Aspects

The economic aspects of appraisal are fundamental as they logically precede all other aspects — this is so because the bank will not finance a project unless it stands assured that the project represents a high-priority use of a region's resources. However, a purely financial analysis normally does not provide an adequate basis for judging a project's value to the economy, since the financial analysis looks at the project only from a limited viewpoint of the revenues entering the project's own accounts. So, an economic or social analysis looks at the project from the viewpoint of the whole economy, asking whether the latter will show benefits sufficiently greater than project costs to justify investment in it.

The economic benefits brought about by a successful project normally take the form of an increased output of goods or services, either directly or indirectly (as in a large class of cost-reducing projects). This increased production will also generate many different forms of additional income, such as increased wages or employment of labour, larger government revenues, higher earnings for the owners of capital, or most frequently, a combination of these income benefits.

In a large majority of cases, it is possible to quantify project costs and benefits, and to çonstruct a rate of return or some other appropriate move. Future costs and benefits are calculated, using either market or shadow prices, as found appropriate. Further both costs and benefits are put under subsidence to initiate the projects' estimated rate of return.

The latter is then compared with the minimum earning power of capital judged appropriate for each country. While the rate of return is an important test that all projects with quantifiable cost and benefits must pass, its significance is usually overestimated. The rate of return is a necessary confirming test of projects that have to be justified within a much wider frame of reference, in which basic project objectives and the nature of project benefits (e.g., foreign-exchange savings, increased employment and improved income distribution) play major roles.

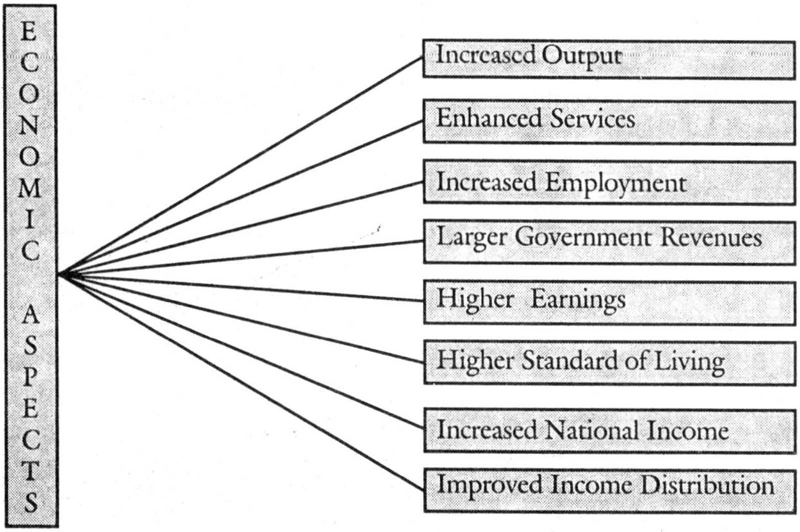

Fig. 10.3 : Economic Aspects of a Project

Organisational Aspects

As a lender and a development institution, the bank places particular stress on the need for an efficient organisation and responsible management for the execution of a project. During appraisal, these two essential dimensions of a project are examined. If one or the other is found wanting, short-term remedial steps are recommended to the entrepreneur and the bank may make a clause for assistance — such as the recruitment of individuals or an organisation qualified to assist in running the enterprise, at least during the initial phase; or those for a longer term, such as a management study, reorganisation or creation of a new autonomous agency to operate the project. In either case, the need for training local staff to fill positions at all levels is examined, and training programmes may well be included as part of the project. The objective of this aspect of appraisal is to make sure that the project is adequately carried out and that a locally-staffed institution, capable of contributing effectively to the development of the sector in question, is created.

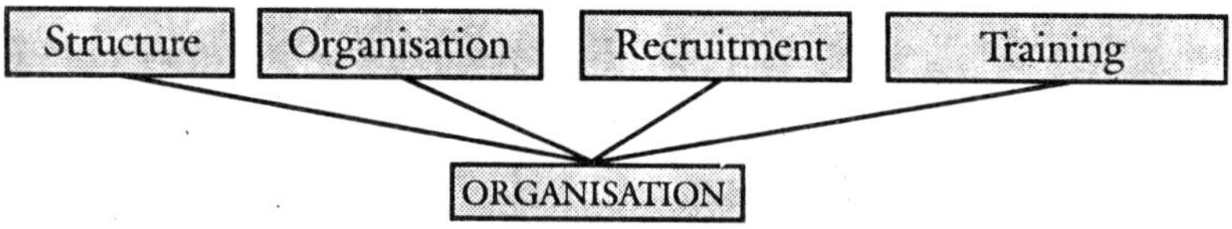

Fig. 10.4 : Organisational Aspects

Managerial Aspects

If the management is incompetent, even a good project may fail. It is rightly pointed out that if project is weak, it can be improved upon, but if the promoters are weak and lack business acumen, it is difficult to reverse the situation. It is, therefore, natural that financial institutions very carefully appraise the managerial aspects before sanctioning assistance for a project.

It may be relevant to recall here that there are provisions which enable financial institutions to exercise control over the assisted units. For example, they now stipulate the condition of option for conversion of loans into equity in respect of loans aggregating Rs. 5 crore or more generally, and in respect of sick units, irrespective of the amount of assistance and the level of shareholding in the assisted company.

Further, there is a provision for appointment by the financial institutions of nominee directors on the boards of all MRTP companies assisted by them. As regards non-MRTP companies, nominee directors are appointed on the boards on a selective basis, especially in cases where one or more of the following conditions exist, viz., *(a)* the unit is running into problems and is likely to become sick, *(b)* institutional holding is more than 26 per cent and *(c)* the institutional stake by way of loans/investment exceeds Rs. 5 crores.

The Companies Act, the Industries (Development and Regulation) Act, etc., empower Government to exercise powers of control over the management, including the take-over of management of industrial undertakings.

All these indicate the importance given to proper managerial strategies to prevent mismanagement.

If a proper appraisal of the managerial aspects is made in the beginning itself, future problems in this area can be avoided to a very large extent. It is, therefore, necessary that the overall background of the promoters, their academic qualifications, business and industrial experience, their past performance, etc. are looked into in greater detail to assess their capabilities for implementing the project for which financial assistance has been sought.

Technical Aspects

The importance of technical appraisal in project evaluation needs no emphasis. Technical appraisal of a project broadly involves a critical study of the following:

Location and Site

An industrial feasibility study aspect refers to the appropriate selection of a geographical area where the project should be located. Towards this end, the required site characteristics shall be kept in mind when selecting the location.

There are a number of important factors that influence industrial location because the site may significantly influence the cost of production and distribution, distribution efficiency, the operating environment, etc.

The problem of site selection gets complicated by the fact that at a particular location where one or a few factors are favourable, other factors may not be so. Selection of an optimum location, therefore, revolves round the combined consideration and evaluation of all the relevant factors.

The important factors that influence industrial location are the following:

1. *Raw Material Supplies:* Certain industries are located near the source of raw materials. This is particularly true of industries based on gross (weight-losing) localised material — industries with a high *Material Index* (the proportion of the localised material to the final product). For example, iron and steel mills are usually located near the ore deposits and sugar mills in the sugarcane cultivating regions. Similarly, the timber industry tend to be closer to forests or riverways leading from forests. Kallayi (near Calicut, Kerala), one of the largest timber business centres of the world, is on the banks of the Chaliyar river leading from the richly endowed Nilambur forests. In certain cases, even industries based on pure materials prefer to be located near source of raw materials. The jute industry in India, for example, is developed in the jute growing region. Similarly, the early development of the cotton textile industry was in the cotton growing region.

Industries using perishable raw materials also tend to be located in closer proximity to the raw material sources.

2. *Proximity of Markets:* Certain categories of industries tend to be located near the market. This is particularly true of the industries with the manufacturing process that involves an increase in weight and/or bulk. In such cases, the transport and distribution costs can be minimised by being closer to the market. Bottling of drinks is a very good example. Industries with fragile and perishable output also have a tendency to be located closer to the market.

When there are large markets geographically spread, nationally or internationally, manufacturing units may be established in close proximity to the major markets.

3. *Transportation Facilities:* Transportation facilities including the cost of transport play an important role in industrial location. No wonder, centres connected with sea, air,

rail and road transport facilities exert a strong pull on industries. It is not only the transportation of the materials and finished products that it is to be considered but also the transportation facilities for the personnel.

In a vast country like India, there may be significant variations in transportation costs between different locations.

Places with a high transport disadvantage are not likely to attract industries. It is due to this reason that the Government of India is providing transport subsidy to industrial units located in certain hill regions and islands with a view to encouraging the industrial development of these regions.

4. *Power and Fuel Supply:* Power and fuel supply conditions have an important bearing on industrial location. Cheap power or fuel and its uninterrupted supply is an important attraction for industries, especially in the era of energy crisis. In the past, certain industries tended to be located near coal deposits. But the advent of electricity has greatly changed the industrial location patterns. Now, it is not very difficult to take power supply to the location of raw material supply so that weight-long materials may be processed at their location.

Electrification of various parts of the country, including the villages, is encouraging decentralisation of industries.

5. *Water:* Certain industries like the paper industry by their very nature require large quantities of water. The quality and properties of the available water are as important as the quantity of water available and the stability of its supply. A number of industries also use the water sources for effluent disposal. While selecting the location, the possibility of the pollution of water by other industries making the water unfit for industrial and domestic purposes should also be considered. The requirements of water for the employees and their families housed near the industrial unit for domestic purposes and its availability should also be considered.

6. *Manpower:* The economic, social and political aspects of labour supply have an important influence on industrial location. Not only the quantity but an assessment of skill levels of the available manpower are very important. In certain regions, abundant cheap labour may be available; but if the labour does not possess the required skill, the industry will have to incur expenditure on training the labour.

Cheap labour is particularly important for industries where labour accounts for a significant part of the total value added. One of the important factors influencing the location of plants in the less developed countries by the multinationals (MNCs) is said to be the cheap labour supply.

For the assessment to be realistic, it is essential that the wage rates be compared with the level of productivity of the labour.

Certain socio-economic characteristics and political affiliations of labour are also important considerations. In certain localities and communities, labour turnover and absenteeism are high. These factors may not only tend to increase expenses but also affect the smooth functioning of the enterprise.

Some regions may be characterised by the dominance of militant trade unions, widespread labour unrest, etc., seriously affecting the smooth functioning of industries. Industries prefer to consider other areas for their location.

It may be difficult to get professional, skilled manpower etc., if the location is very remote and deprived of civic amenities.

7. *Labour Laws and Government Policy:* Labour laws and the government's attitude and policy toward strikes and other labour problems and employee-employer relations, etc., may also influence location decision-making.

8. *Natural and Climatic Factors*: Natural and climatic factors also play an important role in the location of certain industries, as the absence of these conditions will necessitate additional expenditure to create favourable conditions artificially. For instance, a humid climate is conducive to the cotton textile industry. Favourable climatic conditions and other environmental factors played a major role in the location of these industries.

9. *Strategic Considerations:* They also influence the location of industries. It is not likely that major industries will be located in strategically sensitive areas even if all economic factors favour such a location. Especially in the case of strategic industries, special care is taken to ensure that the location chosen is not easily accessible to the military forces of other countries. For defence industries, strategic location may be the sole criterion.

10. *Taxes and Fees:* Variations in taxes, fees and charges may also influence industrial location.

11. *Incentives and Disincentives:* Certain incentives and disincentives may also affect industrial location. For instance, in India, the Union and State Governments offer a number of fiscal, monetary and physical incentives for industries in the notified backward regions.

Certain disincentives like higher taxes may discourage industries in certain regions. Government may even ban new industrial units in congested areas, large urban areas or developed regions.

12. *Site and Services:* Some industries require a large area which may not be available in a locality where all other factors are favourable. Availability of the required type and quantity of land at reasonable prices is, thus, an important factor.

With a view to developing industries in certain regions, Government has been providing developed sites and necessary facilities and services. Certain such locations like Hosur (Tamil Nadu) have been very successful in attracting industries.

Similarly, industrial estates have been established in different parts of the country to encourage the development of industries.

13. *Socio-economic and Political Factors:* Socio-economic and political factors are also sometimes very important, especially in respect of location of public sector units. Some large-scale public sector units are located in backward regions on such considerations. Social and political considerations sometimes favour industrial location in certain sensitive regions.

14. *Miscellaneous Factors:* There are also a number of other factors that may influence industrial location — the attitude of the local community, proximity of complementary industries, prospects of development of the region, service facilities required by the industry, recreational and social facilities, proximity to important centres like metropolitan centres, personal factors, historical factors, etc.

Site

There are a number of important factors to be considered in the selection of the site. These include the load bearing capacity of the site or towards flood and earthquake hazards, access to transport facilities, facilities for water supply and effluent discharge, ecological factors, etc.

The nature of the industry has a bearing on site selection. For example, some industries like the paper industry need an abundant supply of water. For some industries, effluent discharge is a major problem. Environmental pollution is a serious problem that certain industries have to contend with. All these factors influence the selection of a site.

As stated earlier, the Government provides 'site and service' in specified locations. However, some of the facilities needed for certain industries may not be available on these sites.

Size of the Plant/Scale of Operation

The size of the plant or scale of operations is an important factor that determines the economic and financial viability of a project.

In many industries, there are certain technological plant capacities which are economical. If the size is sub-optimal, there will be diseconomies of scale.

This is one of the important reasons for poor performance of many industrial units in India. Diseconomies of scale result in high costs and make survival in a competitive market, particularly in the international market, very difficult. The Government of India in this context, has emphasised that the plants or scale of operations should be of economic size.

An important aspect of technological size is that the available process technology and equipment are often standardised at specific capacities in production sectors. Operative capacities in such sectors are, therefore, available only in certain multiples.

There are, however, certain factors that may come in the way of optimal scale. For example, there may be demand constraints, i.e., the market demand may be so low that it cannot absorb the output of a large plant. In some cases there may be resource and input constraints. For example, the available raw material in a region may not be sufficient to feed a large plant. When there is import control, non-availability of economic size plants or equipments domestically makes the adoption of optimal scale impossible. Sometimes, there will also be scarcity of finance.

Another factor that may discourage the establishment of large-scale facilities is the risk of rapid obsolescence of technology or the product.

Technical Feasibility

Appraisal of technical aspects of a project involves scrutiny of such aspects of the project as:

- Manufacturing process/technology selected.
- Technical collaboration arrangements made, if any.
- Capacity/size of the project and the scale of operations.
- Location of the project.
- Availability of physical and social infrastructural facilities.

— Availability of various inputs covering raw materials as well as utilities.

— Selection of plant, machinery and equipment together with background, competence and capability of machinery/equipment suppliers.

— Plant layout/and factory building.

— Technical engineering services.

— Project design and network analysis for assessing the project's implementation schedules, etc.

The technical feasibility study should consider the adequacy and suitability of the plant, the equipments and their specifications, plant layout, balancing of different sections of the plant, proposed arrangements for procurement of the plant and equipments, reputation of the machinery suppliers, etc.

The feasibility study should also consider the technology required for a particular project, evaluate technological alternatives and select the most appropriate technology in terms of optimum combination of project components. The various implications of the acquisition of such technology should be assessed, including contractual aspects of technology licensing where applicable, etc.

The Government of India's policy in this respect clearly states that while evaluating applications for industrial licensing, the following factors will be specifically considered:

(i) Whether the proposed capacity is of economic size.

(ii) Whether the processes proposed to be adopted are efficient from a techno-economic point of view.

(iii) The extent to which diversification and expansion proposals will result in fuller utilisation of capacity and economies of scale.

Besides these proper evolution of alternative technologies is essential for selection of the appropriate one. This evaluation should be related to plant capacity and should commence with a quantitative assessment of output, production build-up and gestation period and qualitative assessment of product quality and marketability.

The selection of technology has to be related to the nature of the principal inputs that may be available for a project and to an appropriate combination of factor resources for both short and long periods.

Financial Aspects

The purpose of the appraisal of financial aspects of a project is generally to ensure its initiation of financial conditions for the sound implementation and efficient operation. The scope of this aspect of appraisal varies, of course, considerably with the nature of the project and whether it is revenue-producing (e.g., industry, utilities, agriculture) or not (e.g., education, most highway projects).

For projects which involve the marketing of a product or service by an entity, the appraisal includes in investigation of the availability and cost of raw materials power, labour, and services needed for production, and the prospects for marketing the product or service profitably.

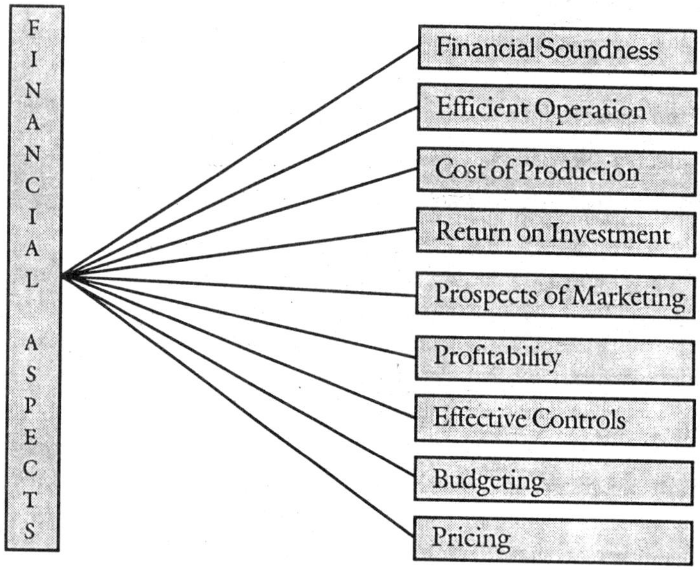

Fig. 10.5 : Financial Aspects of Project Appraisal

In every case, it is necessary to ensure that satisfactory accounts are maintained for effective control over expenditure and revenue, and to disclose the project and entity carrying it out. Also, since the banks finance only a part of the investment cost of a project, it is necessary to ensure that funds from other sources are available on acceptable terms to meet the balance of the cost. This may be relatively simple where the government is able, without difficulty, to provide the rest of the necessary funds from budgetary sources; or it may be complicated, as in a project to expand or modernise a revenue-earning concern, where all the financial requirements of the concern during the construction of the project must be considered.

Financial appraisal also evaluates capacity of revenue-producing investments from the standpoint of the entity. Industrial sponsor or other investor who would make them, in order to ascertain whether it is sufficiently attractive to warrant their participation. Establishing that the entity carrying out the project is in a position to manage its business in a cost-effective fashion is another important aspect.

The financial aspect of project appraisal covers the following areas:

(i) *Cost analysis:* In the case of cost analysis it is to be decided or to be worked out what would be the cost of production. There are different methods of finding out the cost.

(ii) *Pricing:* This strategy concerns the fixing of the product's price. Price fixation is a very tedious job. The price must be fixed very judiciously, because the price is the cause of demand. If the price is high, the demand may be low and *vice versa* and a low price may mean a lower rate of profit also.

(iii) *Financing:* The funds needed to finance the project are an important aspect of project appraisal. It is concerned with raising the funds and their most efficient use. The funds must be raised from sources where the rate of interest is lower.

(iv) *Income and Expenditure:* The income and expenditure profile is concerned with the estimates regarding the income expected and expenditure involved in the project. This helps in ascertaining the cost involved in production and profit expected therefrom. Detailed proposed accounts should be made for future reference to know whether the plans are working out properly or not.

Financial institutions examine the project to ensure economic justification of investment details. They study the marketing scope of the project and also its worth to the national economy by analysing the consumption pattern and the potential demand for the project.

Market/Commercial Aspects

In setting up an industrial project, estimation of demand for the product/group of products proposed to be manufactured by a promoter is the first important step. Ideally, the market analysis should give a comprehensive account of the market opportunity, as well as of the marketing strategy appropriate for converting the opportunity into a reality. Marketing strategy in this context could be defined as an ever-evolving design or blueprint consisting of a set of inputs like product quality, price, design, dealer/agency discounts, distribution network/channels, packaging, etc.

To be of maximum benefit to a promoter, whether new or already established, market analysis should cover the following major aspects :

(i) Analysis of market opportunity and specifying marketing objectives. This involves a scientific assessment of (a) total size of the market for a product; and (b) the share that could be secured by a firm, existing or new.

(ii) Planning the process of marketing the product.

(iii) Organisation of the marketing process.

(iv) Control of the implementation of the marketing plan which facilitates taking corrective action when the actual results deviate from the estimates or expectations.

An intensive scanning and analysis of the proposed environment in which the industrial unit has to function should form the basis for analysing market opportunities as well as for specifying the marketing strategy. This is because the ever-changing environment in which the industry sector functions, restricts or expands the opportunities available to and the threats to be faced by an industrial unit.

Market opportunities expressed in terms of demand forecasts and market shares are based on a host of factors outside the control of the promoter, whereas marketing strategy and marketing process are largely under his control. Hence, the formulation of a detailed marketing plan, specification of a proper marketing strategy, and the manner in which the marketing process should be undertaken would enable the promoter to cope with the uncertainties in the market place more effectively than otherwise. It is also a fact that the estimated market share of a promoter and his marketing strategy influence and reinforce each other and should never be viewed in isolation.

Answers to the following questions would indicate the safeguards that may be necessary to take in the likely weak areas in the project:

(i) What is the management culture in which the entrepreneur has been brought up?

(ii) Is the entrepreneur's approach to project planning scientific and consistent with the requirements of the proposed project?

(iii) In the initial stages of project planning, is the entrepreneur enlisting the support of mere helpers or of professional managers?

(iv) How has the entrepreneur drawn up the organisational structure of the unit? Does it show *ad hocism* or indicate that he has tried to merely fulfil certain legal/other obligations or is it purposeful and does it indicate a good deal of foresight on his part?

The difference between an entrepreneur and manager has been dealt with earlier.

Political and Labour Considerations

Financial institutions also pay attention to political environment and labour conditions of the area where the project is to be located. Strikes, lockouts, industrial peace and communal harmony in the area play a decisive role in examining success or failure of the project.

The lending institutions examine the project to study its soundness on technical, economic, commercial and managerial grounds. If the appraisal report is found satisfactory, the loan application will be favourably considered. The manager then communicates his decision to the borrower and terms and conditions will be negotiated. The most important areas for the borrower and lender to negotiate are: timing in relation to negotiations, method of financing based on certificates of work done, repayment schedule, rates of interest, commitment fees, security options, and monitoring and control requirements.

Technical Collaboration Arrangements

The Government of India has issued an illustrative list of industries where no foreign collaboration, financial or technical, is to be allowed in view of indigenous technology base having been well-established. However, looking to the need for constant upgradation of production technology in line with that of developed countries, the Administrative Ministries and Foreign Investment Promotion Board (FIPB) may permit import of technology in those field where:

— indigenous technology developed for items in the list is too closely held and is not available for use by new entrepreneurs on competitive terms;

— technology is required for updating of existing technology in India to meet domestic requirements efficiently or to be competitive in the export market; and

— such import is required for the manufacture of items with substantial exports, backed by buy-back guarantees.

The terms in the collaboration agreement are examined in detail by the appraising institutions with reference to the technical know-how, engineering services, procurement of imported equipment, price comparison with indigenously available equipment, performance guarantee by the collaborators, penalties for non-performance specified in the agreement, deputation of foreign experts during construction, initial and post-operation period, provision for training of Indian technicians etc. The reputation of the collaborators and past experience concerning tie-up arrangements with them, the competitiveness of the terms of collaboration in relation to the requirements of the project, the rationale of financial collaborations and other costs by way of down-payment and royalties, as also restrictive clauses in regard to marketing areas etc., are also looked into and worked upon by the appraiser.

In the case of financial collaborations, the terms relating to the right of participation of the foreign collaborator in management and future issues of share capital are also critically examined and considered. The financial standing and reputation of collaborators, where necessary, are checked through the Indian Consulates/Missions abroad as also through the India Investment Centre.

Research and development is also studied in depth and it is ensured that during the validity of the collaboration period, the borrower is allowed free access to the latest developments that may take place at the collaborators' end. The collaborators are also required to agree to provide facilities to the borrower in establishing his own uptodate R & D organisation, both in terms of equipment and manpower.

Conclusion

To sum up, project appraisal is a science as well as an art. While the basic principles of appraisal could be mastered in a short time span, the successful practice of the art of carrying out appraisal requires keen observation, a knack for details, objectivity, decision-making. It is also necessary to look ahead of the project. Project appraisal is a key to broad-based, balanced industrial growth of the country. In a way, it calls for judicious judgement and foresight. It is, therefore, aptly viewed as a composite process of development.

ANNEXURE I

TECHNICAL APPRAISAL REPORT OF A SMALL-SCALE UNIT

A technical appraisal report prepared by the Technical and Consultancy Department of a bank is given below for the study of the readers.

Name of Unit: K.C. Industries, Mumbai

Background of Proponent, Product and Technical Know-how

Proponent is a proprietary SSI concern engaged in the manufacture of "Drawn Copper Conductors" utilised by electrical equipment manufacturers since the past two decades. It is learnt that the proponent was enjoying working capital facility with the... Bank in the past. It is essential to verify the proponent's report from... Bank to its own satisfaction. The proponent has approached us for financial assistance towards working capital requirements.

Proprietor is Shri... and he is also interested in a similar unit as partner in the firm XYZ... Corporation. It is learnt that this unit has been recently floated.

Technical know-how involved in 'Copper Wire/Strip-drawing activity' is available with the proprietor and the employed technicians.

Location

Proponent's factory is situated at ownership in .... Mumbai. Aggregate built-up area of both the galas is 120 sq. mt. (app.) and is sufficient for the manufacturing activity. Branch to verify the title of factory premises/gala to its own satisfaction.

Proponent is registered as SSU and has received the necessary permissions from the municipal authorities along with sufficient power connection of 80 kw. The proponent has employed 25 persons on a single-shift basis and is expected to employ an additional 20 persons for working on a double-shift basis. Sufficient water supply is expected at the factory premises.

Infrastructural facilities are satisfactory in general.

Raw Materials

The required raw materials are electrolytic Grade Copper Rods which are available from the local market and M.M.T.C. Raw material prices are susceptible to change.

Marketing

The proponent's product is being manufactured and sold directly to ... against firm and repeat orders.

The proponent has registered annual sales of Rs. 28.36 lakhs (appr.) and Rs. 93 lakhs (appr.) during year SY 2043 and 2044 respectively.

The present position of orders on hand aggregates to Rs. 22.70 lakhs.

The proponent is expected to register a projected annual sales of Rs. 135.25 lakhs during the SY 2045 under normal conditions.

Plant and Machinery

The proponent's machinery and equipment is as per attached annexure and annual production capacity is estimated at 60 MT on a double shift basis.

The initial hot drawing operation is being done by a third party on job basis.

Working Capital

The proponent's working capital requirements or inventory level for estimated annual sales of Rs. 135.25 lakhs during the current year SY 2045 are given below:

	Period	*Total Rs. in lakhs*
1. Raw material paid stock	30 days	7.25
2. Work in process & finished goods	negligible	N.A.
3. Sales receivable from first-class party	75 days	27.75
		35.00

Note:

(1) Normal margins to be stipulated.

(2) Transactions with sister concerns to be viewed with care.

Profitability

Estimates towards cost of production are satisfactory in general.

The proponent is expected to register a pre-tax profit of Rs. 5.40 lakhs for the estimated annual sale of Rs. 135.25 lakhs during the current year SY 2045 under normal conditions. Variable cost is estimated at 86% of the sales prices.

Comments

(1) The proponent's operations are technically feasible and economically viable.

(2) Working capital facility may be considered in the light of observations made hereinabove and as per usual banking norms.

Technical Officer
Technical & Industrial
Consultancy Division
HEAD OFFICE

14th December, 1996.

ANNEXURE II

PROJECT APPRAISAL FOR TERM LENDING

A PROJECT VIABILITY

To enable the appraiser to arrive at a decision at this stage a product viability score table has been developed which is given below. The credit appraiser may accept or reject a proposal on the basis of score obtained from this table:

Product Viability Score Table for Project Appraisal

1. Product has widespread use.
2. Customers are restricted to a special class.
3. Product satisfies basic need.
4. Luxury product.
5. Product will sell itself. Repeat sales likely.
6. Intensive sales effort required.
7. Some amount of sales effort required.
8. Large international and domestic market.
9. Export market only.
10. Domestic market only.
11. Market not crowded. Competitors relatively small.
12. Large competitors dominate the market.
13. Product needed both in good times and bad.
14. Demand will fall fast in bad times.
15. Steady demand of the product in all seasons.
16. Demand is seasonal.
17. Product is protected. No possible threat from international competition.
18. Product is open to international competition can be imported any time.
19. No single competitor can affect market share substantially by reducing price.
20. Powerful competitors can capture substantial market by reducing price.
21. New product — can be protected by patent.
22. Product design difficult to protect. Can be copied easily.
23. Raw materials widely available domestically.
24. Mostly imported raw materials are required.
25. Raw materials available domestically but are closely controlled.
26. Raw materials are in short supply.
27. Project is located within a reasonable distance from the source of raw materials.
28. Project is far away from the source of raw materials.
29. Skilled workers are locally available.

30. Skilled workers are to be brought from other areas involving high wages.
31. Technology of production is reasonably stable.
32. Produce and process of production can be easily modified in response to new technology.
33. Technological advances in the product and process are very rapid.
34. Product does not create environmental hazards. No control is likely.
35. Product creates environmental hazards. Controls are likely to be imposed.
36. Market is within the command area of the factory involving low transportation costs and low inventory of finished stocks at various distribution points.
37. Market is widely dispersed involving high transportation cost and large inventory of finished stocks at various distribution points.
38. Project located in backward area
    (i) Are the markets for raw materials and other inputs stable or is there likelihood of a sudden supply shortage?
    (ii) Range of substitutes already available in the market and the possibility of future substitutes concession by Government.
    (iii) Price structure of similar products in the market and the sensitivity of consumers to a variation in price.
    (iv) Who are the major buyers; government or private consumers?
39. Project not located in backward area.

Instructions: Attributes of a product are given in the above table. Tick the most appropriate ones. Award the following marks against each attribute ticked:

	Serial no. of attribute	Marks to be awarded
(a)	1, 3, 5, 8, 11, 12, 15, 17, 19, 23, 27, 29, 31, 34, 36	3 for each attribute.
(b)	2, 4, 7, 10, 16, 21, 24, 25, 32, 35, 38	2 for each attribute.
(c)	6, 9, 12, 14, 18, 20, 22, 26, 28, 30, 33, 37, 39	1 for each attribute.

Add up the total scores and then decide the viability or otherwise of the product in the following manner:

Most viable	Viable	Non-viable
50 — 40	39 — 40	Below 30

ANNEXURE III

GLOSSARY

Accounting Rate of Return : It represents the ratio of average profit per year to the total investment on the project.

Benefit-cost ratio : It is the ratio of present value of benefits to the present value of investment.

Break-even analysis : It seeks to determine the plant capacity level at which the variable operating costs are fully recovered, and the difference between sales revenue and variable operating cost is equal to fixed costs.

Capital rationing : It is the limiting of funds for different projects when the total funds available are insufficient to meet the requirements of all projects.

Debt-Service coverage Ratio : It denotes the ability of a firm to repay its long-term debt out of its profits after tax but before depreciation and interest.

Demand forecasting : It is the estimation of demand for product/service using a scientific method. Trend projection, consumption level, End use, Leading indicator, and Econometric methods are used for demand forecasting.

Economic appraisal : It is the evaluation of projects on the principle of opportunity costs and benefits from a macroeconomic point of view, which includes the social perspective.

Financial viability : It refers to the financial soundness of the project in terms of profitability and adequate availability of funds.

Internal Rate of Return : It is the discount rate at which the present value of cash outflows is equal to the present value of the cash inflows.

Market feasibility : It is the estimation of market size for the product/service and the anticipated yearly growth.

Market survey : It is a means of collecting primary data on the product for comprehensive demand and market analysis.

Net Present value : It is the net difference between the stream of future cash inflows discounted at the rate corresponding to cost of capital and the current investment representing cash outflow.

Payback period : It is the period required to recover the original investment outlay through profits earned.

Plant capacity : It refers to the number of units that can be produced during a period from a plant facility.

Product Mix : It is the combination of two or more products which are manufactured to achieve a particular objective such as maximisation of earnings, or minimisation of cost.

Project appraisal : It is the evaluation of project from technical, market, financial, economic and social perspective before committing funds for investment on the project.

Project layout chart : These charts, based on data relating to plant capacity, technology, equipment, civil works, plant site, etc., are used for detailed engineering and estimation of production and investment costs.

Risk analysis : It seeks to measure the degree of risk involved in a project; that is, the measure of probability of a project's profitability.

Sensitivity analysis : It seeks to determine the effect of changes in the values of key variables such as sales volume, selling price, or unit costs on the profitability of the project.

Work Schedule : It refers to the plan of work relating to the installation and initial operation; its purpose is to anticipate problems likely to arise during installation and to suggest ways of coping with those problems.

Chapter - 11

REPORTS

A report is a logical presentation of facts and information. The information is needed for reviewing and evaluating progress, for planning future course of action and for taking decisions. Reports provide feedback to the managers on various aspects of the organization.

Every organization has a system of routine periodical reporting on the progress and the status of different activities. Besides, management may assign certain special studies for the purpose of taking decisions.

Special Reports may be written by an individual or by a group of persons to whom the task has been assigned. The report is submitted to the authority that has assigned it. Reports are written for various purposes. They may be required to review performance, keep a check on a continuing activity, plan for the future needs of the organization, survey the market, submit standardized information, etc.

TYPES OF REPORTS

Reports may be routine or special. Routine reports are periodical and are usually prepared by filling in printed/cyclostyled forms, to convey information about the progress or status of work/tasks. They are submitted at regular intervals or soon after the completion of the task.

Special reports are required when a special situation or problem arises. An individual or a committee of persons who have knowledge and understanding in the field /subject, is appointed to investigate and study a specific problem, collect information related to it, and make suggestions to help the management to take a decision.

The following diagram gives an idea of the types of reports:

Types of Reports	
Routine	*Special*
Progress	F.I.R.
Inspection	Investigation
Performance	Feasibility
Appraisal	Survey
Periodical	Project

Routine Reports

Routine reports are usually forms in which blanks have to be filled in or multiple choice statements are to be ticked. Report forms must be prepared carefully to ensure that the management gets complete information.

The following are routine reports:

(a) Progress report gives information about the progress of a project or a task which is in the process of being completed, such as construction of a building or manufacture of products or implementation of a scheme. This report is also prepared by filling in a standard form periodically. (b) Inspection report is submitted as soon as an inspection is carried out. It is necessary for detecting any irregularities or deviations from standard practice, in day-to-day work; for example, internal audit reports. Inspection of machinery, buildings, and property may be done at regular intervals. Audits and inspection of work and systems may be done by surprise check in order to ensure that they work properly at all times. Printed forms and guidelines for checking may be provided by the authorities; otherwise, experts in the field, like engineers, auditors, etc. use their own guidelines and formats for inspection reports. (c) Performance Appraisal report is periodical and is usually prepared by filling in a form. It is meant for assessing and recording the performance of an employee. Every supervisor has to fill in an assessment report for each of the subordinates, annually. Performance appraisal helps the superiors to assess performance of individual employees. It also helps employees to get feedback on their performance. On the basis of these reports, decisions about promotions and other benefits are taken. (d) Periodical report is prepared at regular intervals on the working of a section or a department. The information required is of a routine nature and can be easily tabulated; hence it is prepared by filling in a form.

Special Reports

(a) First Information Report (F.I.R.) is required when there is a disaster like fire, building collapse, robbery or accident in an organization. It is prepared by a responsible person on-the-spot or the person in charge, for submission to a higher authority, for example the branch manager prepares it for submission to Regional Office or Head Office. The report has to give all the information which is available immediately after the incident occurs. It must state what happened, about what time, who first noticed it, and what steps were taken immediately. It also states the extent of destruction or loss of life, property, important papers, etc. as can be estimated immediately. A First Information Report is always written by an individual.

(b) Investigation report is written after making a thorough study and inquiry. An investigation is made when there is a problem and the management needs to find out the causes of the problem, and needs suggestions for solving it. For example, falling sales, declining deposits in a bank, many customer complaints, losses in a branch, etc.

A committee may be appointed to find out the causes of the problem, and suggest measures to solve it and prevent it from occurring again. It requires collection of facts which are not always easy to get. The collected information has to be analyzed; conclusions have to be drawn and recommendations may have to be made.

Since such reports require a great deal of work, thinking, discussion and consideration, they are usually assigned only to a committee of competent and experienced persons. A simple investigation of a small problem may be assigned to an individual who has knowledge and experience in the field.

(c) Feasibility or Survey Report is required when an organization intends to launch a new product in the market, introduce a new service, or make any major changes that may affect the company's customers. The proposed field or area has to be surveyed, and its conditions observed and recorded. The factors to be examined and recorded depend on the purpose of the survey. The purpose may be to consider the suitability of a site for a factory, to evaluate the feasibility and financial viability of a proposal, to survey the market, to estimate damage. For some purposes only a physical survey and inspection of the area may suffice; for others, availability of essential requirements in the area, attitude of the local people, State Government's policies, possible expenses, etc. will be needed. A survey may be made by an individual or by a committee, depending on the size of the survey to be made. For example, if a factory is to be established, the survey involves a great deal of work, and a committee would be appointed; if damage to a piece of machinery is to be surveyed for the purpose of estimating the loss, an engineer can do it alone.

(d) Project Report is written after a proposal takes shape, and after the preliminary survey has been completed. It describes the proposal as projected into the future, showing the cash flow and expected results. It is used for planning and also for convincing others, especially sanctioning and funding authorities like government departments and banks.

A project report may be prepared on their own by persons who want to get their proposal approved or sanctioned.

STRUCTURE OF A REPORT

A report is divided into sections with headings so that the collected information can be presented in a form that is easy to read and refer to. A covering letter usually accompanies the report.

Reports are read by different persons for different purposes. Some are interested only in the findings and/or conclusions; some may want to know only the recommendations; yet others may want to check the procedure followed for data collection; most might want to know with what terms of reference the report writer was working. All these details have to be included and presented in a logical format.

A report may be written by an individual or by a committee. Both are formal and must follow a logical order. An individual report may be a little more personal in tone, while the committee report is impersonal in tone.

An Individual Report is written by one person. It follows the same logical presentation as the committee report.

If the report is short, it is written in letter form with numbered and sub-titled paragraphs. It is addressed to the person or the body that has authorized /assigned the report; it does not have the complete inside address as it is internal communication and is typed on the organization's letterhead. It is dated on the day of submission or a day earlier. The salutation is Sir, or Madam, as required, and the complimentary close is Yours faithfully. If the report has enclosures, these must be indicated. At the end, the report usually records acknowledgement of the help received in making the study.

I am grateful to Mr. Rakesh Shah, Chief Accountant, and Ms. Naina Parikh of the computer department, whose help enabled me to access past and current records of the company.

The last line offers to make further study, if necessary:

I shall be glad to undertake further study if required.

If the report is long and includes complex details, it is written in the schematic form with sub-headings, and is submitted with a covering letter.

A Committee Report is written by a group of persons who have been assigned the work as a committee. It is impersonal in style and written in the passive voice. The words 'we or our', are not used; the committee is used when necessary. It is never written in the form of a letter; it must always be presented in schematic form with sub-headings. The report is typed on plain paper and submitted with a covering letter.

The covering letter is typed on the organization's letterhead. It is addressed to the appointing authority, and has the date of submission of the report. It is signed by the convener/ chairperson of the committee. The letter states what work was assigned, that the work has been completed and is being submitted. It ends with a courteous message, offering to undertake further study if required.

Review

1. Name the types of routine reports.
2. Name the types of special reports.
3. Fill in the blanks using as few words as possible:
    (a) Reports are required by an organization for —.
    (b) An individual report may be in — form.
    (c) A committee report must be accompanied by a —.
4. Are the following statements true?
    (a) A committee report may be written in letter form.
    (b) A committee report must be signed by all the members of the committee.
    (c) An individual report may be in letter form or in schematic form.

Parts of a Report

A report has several parts which enable the writer(s) to lay out all the complex information in an easy-to-read form. All reports do not require all the parts; but long reports need to include all the parts. The parts from the title to the signature are essential and must be included in all reports.

Title

A report must always have a title indicating the subject of the study, the period and the location of the study. A long report has a full title page which gives the title, the name of the person who assigned the report and the name/s of the person/committee who prepared it, with month and year of submission. In a short report, the title appears at the top of the first page, before the text of the report, as follows:

Report of Committee
appointed to investigate
the decline in sale of cycles
in
Tamil Nadu
between January and June, 2000

In an individual letter form report, the title is in the form of subject line, indicating only the topic, for example:

Subject: Decline in Sale of Cycles in Tamil Nadu between January and June, 2000

Terms of Reference

This is the first section of the report and is numbered I. It gives (i) details of the assignment and, (ii) the purpose and scope of the study.

(i) Details of assignment include : who assigned the report (and/or appointed the committee), on what date and how the appointment was made (that is, by a resolution at a meeting, or by letter or office order). In the case of a committee, the names of the members of the committee are included. It also states what is the assignment, what is the date for submitting the report, and whether the report is expected to make recommendations. For example:

The committee was appointed by the following resolution adopted at the meeting of the Board of Directors, held on 8 July, 2000:

Resolved that a committee consisting of Mr. A (Convener), Mr. B and Mr. C, be, and is hereby, appointed to investigate the decline in the sale of cycles in Tamil Nadu between January and June, 2000, and to report with recommendations in one month's time.

If the assignment is made by letter by the CEO or any other authority, the terms of reference must give the number and date of the letter, the name and title of the appointing authority, the purpose of the report, and the time allowed.

According to the D/O letter no. xxx, dated xxx from Ms. Zarine Chowna, M.D., a committee consisting of Ms. ABC, Mr. DEF and Ms. PQR was formed to examine the complaints of customers in xxx region. The committee was asked to report with recommendations in three weeks.

An individual writing a letter form report includes the authorization in the first paragraph of the letter.

- *In accordance with your letter no xxx dated xxx I have examined xxxx and am presenting the report below.*
- *As you requested, I have investigated xxx and am happy to present my findings as follows.*

(ii) Purpose and Scope include : information about the area surveyed/ problem examined, and the limitations imposed on the study by constraints like time, finance, non-availability of data.

- *Owing to constraints of time, the committee limited its study to five most populous cities in Tamil Nadu.*
- *As data related to xxx was not available, this study is limited to xxx only.*

Procedure

This is the second section of the report and is numbered II. Methods used for collecting information are stated in this section. It begins with the meetings held by the committee, for example:

- *The committee met three times, on 26 July, and 12 and 20 August, 2003.*

Other methods of collecting information depend on the nature of the study. There are several methods.

(i) Records of the organization can provide data on production, sales, recruitment, marketing, expenditure, etc. A comparison of figures for different periods may suggest useful conclusions.

(ii) Observation consists of watching certain phenomena involved in a problem, and recording what is systematically observed. This method is useful for problems like wastage of time in movement of material in a factory, or the circulation of traffic during certain hours or buyers' behaviour at the point of purchase.

(iii) Interrogation is the method of asking questions. It may be done by (a) interviewing, if the number of persons to be questioned is small, (b) getting questionnaires filled in, if the number is large, (c) meeting experts and asking for their opinion, (d) informal talks with randomly selected concerned persons can be used for collecting information, provided that questions are asked skilfully.

(iv) Reference to books, directories, standard publications.

(v) Visits and personal inspection are necessary when suitable sites are being surveyed.

(vi) Experimentation is done by various kinds of tests for different kinds of inquiries.

The committee's work of investigation is recorded in passive voice, for example,

- *Meetings were held with the members of the panchayat.*
- *All the three sites were visited by the committee.*
- *Buyers' choice decisions were observed for three days.*

The value of the findings, conclusions and recommendations depends on the thoroughness of the investigation, and the methods used. Therefore, a report must indicate the methods used for collecting information.

Findings

This is the third section and is numbered III. Presentation of findings is the main part of the report. The collected facts and information have to be organized into a presentable form, with headings and sub-headings. The mass of collected information is analyzed and divided for easy and readable presentation and the units are joined by a numbering system. The usual form of numbering is:

I first division

A. sub-division

1. second sub-division

(a) third sub-division

(i) fourth sub-division

The basis for division into units may be time periods, or geographical location, or cause-and-effect or any factors which enable classification of the data.

The sub-divisions must be named carefully; there should be only one or two words, for example, Raw material, or Competing products. Sub-titles of equal importance must be in the same grammatical form, preferably a noun phrase, for example:

(a) *Lagging machine output*

(b) Increase in marketing cost

(c) *Difficulty of attracting skilled labour*

Details may be in the form of numbered statements, for example:

(i) Unemployed villagers are migrating to cities in search of jobs.

(ii) Failure of the monsoon, leading to drought conditions, has encouraged migration to cities.

(iii) Exposure to city life-styles has popularized the use of consumer durables. As a result the villagers have little surplus income left to deposit in bank accounts.

This section may end with a brief summary of the most important findings or some conclusions which emerge from the findings. If the conclusions are very important and significant, there may be a separate section with the heading 'Conclusions.'

Use of Illustrations

A report becomes much more readable, clear and effective if the findings are explained with relevant illustrative data like diagrams, graphs, charts, plans or maps. There are several advantages in using illustrations.

- They clarify and support the verbal analysis.
- They can present a large amount of complex data in a compact form and with precision.
- Comparisons of data can be seen at a glance in a graph or chart.
- Pictorial representation is more attractive and interesting to most people.

Every illustration should have a number and a title and should be mentioned in the text of the report. A table has a Roman number (I, IV, IX are Roman numbers) and title placed above it. A figure has an Arabic number (1, 4, 9 are Arabic numbers) and title placed below it.

An illustration should be placed as near as possible to the point where it is mentioned for the first time in the text. Complicated illustrations are given as Appendices. All diagrams, graphs, charts, maps etc. used as illustrations must have:

- proper labels to show what information is being represented
- the scale used
- the key to colour/shading/symbols used
- the date of the information it contains

Recommendations

This is the last section and is numbered IV (or V or any required number depending on the number of previous sections). Recommendations are proposals for action suggested by the report writer(s) to the appointing authority.

This section is included only if the assignment has asked for it. Sometimes an assignment may be only to present findings without recommendations. Usually, very senior persons in responsible positions are asked to include recommendations. A person or committee of persons in junior position may make suggestions; since they have studied the problem in depth, they are in a position to suggest ways to solve the problem.

Recommendations should be written in the same order as the problems are stated in the findings, as far as possible. They may be numbered, and must be in the same grammatical form. Recommendations may be introduced with a sentence like,

- *The committee makes the following recommendations:*
- *The sub-committee recommends the following steps:*
- *The following steps are recommended:*

The recommendations may also be written without any introductory sentence, for example,

(1) A scheme of loans to educated boys and girls should be introduced to encourage self-employment.

(2) Loans should be given for minor irrigation projects to combat the drought conditions.

(3) The possibility of establishing a hire-purchase scheme through the bank for consumer durables should be explored.

Signature, Place, Date

A committee report must be signed by all members of the committee. The signatures are on the right. The place and date are on the left. The date is the day of submission of the report.

Place : Mumbai

Date : 23 May, 2000

R. B. Dabholkar, Convener
C. K. Puranik
J. J. Mehta

These are the essential parts of a report.

Other Parts of a Report

A long report which is divided into several chapters or sections has some ancillary parts to make it easy for the reader to find different parts or sections.

Table of Contents is given after the title page. It is a list of the chapters by number (and name if any), with the page number on which the chapter begins. It is like the table of contents in any book.

Acknowledgements can be written in one paragraph or a few short paragraphs; it is a list of names of persons who helped the writer of the report with information, references, discussion, etc. It appears before the first chapter.

Appendix (plural: appendices or appendixes) is supplementary material given at the end of the report. This may be a copy of a questionnaire used, or plans of buildings, maps or other material which is referred to in the body of the report, but need not appear in the body. Any interested reader can refer to it since it is mentioned in the report. If there is more than one appendix, they are numbered.

Bibliography is the list of books and articles used by the report writer. It is arranged in alphabetical order of the surnames of the authors.

Review

1. Name the essential parts of a report. 2. Explain in two or three sentences, the following parts of a report. (a) bibliography (b) appendix. 3. Name some non-verbal methods of presenting information in a report.

Specimen Reports

15 June, 2003

The Managing Director
XYZ Paints Ltd.

Sir,

Re: Working of Nagpur Branch

In accordance with your instruction by telephone, on 4 June 2003, I visited the Nagpur Branch for a surprise inspection last week. I observed the working of the branch office for three days and also inspected the office and the records. I am sorry to report that the branch office is run in a most unsatisfactory manner.

When I reached the branch office on 10 June at 10.15 a.m., which is 15 minutes after opening time, I found that there were only a peon and two clerks. Taking me for a client, they informed me that office work started only at 11.00 a.m. The manager, Mr. R.S. Tatki arrived at 11.30 a.m.; lacking discipline himself Mr. Tatki is unable to maintain any discipline among the staff.

The stock register and the account books have not been properly maintained for the last three months. It also appears that office stationery and small articles are freely used and taken away by the staff. The general indiscipline, if not controlled at once, is likely to result in heavy losses. Already there is loss of business since many of our clients have turned to our competitors owing to the poor service rendered by our branch office.

Since the situation is quite bad, it will be necessary to take drastic steps to restore discipline in the branch office. I recommend that Mr. Tatki should be brought to the H.O. and kept in a subordinate position. Mr. G.K. Nayyar, Assistant Manager of Pune branch has proved himself quite able; he may be promoted as Manager and posted at Nagpur.

Yours faithfully,
ABC
Secretary

Date ....

The Managing Director
Glazed Tiles (Pvt.) Ltd.

Dear Sir,

Sub: Decline of Sales of Tiles

In accordance with your instructions I have enquired fully into the causes of the decline in the company's business in the last two years till July 2003, and submit my report as follows:

Several new companies have put out glazed tiles in the market. Some of the companies have introduced artistically designed tiles in a variety of colours. Besides most companies make square tiles in four sizes and rectangular tiles in two sizes.

We have limited our production of tiles to six standard colours without design, and to only two sizes.

Tiles are used extensively in kitchens of homes and hotels but the demand is for designed tiles, and for sizes other than those we make. Hence, while the market for tiles has gone up, we have not been able to keep our share of the business.

Recommendations

1. An experienced designer should be appointed to create new designs for our tiles.
2. A colour technician should be appointed to assist the designer.
3. Some of the more popular sizes and shapes should be introduced.
4. An intensive advertising and sales campaign should be launched in order to win back the lost market.
5. Follow-up correspondence should be maintained with all former customers in order to regain and build up old contacts.

Yours faithfully,
XYZ
Secretary

The following report by Auditors to Directors of a company where indiscipline has led to losses was assigned to a firm of Chartered Accountants.

15 September, 2003

The Directors
Rosa Glass Works (Pvt) Ltd.
Mumbai

Sirs,

In accordance with the instructions in your letter dated 1st September, 2003, we had two experienced persons from this firm observe the working of your company for two weeks to investigate the methods of running the business, and the daily conduct of the staff.

From the observation, the following defects were noted:

1. The Secretary's age and continued poor health has made him lose interest, and the Registrar is too indecisive to control the office staff who disobey his instructions. As a result, the work as a whole is not carried out according to the instructions of the Managing Director, and is often seriously delayed. Customers complain about delays and some even cancel their orders owing to the delays in delivery.
2. The departmental managers at the works, with the exception of the one in the Stores Department, have become too friendly with the workers. Their authority is thus weakened, and the workers waste a great deal of time. The production is seriously slowed down, and the goods are not finished to the required high standard. This has resulted in rejection by customers, and general loss of business, apart from the loss of man hours, power and raw material. This matter

has been reported twice to the Secretary by the Works Manager, but no action has been taken.

3. The Accountant, owing to ill-health, has not kept his professional knowledge up-to-date, and has made no effort to find the best system of costing to suit the company's business. Prices quoted for some contracts have been far below the actual cost, and some of the contracts carried out have resulted in losses. When an attempt was made to correct this, unreasonably high prices were quoted, leading to loss of business.

The following recommendations are made:

1. The Secretary should be superannuated, and the Registrar demoted to the position of superintendent. The positions of Secretary and Registrar should be filled by competent and efficient men who are able to impose discipline on the staff.
2. All the departmental managers at the works, except the Stores Manager, should be dismissed immediately, with one month's salary.
3. The Accountant should be superseded, and a person with up-to-date knowledge should be appointed above him.
4. A staff meeting should be called to explain the need for discpline and to point out that disobedience to orders of superiors will be punished with immediate dismissal. Notices announcing this warning should be put up in all the departments of the office and the works.

Yours faithfully,
XYZ
Partner, Sanghvi and Shah
Accountants

The schematic form may be used for presenting a complex report. The details are arranged under headings. The passive voice is used for most statements in a formal style.

Report on Workers' Unrest at Pyramid Plastic Works Factory, Wadala, Mumbai

I. Terms of Reference

To report on the workers' unrest and make recommendations to remedy the situation. The report was assigned by Board of Directors at its meeting held on 2 December, 2003.

II. Procedure

(A) The Works Manager of the factory was met twice, and detailed discussions were held, once alone, and the second time in the presence of his Assistant.

(B) The committee's report is always in the schematic form. The following are examples of a report in schematic form: two meetings were held, one with the foremen alone, and one with the foremen in the presence of the Assistant Works Manager.

(C) Twenty workers, chosen at random, were interviewed personally, and their views ascertained.

III. Findings

(A) Extent of Unrest: The discontent and apathy, and the unrest that followed were observed among the workers in the month of September for the first time. To begin with, there were only signs of occasional outbursts of ill-temper or lack of interest in work. These were followed by group meetings and discussions of workers. Finally at the end of October a meeting of all the workers was held and a memorandum was presented to the Works Manager. A report was sent by the Works Manager to the General Manager, but the workers' representation was not sent.

Several foremen felt that unless remedial steps were taken, the situation might get out of hand, with the possibility of total strike.

(B) Causes of Unrest: Resentment was felt by workers at the insistence of the new Works Manager on punctuality and greater efficiency while conditions in the factory have become too uncomfortable for efficient functioning. Complaints were made by workers that:

1. There was no suitable bus service available from the Railway station to the factory. Even a slight delay in starting the machines was ticked off by the Works Manager.
2. There was not enough room in the canteen; workers' strength has been doubled during the last two years.
3. Machines were kept too close to each other and workers were unable to operate them with ease as they used to, before additional machines were installed.

IV. Conclusions

The complaints made by the workers seemed just.

(i) Workers who travel by train find it difficult, occasionally, to arrive in time, owing to irregular bus service from the station to the factory. However, the delay has never been more than seven minutes.

(ii) Owing to lack of space in the canteen, workers have to spend part of their lunch hour in waiting for a seat in the canteen. They are often forced to eat hurriedly to be in time after the lunch hour.

(iii) Additional machines installed in the month of August have been installed in violation of the Factories Act which lays down the minimum space between machines.

V. Recommendations

1. A bus service should be operated between the factory and the station, to be run four times daily to coincide with the two shifts.
2. The store-room adjacent to the canteen should be cleaned up and handed over to the canteen for additional space.
3. The Works Manager should be advised to keep some of the machines in the crowded parts of the factory unused, so as to prevent hazardous occupation of workers at the machines, until the machines are moved to new premises. Work should be suitably rescheduled.
4. The contractor should be advised to hasten the construction work so that the extension of the factory is completed within two months.

5. The Works Manager should be advised to take a more humane view of the problem until the extensions are completed and conditions are made more comfortable.

18 December, 2003

James Mason
Secretary

Report of Sub-committee on Decline in the Circulation of the Company's Magazine "The Indian Woman"

To the Board of Directors
Popular Magazines Pvt. Ltd.

I. Terms of Reference

The sub-committee was appointed by the following resolution of the Board passed at the meeting held on 8 February, 2003.

"Resolved that a sub-committee consisting of Mr. Dalal, convener, Dr. Gulzar and Mrs. Ahuja be, and is hereby, appointed to investigate the causes of the decline in the circulation of 'The Indian Woman' and to report with recommendations in a month's time."

II. Procedure

(i) The sub-committee met three times, on 11th and 23rd February, and 5th March.

(ii) Three of the large distributors in Mumbai were contacted and their views noted.

(iii) Twenty small magazine shop owners were questioned to find out their experience with the sale of women's magazines.

(iv) Fifteen hundred questionnaires were collected from various readers including our past and present subscribers and members of women's associations. Their interviews were sent out for filling in the questionnaires.

(v) Other women's magazines available in Mumbai were carefully compared with our magazine.

(vi) Circulation figures of the last 3 years for our magazine were studied, and the company's budgeting policy reviewed.

III. Findings

From the investigation, the sub-committee arrived at the following conclusions:

The decline in the circulation became sharp in May 2001, although there was a gradual decline over the six months before that. The fall by over 30% in January 2002 coincided with the arrival of a new women's magazine, 'Eve's Era,' on the market. While our two competitors, 'Women Today' and 'High Fashion' were able to withstand the impact, our magazine failed to retain its share of the market. This is largely due to the fact that the quality of our magazine had already begun to deteriorate.

The deterioration in quality was traced to the decision to make no increase in the expenditure on paper and to purchase paper in bulk for all the company's publications. The women's magazine editor had always been given freedom to select the paper in view of the sophisticated readership of the magazine and the need for good reproduction of photographs, drawings and various other illustrations. The magazine suffered an immediate set-back when it was allotted the ordinary newsprint.

As a result of using the ordinary newsprint, the photographs and illustrations became poor in reproduction. This caused reputed photographers, artists and illustrators to refuse to contribute to our magazine. Gradually, reputed writers who used to write regularly for our magazine began to contribute feature articles to other periodicals. Hence there was a general fall in the quality of the magazine.

IV. Recommendations

(i) Adequate funds should be allocated to the magazine, and the Editor authorised to purchase good quality paper for the next issue.

(ii) The Editor should be instructed to write letters to reputed writers inviting contributions and offering an attractive honorarium.

(iii) The services of good artists and photographers should be procured by offering attractive terms.

(iv) An intensive publicity campaign should be launched to impress upon the public, the improved quality of the magazine.

Sd-
A.G. Dalal, Convener
B.V. Gulzar
(Mrs.) S.T. Ahuja

Date : 12 March, 2003
Place : Mumbai

Report of Sub-committee on the choice of a suitable site for a branch factory in Maharashtra

To the Directors
Crystal Glass Works

I. Terms of Reference

The sub-committee was appointed by Resolution No. 845 adopted at a meeting of the Board of Directors, held on 10 January, 2003. The sub-committee, consisting of Mr. Pea, convener, Mr. Que and Mr. Are, was authorised to choose a suitable site for a branch factory for producing glassware in Maharashtra and to report in two months.

II. Procedure

The sub-committee held three meetings, on 13 and 29 January and 28 February.

The members of the sub-committee visited Mumbai, Pune and Nagpur between 20 January and 10 February, and saw several sites available for industrial units.

The members also met the Government and Municipal authorities to enquire about permission, licences, water and power connections.

III. Findings

The sub-committee felt that Mumbai is the most suitable city for a glass works factory, owing to the local market as well as export facilities.

Other conditions are described below:

A. Raw Materials: All the components for the manufacture of glass are available in Mumbai since there are several other glassware factories. Fine sand is regularly supplied by specialised agents, from the banks of the Narmada, the Tapi, and the Godavari rivers.

B. Staff and Workers: Supervisory staff, and skilled and unskilled labour are available. The salaries and wages are higher than in the other cities but the quality of the work is of a high standard. Highly qualified technicians and designers receive very high salaries in Mumbai, but the expense of such staff will be compensated for by the market.

C. Power and Water: The Government authorities have agreed to give electricity and water connections and to supply the required quantities of power and water.

D. Scope for Expansion: The company's market can be extended to foreign countries through the Export Promotion Council as well as the consulates in Mumbai.

E. Site: There are three suitable sites of 4, 5 and 6 acres at Vikhroli, Borivli and Mulund respectively. All are available on a 99 years' lease. Details of the 3 sites are in Appendix I.

IV. Recommendations

The sub-committee recommends that:

1. One of the sites be chosen in consultation with the Company's Architects.
2. Negotiations be started immediately to acquire the selected site.
3. The Secretary be authorised to invite tenders for the construction of the factory and to apply to the Government of India for licence to import the required machines.

Date: 5 March, 2003,
Place: Surat

N. O. Pea
O. P. Que
P. Q. Are

EXERCISES

1. The Chief Marketing Executive of Udai Garments, visited Germany to explore the possibility of entering the European market. He found that the company's garments were criticized for dull colours, and limited range of sizes. Write the Executive's report to the company's Directors recommending changes to be made in the production designs to enable the company to sell in the European market.
2. There has been some unrest among the employees of a pharmaceuticals firm. The employees are all women. Write the report of the Human Resources Manager who was asked to make an inquiry.
3. There has been remarkable decline in the sale of sports goods manufactured by a company. The Marketing Manager has been asked to report with recommendations for stopping the decline. Prepare the report.
4. Many complaints have been received about delays in delivery, and shortage in the consignments of a company's edible oils dispatched to Gujrat. A senior marketing official from the company has been asked to look into the causes of the complaints and report to the Board of Directors within fifteen days. Write the report.
5. The Principal of a college has appointed a committee of two teachers and three students to suggest new directions in which students' co-curricular activities can be developed. Write the committee's report.
6. As the Librarian of your college, you have been asked by the Principal to suggest reorganization of the college library so as to make the maximum use of space and

facilities available. Prepare the report, recommending computerization of the library's catalogues and lending system.

7. The results of a college have been very poor for the last five years. The Managing Committee of the Society which runs the college has asked the Principal to make a recommendatory report for improving the results. Write the report including a brief statement of the finance required.
8. Three management trainees have been appointed to a committee to look into the problem of theft and pilferage from the factory premises. Write their report.
9. A manufacturing company proposes to start a Welfare Centre for its employees. The Personnel Officer has been asked to make a report presenting a plan for the Centre. Write the report.
10. A manufacturing company (product of your choice) from Himachal Pradesh proposes to open a sales depot in Pune in Maharashtra. Prepare the report to be submitted to the Board of Directors by a subcommittee of three of the Directors.
11. Madhusagar Fruit Canning Company, Nagpur, proposes to open a branch factory in Goa in order to take advantage of the different variety of fruit available in the region. A sub-committee of Directors has been appointed to examine the feasibility of the proposal. Write the report recommending a suitable location for the factory.
12. There has been significant decline in the business of the urban branches of a nationalized bank. A committee of five Regional Managers has been appointed to look into the causes. Write the report recommending computerization of the branches and customer relations training for the staff.
13. It has been proposed that the working hours of your bank branch be changed to morning and evening hours, for the banking convenience of customers. You have been appointed convener of a committee to look into the feasibility of implementing the proposal. Prepare your report with recommendations.
14. A committee consisting of the Factory Manager, the Personnel Manager, and the Chief Engineer has been asked to look into the possibility of holding regular refresher courses for all supervisors of the factory workers. Draft the report to be made after completing the survey, giving recommendations.
15. There have been constant complaints from your customers about late delivery of goods and shortage in the goods supplied. As Head of the dispatch section you have been asked to look into the matter and report with recommendation. Draft your report.

Chapter - 12

LAYOUT OF A BUSINESS LETTER

A business letter has a distinctive structure and appearance. Each of the parts has a specific style, position and function which has been established by custom and is followed because it is convenient for handling and processing correspondence in an organization's office. A letter is usually an organization's first visual contact with another organization or person, and makes an important impression.

APPEARANCE OF A BUSINESS LETTER

A letter makes a visual impression before it is read, and the first impression is often decisive. Everyone is attracted by a good, presentable appearance.

The appearance of a letter depends on all the things that make up the letter.

Stationery must be of good quality. Most companies prefer to use pure white paper, with black print for the heading. The envelope must be of the same quality paper with the same type of print as the letterhead.

The printers and typewriters must be maintained well and cleaned regularly; the ribbons need regular attention. Good quality carbon paper must be used for making copies.

Typing must be neat, without cancellations or corrections. There should be equal spacing between words and between lines, and double spacing between paragraphs and different parts of the letter. The letter should be placed carefully in the centre of the page, leaving equal margins on the sides and at the bottom. The margins are usually one-and-a-half inch on the left, one inch on the right, and at least one inch at the bottom. If a continuation sheet is used, it must have the same margins as the first page.

A suitable style of layout is selected by every organization and all typists are expected to use the adopted style. Most word processing packages offer the choice of full block or modified block style of layout.

Paragraphing is necessary for breaking up a composition into readable, logical and progressive units. It is also needed for a pleasing appearance. A large block of writing is not pleasant to see; it is restful to the eyes to see a good amount of white space between the reading material. In a business letter, paragraphing is important for appearance as well as for composition. Usually, a letter has three to four paragraphs: a short opening paragraph which may have only one or two sentences; one or two longer middle paragraphs which carry the main message of the letter; and a short closing paragraph which may be only one sentence.

Folding of the letter must be neat. It makes a poor impression if it is badly folded. The size of folded letter must be such as to fit in the envelope leaving enough space for cutting the envelope open.

Address on the envelope is typed halfway down and one-third in from the left in order to ensure that the post office franking or stamping does not efface it. It is typed in block form. Its appearance is as important as that of the letter as it is seen before the letter. Note that the practice of writing *To*, is outdated.

STATIONERY

Every office has certain standard stationery required for correspondence. The sizes of the sheets and envelopes are standard, but some organizations have distinctive sizes. The quality of the stationery, the designing of the letterhead, the layout and printing/typing together make the first visual impression on the receiver.

Letterheads

Letterheads can be got in several sizes. Most companies have letterheads of at least two sizes: the standard 8.5 × 11 inches for most letters, and smaller 5.5 × 8 inches for short letters. The appearance and the quality of the letterhead makes an important first impression on the receiver of the letter. Good quality, white paper should be used for letter stationery. Letterhead can be designed in consultation with a commercial artist or a computer graphics firm. Simple, elegant, stream-lined designs are in keeping with modern style.

Continuation Sheets

A continuation sheet is used if a letter does not fit on a single sheet. The continuation sheet is of the same size and quality as the letterhead. The company's name is printed across the top of the sheet in the same colour as the print on the letterhead. The name of the receiver, the page number, and the date of the letter are typed at the top, in one line. The top margin should be one inch, and the side and bottom margins should be the same as those on the letterhead on which the letter begins.

Envelopes

Offices usually have envelopes of several sizes for use according to the size and quantity of the material to be dispatched. The company's name and address are printed at the bottom on the left; some companies have it printed on the flap of the envelope. The receiver's address is typed, or the address label is affixed neatly on the back of the envelope.

The quality of the paper and the colour of the envelope must match those of the letterhead. Some offices also have brown paper envelopes for dispatch of printed material.

Window envelopes have a transparent panel in the place where the receiver's address is to be written. The letter is folded and inserted in the envelope in such a way that the inside address can be seen through the window of the envelope. Window envelopes are most useful for sending out circulars as they eliminate the need for addressing the envelope. They are not generally used for confidential communications.

PARTS OF A LETTER

An official letter looks different from a personal letter and from other types of business documents. Convenience and custom have laid down certain requirements as parts of a letter. Since letters serve as records, some routine details are necessary in the make-up of a letter.

Different parts have their own fixed location on the sheet; there is a slight variation from left to right in the different styles of layout; their order of appearance from top to bottom, is the same in all styles.

The main parts of the letter, apart from the text of the message are: Heading, Date, Inside address, Salutation, Complimentary close and Signature. In addition to these, the following details are included, according to the requirement of each letter: Reference number, Delivery mode, Subject line, Attention line, Enclosures, Courtesy copies, Sender's & Typist's initials. The letter wizard in Word 97 guides you through all the parts of the letter.

Heading

The heading is printed at the top. It includes the company's

(a) name and business

(b) emblem

(c) postal, telegraphic, and e-mail addresses

(d) telephone, telex, and fax numbers

Some companies include the names of directors or of the Chairman or of the Managing Director. Most companies prefer to have letterheads with a streamlined appearance; the printed portion does not occupy more than one-fifth of the sheet. It is printed in a simple attractive design in a single colour, usually black. The printed sheet is called letterhead.

Educational Publishers
Himalaya Publishing House
"Ramdoot", Dr. Bhalerao Marg
Kelewadi, Girgaon
Mumbai 400 004

Ref....

Date...

Date

Every official document must be dated. The date provides an important point of reference in further correspondence and in following up the issues dealt with in the letter. The date is placed two line spaces below the heading, on the right. In full block and NOMA styles, the date is at the left margin.

In all formal letters, the name of the month is spelled out in full; the year is written in all four figures. The figure of the year is separated from the date and month by a comma. The date can be written in either of the following ways:

16 June, 2003

June 16, 2003

The practice of writing ordinal numbers, 1st, 2nd, 3rd, 4th, has fallen out of use.

Reference Number

Reference number appears on the left on level with the date. The words *Ref. no.* may be printed on the letterhead; some companies have both, *Our ref. no.* and *Your ref. no.* printed on the letterhead, and give both numbers in their letters. The reference number gives the letter number, file no. and other filing details; a letter is filed and can be located among office records, by its reference number.

Inside Address

Inside address is the name and address of the receiver. It is typed in block form; only a very few old-fashioned companies use the indented form.

In the indented form the first line begins at the margin and the subsequent lines begin two spaces away from the beginning of the previous line; a comma follows each line and a full stop is placed after the last line. The indentions and the punctuation take more time to type, and also present a cluttered appearance. This style is now obsolete.

In the block form all lines begin at the margin and there is no punctuation at the end of any line. This style looks neat and takes less time to type.

Block	**Indented**
Neil Publishing House	*Neil Publishing House,*
896, Mahatma Gandhi Road	896, Mahatma Gandhi Road,
Kolkata 700 001	Kolkata 700 001.

Note that the practice of writing *To* before the address is outdated now.

Attention Line

Attention line is used only if, from previous communication, you know the name of the person in the organization who is handling the matter about which you are writing. The letter is addressed to the organization, but directed to the attention of the individual, by name, so that the letter is sent to that person without delay.

The Attention line placed between the inside address and the salutation, either at the margin or in the centre. It does not affect the salutation. The salutation must match the first line of the inside address, e.g.,

The Blank Foods Manufacturers
Tagore Road
Kolkata 700 001

Attention: Miss A.C. Biswas

Gentlemen:

If the letter is addressed by name to an individual in the company, there is no attention line. It is used only when the letter is addressed to the company or a department in general.

Subject Line

Subject line gives a brief and quick indication of the subject of the letter. It adds to the clarity of the letter, especially if the letter is long. It helps to classify and file the letter.

It is placed either above or below the salutation at the centre; in full block form, it is placed at the left margin. When there is an Attention line, the Subject line is placed after the Salutation.

It is introduced by the word *Subject*: or *Sub*. or the Latin word *Re:* for example:

> Subject: Your insurance policy no. 8873265
>
> Dear Sir,
>
> Or
>
> Gentlemen:
>
> Sub: Your order no. YA-42
>
> (Note: Re is a Latin preposition meaning "in the matter of" or "in the case of"; it is not the short form of any English word; it is not correct to write ref. or reg. for the subject line.)
>
> In more modern practice, the subject line is placed at the margin below the salutation, without any introductory word. It may be in capitals or initial capitals and underlined; e.g.
>
> Dear Mr Lulla,
>
> ORDER NUMBER 5476

Salutation

The Salutation begins at the margin, two line spaces below the inside address. It is followed by a comma. In American practice it is followed by a colon; in full block style it has no punctuation mark.

The salutation matches the first line of the inside address. If the letter is addressed to an organization, the salutation is plural: *Gentlemen* or *Dear Sirs* or *Sirs*. If the letter is addressed to a particular official mentioned only by designation, e.g., "The Sales Manager" the salutation is singular: Sir or Dear Sir. If the official is a lady, the salutation is *Madam* or *Dear Madam*.

It is quite common, now, to address business letters to an official by name and designation, e.g., *Mr. A.P. Shah, Sales Manager*, or *Ms A.B. Coelho, Finance Manager*. In this case, the salutation is *Dear Mr. Shah* or *Dear Ms Coelho*. Ms can be used before a lady's name as it stands for both Miss and Mrs.

Review

Fill in the blanks using the minimum number of words for each blank.

(a) A letter addressed to Tristar Computers Ltd and directed to the attention of Mrs. Anita Dasgupta may have the salutation —.

(b) The commonly accepted styles of writing the date are — and ——.

(c) The purpose of the reference number in a letter is —.

(d) The attention line is used only when — in order to —.

(e) In a letter which has an attention line, the subject line is placed —; otherwise it is placed —.

(f) If a letter is addressed to The Sales Manager, the salutation would be —; if it is addressed to The Sales Department, the salutation would be —.

Complimentary Close

The complimentary close is written two line spaces below the last line of the text of the letter; it is placed on the right and is followed by a comma. In full block style and NOMA style it is placed at the left margin and has no comma. The first word begins with a capital letter.

The most common form is : *Yours faithfully*; Other common forms are: *Faithfully yours*, *Yours truly, Truly yours.*

If the addressee's name is used in the salutation, the complimentary close is *Yours sincerely*, or *Sincerely yours.*

Respectfully is used only when writing to a high public official.

Signature

The signature is placed just below the complimentary close. The name of the signatory is typed in brackets three or four line spaces below (to leave space for the actual signature), and the designation/title is typed below the name. The complete signature includes the name of the company, either above or below the name and designation of the person who signs; but many companies do not put the company's name in the signature as it is already in the heading.

The following styles are in common use:

Yours truly,	Yours truly,
ABC Publishers	(William Lyle)
(William Lyle)	Sales Manager
Sales Manager	ABC Publishers

Per pro (Per procurationem) signature is used when the person who signs is not personally liable but has been given power of attorney to sign on behalf of the person or company who will be responsible. The words per pro or P.P. are put before the name of the person or company on whose behalf the letter is sent.

Reference Section

The reference section includes: enclosures, names of parties to receive copies, the type of delivery service to be used, and initials of the persons who dictated and typed the letter. Most of the details are for the convenience of the dispatch department. They are placed at the left margin after the signature.

(a) **Enclosures:** Enclosures are related documents sent with a letter; bills, cheques, quotations, brochures, price-lists, etc., which have been mentioned in the letter are sent as enclosures. They are folded and placed behind the letter in the envelope. If there are many enclosures, they are numbered and placed in the order of their serial number.

The enclosures are indicated in the letter by writing *Enc(s)* or *Encls*: at the bottom corner of the letter, after the signature. If there is more than one, the number is also indicated, e.g. *Encls: 2*. Sometimes the enclosure is named, e.g. Encl: pro forma invoice.

(b) **Courtesy Copies:** When a matter concerns more than the two parties, a copy of letters related to the matter is sent for information to the other parties who are concerned. This is indicated by writing:

c.c.: Mr. A.C. Sheth

or

c.c.: 1. Mr. A.C. Sheth
2. *Accounts Manager, ABC Transport Service*

Note that, cc also stands for "carbon copy."

(c) **Delivery Service:** The type of delivery service to be used is indicated as Air Mail, Registered Mail, Express Delivery, Hand Delivery, Courier, Fax, etc.

(d) **Initials:** The dictator's and the typist's initials are placed at the bottom. This is for future reference in the sender's office; the person who prepares or dictates a letter is not necessarily the person who signs it. The letter may be dictated by a senior clerk or a junior officer; it will be signed by the manager or a person who is authorized to sign for the company. The initials may be shown as: *PSW:rd* or *CRT gt* or *MRO/cs* or any such style.

Postscript

Postscript is a bit of writing, not more than three lines, added to the letter after the signature and after enclosures; it is signed again, without the complimentary close, by the same person. It is used for conveying a small bit of information which is not a part of the main message of the letter; it is an extra or unrelated point and is often written in hand at the time of signing the letter.

Postscript should never be used for adding something which was forgotten while preparing the letter. The idea of using PS to add a forgotten point is outdated with word processors. Even if a manual typewriter is being used, the letter must be typed again.

The postscript can be used to add a friendly personal note to a formal letter; it may be just a line, but it can successfully establish personal contact by referring to some common experience or by making a friendly personal enquiry. For instance:

- *P. S. It was nice meeting you at the dinner last Sunday.*
- *P. S. How's your new venture in Guwahati coming up? Wish you the best of success.*

The Postscript can be used effectively in a sales letter to impress an "action incentive" sentence on the reader's mind.

- *PS: There's an early bird prize for the first seven orders.*

It can also be used to make an impact at the end of a "stunt" collection letter.

- *PS: Do clear your account before the fast approaching festival season.*

Review

Complete the sentence by choosing the correct answer.

(1) An acceptable form of writing the complimentary close is —

(a) yours Faithfully,

(b) Your's faithfully,

(c) Yours' faithfully,

(d) Yours faithfully,

(e) yours faithfully,

(2) When the salutation is Dear Mr Adhikary, the correct complimentary close is —

(a) Yours obediently,

(b) Yours faithfully,

(c) Yours affectionately,

(d) Yours sincerely,

(3) Fill in the blanks.

(a) The reference section includes —, —, —, and —.

(b) A letter addressed to Comfort Furniture, with the salutation *Gentlemen,* may end with *Yours* —.

(c) Courtesy copies are sent to — for the purpose of —.

(d) Any documents sent together with a letter are indicated by ——.

(e) Postscript is indicated by writing — and is used for —.

STYLES OF LAYOUT

Layout means the design in which the different parts of the letter are placed on the letterhead. The parts are placed in the same order from top to bottom in all forms or styles; the variation is in the indention and the paragraph styles.

Indented Form

This is the oldest style and is now outdated. In this form, the inside address is in indented style as shown earlier, and every paragraph begins three to five spaces away from the left margin. The indention causes the letter to look uneven at the left margin. Besides, it takes more time to type because of the indenting. This style is not used today.

Full Block Form

This is the most modern style. There is no indention from the left margin at all; every line, including the date and the complimentary close, begins at the left margin. The address has no punctuation at the end of the line. The salutation and the complimentary close do not have a comma at the end. There is double line space between the parts and between the paragraphs.

Typists have an advantage in this form; it takes less time to type because it requires no change of margin and has less punctuation.

Some companies do not like this form because it looks heavy on the left, and rather blank on the right.

A clear disadvantage of this form is that, after the letter has been filed, the date and the signature cannot be seen unless the file is fully opened. The date of a letter is an important item and is often referred to for many purposes. Quick reference to date and to signature is not possible in this form.

Modified Block Form

This style is a modification of the full block form. It eliminates the shortcomings of the full block style by keeping the date and the complimentary close on the right in their usual position. The inside address is in block form. The salutation and the complimentary close are followed by a comma. All the paragraphs begin at the left margin, and there is double space between the paragraphs.

This is the most popular form, as it has many of the advantages of the full block form without its disadvantages. Its appearance is balanced and neat.

Semi-indented Form

This form is also called Semi-block form. It has the inside address in block form but the beginning of every paragraph is indented. The date and the complimentary close are on the right side. The salutation and the complimentary close are followed by a comma as in the traditional style.

Hanging Indention Form

In this style, the inside address is in block form. The date and complimentary close are on the right. The beginning of every paragraph is at the left margin, but the subsequent lines of every paragraph are indented three to five spaces. The margins for the first line and subsequent lines can be set on a computer, but it takes more time to type on a manual typewriter.

This style is adopted for sales letters, brochures and other documents in which striking appearance is useful. The opening line of every paragraph "hangs out", and can be used for highlighting important points. If this style is used, the opening words of every paragraph should be important and worth highlighting.

NOMA Form

This is the most recent experiment in layout style. It is recommended by National Office Management Association of America (the name NOMA is an acronym). It has been accepted in the UK by the Institute of Office Management.

It has most of the features of Full Block form: all lines begin at the left margin, and the inside address is in block form. The special features of this form are: (i) it has no salutation and no complimentary close; (ii) the subject line is in capitals three lines below the inside address; (iii) numbered items of a list begin at the left margin, but if there is no number, the items are indented five spaces; there are no full-stops at the end of items; (iv) the writer's name and title are typed in capitals in one line below the space for signature; (v) the typist's initials are in the left bottom corner. This style is not popular as it is too far removed from the familiar, conventional styles. Some people feel that this style saves time and sensibly omits meaningless salutation and close; but most people feel that this omission makes it impersonal, distant, and lacking in feeling.

Review

Answer in two or three sentences.

(a) What are the main differences between the full block form and the modified block form?

(b) What is the distinctive feature of the Hanging Indention form?

(c) How would you use the distinctive feature of the Hanging Indention form?

(d) Why do some people dislike the NOMA form?

An organization decides on its letter layout style and appearance after careful consideration and all typists are expected to conform to the standard of typing set up by the company.

Illustrations of all the styles are given below:

18 November, 2003

Excello Typing Institute,
14, Green Avenue,
Kolkata 700 053.

Dear Sirs,

This is the Indented form which is considered old fashioned now. The inside address is indented, i.e., each subsequent line is indented 2 spaces from the previous line; each line is followed by a comma, and the last line by a full stop. Each paragraph begins five spaces away from the margin.

This form was used in the days before the typewriter when all letters were hand-written. Today even handwritten letters are not written in this style.

The appearance of this style is not very neat; besides, it wastes typing time because of the indentions.

Yours faithfully,

Office Superintendent

Indented Form

2 May, 2003

Windsor Stationery Mart
86, Main Avenue, Salt Lake
Kolkata 700 054

Gentlemen

This letter is in Full-Block form. Every part of the letter, including the date and complimentary close, begins at the left hand margin.

The inside address is in block form with no end-of-line punctuation. There is no punctuation mark after the salutation or after the complimentary close.

As there is absolutely no indention, this form takes the shortest time to type, and is very useful in a firm which sends out a large number of letters. It is the latest in styles of layout, but it has already become quite popular and is used in a number of firms.

The drawback of this form is that it looks rather blank on the right side and heavy on the left. Besides, when the letter is filed, it is difficult to refer to the date and the signature without taking out the file and opening it fully.

Yours faithfully

Correspondence Supervisor

Full-Block Form

10 September, 2003

Pinto Commercial Institute
23, Rampart Row
Kolkata 700 001

Dear Sirs,

This is the Modified Block Form, and is in most common use today. Most companies adopt this form as the most convenient and also the most attractive.

The date and the complimentary close are at the right. The address is in block form, that is, all lines begin at the margin and there are no punctuation marks at the end of any line. The paragraphs begin at the left margin and are separated only by double spacing. As most of the lines begin at the left margin, this form saves the time of the typist.

This form is neat and balanced in appearance. It is a modification of the ultra modern Full Block Form.

Yours truly,

Supervisor

Modified Block Form

15 July, 2003

Modern Typists
29, Mount Road
Kolkata 700 002

Sirs,

The Semi-Block form combines the indented and block forms. Some of its features are taken from the old style and some from the new style.

The date and the complimentary close are on the right. The address is in block form and the paragraphs are indented five spaces away from the margin. Many firms use this form although it does not look so streamlined as the modified block form.

This form will probably fall out of [illegible] letters and will be used only for handwritten letters.

Yours faithfully,

Sales Manager

Semi-Block Form

20 August, 2003

Expert Advisory Service
Beach View
Warden Road
Kolkata 700 026

Gentlemen:

This is the Hanging Indention form. It has the address in block form, every paragraph starting at the margin, and subsequent lines of every paragraph indented a few spaces from the margin.

As the first line of every paragraph 'hangs' out, it attracts attention. Sales and stunt collection letters are written in this style in order to catch the eye. The opening words of every paragraph must be striking and the drafting must be done carefully.

Typing time is wasted in this form because of the large number of indentions. It is not used for routine letters.

Yours faithfully,

Sales Manager

Hanging Indention Form

11 May 2000

Expert Advisory Services
Beach View
Kolkata 700 026

NOMA LETTER LAYOUT STYLE

The name NOMA is an acronym of National Office Management Association. This American organization has recommended this style. It has been accepted in Britain with some modifications.

Most of its features are the same as those of the full block style. The address is in block form with no punctuation at the end of the line. All lines begin at the left margin.

This style has the following special features:

(a) Salutation and complimentary close are omitted.

(b) Subject is in capitals three lines below the inside address.

(c) Enumerated item lists, like this one, begin at the left margin. Lists of items without number/letter are indented five spaces.

(d) There is no full stop at the end of the items in the list.

(e) The writer's name and title are typed in capital letter in one line at the left margin at the end of the letter, leaving space for the signature.

(f) The typist's initials are at the bottom left corner.

Some people like this form as it eliminates the needless salutation and complimentary close, but it is impersonal, distant and too far removed from the familiar conventional styles.

KAMAL BHUTA - REGISTRAR
vsd

NOMA Form

EXERCISES

1. Fill in the blanks using as few words as possible.
   (a) A window envelope has —; this saves office time because ——.
   (b) On envelopes, the sender's name is printed at — or —.
   (c) On a continuation sheet, — is printed; you have to type —, — and — at the top.
   (d) Companies have letterheads and envelopes in several sizes because —.
   (e) Appearance of a letter depends on —, —, —.
2. Are these statements true?
   (a) Continuation sheets may be of a lower quality paper than letterheads.
   (b) Letterheads used for official letters should be colourful in order to be attractive.
   (c) Envelopes match the letterheads in quality, colour and printing style.
   (d) The manner in which a letter is prepared for dispatch affects its appearance and the impression it makes on the receiver.
3. How will you ensure that your letter makes a good visual impression?
4. Write notes on:
   (i) Letterhead and heading
   (ii) Date and reference no.
   (iii) First line of inside address
   (iv) Inside address and salutation
   (v) Attention line and salutation
   (vi) Subject line and attention line
   (vii) First line of inside address and salutation
   (viii) Salutation and complimentary close
   (ix) Complimentary close and signature
   (x) Reference section
   (xi) Enclosures
   (xii) Postscript

5. Write a note on the stationery required for letter writing.
6. Write notes on:
   (i) Advantages and disadvantages of full block form
   (ii) Modified block form
   (iii) NOMA form of layout
   (iv) Disadvantages of Indented form
   (v) Features of Hanging indention form of layout
   (vi) Semi-indented form of layout
   (vii) Continuation sheets
   (viii) Letterheads
   (ix) Envelopes
   (x) Window envelopes

   Say whether the following statements are true of false:
   (a) A letter addressed to United Insurance Corporation with an attention line to Ms Radhika Bose should have the salutation "Dear Madam."
   (b) In the modified block form, the date and the complimentary close are on the right.
   (c) It is acceptable to write the date in the form 23 Dec, '03.
   (d) A letter addressed to "Omega Watches (Pvt) Ltd" should have end with "Yours sincerely."
   (e) Hanging indention form of layout is most suitable for routine letters.
   (f) Postscript is used for adding a point which was forgotten while typing the letter.
7. Fill in the blanks in the following sentences using the fewest possible words:
   (a) In the Hanging Indention form, the paragraphs begin — and the rest of the lines of the paragraph —.
   (b) The disadvantages of the full block style of layout are that — and —.
   (c) If a letter begins with the salutation "Dear Sirs," the complimentary close should be —.
   (d) Post script can be effectively used for —.
   (e) The abbreviation Ms stands for —.
   (f) The full form of NOMA is —.
8. Choose the correct answer.

   In an official letter, the date may be written in the form —
   (i) Jan. 12, 2003
   (ii) 12 Jan. '03
   (iii) 12 January, 2003
   (iv) 12th January, '03

9. Discuss the advantages of the different forms of layout. Which form would you select for letters to be sent out by your office? Give reasons for your choice.
10. What is wrong with the following extracts from letters? Make the correction.

> Dear Sir,
>
> Sub: Negligence in delivering goods
>
> Thank you for delivering the two steel cupboards which we had ordered.

> Confidential
>
> Zen Graphics (Pvt) Ltd.
> Green Avenue
> Mumbai 400 004
>
> Sirs,
>
> Sub: Condolence on death of your partner

Chapter - 13

LETTERS OF OFFER

Offers are sent to potential buyers. Sometimes an offer is made in reply to a customer's enquiry; sometimes a seller may make an offer to build up business and make new customers. The direct approach is used in such letters to save time. The letter is short; formalities are not required, and you can get straight to the business.

Enquiries

To ask for information, you can begin with a question like:

*Could you give us the following information?

or a sentence like:

**Please send us the following information:*

or

*I would appreciate receiving the following information from you:

Indicate the purpose for which the information is needed; in some fields, the information is very vast and only some of it is needed by different users; for example, a dealer in computers will be able to give useful information and a quotation only when he knows the buyer's specific need. The letter may begin with an explanation of the need as in the following examples:

*We intend to set up a computer laboratory with capacity for 40 students to work at a time. The room in which the laboratory is to be set up measures 6x7 metres.

*We have been awarded a contract for the construction of a railway bridge across River XYZ. This river is prone to tidal waves. The work is to be completed in four years. We would appreciate receiving the following information from you:

A series of direct questions may follow this opening paragraph. End the letter with a friendly comment which will leave a sense of personal relationship. Avoid old-fashioned endings like "an early reply would be appreciated" or "Thanking you in advance." It is more effective to end a letter with an informal sentence like the following:

*We could discuss this personally, if you could meet me in my office next week.

*If you could get this data to me by Tuesday, I shall be most grateful.

The following letter illustrates these points.

Dear Sirs,

During a recent Trade Fair held here, I saw some samples of your new granite tiles for flooring. I would like to make use of them for the interiors I am designing for a new housing complex. Please give me the following information:

(1) In what sizes, colours and designs can you supply the tiles?

(2) Are the tiles likely to be affected by rising moisture?

(3) Is any special processing of the under-flooring required?

I shall be most grateful if you could send me answers to these questions by Friday, the 17th.

Yours faithfully,

Points included in the letter are:

1. Courteous request for information, giving its purpose
2. Statement of what is wanted (or a list of questions)
3. Request that the information may be given by a certain date

Letter of Offer

Always give prompt attention to when a customer makes an enquiry whether by letter or by telephone. In the letter of offer, make every effort to work it up to an order.

Your letter must do a sales job. Tell the potential customer what he wants to know, and something more. You need persuasive skill and good judgment in giving information.

Present the facts so as to show the customer the benefits of buying the product/service from you. If you send a brochure, catalogue, price-list or samples send a letter with it; give the relevant page numbers or models which will be suitable to the customer. Ask for an appointment to meet the customer for a discussion. It is not enough to say, "We hope that the samples will meet with your approval." You must show the advantages of the product.

The letters below illustrate these points.

Dear Sir,

Thank you for your request for our catalogue and price-list of moulded plastic chairs and desks. They are enclosed.

You will find models shown on pages 3-4 particularly suitable for your purpose. We have supplied these chairs and desks to many schools, both in Mumbai and in small towns around Mumbai.

The schools have found them highly satisfactory as they require very little maintenance and are easy to clean. Their pleasant appearance adds to the attractiveness of the surrounding. We shall be very happy to discuss your requirements personally. Please call us at any of the numbers given above for an appointment for our representative to meet you.

Yours truly,

Dear Sir,

Thank you for your enquiry of 22 October about our new PVC tiles for flooring. We have enclosed a copy of our catalogue showing the designs and range of colours in which the tiles are available.

Messrs. Dhruv & Co, 23 M.G. Raut Road, Dhulia, are a reliable firm and handle all our products in your area. We have asked Mr. Dhruv to get in touch with you; he will inspect the premises and advise you whether moisture would give rise to any problem. Our new PVC tiles are hard-wearing and, if they are laid according to the instructions provided by us, will give you lasting satisfaction.

Yours faithfully,

Voluntary Offers

A seller may make offers to potential customers without receiving any enquiry from them.

Credit may be offered to customers of long standing in order to create goodwill. It is also offered to individuals or firms of high repute and known credit standing to win them as customers. The following is an example of a letter offering credit.

Dear Sir,

You have been buying from us for over five years now, and we feel that you would like to enjoy our credit privilege.

With credit facilities you can keep good stocks and pay for the goods only after most of the goods have been sold, and your profits made. You can also buy in large quantities and take advantage of bulk purchase discounts. We hardly need to enumerate further, the various benefits that credit customers enjoy.

Please fill in and return the enclosed card and we would be glad to open a charge account for you.

Yours truly,

Asking for Quotations

When you intend to buy a product or service, you ask for quotations from several suppliers and then select the one most suitable to you. If your order is likely to be large or might lead to further orders, indicate it in your request; suppliers offer special terms to large buyers.

Mention all details of your requirements when asking for a quotation; if it is for service like painting, renovation, air conditioning, or a machine whose working you would like to see, ask for a representative to be sent.

Points:

1. Polite request for quotation
2. Details of requirements with quality and quantity of goods
3. Place and time of delivery of goods required, carriage paid or carriage forward. Any special request about mode of delivery or packing.
4. Suggestion that the volume of business will be large if the quotation is favourable.

Sirs,

We intend to purchase large stocks of notebooks for our newly opened Department of Stationery in our Departmental Store at Salt Lake, and invite you to submit your most competitive quotation.

If your prices and terms are favourable, and your goods and services of a high standard, we shall consider giving a five year contract for the supply of notebooks. Please send your quotation, carriage paid, within a week.

Yours faithfully,

Gentlemen:

The dining room and the conference room of our hotel are to be redecorated. We invite you to submit designs and estimates for carrying out the work. The building is on M.G. Road, Jadavpore, and is about 20 years old. The area of the rooms is 15 x 20 x 10 meters and 20 x 30 x 10 meters. Air conditioning is to be installed in both rooms.

Please send your representative to inspect the rooms and discuss the matter personally. Please call us to fix an appointment for your representative's visit.

Yours faithfully,

Giving Quotation

When market conditions are normal, the usual quotation is given. If the customer seems likely to place a large order, an exceptional quotation may be given. A tabulated quotation may be enclosed with a letter. Point out the advantages of the quotation and the benefit of buying the goods.

Points:

1. Thanks for the enquiry
2. Statement of prices and terms
3. Attempt to win the customer

Sir,

We welcome the opportunity you have given us to introduce some of our products to you. We have sent you samples of our food colours and flavour concentrates. The enclosed price-list will show you that our prices are competitive. We give 7% discount on orders of Rs. 100,000 and more, and 2% cash discount for payment in cash within 7 days of the date of the bill. An order form is enclosed for your convenience. We are looking forward to the beginning of a pleasant business relationship with you.

Yours faithfully,

Firm offer **is a promise to sell the goods at the quoted price provided the order is received within the stated time, usually 3 to 7 days.**

A firm offer is made when the price of a product is expected to rise or when the price is fluctuating, and quoting a definite price is difficult. It is also made when the supplies are short of the demand. The letter states the reason for making the offer firm, and the date up to which it is firm. A firm offer is a moral obligation but not a legal obligation. It builds goodwill with important customers.

Dear Sirs,

Thank you for your letter of the 13th, asking for a quotation for the supply of 3000 units of LG microwave ovens.

Our price-list is enclosed; we give a discount of 7% on all orders of 1000 units and above, and deliver goods carriage paid within the city of Mumbai.

Please note that this offer is firm only till 30 September. The demand for microwave ovens has increased considerably, and the production cannot keep pace with the added demand just before Diwali festival. As your order is large, we shall hold the goods at your disposal for 5 days.

We urge you to take advantage of this offer and send us your order by 30 September.

Yours truly,

Offering a Substitute: **If the requested goods are not available, you can offer a substitute. An enquiry means a possible customer; make the effort to win him. The customer can be interested in another product which satisfies the need. The substitute you offer must satisfy the purpose and need of the customer. It must be the nearest in quality and price; if it differs, explain why. A substitute must be offered with confidence. Win the customer's confidence for the substitute product; send a sample with the quotation or offer a "trial lot" on approval.**

Explain briefly why you cannot supply the product which the customer has asked for; just offering a substitute without explanation may give rise to mistrust. The letter that follows embodies these suggestions.

Dear Sir,

We thank you for your enquiry of January 12, about the supply of 20 facsimile machines. The Corel machines which you have asked for are out of stock and not likely to be available for at least four weeks. We suggest the Twinkle Fax machines which have become very popular and have a good reputation for trouble-free service. There is a range of six models which allows you to choose a different kind for each desk according to the needs. These machines also have the additional feature of storage of 100 addresses and telephone/fax numbers.

The prices of Twinkle Fax machine range are a little higher than the prices of Corel but the Twinkle machines have a guarantee of five years and can use several types of paper.

We would be happy to demonstrate the Twinkle Fax machine on any day and time suitable to you.

Yours faithfully,

Withholding quotation: If a particular customer repeatedly asks for quotations for the purpose of comparing with other quotations and does not place any orders, you may avoid giving a quotation. Write a tactful letter saying that the market is uncertain and you would quote only for a definite contract, or make a firm offer for a very short period.

Dear Sirs,

Thank you for your letter of 29 July, asking us to quote our rates for printing 5000 copies of your catalogue. As the price of paper is fluctuating and has to be negotiated for every order, we are unable to give a standard quotation. We shall be able to give a quotation only for a firm order. Our rates and terms for the printing job are the same as we had quoted for your brochures in April.

We shall be happy to negotiate the price of paper on your behalf as soon as we hear from you.

Yours faithfully,

Review

1. Fill in the blanks using as few words as possible.
   (a) A firm offer is made to a — customer when — for the purpose of —.
   (b) When you offer a substitute, you can win the customer's confidence by —.
2. Is this a good sentence to write in a letter? "Since you do not place any orders even when we send you a quotation, we do not wish to send you a quotation now, when the prices are fluctuating,"

Bargaining Letters

Final price is usually negotiated in a face-to-face discussion. But some negotiation of prices and terms may be done by letters.

On receiving a quotation, a customer may try to persuade the seller to offer better terms. If the order is likely to be large, the buyer can point this out to persuade the seller to give better terms. The buyer may also indicate that other suppliers are willing to give more favourable terms. It is useful to make a specific request.

Points:

1. Expression of thanks for the quotation
2. Specific request for more favourable terms and attempt to show that the supplier will benefit if he gives the requested terms
3. Suggestion that large/frequent orders will be placed if the request is granted

Dear Sir,

Thank you for your quotation for washing machines. We approve of your model Nos. X and Z and would like to place an order immediately for at least 10 machines, five of each model.

However, we feel that your carriage forward terms are high. We usually get our supplies on carriage paid terms, and request you to reconsider this. We are planning to open launderettes in several places, and will be placing further orders if we find your products and terms satisfactory. You will be compensated by the large orders we shall be placing.

As we are about to equip our newly opened launderettes, we would like to have your reply within a week.

Yours faithfully,

Seller's Reply

It may or may not be possible to reduce your quotation. Either way, try to win the customer.

Agreeing to reduce your price should not give the impression that the originally offered terms were not fair, or that the sales are so poor that you are eager to get an order at any price.

If you agree to the request, try to put some condition like offering a special discount for a large order; mention specific amount in terms of worth in money or number of units purchased. Discount may also be offered for a long-term contract.

A request or a favour should be granted with dignity. A grudging or condescending tone will not be liked by the customer.

> Dear Sir,
>
> We are glad to learn from your letter of 19 February that you have undertaken a project to establish launderettes in several places in the city, and we are happy to be able to cooperate with you in the project. Since this is a long term project and there will be continuous business for quite some time, we are prepared to supply our washing machines on carriage paid terms as you have requested.
>
> Our machines are guaranteed for 5 years and are backed up by our excellent after sales service. We undertake to ensure your complete satisfaction with our products. Our representative will visit you within four days to inspect the location and check the facilities for installation of the machines.
>
> Yours faithfully,

If you have to refuse the request, remember all the skills of handling negatives discussed earlier.

> Dear Sir,
>
> We have given careful consideration to your request that we should give a 15% discount on our washing machines. Unfortunately, our overheads have risen sharply in the last 10 months, making it impossible for us to reduce prices to this extent without compromising on our standards of quality.
>
> Since we cannot do this, we suggest that we will deliver goods carriage paid on all your orders for five or more machines.
>
> We are sure you will understand that our pricing is done after taking into account the cost of maintaining high quality and after sales services. We request you to accept this offer and give us the opportunity of doing business with you.
>
> Yours faithfully,

Getting Back Lost Customers

Along with the effort to get new customers, you have to make efforts to keep old customers' goodwill. It is far more expensive to win new customers than to keep the old ones. You have to keep in touch with all customers and make sure that they are not attracted by competitors.

With increasing competition and more demanding customers, it is easy to lose your customers. Efforts must be made to get back any customers that have stopped buying from you.

There are several reasons why a customer stops buying:

- Attracted by lower price or better service elsewhere

- Dissatisfied because of unadjusted complaint
- Influenced by competitor's sales effort
- Gone out of business or shifted to another place

Only the last one who has gone out of business is really lost; the others can be brought back. The commonest reason for loss of customers is that the seller does not make effort to retain them and so they go to other sellers.

A timely letter to a drifting customer can save a loss. By making a periodical check of your record of orders you can see if any old customer has dropped out. It is useful to write a letter to a customer who has not placed an order for a long time.

A short letter of offer should suffice; if you send the latest catalogue, or samples of the latest designs/products or details of new services, it may make an indifferent customer feel that he is remembered by you and ought to buy from you. In more competitive business, you may have to offer discounts/concessions, additional service etc. Also make a telephone call so that the contact is more personal. Address the letter to a specific person by name, and include these points:

1. Statement that the customer's communication has been missed (never mention "records") for some time
2. Tactful enquiry about why s/he has been silent
3. Information about new product/service or special offer
4. Request for order; assurance that satisfaction will be ensured.

This should be followed up by a personal visit.

Dear Mr. Das Gupta,

There has been no communication from you for a long time; I am anxious to know the reason. Did I unwittingly given you cause for dissatisfaction? If so, please tell me, and I shall gladly make adjustments. I am able to offer the most competitive prices and terms now, owing to re-organization of the business. The new price list is enclosed. Delivery is free for long standing customers like you.

I am enclosing a new easy-to-fill order form. Your requirements will reach you on the same day as I receive your order. Your convenience and comfort is my business.

Yours sincerely,

Dear Ms Mukherjee,

We have waited for the long period of six months without any communication from you.

We are about to launch a range of new products. As we always offer the special launching discount prices to our long standing patrons first, we are enclosing brochures and catalogues of our new range of skin care products which we have just started manufacturing.

As you will see from the brochure, we are giving a number of services and facilities to beauty parlours. Packing, shades of colour and potency of some of the products can be adjusted to your special requirements. Here are also special launching discounts to beauty parlours.

Our representative, Ms Nivedita Bose will visit you on Monday, the 16th with our new catalogue and samples of the full range of our new cosmetic products. She will explain the special features of the products and also the scheme of special discounts.

A trial order form, exclusively for longstanding customers, is enclosed. Nivedita will help you to select the products for your trial order.

Yours sincerely,

Credit terms may be offered to win back a lost customer as this letter does.

Dear Mr. Adhikary,

It is a long time — over six months — since we received your last order. Perhaps you did not need stocks of stationery as this is not the peak season for these goods. We expect your order soon, however, and are glad to inform you that we are offering credit terms to a few of our customers. You can now place your orders on credit, with bills payable every three months, or when the amount comes up to Rs. 50,000/-. This will enable you to benefit from bulk purchase discounts and also to put your capital to other uses. We are sure you will take advantage of this offer and place your order soon.

Yours sincerely,

Review

Are these statements true?

(a) Following up customers who do not place orders requires personalized letters.

(b) "We noticed from our records that you have not placed any orders with us for six months," is effective for winning back a customer.

(c) Most customers are lost because they are dissatisfied with the goods/services.

(d) Keeping in touch with customers helps to retain them.

EXERCISES

Inquiries

1. **You have bought a place for starting a Computer Education centre. Invite quotations from re-construction firms for carrying out restructuring of the place. Give details of your requirements and ask for designs for interior decoration.**
2. As the owner of Mahatma Computer Education Centre, Kolkata, you intend to advertise in the computer journal COMPUTECH. Draft a letter asking for a quotation for 12 back cover weekly advertisements.
3. Popular Tours intend to print 1,000 copies of a brochure of their holiday tours to South East Asian countries. They write to New Image Graphics asking them to quote their terms for the designing and printing of the brochure. Draft the letter.
4. A college library intends to buy display boards and racks. Write a letter from the Librarian to Jupiter Displays, asking for their catalogue and terms and conditions

of supply. The letter should point out that a substantial concession is expected as it is for an educational institution.

5. You are the Secretary of your College Co-operative Store. Write to a supplier of stationery that you are planning to give a contract for the supply of pencils, ball-pens, paper clips, notebooks, and other stationery items for a period of ten months, from July to April. If the terms and conditions are satisfactory, you will consider renewing the contract for three years. Request the supplier to send a representative to discuss the terms.
6. A Pharmaceuticals Company requires glass bottles of assorted sizes; they ask Borosil Glass Works Ltd. to submit a quotation, carriage paid, for the supply of 50,00,000 bottles, to be supplied at their factory in one month after the order is placed.
7. Invite a marketing agency to quote terms for designing a marketing campaign for a new product you intend to launch shortly.
8. Your college theatre, with a capacity of 500, needs to have the seats repaired. As Secretary of the College Trust, write to a firm of furnishers asking for their quotation to carry out the work. You require foam rubber and rexine covering. Ask for samples of rexine and request a visit from a representative.
9. Your class has decided to go for a picnic. Write a letter to the owner of a bus service, making enquiries. Give all required details.
10. You need an intercom system for your office. Draft a request for a quotation, giving all details of your requirements, to be sent to manufacturers of the system.
11. Unistar Computer Services need to get their premises treated for termites (white ants). As the owner, write to Pest Control (India) for a quotation, and request them to inspect the premises immediately.
12. Your organization is celebrating its golden jubilee this year. You are the secretary in charge of organizing a seminar as a part of the celebrations. Draft a letter to a firm of caterers to arrange for lunch for the guests.
13. You have seen an advertisement for a new electronic Xerox machine which can be programmed to make up to thirty copies of 10 pages and sort the copies into sets. Write to the advertiser asking for a demonstration as you want to purchase one for your office.
14. Draft a letter to Godrej Boyce & Co. asking for information about their new ergonomic furniture for your office. Give detailed specifications of your requirements.

Quotations

15. In reply to an enquiry from Mahatma Computer Education Centre publishers of COMPUTECH (a computer journal) send the schedule of advertising space rates and state the discount allowed on booking of space for 15 weeks.
16. You had sent a quotation by telegram to a customer who wanted it urgently. Write a letter confirming the quotation. Give sales value to the letter and enclose an order form.

17. New Image Graphics reply to Popular Tours stating their price for designing and printing 1,000 copies of their brochure giving information about their tours to South East Asian countries. They enclose some samples of designs.

18. A manufacturer of glass products has been asked for a discount and a special window dressing equipment and material, for an exhibition for one week, by a retailer in a small town. He can supply a sample lot of glass products and a standard window lighting plant at a rent of Rs. 3000/- per week. But he cannot give a discount of more than 5% because of a narrow margin of profit. Draft the letter.

19. As a supplier of stationery, reply to an enquiry from a college cooperative store about the supply of stationery for the period from July to April. Send your price list and inform of the day and time when your representative will visit to discuss the details.

20. A highly placed official in Wipro Ltd. has just been transferred to your city. Write as from a well-known department store offering him credit terms in an effort to win him as a regular customer.

21. You have received a request for a quotation for the supply of examination answer books from a customer who often asks you for a quotation but uses it only to compare it with other quotations and never places an order. Reply tactfully avoiding giving a quotation.

22. Draft a letter to be sent to a College Principal who has not placed any order with you for two years though she used to buy large quantities of answer books from you every year. Offer an inducement to get her to place an order.

23. You have received a letter asking if you can supply steel furniture within 15 days, for an office. Reply stating that you can deliver only 10 writing desks immediately, and can send the rest a week later; computer tables and chairs are not in stock and can be delivered only after a month; filing cabinets with 4 drawers are not available at present, but you can supply cabinets with 5 drawers immediately.

24. A retailer has requested you to supply 6 fax machines at 20% discount for an important customer. It is not possible for you to give the large discount. Draft a reply explaining why the rate of discount cannot exceed 15%. Make an attempt to get the order.

Chapter - 14

ORDERS

Orders are routine letters and their effectiveness depends on the accuracy of the details. Most of the contents of an order can be tabulated.

Replies to orders are treated as opportunities to build up goodwill and relationship with new customers, uncertain customers, regained customers as well as long standing loyal customers. Taking interest in replying to orders goes a long way in creating goodwill.

ORDERS

Before placing an order, get all the details of what you want to buy. Group the details under headings as follows:

Product, its Specifications and Quantity

Some products come in a variety of sizes, colours, models and so on. Many products are sold in packages of different sizes. Liquids and small products have packing of various quantities; shampoos are packed in 100ml, 200ml, etc.; tablets come in strips of ten or bottles of 50, 100, etc. Some products are available in different types of packing like bottles, tins, sachets. This should be specified in the order.

Identify the exact product and item you want by giving specifications of (i) size (of the product or the packaging), (ii) colour, (iii) catalogue number, (iv) model number, (v) unit price.

If you have selected the item after approving or testing of a sample, you may reserve the right to reject the goods if the delivered goods do not tally with the sample.

Mention the correct quantity required. Different products are sold in different measures: liquids in litres; solids in kilo-grams; dozens or hundreds; large products ·like cupboards or refrigerators, in units.

Packing

Packing a consignment of goods suitably for transport is the responsibility of the supplier. Buyer's instructions are needed only if the goods are to be specially packed for any special purpose, such as for export.

Delivery

The place, time and mode of delivery have to be indicated at the time of placing the order.

(a) *Place:* Give the full address of the place at which the goods are to be delivered. You may want the goods to be delivered at your retail shop or at your warehouse/ godown or at your showroom.

(b) *Time:* If the order is urgent and you require the goods within a certain time, give the date by which the goods should be delivered. When the question of time is very important, and you have no use for goods delivered late, you may reserve the right to reject the goods if they are not delivered within the specified time.

(c) *Mode:* The mode of delivery is required only if there is any special requirement. For construction work being carried out at a far-off location, you may want cement to be delivered in lots at specific intervals. Mode of transport need not be mentioned unless it is carriage forward.

Settlement of Account

Mention the agreed prices and terms and refer to: (a) discount or concession given (b) mode of payment of the bill.

Order Forms: Details to be given in an order are easy to tabulate, and hence printed forms are used for placing orders. Sellers prepare the forms with columns required for their products. This ensures that no essential detail is left out; the form makes it easy for the customer to place an order. There is arrangement for the required carbon copies in the pad. Regular customers are given pads of the forms. A set of forms is sent with a quotation to encourage a potential customer to place an order.

Drafting Orders

After the prices and terms are settled by a quotation and discussion, and samples are approved, the buyer may place a trial order to make sure that the seller gives efficient service, that is, proper packing, delivery of goods in time, prompt receipts for payments etc. A retailer may also place a trial order to find out the demand for a new product. Only a small quantity is ordered for trial.

Any of the following situations may lead to a first order:

(i) Seller's samples and/or quotation are approved

(ii) A bargain has been concluded

(a) request granted

(b) buyer convinced to order on offered terms

(iii) Buyer is willing to try an offered substitute

(iv) Buyer intends to try a product in a new area

The opening and the ending for each of these are given below:

(i) Open with a reference to the received quotation.

**Your quotation for ... is approved and we are pleased to place an order for the following:*

*Thank you for your quotation for.... We are glad to place a trial order with you as follows:

When you have reason to be very particular about the quality of the product as in the case of medicines or precision goods, testing of samples leads to the order. Start the letter by mentioning satisfaction with samples.

*We have tested your samples of... and found that sample No. 099 suits our requirements.

**We are glad to say that we approve of your samples of terry wool suiting, and would like to receive supplies as follows:*

End with the expectation that the trial order will be satisfactory and lead to regular business.

We hope to find everything satisfactory and are looking forward to placing frequent orders with you.

If you order goods on the basis of a sample, you may refuse to accept the goods if they are different; mention this at the end of the order.

* *We expect that your goods will be of the same high standard as the sample which has led us to place this order.*
* *It is essential that goods supplied should be of the same quality as the selected sample and we reserve the right to reject goods which do not tally with the sample.*

(ii) (a) When the seller has agreed to a bargain, open the order letter with a reference to it.

* *We thank you for agreeing to give us special packing at no extra charge.*

The corresponding ending would be:

* We assure you that a large amount of business will follow if the trial order is found satisfactory.

(b) If you are convinced that the seller cannot give better terms, but still wish to place the order, mention this in the opening.

* *We understand that it is not possible for you to give us export packing without charging extra, but we are wiling to take a trial lot of your Cheese Powder tins.*

End with expectation of high standard of goods/services.

* *We hope to find your goods and services of a high standard to justify our placing orders with you.*

(iii) If you decide to try an offered substitute, you may order a small lot.

* *We are willing to try the A1 disinfectant cleaning fluid which you have offered instead of Yellow Bond phenyl we had asked for.*

End by suggesting that more will be ordered only if the trial order proves satisfactory.

* *We shall ask for further supplies if we find it suitable for our requirements.*

(iv) A buyer may place an order on his own initiative on seeing an advertisement if he feels that a certain product has a potential demand. The opening sentence refers to this.

* *There is a reasonably good demand for cotswool shirts in this town and we would like to have a trial consignment according to the following details.*
* *We have received several inquiries from local customers about your PVC tiles; as there is no supplier of your products in this area we would like to try the market. Please send us a trial consignment according to details given below:*

End with the hope that a regular demand will be established.

*We hope to establish a good demand and expect to place frequent orders with you.

Points to be included in an order:

1. Reference to previous communication (for first order) and request to send goods.
2. Details of required goods, instructions for delivery and reference to terms of payment.
3. Goodwill message.

These points are embodied in these examples.

Dear Sirs,

We have tested your samples of adhesive paste and found that No. 27 is suitable for our requirements. We are glad to place an order for 500 large tins of this paste. Please deliver the tins at our factory at Jadavpore. Our cheque for Rs.— in advance payment, and our Sales Tax declaration form are enclosed.

The material supplied should be of the same quality as the sample and we reserve the right to reject material of any other quality.

Yours faithfully,

Sir,

We are willing to try the range of A1 disinfectant cleaning fluids which you have suggested instead of the Yellow Bond phenyl we had asked for.

Please send a trial lot of all the disinfectant products, suitable for hospital use, to our address given above. We shall consider placing an annual contract for the supply of the products if the quality is suitable for our requirements.

Yours faithfully,

Confirmation of Order

An order placed by telephone or telegram needs to be confirmed by a letter because a signed, written document is necessary for a contract. The letter opens with a reference to the order already placed, and the confirmation, for example:

**We confirm our order for (name product) placed by telephone this morning.*

All details of the order must be given just as in a letter of order.

Ending may be similar to that of (i).

Dear Sirs,

We confirm our order for 5000 sheets of A4 size bond paper placed by telephone this morning. Enclosed is our cheque for Rs.— as advance payment. Please deliver the package on the 16th at our address given above. The balance of Rs.— will be paid after delivery. We shall be placing similar orders with you if we find that your products and services are of a high quality.

Yours faithfully,

Review

1. Collect the order forms of four or five companies selling different kinds of products and compare them. Order forms are also available on the web sites of companies. How are these different from printed forms?

Changes in Orders

The customer might have to make a change in an order which has been placed; it may be a correction on finding a mistake or a request for a change in the quantity required or the date or the place of delivery.

Points:

1. Reference to order
2. Statement of change required, and explanation of the reason
3. Offer to cooperate/adjust
4. Apology for the inconvenience caused.

The following example embodies these points:

> Dear Sirs,
>
> Please refer to our order no. xxx, dated 28 October, for the supply of 100 units of IBM PCs to be delivered on 3 December.
>
> The computers are to be installed in our training centre which we intend to start on 1 January 2004. Unfortunately, the final touches to the reconstruction of the rooms will be a little delayed. We request you to delay the delivery by two weeks; we shall be able to take delivery on 18 December.
>
> Please excuse us for any inconvenience that might be caused by this delay, which we could not avoid, and please confirm the revised date of delivery.
>
> Yours faithfully,

> Dear Sirs,
>
> Please refer to our order no yyy dated 15 January, for the supply of 100 washing machines to be delivered on 22 April, at our new apartment complex at 16, MG Road.
>
> The construction work has been completed earlier than we had expected and we would like to begin renting out the apartments by 29 March, as a number of enquiries have already been received. We would appreciate it if you could make the delivery a month earlier, by 22 March. This would enable us to complete all the installations in the apartments in good time.
>
> We are willing to pay additional charge to cover a part of the cost of earlier delivery. Please confirm immediately, as we intend to make announcements in the Press about the date from which the apartments will be available.
>
> Yours faithfully,

Reply to Seller's Request for Change

The customer has to make adjustments and may have to give instructions about delivery of goods in case of delay or early delivery etc.

> Sirs,
>
> We do not mind accepting early delivery of our steel shelves and cabinets which were to be delivered on the 18th. However, it is not possible to keep them at our

showrooms at Hutatma Chowk owing to lack of space and we therefore request you to deliver them carriage paid at our Thane showroom.

We shall expect delivery of the goods on the 11th as you have suggested, and hope that there will be no inconvenience in delivering them at Thane.

Yours faithfully,

Cancellation of Order

An order may have to be cancelled on account of unforeseen circumstances. There may be a disaster like earthquake, flood, war, which affect either the buyer or the seller. There may be fire, building collapse, strike or other problems that affect the business of either the buyer or the seller. A sudden recession in the market may also cause a buyer to cancel an order if there are no sales of the goods.

Cancellation of an order by either side affects the other because it upsets the plans. If the buyer cancels the order, the seller may incur loss. He might have already incurred expenses in buying raw material and manufacturing the goods; he will be left with no buyer for the goods. If the seller cancels the order, the buyer may find that his business is lost because he has no stock and cannot get it from another supplier.

There is usually a penalty if an order is cancelled. However, if the cancellation is due to unavoidable reasons, the seller may be willing to make some adjustment such as postponing the date of delivery.

A buyer may cancel an order if he finds that the first consignment or a trial lot is found to be defective or unsatisfactory in any way.

Dear Sirs,

Please refer to our order No. XX03 dated 15 June, for steel shelves to be delivered on 15 September.

We are sorry we cannot take delivery of the shelves on 15 September owing to unforeseen circumstances. Our warehouse was destroyed by fire this week, and we have had to remove salvaged goods to our showrooms. It will take at least two months to arrange for storage space and unless you can hold the goods for us, we shall have to cancel our order.

We are sure you will understand the situation and accept our apology for the inconvenience caused. Please let us know whether you can hold the goods for 2 months.

Yours faithfully,

Dear Sirs,

Sub.: Our order no bbb for 500 tons of cement

We are sorry to inform you that the delivery of consignments against our order has been very unsatisfactory. When we informed you by telephone, you promised to ensure that regular consignments would us every 15 days as we require, but we have not found any improvement.

Please cancel our order for the remaining quantity of the cement as it is not possible for us to carry out our construction work in these circumstances.

Since our work has been seriously affected and we have incurred losses on account of your inability to deliver the consignments as required, we intend to charge a contract penalty of Rs. —— on the price of — tons delivered so far.

Yours faithfully,

Dear Sirs,

You are aware of the conditions of civil disturbance in this city for the last one week. Civil life has come to a standstill and there is no sale of any goods at all.

In these circumstances, we are unable to take delivery of any supplies for the next one week. Please cancel our order nos. 111, 222 and 333 dated —.

As and when normal conditions are restored, we shall send you revised orders. We are sorry for the inconvenience caused.

Yours faithfully,

EXECUTION OF ORDERS

Always acknowledge an order as soon as it is received. The acknowledgement can be used to build and maintain good relationships with customers.

Include the following points:

1. Name and quantity of article dispatched or being dispatched
2. Date of shipment and expected date of receipt or the date of delivery of goods
3. Mode of transport, and place of delivery
4. Mode of payment and reference to enclosed bill

Assure the customer that every attention has been paid to the order, and that future orders will receive the same careful attention.

The letter given below includes the following points:

1. Expression of thanks for the order
2. Statement of terms etc.
3. Assurance of satisfactory goods and service and expectation that you will deserve further orders

Dear Sirs,

Thank you for your order for 15,000 cartons with corrugated partitions for packing biscuits.

We shall deliver your goods in 10 days, i.e., by the 20th as required. The bill will be sent with the goods; payment within seven days entitles you to a discount of 2 %. You will find that our goods and services are of a high standard. We are looking forward to a standing contract for regular supplies of packing material for your biscuits and confectionery.

Yours truly,

Refusal of Order

A seller does not refuse an order; in these days of severe competition, no business person can afford to turn away a customer. A customer whose order is refused is most likely to become a lost customer. Therefore every effort must be made to keep the customer by persuading him to change the terms of his order.

If the customer makes an unreasonable demand such as asking for delivery in a very short time when there is limited supply of goods or there is a rush of orders, the seller may not be able to accept the order on those terms. But it is worthwhile to try to make the customer accept a later delivery date.

If goods cannot be delivered at the expected time, contact the customer to negotiate a new date. The purpose of the letter is to get the customer to agree to a later date of delivery.

Points

1. Appreciation of the order and explanation of circumstances
2. Steps being taken to handle the situation, and approximate date by which normal conditions will be restored
3. Apology for the inconvenience and request for confirmation of the order for delivery at a later date.

Dear Sirs,

Thank you for your order for 50,000 units of mobile phones to be delivered in the course of the next one month.

These handsets are imported and we are required to effect deliveries as and when we receive a consignment. Although the consignments arrive regularly, we have a very large number of orders to be delivered in the next three months, and will not be able to undertake your contract on the time schedule you have proposed.

We would be glad to enter your order in our waiting list. We estimate that we will be able to start your delivery schedule by the middle of October.

Please confirm your order for this schedule of delivery. We are sorry for the inconvenience.

Yours truly,

Dear Sirs,

Thank you for your order for stationery items to be supplied by 5 June.

Owing to a rush of orders and somewhat slow supplies, we are not able to guarantee that we can supply your requirement by the required date. We are handling all orders in rotation, and expect to be able to deliver your consignment around 15 June.

We are making every effort to meet the requirements of all our customers and will get in touch with you as soon as we have the required supplies.

In the meantime, we request you to confirm your order for delivery by mid-June.

Yours faithfully,

Dear Sir,

We thank you for your order dated 10 January, for 50 steel bookshelves to be delivered in 2 months. Unfortunately, owing to a strike in the steel industry, there is a shortage of steel sheets in the market. We shall not be able to deliver the shelves in 2 months as you have requested.

Negotiations with the Union leaders are in progress; a final agreement is likely to be evolved only by the end of this month. As we shall be out of production for a fairly long time, we must unfortunately request you to withdraw your present order. We shall get in touch with you as soon as normal production is resumed.

We once again thank you for offering us your business.

Yours truly,

Appreciating Regular Customers' Orders

Take every opportunity to maintain personal contact with all customers, specially, long standing ones. Use any special occasion like a festival or a large order to show appreciation of the customer's regular business. This is largely a goodwill letter, and not just a routine acknowledgement; address the letter by name.

Dear Mr. Das Gupta,

Thank you very much for your large order for 50,000 'Volga' cartons. We take this opportunity to tell you how much we appreciate your regular orders and prompt payments. Business depends on customers like you, but unfortunately, while poor buyers and slow payers get letters, you receive only routine acknowledgements, bill and receipts. As a businessman yourself, you must have experienced the same problem of maintaining contacts with the best of your customers. You will receive your goods as usual. Do accept our sincere thanks for the business you give us.

Yours sincerely,

Appreciating Orders from Regained Buyers

When an order is placed by a regained customer after a long interval, make an effort to re-establish the relations firmly. Show appreciation of a customer who has come back, and also assure him that he will be happy with his decision to return.

Points

1. Expression of gratitude for the long-missed order
2. Statement of routine acknowledgement
3. Assurance of highly satisfactory service

Dear Mr. Mitra,

We are indeed grateful for your order of the 10th which we have received after a long interval. The drums of paint have been dispatched to you by truck and you will receive them by the 17th. The Transporter's Receipt is enclosed. Our bill of Rs.—— is enclosed. We are anxious to make sure that our customers are satisfied with our goods and services; please feel assured that we shall take every care to see that you are happy with your decision to order goods from us again.

Yours sincerely,

Reply to Customer's Request for Change

If the change requested by the customer can be made without much inconvenience or loss, inform him that it will be made. If it involves disturbance, request the customer to cooperate.

1. Agreement to make the change as requested
2. Explanation of problem, if any, and how customer can help
3. Statement of terms for purpose of acknowledgement

Dear Sirs,

Subject: Your letter of 10 November

We are willing to delay the delivery of your 100 IBM PCs, by a month as you have requested. However, since the consignment will be received by us by the end of November, we shall have to store them in a warehouse as there is a shortage of space in our shop.

The cost of storage will be about Rs. 3000/- which will be added to your total bill. If this arrangement is acceptable to you, please confirm.

Yours faithfully,

Dear Sirs,

Subject: Your letter dated 15 February

We are glad to inform you that we can deliver the washing machines you ordered, a month earlier than the date originally fixed, as you have requested. Thank you for offering to pay additional charge for early delivery. We will not charge extra for the early delivery, but as our delivery vans will not be free engaged till 15 April, we request you to release us from the contract to deliver carriage paid, and to make arrangements for the transport of the goods. .

Your consignment will be ready for collection on 22 March. Please let us know about your arrangements.

Yours faithfully,

Seller's Request for Change

Sometimes the seller may request the customer to permit a change in the date or the place of delivery; he may ask for extension of time if his production is held up; or he may request the customer to accept early delivery if he has more orders coming in and wants to free his space.

Adjustments are a matter of goodwill and understanding between the seller and the buyer.

Sirs,

Please refer to your order for the printing of 20,000 copies of your special tour brochures, to be delivered on 8 March.

Owing to a breakdown of one of our machines, there will be a delay in completing the printing work. Immediate repair work has been undertaken and the delay will not be of more than 4 days. Please accept our apologies for the inconvenience caused.

We already have 12,000 copies ready; please let us know whether you would like us to deliver these on the 8th and the rest four days later, or deliver all the 20,000 copies on the 12th.

Yours faithfully,

Gentlemen:

Please refer to your order of 15 January for 50 steel book-shelves. We are sorry that we have to request you to allow us an extension of time to deliver the goods. Our supplies of steel sheets have been delayed by 15 days owing to shortage in the market, and this delay has affected our production schedule. We have been assured of our supplies by 15 February and will be able to complete your order within 20 days of receiving the supplies. We are sorry for the inconvenience caused by this delay.

Yours truly,

Seller's Letters Related to Cancellation of Order

If the customer cancels an order after the seller has incurred expenses, he might have to recover the expenses from the customer, by charging a penalty.

Dear Sir,

We are sorry to learn from your letter of 7 September, that you are compelled to cancel your order for 50 rubber foam mattresses owing to delay in the completion of the hospital building.

Unfortunately, however, if you cancel the order at this stage, we shall be forced to charge a penalty of Rs.15,000 to cover the expenses we have incurred on making the mattresses to your specifications. As an alternative, we shall store them in our warehouse at a rent of Rs. 2000, if you wish. This will save you the penalty charge. Please reply within a week. We hope that you will take advantage of the alternative which we have offered.

Yours faithfully,

The seller may have to cancel an accepted order on account of similar circumstances that disturb business activity.

> Dear Sir,
>
> Sub.: Your order no. 111
>
> We are sorry to inform you that a fire has brought our factory to a standstill. It is not possible to estimate the time that it will take to restore normal conditions.
>
> In these circumstances, we are sorry to inform you that it will not be possible for us to deliver your goods on the above-mentioned order. We regret the inconvenience caused to you and request you to release us from the contract owing to the unforeseen and unavoidable conditions.
>
> Yours faithfully,

After-sales Letters

It is business courtesy and good business practice to contact a customer some time after he has bought a consumer durable product like a computer, a vacuum cleaner, a Xerox machine etc. Often, the salesperson visits the customer within a week of the sale to check whether the customer is making full use of it and is comfortable with it. An after-sales letter after three or four weeks reinforces the contact and the goodwill.

The after-sales letter performs three functions: (i) it checks that the customer is satisfied; if not, the seller has a chance to set matters right. Enquiring about the customer's satisfaction is the mark of a reputable seller; (ii) it reminds the customer about the after-sales service; (iii) it makes way for further business through the customer.

A customer who receives after-sales attention from the seller is more likely to speak well about the company to others. Word-of-mouth publicity through the customer is a very powerful image-builder. Address the letter by name.

The letter below is an example of an after-sales letter.

> Dear Mrs. Bose,
>
> We are writing to ask you about your experience with our Acme washing machine you bought last month. We want you to feel assured that in case you have any difficulty with any of the operations, we shall be glad to send our expert to help you. The booklet of instructions, supplied with the machine will, of course, be helpful in handling the machine.
>
> But please do not hesitate to call us if you need further help at any time. Once you buy one of our machines, you are our customer forever, and may claim our help and services at any time.
>
> Yours faithfully,

EXERCISES

1. Place an order for 300 boxes of coloured crayons subject to the manufacturer's agreeing to pack them in specially designed boxes for Diwali presentation for no additional charge.
2. You have received an order for 300 boxes of coloured magic crayons in special presentation packing for no additional charge. Write to the customer saying that you have dispatched the articles as required, tactfully suggesting that he should not, in future, ask for such concessions unless his order exceeds 5000 boxes.
3. Place an order for 100 bar magnets for use in your factory of electrical goods, and reserve the right to reject them if they do not tally with the sample submitted.
4. Confirm an order given by telephone, for 100 pocket calculators for your school.
5. Popular Tours write to New Image Graphics that they approve of one of the brochure designs submitted by them, and wish to have 5,000 copies in that design. They will send their representative to the Press in the following week to settle the details of the contract. Draft the letter.
6. New Image Graphics inform Popular Tours that owing to the breakdown of their machines only 3000 copies of their catalogue are printed: the remaining copies will be ready within five days. They ask the customer whether the copies that are ready should be sent at once, or retained till the rest are ready.
7. You had ordered 20 computers for a Computer Education class, to be opened shortly. A dispute among the partners has forced postponement of the opening of the class. Write cancelling the order unless the vendor is prepared to hold the order until your classrooms are ready.
8. Beam Personnel Services had placed an order for 100 conference chairs with Comfort Furnishers (Pvt.) Ltd. They now request them to deliver the chairs a week earlier than the agreed date. They are willing to pay for the extra work which will have to be undertaken.
9. Comfort Furnishers (Pvt.) Ltd. are willing to deliver 100 conference chairs ordered by Beam Personnel Services a week earlier than the originally agreed date as requested. They do not intend to charge extra for this but, as their own trucks will not be free at the time, they ask the customer to release them from their undertaking to deliver the goods free of charge. Draft the letter.
10. For the silver jubilee of your firm, you wish to present wall clocks to your staff. Write to a manufacturer of clocks giving details of your requirements and ask him to gift-wrap each clock at no extra cost. Point out how the manufacturer will benefit if he grants your request.
11. You have received an urgent order for 25 vacuum cleaners from a hotel. Owing to a rush of orders there will be a delay of three weeks in delivering the goods. Write asking for extension of time.
12. Rajesh Furnishers have received an order for six steel cupboards, based on an old price list. Prices have increased by 10% since then. Write a reply saying that you are willing to supply the goods at the old price, if the order is worth more than Rs.100,000/-. Mention that this special offer should not be treated as a precedent.

13. Quality Stationery Suppliers acknowledge the first order from Messrs. Mehta & Sons after a long interval, and try to build up goodwill. Draft the letter.
14. A long standing customer has written to cancel an order stating that there is no storage space in his warehouse. Write a reply offering to store the goods in your warehouse for a month, if he is willing to pay the warehousing charges.
15. Acknowledge an order placed by an old customer who has been regained by the efforts of the sales department.
16. You had given a specially low quotation to a potential customer for acceptance within fifteen days, as a price rise was expected shortly. The customer's order comes three days after the expiry of the firm offer when the prices have risen. Write to the customer persuading him to confirm his order at the raised prices.
17. A long standing customer has placed an unusually large order for designing and printing his company's office stationery. Write a letter acknowledging the order and showing appreciation of his regular orders and prompt payments.
18. You had ordered some goods to be delivered by a specified date. The goods did not arrive on time and are of no use to you now. Write to the supplier cancelling the order and pointing out that you have incurred considerable loss on account of his negligence.

Chapter - 15

STATUS INQUIRIES AND RECOMMENDATIONS

Letters related to status inquiries and credit must be written with the greatest tact. You have to get information about the credit standing of customers who ask for credit, and also give credit information about your customers when others make enquiries. Sometimes you may have to tell a customer that credit cannot be granted.

A buyer's credit standing depends on his Capital, Capacity, Circumstances and Character. All these aspects of credit are taken into account before granting credit.

Capital is the cash as well as the stock, the building, the machinery and other property that the buyer owns.

Capacity is the person's skill and ability to use resources properly and run the business/ profession profitably. This may be partly affected by the line of business and the location of the business.

Circumstances are outside the person's control; political conditions, government's financial and economic policies and industrial relations in the region or in the whole country may affect any business or profession. Currently, computerization of business as well as globalization is causing changes in many organisations. Circumstances can change and may either improve or worsen the standing of a business enterprise.

Character is what really makes a reputation; it consists of honesty, ability to work hard, and self-respect.

Sources of Credit Information

The inquiry begins by asking for information from references given by the credit applicant, and may extend further to sources found out from the first references or agencies.

The usual sources of credit information are the credit applicant's bank and suppliers. Organizations like Credit Agencies, Merchants' Chambers and Trade Associations can help in ascertaining the credit standing of potential customers. A somewhat elusive but useful source is market gossip from which organisations gather information. For the purpose of letter writing we are concerned with the bank and other suppliers as sources of credit information.

A **bank** knows several things about its client. The scale of the customer's business is assessed from the amounts paid out and deposited. The business circle of the customer is indicated by the names of the parties on the incoming and outgoing cheques. The customer's peak season and lean season of business are indicated by the timing and frequency of incoming and outgoing cheques. The general standing and conduct of the customer can be gathered from the manner in which the customer operates the account. Bank is generally the most reliable source of credit information.

Other suppliers with whom the customer has already established credit, can give information about the customer's credit standing, general respectability and regularity in settling accounts.

Making Status Inquiries

Information about customers' financial standing and paying habits of the customer is got from the references. The inquiry should be specific and clear. Status inquiry questionnaires are quite useful since the definite questions can bring definite and clear answers from the references.

The reference gives information only as a favour; courtesy demands that the information should be requested politely and with an offer to do return the favour.

Assure the references that whatever information they give will be kept in strict confidence. These letters are marked "Confidential" and are addressed to an individual officer, and not to the company in general.

Points

1. Name and address of credit applicant stating that their name has been given as reference; amount and period of credit requested.
2. Request for information on specific points (e.g., amount and period of credit allowed by the reference, details of delay in payment by customer), and opinion on the advisability of the proposed transaction.
3. Offer to help in return in similar situations and promise to keep the given information confidential.

Dear Sir,

Your name has been given as a credit reference by Messrs. Sanghi & Roy of 87, Green Street, Kolkata 700 004 who have asked us to supply goods worth Rs. 500,000/- on credit. This is our first contact with them and it would help us in assessing their credit if you could give us some information about their credit standing and your experience in doing business with them. A credit information form is enclosed; please fill and return it in the enclosed postage-paid envelope.

We would be glad to help in a similar way whenever we can. Please be assured that the information you give will be treated as strictly confidential.

Yours faithfully,

Dear Mr. Mitra,

We have received a request for credit of Rs. 1,50,000/- for 2 months from the firm of Messrs. J.K. Shah & Sons, 710 Wallace Street, Ballard Estate, Mumbai 400 001. They have given us your name as credit reference.

We would be grateful if you could help us to assess the credit application by giving us information about the number of years they have been your credit customers, the amount and period of credit you grant them, and whether there has been any difficulty in collecting dues from them. Whatever other information you may have about the firm's general reputation in the business circles would also be appreciated.

The information you give will be used with the utmost discretion, in strict confidence and no liability on your part.

Yours sincerely,

Sir,

The Ball Printing Press, Dadabhoy Road, Bangalore 560 002, have given your name as credit reference and requested us to supply paper worth Rs. 300,000/- on 3 months' credit. We do not know much about the proprietors but we have an impression that their business is not large enough to expect a credit of Rs. 300,000/-. Of course, we may be quite mistaken, and would be glad to know your opinion of their business and your experience of collecting dues from them. We would be glad for an opportunity to return this courtesy and help in ascertaining the credit standing of our customers who may approach you for credit. Whatever information you give will be kept in strict confidence.

Yours truly,

Bank References

Banks do not give information about their customers to the public. You have to write to your own bank to take up the inquiry with the prospective customer's bank. The letter to the bank is formal and short. It includes the following points:

1. Name, address and business of credit applicant, with amount and period of credit
2. Name and address of credit applicant's bank and A/c number
3. Request that the bank should take up the reference and advise on the safety of the risk
4. Assurance that the information given will be treated as confidential.

The Manager
Bank of India
Mahatma Gandhi Road
Kolkata 700 001

Sir,

We have been asked for credit of Rs. 75,000/- by Messrs. Sanghi & Roy of 87, Green Street, Kolkata 700 004, who have given the same of Syndicate Bank, Lal Baug Gardens Branch, Kolkata, as their credit reference. Their A/c No. is 4870. Please take up the reference on our behalf and inform us whether the proposed transaction is a safe risk. The information you give will be treated as strictly confidential.

Yours faithfully,

Review

Are these statements true?

(a) To find out about a customer's credit standing, you should write to the customer's banker.

(b) In order to get information about a credit applicant's status from the customer's bank, you must write to your own bank.

(c) A letter asking for credit information about a customer may be addressed to "Image Graphics" with the salutation "Sirs."

Giving Status Information about Customers

Letters giving credit information must be marked "Confidential" and addressed by name to the individual who has signed the inquiry letter.

The information given must be helpful to the inquirer as well as fair to the credit applicant. The behaviour of a customer may not be the same with all his creditors; besides, with a long standing credit relationship, many little faults on either side may have become accepted as routine. The reference can help by giving information about the scale of the customer's business, reputation as a skilled businessman and habits with regard to payment of bills.

Talking about a person's credit is a delicate matter; the letter must be tactful. It is advisable to keep the facts like the length of business relationship with the customer, the amount and period of credit granted, and the longest extension of time the customer has taken to settle his dues. General market opinion can be given to balance personal experience.

The credit standing of a customer depends upon the strength or weakness of each of the four Cs of Credit. Some information can be given about the customer's capital, capacity and circumstances. It is important to be tactful in indicating any weakness. Character should never be mentioned in the letter.

It is also advisable to avoid mentioning the name of the customer, especially if weaknesses are mentioned.

Points

1. Reference to inquiry indicating name (or enclosed slip with name) and length of business relation with the customer
2. Information about personal experience; general market opinion
3. Reminder that information is given in confidence and should be treated with the utmost discretion

These examples show how different kinds of customers can be described.

Sir,

We are glad to be of help in ascertaining the credit standing of our customer, Messrs. Sanghi & Roy of 87, Green Street, Kolkata 700 004.

They have bought from us on credit for the last five years, and we grant them credit up to Rs. 200,000/-. They have always been prompt in paying their bills and are known in the market for their integrity and business acumen. We ourselves would readily grant the credit they have asked for from you. This is our personal opinion of the firm and we request you to treat it as such. We are not responsible in any way for any decision you may take in this matter.

Yours faithfully,

Dear Sir,

The party about whom you inquired in your letter of the 6th (name is on the enclosed slip), have been our customers for the last 3 years.

We grant them credit up to Rs. 100,000/- and have not tried higher limits; we have had no difficulty in collecting dues from them. One of the partners who has recently joined the partnership, has had a good training in business administration, and the firm may be expected to develop rapidly.

Please note that our experience with the firm is limited, and whatever decision you may take is without any responsibility on our part.

Yours truly,

Dear Sir,

We have known the party you mentioned in your letter of 30 August, for seven years.

Our credit dealings with them have been few and they have paid, usually, after a delay of fifteen days. We have had little opportunity of observing their habits of payment with their regular creditors. We suggest that you make further inquiries, and not consider our opinion as anything final or decisive.

Please treat this letter as strictly confidential.

Yours faithfully,

Review

1. Are these statements true? If any statement is not true, give the correct statement.
   (a) The name of the party should always be mentioned in a letter giving information about their credit standing.
   (b) Credit information letters are marked "Confidential."
   (c) Letters giving information about a party's financial status must be addressed to an individual.
   (d) In a reply to an inquiry about a customer's credit standing, you should give definite advice whether to grant credit or not.
2. Choose the correct alternative.
   When talking about a person's credit standing, we should avoid mentioning the person's — (a) capacity (b) capital (c) character (d) circumstances

Informing the Customer

You may decide to grant credit as requested, or give credit for a lower amount than requested by a customer. If you have a small working capital, you may not be able to give a large amount of credit. A letter conveying that credit is granted for a lower amount may include these points:

1. Statement that inquiries have been completed and explanation of the position as seen from the inquiries (e.g., competition is tough; demand for the product is not very high)
2. Decision to grant credit up to a given limit
3. Expression of confidence that the customer will understand the situation and agree to the proposed terms

> Sir,
>
> We have examined your request for credit of Rs. 750,000/- for 3 months to stock microwave ovens.
>
> In the long run, the demand for microwave ovens will pick up, but at the moment we feel that it is somewhat risky to invest a large sum on stocking goods which may be a little slow moving for some time.
>
> We suggest that you buy goods worth Rs. 3,00,000/- on credit and the rest on cash basis in small amounts as and when you require them. You will, of course, have the benefit of cash discounts. Besides, you will have part of your working capital free to enable you to make any quick changes that may be necessary because of rapid changes in the market.
>
> We are sure you will see that this advice is given in a spirit of friendly co-operation between businessmen. Your consignment will be dispatched as soon as we receive your confirmation of these terms.
>
> Yours faithfully,

Refusing Credit

Of all the negative messages, this one is the most unpleasant for the writer as well as the reader. You must take care to analyse this situation carefully before conveying the message. If you show personal interest, you have a better chance of persuading the customer to place his order on cash. Make every attempt to win the customer. It is better not to give vague reasons for the refusal; it is more useful to discuss it in a friendly way with the customer.

Conditions and circumstances do not remain the same; they may change so as to become more favourable to the customer. An offer to reconsider the application at a later date can soften the refusal.

Look at the situation from the customer's point of view, understand his needs and point out the benefits he can get by buying on cash, like

(a) saving capital by getting discounts for cash payments
(b) ensuring fresh stock by buying in small lots (fashion goods, medicines and technological products become outdated rapidly)
(c) lower expenditure on cash buying and passing on the advantage of low prices to valued customers to build up goodwill
(d) freedom from commitments

Taking a positive attitude makes it easier to persuade the customer to buy in small lots on cash.

Points

1. Statement that inquiries related to credit are complete
2. Explanation of what seems to be strengths and what are the weaknesses of customer's position
3. Statement of refusal, with apology
4. Suggestions for improvement, showing advantages of present cash buying
5. Inducements to buy on cash and assurance of co-operation
6. Expression of confidence that the customer will understand the situation and place orders on cash.

Sir,

We have made complete inquiries in connection with your request for credit.

With the development of the locality in Bhoisar, we are sure that your business will grow well. At present, however, owing to the risk of over-stocking we cannot grant the credit. Stocking large quantities of medicines in an area with a small population is risky, especially since medicines have an expiry date.

We, therefore, suggest that you buy on cash, but in smaller lots, as and when required. You will have the benefit of 5% bulk purchase discount if you buy medicines worth Rs. 300,000/- in 3 months. We shall deliver the medicines within 24 hours of receiving your orders. We are sure that you will understand that small cash purchases are to your advantage until the market grows large enough for larger stocks.

Your consignment will be dispatched as soon as we receive your instructions.

Yours faithfully,

Sir,

We have completed inquiries in connection with your credit application and our understanding of the situation is as follows:

As you are going to open a new shop you will have to face a good deal of competition, and it will take some time for you to build up a sound business. The risks at the initial stage are greater and we feel that it is advisable to avoid commitments at this stage.

As soon as you have established yourself firmly, we shall be glad to reconsider credit terms. At present, we suggest that you spread your large order into small cash orders over a period of four months. This will give you the benefit of discounts which we offer on cash purchases. The goods will be delivered promptly when you require them. We are sure that you will understand why we are refusing your request for credit now, and that you will let us have your instructions for dispatching your first consignment.

Yours faithfully,

Dear Mr. Amin,

We have completed inquiries in connection with your application for credit of Rs. 300,000/-Considering the location of your shop in New Panvel which is a distant suburb of Mumbai, we feel that the risk that you are taking is not very safe. Fashion goods and cosmetics cannot have much sale in your area yet. We must therefore request you to place your order on cash terms. The cash discount of 7% will be a saving which you can pass on to your customers.

We shall give you a special bulk discount even if the purchases are spread over a period of 6 months. We also guarantee prompt delivery of goods ordered. We are sure that you will agree with us and find it to your advantage to buy on cash at this stage. May we have your instructions for the dispatch of the first consignment?

Yours sincerely,

Review

1. Fill in the blanks in these sentences:
   (a) In a letter refusing credit, it is better to show the customer the advantages of —.
   (b) Taking a positive attitude while refusing means that you have to —.
   (c) A letter granting credit should include information about —.
2. Choose the correct alternative

   The reader is most likely to respond favourably if we write —
   (a) We regret very much that we cannot grant your request for credit since the market conditions are not favourable.
   (b) We are extremely sorry that we are unable to grant credit terms at present; we shall re-consider your request when the present conditions improve.
   (c) We greatly regret our inability to help you by granting credit terms owing to unfavourable market conditions.
   (d) It is a matter of regret for us that we are unable to grant you credit because the market conditions are unfavourable to us.

EXERCISES

1. A customer has placed an order for goods to be supplied on credit of thirty days, but has not given any information about himself. Write to him asking for credit information.
2. A prospective buyer has referred you to his banker for information about his financial position. Draft the letter you would write taking up the reference.
3. You have been asked about the financial standing of a customer whose credit facility you have temporarily stopped owing to repeated delays in payment. Write a reply which is fair to both the inquirer and the applicant for credit.

4. You have been asked about the credit standing of a partnership firm which has bought from you on credit for 8 years. There has been a recent change in the constitution of the partnership and this has led to some lowering of their credit reputation and you have tightened your credit facilities to the firm. Draft a suitable confidential reply to the enquiry.
5. Tristar Electronics have asked you to supply goods worth Rs. 1,000,000/ on credit. Inquiries show that they have a limited working capital and are probably trying to expand too rapidly; their credit seems to be good up to Rs. 5,00,000/-. Draft a suitable reply, persuading them to buy in smaller lots.
6. You have received an order for the first time, for goods worth Rs. 250,000/- from Messrs. Mitra & Sons. Inquiries you have made indicate that their financial position is not satisfactory. Draft a suitable reply.
7. A newly trained diploma holder of a Computer Programming Course, intending to open a computer training class has asked for credit from a supplier of computer furniture. Draft the supplier's reply suggesting that she should reduce her order by half and pay 50% on delivery and the rest a month later.

   Full credit terms may be considered after six months; meanwhile she would be granted the suggested limited credit.
8. A credit customer who was regular in making payments for three years, has been delaying payments for the last one year, owing to difficulties in business. Write to him tactfully pointing out that in such circumstances, he should stop buying on credit for some time.
9. Inform a customer that owing to his repeated delay in paying his dues you are compelled to deal with him on cash basis only.

Chapter - 16

COLLECTION LETTERS

Collection letters are written to customers who have purchased on credit and not paid their bill on the due date. If a customer does not settle the account when it is due, the creditor has to make efforts to collect the dues. Some debtors pay immediately on receiving a reminder, other may need to be pursued with a series of messages. Telephone calls, telegrams, fax and e-mail messages and personal visits are used in addition to letters. Most companies have a collection policy and procedure to be followed. A collection letter has to do two jobs: get the money and retain the customer's goodwill. In order to do this, the writer needs a good understanding of the particular customer, knowledge of how the customer usually handles his credit account, and knowledge of his present circumstances.

Collection Series

Collection letters are written in a series. Most persons finally take action if reminded often enough, and with increasing pressure. A series makes it possible to increase pressure gradually and gently, from letter to letter. The collection series is both persuasive and constructive; it sells the customer the idea that it is to his own advantage to settle the account. The series allows you to try several approaches that may be suitable to a particular customer's nature and circumstances. Debtors are of several types and the reasons for non-payment can be many; the series can break down the reasons one by one. There is no point in assuming the worst reason for non-payment at the start. It is better to begin with a gentle approach and make every effort to save the relationship even if the customer must be finally lost.

Reasons for non-payment and types of debtors can be listed roughly in ascending order; the letters can tackle each one separately.

Group 1

1. Easy-going; forgets to pay
2. Very busy; overlooks payments
3. Muddled and cannot keep track
4. Has plenty of money; cannot understand that others need it
5. Kind-hearted/indulgent; cannot manage affairs/ employees

Group 2

6. Dissatisfied with goods/services; will not pay because he is angry

7. Troubled by sickness/misfortune; cannot pay because of temporary lack of money
8. Hates to let money go; likes to keep it in the bank instead
9. Large buyer; thinks he is entitled to take time
10. Takes all the time possible; has other uses for his money
11. Has too many credit obligations and is not very particular about all of them

Group 3

12. Will pay only to avoid losing his credit reputation
13. Will pay only when frightened
14. Will pay only when convinced that he must, in order to avoid trouble.

The three groups roughly correspond to the three stages of the collection series. The first group will respond to repeated reminders with increasing insistence; this part of the series is the Reminder Stage. The second group has a variety that must be matched with a varied approach; it may not be necessary to go through every approach for every customer; this stage of the series is elastic and it may be shortened or lengthened by using less of more letters; this is the Enquiry-Appeal Stage. The last group is composed of tough people who will not yield easily to persuasion; with them the hard line is the only way, but you may still try to save the customer; this is the Warning-Threat Stage. A company usually tries to save its customers and will avoid coming to the last stage as long as possible. Besides, legal action is an expensive and bothersome process. Only very large debts are worth collecting by legal action; small bad debts are written off.

The number of letters to be written to a particular debtor will depend upon the company's collection policy and on the kind of risk the customer represents. The series, as well as each letter in the series, must be customized to match the circumstances and the nature of the particular customer.

Timing the Collection Series

Timing is an important factor in the success of the collection effort. The strongest pressure to pay should be applied at the time when the customer's business is in its best season and the highest profits are being made. For example, the owner of a book-shop selling textbooks has the best business in June-July; the owner of a hill-station hotel makes the greatest profit in April-May. It is expected that when there are profits the dues will be paid. If they are not paid at the best time, it is likely that they will not be paid unless persistent demands are made by the creditor.

The intervals between the letters can be arranged in such a way that the last three letters of the enquiry-appeal stage are sent when the customer has his best season. The number of letters to be used for a particular customer can also be decided according to the time available so as to reach the high pressure stage at the right time.

In the case of customers who do not have a seasonal business, the creditor has to decide how much time to allow a particular customer, and how fast he will come to the highest pressure point.

Writing Collection Letters

All collection letters can be written on this pattern:

1. Express regret that the account is still unsettled; refer to amount of bill, due date and reminders already sent.

2. Try to persuade the customer to pay (main argument depending on the stage).
3. Motivate action (enclose stamped envelope/ fix date for payment/ pointedly state customer's advantage etc.).

To be effective, keep these points in mind while drafting the letter:

- Be sincere in the arguments used.
- Never use "red pepper" words like *neglect, ignore, fail, careless, debt*, which hurt the customer's feelings.
- Do not humiliate the customer by putting on a superior air.
- Write in personal style, not in jargon phrases.
- Never suggest alternative courses of action; if a choice is offered, the reader may postpone decision.

Reminder Stage

This stage can be lengthened by increasing the number of reminders and/or the interval between the reminders. The first reminder is sent within a week of the bill or its duplicate copy. It may be a form letter which has the advantage of looking like mere routine with no personal implication. A second reminder may be sent in a week or in a fortnight; this is a personal reminder that the bill has been rendered, and indicates expectation that it will be paid soon.

> Dear Sir,
>
> Your account today shows an unpaid balance of Rs.—. It is not a large sum, so we thought you had probably overlooked it.
>
> Will you remit the amount today?
>
> Yours faithfully,

The third reminder is more pointed and urges the customer to settle his account early. The writer assumes that the customer has forgotten because of the pressure of business.

> Dear Sir,
>
> We reminded you earlier that your account is past due, as shown in the enclosed statement. We have not received the payment yet. May we remind you again to send your cheque as soon as possible?
>
> If you have already sent your cheque, please accept our thanks and ignore this reminder.
>
> Yours faithfully,

Humorous Collection Letters

Stunt collection letters are a part of the reminder stage. If there is no response after two or three reminders, you may try a letter with an out-of-the-way approach to get attention; an unusual letter has a better chance of getting a response. The letter may be unusual in its content or its layout. Collection letters can use the tricks and stunts of sales letters. The attention device may be anything like a picture, coloured paper or type, or a little article enclosed with the letter.

One picture is worth a thousand words. You can effectively use a little cartoon or any graphics; some ideas for this are given below:

- A picture of a man emptying the contents of a drawer or a waste paper basket; letter reading: We're searching for your cheque everywhere.
- A picture of a very fat man; the letter reads: It's harder to reduce as we get older.—Yours sincerely, Old Bill.

A small object may serve as a good reminder when properly connected with the message.

- A rubber-band enclosed with a letter reading: Stretch the rubber-band to this —x point and it will snap back, brand new. But stretch it to this———— x point and S-N-A-P! Credit is like a rubber-band: you cannot stretch it beyond a point.
- A small coin enclosed with a letter reading: It's said, Money attracts money; we're sending this penny to attract your cash to pay our bill.

Other interesting tricks include variation of the shape, size and colour of the paper, or the message of the letter.

- Typed on a letterhead ¼ of the usual size: Your account is so small that we are sending this very small message to remind you of it.
- Typed on a letterhead 4 times the usual size: We're trying to make this silent messenger shout to get your attention to the bill.
- Typed in red: Help!—

— Help us to get your account out of the red.

Stunt collection letters are to be used with caution; use them only when you know that humour will be appreciated by the particular customer. Although humour is very valuable in business, it may not be appreciated by conservative customers.

Review

1. Are these statements true?
   (a) If a customer does not pay his dues, he should be threatened with legal action.
   (b) It is possible to use humour in collecting debts.
   (c) You should try to keep the customer's goodwill even if the customer has to be reminded often, to pay his dues.
2. Fill in the blanks using as few words as possible.
   (a) Advantages of a writing collection letters in a series are:
      (i) —
      (ii) —
      (iii) —
   (b) Giving a choice of action at the end of the letter is not effective because —.

Enquiry-Appeal Stage

At this stage, the tone becomes serious and each letter has a definite argument for payment. The letters get progressively more insistent and there is a close connection between one argument and the next.

This stage has two aspects: first to ask about the customer's satisfaction and see if s/he has any problems with the products/services or with the business; and second to appeal to the customer's pride, sense of honour and sense of fear to motivate him/her to pay.

1. **Asking about the customer's satisfaction**: This serves a three-fold purpose: (i) it compels the difficult, 'silent' customer to say something; (ii) it makes sure that the customer does not complain later, about the product/service; (iii) it conveys the message of "customer first."

> Dear Sir,
>
> Our letters of the 10th and 18th, calling attention to our bill of Rs. 100,000 have not brought any reply from you. We are afraid that you might have some reason to be dissatisfied with our goods or services, and this probably keeps you from settling the account. If so, please let us know and we shall be glad to make a suitable adjustment. We want you to feel sure that you can buy from us with satisfaction.
>
> If, on the other hand, you are satisfied with our execution of your order, please send us the payment so that your account may be fresh for your next order. May we expect your reply within this week?
>
> Yours faithfully,

2. **Enquiring about the customer's state of affairs**: This has to be done tactfully. If some problem (like losses) affects the business, the customer may be embarrassed, and not willing to tell the creditor. It is useful to assume that the customer is anxious to be free from the debt; you can offer to help by accepting payment in instalments or accepting return of any goods that the customer finds difficult to sell or use. Your desire to help must be strongly stressed.

> Dear Sir,
>
> Since you have not replied to our letter of the 25th asking whether you are satisfied with our goods, we assume that everything was all right. Our bill of Rs. 100,000, however, still remains unpaid.
>
> We are quite willing to accept payment by installments, if you are a little burdened at the moment. As a business associate, please do not hesitate to tell us if you are facing difficulties in disposing of the goods; we can also help by accepting back some unsold goods if you wish to return them. In any case, it would benefit both of us if you tell us what the trouble is, so that we could together work out a plan for the settlement of the account without too much strain on resources. We are sure you will communicate with us so that we can tide over temporary difficulties in co-operation.
>
> Yours faithfully,

3. **Appealing to sense of customer's sense of fairness**: If offers to adjust and to help, both fail, an appeal to the customer's sense of honour may bring a response. Normally, a debtor would feel a little ashamed to misuse the trust placed in him by the creditor, and is likely to respond to an appeal to his sense of honour.

The essence of the argument is to point out that although you have done your part of the transaction satisfactorily, the debtor has not done his part. Such a long extension of time taken by the debtor is also not fair to other customers who pay on time. Besides, interest goes on accumulating if the payment is delayed. The following letter illustrates the use of some of these arguments.

> Dear Sir,
>
> We are sorry to see that you have not replied to our letters asking for payment of our bill of Rs. 100,000, outstanding since 20 March.
>
> You will agree that the bill is long overdue. We delivered your goods to your satisfaction but you have not done your part of the transaction with equal promptness. Usually, we do not extend credit for more than three months and in allowing your account to remain unsettled for so long we have been unfair to other customers from whom we collect payments in three months. Besides, you are not being fair to your own name as a reputed businessman, in this delay. We do hope that you will live up to your reputation and settle your account this week.
>
> Yours faithfully,

4. **Appealing to self-interest**: Some debtors may not be affected at all by appeals to honour; a harder line has to be tried with them. An appeal to self-interest may be effective. The success of the letter using this appeal depends on the fear aroused; the fear of losing credit may move such debtors to pay. This appeal can be used in letters of varying degrees of firmness as the following examples show.

> Dear Sir,
>
> We are surprised at your silence about our bill of Rs. 100,000/- due since 20 March, in spite of our several letters.
>
> Until now, all was well and our bills were paid promptly. Surely, at least an explanation of this delay is due to us. Non-payment combined with silence does not inspire confidence in creditors, as you must know from your own experience. Besides, creditors are sometimes asked to supply confidential information about their customers, and we would hardly know what to say if we were to be asked about your handling of your credit account with us. Please send your cheque in the enclosed envelope, so that your credit with us will remain clear as before.
>
> Yours faithfully,

> Dear Sir,
>
> We are really uncomfortable about your indifference to our letters about our outstanding bill of Rs.100,000/- for goods supplied in January.

This delay is not doing any good to your credit reputation and you know how difficult is to build up a good one. Will you now allow your credit to be tarnished by just ignoring our requests for payment?

We hope that you will not create an awkward situation by remaining silent even after receiving this letter. We are expecting your cheque by return of post.

Yours truly,

Warning-Threat Stage

When all appeals fail to bring any response from the debtor, the collection series enters the last stage. This stage is rigid, and can be extended to three letters, at the most. The first letter pleads with the debtor to settle the account and avoid legal action; no date may be set for the legal action. The second letter fixes the date for legal action but allows a period of time for the debtor to pay the bill. The last letter merely tells the debtor that the account has been handed over to the company's lawyer.

The tone and style of these letters varies considerably; the only fixed and inviolable rule is, never to forget courtesy. The following are examples of such letters.

Dear Mr. Ghosh,

We have begun to feel that our judgement of you was too generous; you have maintained complete silence about our bill of Rs. 100,000/- in spite of every kind of effort we made to elicit some response from you.

If for any reason you were unable to pay, you would surely have informed us in order to protect your credit. But you have left us only one course of action — legal. That will be tiresome and expensive for both of us.

It is now in your hands to save the situation by sending your cheque within five days.

Yours sincerely,

Dear Sir,

We have written to you repeatedly, calling your attention to your unsettled account of Rs. 100,000/- but unfortunately have not received any response.

We are sorry to inform you that, unless the account is settled by 30 May, we shall be compelled to place the matter in the hands of our solicitors.

We hope that you will not force us to take this unpleasant step.

Yours faithfully,

Dear Sir,

You have not replied to our letters asking for a settlement of your account of Rs.100,000/-. It appears that you are not prepared to make a settlement.

We have today handed over your account to our lawyers for collection. However, we have instructed them to wait for four days before issuing you a legal notice.

We sincerely hope that you will take this opportunity offered and save both yourselves and us from irksome legal action. If your payment is received by Tuesday, we shall gladly instruct our solicitors not to proceed.

Yours faithfully,

Review

Fill in the blanks:

(a) It is useful to offer adjustment to a defaulting customer because —.

(b) The enquiry-appeal stage can be made shorter or longer by reducing or increasing — and —. Are these statements true?

(a) The Warning-Threat stage is flexible and can be lengthened.

(b) Letters in the final stage must be written courteously.

EXERCISES

1. Write a letter to a retail store reminding them that they have neither settled their account, nor replied to your earlier reminders. Offer to take instalment payments to help them to settle the account.
2. One of your customers has failed to pay his dues in spite of several reminders. Write to him appealing to his sense of fairness and honour.
3. Messrs. Dey & Co. have not paid their bill of Rs. 50,000 although several casual reminders have been sent. Write to them to ask whether they have any complaint about your products or services.
4. All your reminders, requests and offers have failed to bring a reply from Messrs. Bose & Sons who owe you Rs. 1,000,000 for computers supplied three months ago. Write to them drawing their attention to their poor rating of their own credit reputation.
5. Draft a letter to Messrs. Mitra, Roy & Co., firmly requesting payment of a bill of Rs. 300,000 for goods delivered some months ago. Make it clear that unless the bill is paid within a week, legal action might be the only solution.
6. A letter asking for immediate payment has been sent by mistake to a customer who has already settled his account in full. Write to him apologizing for the mistake.

Chapter - 17

CLAIMS AND ADJUSTMENTS

In any business there will be some mistakes and some accidents; you may not get the goods and services as you had ordered. If things go wrong, you have to bring the faults to the notice of the supplier and see that the mistakes and faults are corrected and adjustments are made.

The purpose of writing a claim letter is to get correction and adjustment. The first thing to do is to make a phone call to the supplier to inform the supplier of the deficiency, and then confirm it immediately with a letter. If the supplier is a reputable company, it is usually enough to point out the mistake in the execution of the order and leave it to the company to make the adjustment.

When there is a mistake in the execution of an order, two things are involved: (i) the buyer suffers inconvenience; (ii) there is a loss of money. These two things are not to be confused; it is not necessarily the buyer who loses the money. The buyer definitely suffers inconvenience and must ask the supplier to take steps to reduce the inconvenience and make adjustments. If the buyer states clearly what mistake has been made and what inconvenience has been caused, the seller can take steps to reduce it. The buyer can help the seller by suggesting what can be done so that things can be put right and adjusted as quickly as possible, and with the least trouble to all concerned.

The spirit of co-operation is useful in pointing out errors. Keep in mind the Cs of good letter writing; state the problem correctly and clearly, and without exaggeration. It is sensible to be factual, concise and exact in describing the problem.

Courtesy is of great importance; resist the temptation to accuse the seller of carelessness, negligence, inefficiency and indifference to customers. Courteous mention of error will earn the gratitude of a self-respecting seller. Firmness, emphasis and insistence on your rights can be done without discourtesy. Courtesy requires that offensive and unpleasant words should not be used. Words like *dishonest, careless, unfair, false, disgusted, useless, inefficient,* are offensive and discourteous. Any error must always be pointed out courteously; it is impolite to say: "You have done a careless job of dispatching our consignment of crockery."

It is better to use passive voice to talk of errors, and choose words tactfully. It sounds more polite to say, in passive voice,

"Our consignment of crockery was not packed with the necessary care,"

than to say "You packed our consignment of crockery carelessly."

Do not attribute errors and faults to anyone unless you are sure. It is the seller's responsibility to find out who made the mistake.

Review

1. Are the following statements true?
   (a) A complaint letter should be written in legalistic style in order to impress the supplier.
   (b) In a letter of complaint you should not accuse and blame anyone angrily even if you know whose fault it was.
   (c) Words like *"cheating"*, *"failure"*, *"useless"* should not be used while pointing out errors.
   (d) *"Your negligent and careless attitude to my order has caused us a great loss and you will have to compensate us for it,"* is a good sentence to use in a complaint letter.

Occasions for Writing Complaints

A buyer may have one or more of the following grievances:

1. Goods arrive in a damaged condition
2. Delivered goods are not what you had ordered
1. Delivered goods are not according to the specifications given
2. Quantity of goods is different from what you had ordered
3. Goods are delivered at the wrong place
4. Delivery of goods or completion of work is delayed
5. Work undertaken is done unsatisfactorily
6. A product does not function properly
7. Discourtesy from staff of shop or office
8. Mistakes in a bill, or reminders for payment after you have paid the bill.

Your claim and your expectation of the seller's response will depend on whether you are a commercial buyer or a consumer. As a commercial buyer you make adjustments, so that the inconvenience and the hindrance to business are minimised; there is more inconvenience than personal loss. You also have greater power to get adjustments and compensation because, as a regular buyer, you have a hold on the seller. As a consumer, you may suffer personal loss on account of the seller's fault or negligence. You will expect correction and compensation, but a small individual buyer has less power in the market to get grievances redressed.

Letter of Complaint

The letter should include the following points:

1. Reference to the order, its date, number
2. Clear description of the mistake or deficiency
3. Clear statement of the inconvenience or loss caused, and the action the supplier should take to lessen the inconvenience
4. Request for adjustment and/or investigation

The letters below illustrate how these points are included.

Dear Mr. Dutt,

We had placed an order with you on 8 October for 60 pocket calculators to be delivered by the 20th of this month. Unfortunately, we have not yet received them. As we do not have any information from you about the delay, perhaps something has gone wrong somewhere. Will you please let us know when we may expect delivery?

Yours sincerely,

Dear Sirs,

We had ordered 4 filing cabinets, 3 shelves, 10 office chairs and 5 tables to be delivered to us here, on 23 September, in time for the opening of our new branch office.

The shipment has just arrived here and we find that 1 kitchen cupboard, 2 wardrobes and 3 garden tables have been delivered to us. It is probable that there was confusion between two shipments and the wrong one was delivered to us.

Our branch office is to be opened on the 25th and we would like our furniture to reach us in time; the customer whose goods you have delivered to us must be equally unhappy with the office furniture delivered to her.

We expect that you will act immediately.

Yours truly,

Dear Sir,

We have received the consignment of 5 Launderwell Washing Machines we ordered on 6 October. The crate was damaged. Three of the machines are also damaged, while the other two are dented and scratched. It appears that the consignment was handled carelessly.

We have made a note of the damage on the carrier's copy of the delivery challan. We are enclosing instant photographs of the damaged machines for your reference. Please arrange for an immediate inspection.

We would like the damaged goods to be removed from our premises, and replacement to be delivered immediately.

Yours faithfully,

Sir,

We regret the manner in which our order for 5000 pairs of sunglasses was handled. Only 2000 were delivered on the 21st and the rest have been delivered now, after the event for which they were required, is over. We had placed such a large order only in order to take advantage of the opportunity to sell the sunglasses on the occasion of the Air Force Day Celebrations held this morning. Your indifference in executing our order has cost us dearly.

As we no longer require the sunglasses we request you to make immediate arrangements to collect the 3000 pairs delivered to us today.

Yours truly,

Sirs,

The answer books we had ordered from you have just been delivered and I am sorry to say that I sorely regret having placed the order with you.

The consignment arrived without any prior notice, at 9.45 a.m. when the office staff and peons were engaged in the work of an examination to be started at 10.00 a.m. The candidates were arriving and were being guided and helped to find their seats. The lobby and the space around the college office was crowded with candidates. The delivery persons refused to wait even until the examination was started and the space was cleared. They dumped the bundles wherever they could see space on the office floor.

The bundles are so badly packed that the wrappers of many of them are torn and the answer books are soiled and damaged.

When we protested to the delivery persons, they rudely replied that they were only the transporters and delivered goods as and when instructed and had no responsibility to inform the customer or for the condition of the packing.

In addition to the bad delivery, there are also defects in the answer books. An inspection of a few of the answer books revealed the following:

(i) They measure 1 cm. less than the given size, both in length and in width, thus reducing the writing space.

(ii) The quality of the paper is so poor that printing on the cover page is seen on the back of it making it impossible for candidates to write on the first page. We are led to conclude that the writing will be seen on the back of every page.

(iii) The printing on the cover page is so poor that it can hardly be read, and gives the answer books a shabby appearance.

All this is not in keeping with the quality of material and service that we expect and receive from our suppliers.

It is not possible for us to use the answer books you have supplied. The bill will not be passed for payment. This incident will be taken up for discussion with our Education Society's Executive Committee meeting on next Saturday.

I expect you to arrange immediately to remove the bundles from the floor of the college office where they are causing serious inconvenience.

Yours truly,

Sometimes, a strong letter may be required. If the seller does not respond to a telephone call and a fax and a letter, this experience of the supplier's indifference justifies a strong letter. Rudeness is not justified; but a letter demanding immediate attention can be made effective by arousing the seller's self-interest. The following letter is an example.

Gentlemen:

It is over a fortnight since we informed you of the defects in the office table delivered to us on 12 August.

When we telephoned to remind you on 25 August, you promised to collect the table for the necessary modifications but the table is still here and it is of no use to us until it can stand on its legs evenly. We do not think the treatment you are giving us will lead us to place further orders with you, or to speak well about your services to our business associates. In any case, the shaky table standing in our well laid-out office attracts many questions from every visitor and is eloquent testimony to the kind of service you render here.

You can at least prevent further damage to your image by replacing the table at once. We expect you to call for it within the next two days.

Very truly yours,

Adjustment Letters

Attention and response to customers' complaints is an important part of customer service. There is growing competition, increased customer awareness, and legislation to protect consumers. Providers of goods and services have to ensure customer satisfaction and to pay prompt attention to any dissatisfaction. It builds up goodwill if you convey to customers the message, "If you are dissatisfied, tell us; if you are satisfied, tell others." The success of a business depends on the satisfaction of the customers, and it is important for the company to know whether the customers are satisfied with its goods/services or not.

Dissatisfied customers are likely to talk about their dissatisfaction with a product/service and may write to grievance columns of newspapers; this is bad for the reputation of the company. When a customer complains, you get a chance to correct any faults, to make adjustment, to explain, and to help the customer to use the product properly; you get a chance to be in touch with the customers and to make sure that they are satisfied with your product/service. In competitive companies, all employees are trained to be alert to customer needs.

Drafting an Adjustment Letter

Whether the claim is to be granted or not, the letter must follow certain principles in order to fulfil its function of maintaining good customer relations.

Customer is King; the letter must reflect the seller's respect for the customer's feelings and needs. When your customer finds something wrong with your goods or services, his/her confidence in you may be a little shaken; your reply to his/her complaint must restore the confidence. The customer may be feeling angry and cheated at not getting what he/she had expected for the money; your reply should regain any lost goodwill. The Adjustment letter must express regret for the inconvenience caused; it must take pains to explain why things went wrong, and what is being done, speedily, to put them right, no matter whose fault it was.

You must have a proper frame of mind and a positive attitude for writing a good adjustment letter. First of all, you must take an objective attitude to error; you must be able to

(i) locate the error; find out where it occurred and who was responsible for it;

(ii) control the error; know what steps to take in order to put matters right speedily, and also know how to prevent such mistakes from occurring again;

(iii) forgive the error; use courteous words, and show human consideration while mentioning or describing the cause of the error, and not accuse either employees, associate businessmen, suppliers or the customer.

This helps you to take a positive attitude which is reflected in the letter. Secondly, be helpful and sympathetic. Reassure the customer about using the product and help him/her to understand how to avoid trouble and get the best service. Use "You" attitude to get a favourable emotional response from the customer. For example,

- *You will get trouble-free service from the copier if you allow it to be used only by trained persons.*
- *You will not be inconvenienced in future, if you let us know in advance, the address of the place where you want the goods delivered.*

Thirdly, remember that loss of money is different from inconvenience suffered. The inconvenience is always suffered by the customer, no matter whose fault it was. It is the customer who has a broken-down machine to deal with, or damaged goods occupying space, or some other problem on account of not getting what was needed. It is therefore important to assure the customer about what action is being taken to reduce the inconvenience. The question of who bears the loss is not to be confused with who takes action to satisfy the customer's need; the action must be taken by the supplier.

Things to avoid while answering claims

DO NOT —

1. — say "your complaint", "you claim that", or "you complain that"; these are unpleasant phrases. Say, "your request for explanation" or "misunderstanding."
2. — express surprise on learning of the customer's dissatisfaction; you sound as if you doubted the customer if you say, "We are surprised to read in your letter that you are not satisfied with our service." It is also discourteous to say that such an error has never occurred before, and that no other customer has complained. The customer will resent this attitude to his problem.
3. — pass on the blame to someone else, such as employee or carrier; admit any error on the part of the company without trying to avoid responsibility for it.
4. — repeat any ugly details of a fault which the customer might have given; the customer may have complained that she found "two dead spiders in the packet of corn flakes," but if the reply repeats it saying, "We are sorry to learn that you found two dead spiders in one of our packets of corn flakes," the customer is needlessly reminded of it.
5. — give details of any confusion which might have led to unsatisfactory work. It is better not to tell the customer what a fine mess there was.
6. — sound unwilling or patronizing when granting an adjustment; the customer is not asking for favours; he only wants justice. Making the customer feel humiliated in any way will create ill-will.
7. — try to explain a refusal by saying that "company policy" does not allow it. The customer has the right to know why the claim is refused.
8. — make a promise that a fault will never occur again. The letter must assure the customer that steps have been taken to prevent the repetition of such errors.

Review

Are these statements true? If any of them is not true, give the correct statement.

(a) Customers' complaints are a great inconvenience to a seller.

(b) A reply to a complaint must make every effort to regain the customer's confidence.

(c) "We are surprised to learn that you are not satisfied with our services" is a good sentence to begin a reply to a complaint.

(d) "We are sorry that we cannot help you in this matter" is a friendly way to end a letter.

(e) A reply to a complaint should always end with "Assuring you of our best services at all times."

Types of Adjustment Letters

Letters of adjustment may be classified as follows:

1. Granting adjustment
2. Refusing adjustment
3. Offering a compromise (partial adjustment)
4. Apologizing for errors when the damage cannot be put right
5. Offering to make adjustment on the assumption that the customer is dissatisfied
6. Stop-gap letter informing the customer that investigation is being made
7. Answering a complaint in readers' grievances column.

Letters that Grant Adjustment

An adjustment is granted when there is a fault in the execution of the order or the goods are defective or damaged. Briefly explain the cause of the unsatisfactory delivery. The attention given to the complaint must be conveyed to the customer. This wins the customer's respect and goodwill.

Points

1. Express regret and sympathy for the customer's inconvenience
2. State the adjustment being made and what is being done to reduce the inconvenience
3. Briefly explain the error and the steps taken to control it
4. Show appreciation of customer's co-operation in maintaining standards.

Dear Madam,

We dispatched, today, 20 sets of Bone China Glassware to replace the damaged ones which you received on 31 January. We are sorry for the inconvenience caused to you. Temporary employees had been entrusted with the packing of the earlier consignment owing to a rush of orders and high pressure of work in the packing department. This time the packing has been done by the usual, experienced persons. Besides, more supervisors have been appointed to oversee the packing work.

Please accept our apologies for this trouble and delay in getting your goods.

Yours truly,

Review

Say whether these statements are true or false:

(a) A letter granting an adjustment should always promise that such a problem will never arise again.

(b) You should give a long and detailed explanation of the cause of the problem in order to convince the customer of your sincerity.

(c) A customer with a complaint is mainly interested in knowing what you are doing about his/her problem.

Letters that Refuse Adjustment

Take a positive attitude even when you are refusing something. Refusing an adjustment means convincing the customer that the repair or replacement cost will have to be borne by the customer. You can never refuse service to the customer although you may not agree to bear the cost. It is poor customer relations to refuse to do any work such as repairing, or delivering goods again. You must willingly agree to render the service but explain why the customer will have to pay for it.

Points

1. Express regret for the customer's inconvenience
2. State what the investigation shows as cause of the trouble
3. Politely explain that the customer must bear the cost of repair or replacement
4. Offer to repair and reassure the customer that his trouble will be removed. Make every effort to retain goodwill.

Dear Mr. Das Adhikary,

We are sorry that you have missed your favourite TV programmes these two days because of the poor reception of the set you bought from us six months ago.

Our mechanic has examined the TV set and found that it has been opened and some parts have been replaced. The replaced parts are not of standard quality and the repair work seems to have been done inexpertly. It is true that our TV sets are guaranteed for five years against defective material or workmanship, but the guarantee ceases to be valid if the TV set has been repaired by unauthorized persons. We shall repair your TV set and replace the parts which have been changed; the cost of the parts will be Rs.—. There will be no charge for the work. It will take only one hour to complete the repair work.

The repair work will be done by the mechanic who brings you this letter, on receiving your instructions.

Yours sincerely,

Dear Mrs. Bannerji,

We were sorry to learn from your letter dated 28 September, that the PC you bought from us in April has not been working properly.

Our service engineer, Mr. Ashutosh Sen has examined it and found that there is extensive corruption of some of the files. The PC seems to have been used for playing games downloaded from some websites on the internet. A PC used for business purpose should not be used for playing games; besides, downloading material from websites is definitely dangerous. It has been our experience that users of PC for entertainment do not take as much care as business users do, and files get corrupted and infected by virus in a PC used for playing games.

It will be necessary to carry out a de-virus operation; it will take about six hours and will be done on your premises, by our service engineer Mr. Sen. The cost of the operation will be Rs. ——.

Please ensure that you use only your own floppies and do not allow any floppies from outside to be used by unauthorized persons. Also, it is advisable to keep the computer locked and inaccessible when your work is completed. This way it will remain free of any virus.

Our engineer will visit your office on Friday, 5 October to clean out the virus. Please confirm the appointment by telephone.

Yours sincerely,

Review

Fill in the blanks:

(a) When the customer is at fault and the adjustment is refused, the letter must convince him/her that — .

(b) Even if the claim is refused, the seller must offer to —.

(c) A good beginning for a letter refusing a claim would be "—

(d) "We are surprised by your complaint..." is a poor beginning because — and — (two faults in the sentence).

Letters that Offer a Compromise or a Partial Adjustment

A compromise is offered when there is a difference of opinion about the standard of service or quality of goods, or when the cause of the complaint was outside the control of either party, and not covered by insurance. It is done in order to maintain good relations and, sometimes, to avoid litigation.

Points

1. Express regret that the customer has been inconvenienced
2. Explain the cause of the grievance and state the adjustment being offered
3. Make efforts to get the customer's agreement.

Dear Mr. Biswas,

We are sorry to learn from your letter of 20 July that four of the wall clocks in our shipment of 6 July were received in a damaged condition.

Ordinarily, we should replace any goods which a customer has received in a damaged condition. However, claims for damaged goods have to be made within seven days of the receipt of the shipment. When claims are made within seven days, we can make a counter claim on the transport company which is, in most cases, responsible for the damage.

Although we cannot replace the clocks in this case, we shall make the required repairs, charging you only 50% of the cost of repair. Our representative will collect the damaged clocks from your office this week.

We are sorry that you have been inconvenienced; we assure you that the clocks will be put into first class condition again.

Yours sincerely,

Letters of Apology for Irreparable Loss

There are some unfortunate situations when an error is discovered too late for any adjustment to be possible. A customer orders goods for a special occasion and the goods reach him after the event; an important customer is treated discourteously by a clerk and you find out about it only after the customer has given a large assignment/ contract to your competitor. Getting back the offended customer is a salvage operation. There is no hard and fast rule by which it can be done. Writing a letter of apology in such a situation needs tact, sincerity and humility.

Points

1. Express regret for the customer's inconvenience and thank him for pointing out the error
2. Assure the customer that every care will be taken to prevent such errors
3. Request the customer to give the company another chance.

Dear Sir,

We are extremely sorry that the 5000 pairs of sunglasses you had ordered for 3 April reached you on the 5th. Please accept our apologies.

The sunglasses were packed and handed over to the transport agent on the 29th, but there was a flash strike of truck drivers which caused the transport to be delayed by 2 days. The goods were held up in transit.

We understand that this delay has cost you an excellent opportunity, and sincerely regret that we were not able to help. We must thank you for giving us this opportunity to explain our position.

Since you do not wish to retain the sunglasses, we are collecting the consignment. Please hand it over to the bearer of this letter.

We earnestly hope that there will be another opportunity, soon, for us to do business together.

Yours faithfully,

Letters Offering Adjustment

You can do this to try to regain a lost buyer. If a review shows that a customer has not placed orders for a long time, contact him and make efforts win his goodwill. Make sure that the customer has had no cause for dissatisfaction since many customers do not tell the seller when they are dissatisfied. Offer to make any suitable adjustment.

You can also make an offer to adjust any complaint as a part of the strategy to collect overdue payments. Send a letter to the debtor asking whether he has withheld payment because he has a complaint about the goods/services.

Points

1. Express regret that the customer's orders have been missed for a period of time
2. Ask for the reason for not buying, and offer to make satisfactory adjustment if there is a grievance
3. Persuade the customer to respond.

It is better to write these letters to a particular person, by name, rather than to the company. You can give the letter a personal touch if you write to an individual.

> Dear Mr. Gohil,
>
> I am sorry that we have missed your orders for the last three months.
>
> Have we given you any reason to be dissatisfied with our goods or services? If so, please tell us and we shall be only too glad to make an adjustment. After all, business depends on long standing customers who not only buy and pay but also tell us when we err.
>
> May I expect your reply within a week in the enclosed self-addressed envelope?
>
> Yours sincerely,

> Dear Mr Gupta,
>
> You will agree that it is poor business to let a long standing customer stray. You follow him if, after a reasonable period, he does not buy again.
>
> You have not placed orders with us for a long time and we are beginning to fear that this may be due to some fault of ours. If so, we are anxious to take steps to put matters right. Won't you please help us by answering the questions on the attached check-list? A stamped self-addressed envelope is enclosed for you to return the check-list.
>
> Yours sincerely,

Letters Informing Customer that Claim is being Examined

When a customer complains of non-delivery or delay in delivery of goods, or delivery in a damaged condition, you check in your office to see if anything went wrong. You may find that the goods left the company premises on time, and properly packed. The source of the trouble is outside your office (for example, the transport agency) and you have to take up the matter with a third party. But the customer cannot be kept waiting while you investigate and recover compensation from the carrier or any other party responsible for the problem. It is essential to take immediate steps to reduce the customer's inconvenience, and to write to the customer at once, informing him about it. Any dispute as to who is to bear the loss can be settled after investigation is completed; meanwhile, business arrangements must not be allowed to get upset.

Points

1. Express regret for the inconvenience caused and state what steps are being taken to reduce customer's inconvenience
2. Explain that the error is probably caused by a third party and is being looked into
3. Advise the customer if he has to take any action and what he should do with the damaged consignment.

> Dear Madam,
>
> We are sorry to learn that you have been inconvenienced because the sewing machine that you bought from us last month would not run properly.
>
> Our mechanic will visit you this Saturday at 11 a.m. to examine the machine. If there is any minor adjustment he will make it. In case there is any major work to be done, we shall let you know when we get the mechanic's report. Please be assured that everything will be done to see that you have a machine that is perfectly satisfactory.
>
> Yours faithfully,

Review

1. *Are these statements true?*
   (a) If a complaint has been caused by the negligence or fault of a third party, the seller should deny all liability in the reply to the customer's complaint.
   (b) If the nature of a customer's complaint is such that it cannot be adjusted (e.g., the event is already over), there is nothing you can do to win back the customer's goodwill.
   (c) In an adjustment letter, how you talk about the error is crucial to the effectiveness of the letter.

EXERCISES

Claims

1. A TV set and a VCR which you had ordered for your office conference room from Messrs. G.K. & Sons, Kolkata, have been delivered in a damaged condition. Write to the supplier.
2. Sparkle Steel Goods Manufactures have found that goods manufactured from the material supplied by Brite Steel Suppliers, have rusted and caused dissatisfaction among their customers. Draft their letter claiming compensation.
3. Twice within the last six months you have received bills for goods for which you had paid cash on delivery. Write to the supplier.
4. Some steel cupboards and filing cabinets which you had ordered for your office have arrived in a damaged condition; you have reason to believe that they were carelessly handled while being transferred from the trucks to your office rooms. Write to the supplier asking for an inspection of the goods and claiming compensation.

5. Deluxe Decorators were given a contract for the renovation of your computer class premises in a month's time. The work was completed one month late and the lighting arrangement is uneven. Write to the Decorators expressing dissatisfaction with the work and your intention to charge a penalty for the late completion of the work.
6. You had placed an urgent order for some goods (product of your choice) and the supplier had promised to deliver them in 24 hours. They have not been delivered even two days later. Write to the supplier.
7. You have just received a consignment of computer printing paper which you had ordered for your office. You find that there is substantial shortage in the supply. Write to your supplier claiming compensation. Give full details.
8. You have been buying from a Departmental Store ever since it was opened. When you visited it this morning, you did not receive proper attention from the salesmen even though there was no crowd at the shop at the time. Draft a letter to be sent to the proprietor of the shop.
9. You have paid Rs. 6000/- for an annual maintenance contract with the firm from which you purchased a P.C. for your office. You find their service very poor; they do not send their engineer in spite of repeated telephone calls and letters. Write to the General Manager (Sales) expressing your dissatisfaction with the service.
10. The trucks of a factory next to your office are parked in front of your gate, causing inconvenience to your staff and customers. Write to the manager of the factory, pointing out the problem and requesting his cooperation.
11. Write a letter to the Manager of your bank, complaining that your peon is kept waiting every time he visits the bank to make deposits or collect cash for the office.
12. You had placed a large order for art paper with Bombay Paper Mart. The quality of the paper supplied by them is inferior to that of the sample you had selected. Write a complaint letter stating that you will be compelled to cancel the contract if the matter is not adjusted satisfactorily.
13. After your Annual Social Gathering at Shalimar Hall, the Manager has sent you a bill for damage to seats. Draft a letter refusing to pay the bill, stating that the seats had been damaged earlier and you had pointed out the damaged seats when you took charge of the hall.
14. As a retailer, write a letter of complaint to the manufacturer, drawing attention to the manufacturing defects in the goods (product of your choice) supplied two weeks ago. Ask for suitable redress.
15. Premier Plastics write to Modern Graphic Art Printers that they are not satisfied with the first lot of their print order for catalogues which have been delivered. They claim that the catalogues have been printed on very old paper. They are returning the stock and threaten to cancel the entire order unless all the copies of the catalogue are printed on good quality paper.
16. You purchased a TV set from Messrs. Pinto & Sons, a month ago. You now find that both the audio reception and the picture quality are not clear. Write a letter complaining about the poor quality of the TV set, and ask for a replacement.
17. Write a letter to the Health Officer of the Municipal Corporation complaining about the poor garbage collection work in the area where your factory and office are located.

Adjustments

1. Golden Square Housekeeping Equipment delivered a micro wave oven to a customer a fortnight ago. She now claims that the oven was delivered in a damaged condition and demands a new one. Write a tactful reply as from Golden Square Housekeeping Equipment explaining why this is not possible.
2. Mr. Sohail Kapadia bought a video camera from you five months ago. He now claims that it is defective and asks for an exchange. Inspection shows that it has been carelessly handled. Write a suitable letter to the customer.
3. An organization whose staff you regularly train in using computers has suddenly sent its staff to be trained at a competitor's institute. Inquiries with your staff reveal that one of your new employees had been rude to the trainees during a training program. As proprietor of the computer institute, write to the Training Manager of the organization, trying to win back his goodwill.
4. A retail agent of Spry Hair Driers has written to the manufacturer that several customers have complained about the product in the last two months and demanded replacements. On investigation the manufacturer finds that there is a defect in one of the machines in the factory which caused the hair driers to be defective. Draft a suitable reply from the manufacturer to the retailer.
5. A customer has returned a bill stating that he has been charged for goods that were not delivered to him. Draft a letter to be sent with the corrected bill.
6. Blue Diamond Interiors have inspected the renovation work carried out by them in a Computer Centre on receiving a complaint about the work. They agree that the lighting is uneven and they will rectify it. But they do not accept liability for delay in completing the work because rains and moist weather had delayed the drying of the plaster and the paints. However, to avoid litigation, they are prepared to submit to a penalty of Rs. 50,000/-. Draft the letter.
7. Write a conciliatory letter to a customer who has complained that she received poor treatment when she visited in your office a few days before.
8. Messrs. Philip and Sons receive an angry letter from a lady customer who purchased a frost-free refrigerator five months ago. She claims that the refrigerator is a defective piece and has demanded a new one. Draft a tactful reply explaining why this is not possible.
9. You have received a complaint about the quality of answer books supplied to Presidency College, for their examination work. Your investigation shows that the complaint is baseless. Draft the reply.
10. A company which regularly organises its conferences in your conference room, has complained about poor service. Draft a reply as from the Customer Relations Manager.
11. A customer who had bought a washing machine from you three months ago has complained that it is defective, and demanded that it should be exchanged. Examination of the machine shows that the washing programme has been constantly changed midway during the process, thus causing damage to the programming system. Draft a reply explaining that the machine cannot be exchanged.